Praise for *American Aristocrats*

"*American Aristocrats* introduces the absorbing family story of the Andersons and their westward movement. More than that, it illuminates the centrality of land acquisition and capital to the development of the nation, focusing on the winners and losers, the patriarchs and the women who kept families intact across distances. In sparkling and elegant prose, Harry S. Stout prompts us to sober reflection on the greatest land grab in US history."

—LAURIE MAFFLY-KIPP, WASHINGTON UNIVERSITY IN ST. LOUIS

"Harry S. Stout's chronicle of an extended family's rise to wealth and influence documents the innumerable ways American prosperity was rooted in native dispossession and African American enslavement. This compelling history reminds us once again that the personal has always been political."

—JOHN MACK FARAGHER, HOWARD R. LAMAR PROFESSOR OF
AMERICAN HISTORY EMERITUS, YALE UNIVERSITY

"As in a sweeping, multigenerational historical novel, in *American Aristocrats*, characters the reader comes to know intimately brush up against famous historical figures—George Washington, Henry Clay, Robert E. Lee, and many more. The Andersons are not fictional creations, however, but real people who left an extraordinary collection of letters and diaries that Harry S. Stout exploits with rare skill. In this intertwined history of family and nation, we see the Andersons trying to make sense of their lives as they experience the great events of the age, from the Revolution through the collapse of Reconstruction. Through the Andersons, who built their fortune primarily through the anxious acquisition of land, Stout explores the personal dynamics of American expansion and how middling white men experienced the rise to wealth and power."

—CHRISTOPHER GRASSO, PROFESSOR, DEPARTMENT OF HISTORY,
COLLEGE OF WILLIAM AND MARY

"Harry S. Stout's insightful story of the Andersons and their times illuminates the very personal ways privilege and acquisitiveness have operated in the capitalist United States. *American Aristocrats* is an important work that enables readers to understand how the past shapes the present."

—RICHARD D. BROWN, AUTHOR OF *SELF-EVIDENT TRUTHS: CONTESTING EQUAL RIGHTS FROM THE REVOLUTION TO THE CIVIL WAR*

"Harry S. Stout's story of the Anderson family provokes a new understanding of American social life from the War for Independence through Reconstruction. Avoiding simplistic moralization, he reveals a family history shot through with ambiguity as its members seek land and more land on the frontiers of Kentucky and Ohio: democratic aspirations and disregard for the lives of native inhabitants, heroic successes and speculative failures, family tenderness and constant warfare, capitalist opportunities and crushing anxieties. This account of American, land-based capitalism offers marvelous insights given through a compelling narrative."

—MARK VALERI, JOHN C. DANFORTH CENTER ON RELIGION AND POLITICS, WASHINGTON UNIVERSITY IN ST. LOUIS

American Aristocrats

AMERICAN ARISTOCRATS

A FAMILY, *a* FORTUNE, *and the* MAKING
of AMERICAN CAPITALISM

—

HARRY S. STOUT

BASIC BOOKS

New York

Basic Books
Hachette Book Group
1290 Avenue of the Americas, New York, NY 10104
www.basicbooks.com

Printed in the United States of America
First Edition: November 2017
Published by Basic Books, an imprint of Perseus Books, LLC, a subsidiary of Hachette Book Group, Inc.

The Hachette Speakers Bureau provides a wide range of authors for speaking events. To find out more, go to www.hachettespeakersbureau.com or call (866) 376-6591.

The publisher is not responsible for websites (or their content) that are not owned by the publisher.

Print book interior design by Jack Lenzo

The Library of Congress has cataloged the hardcover edition as follows:
Names: Stout, Harry S., author.
Title: American aristocrats : a family, a fortune, and the making of American capitalism / Harry S. Stout.
Description: New York : Basic Books, [2017] | Includes bibliographical references and index.
Identifiers: LCCN 2017022134 (print) | LCCN 2017035453 (ebook) | ISBN 9780465098996 (ebook) | ISBN 9780465098989 (hardcover)
Subjects: LCSH: Anderson, Richard C. (Richard Clough), 1750–1826—Family. | Anderson, Richard Clough, 1788–1826. | Elite (Social sciences)—United States—Case studies. | Wealth—United States—Case studies. | Landowners—United States—Case studies. | Capitalism—United States—History—19th century. | United States—History—19th century. | United States—Politics and government—19th century.
Classification: LCC E207.A5 (ebook) | LCC E207.A5 S76 2017 (print) | DDC 973.5—dc23
LC record available at https://lccn.loc.gov/2017022134

ISBNs: 978-0-465-09898-9 (hardcover); 978-0-465-09899-6 (e-book)

LSC-C

10 9 8 7 6 5 4 3 2 1

To my wife, Debbie, who was there through it all.

"Do you stand there, Scarlett O'Hara, and tell me that Tara—that land—doesn't amount to anything? . . . Land is the only thing in the world that amounts to anything," he shouted, his thick, short arms making wide gestures of indignation, "for 'tis the only thing in this world that lasts, and don't you be forgetting it! 'Tis the only thing worth working for, worth fighting for—worth dying for."

—MARGARET MITCHELL, GONE WITH THE WIND

Contents

Introduction

This is the story of a family named Anderson. But unlike in many conventional family histories, the protagonist in this story is land and the theme is anxiety over acquiring and holding the wealth that land represents. Though largely invisible in American history texts and secondary monographs, the Andersons left a substantial corpus of letters and writings that speak to the evolution of the American gospel of private property and accumulated wealth. In all there are more than two thousand surviving letters and diaries in key archives stretching from Richmond, Virginia, to Pasadena, California. Only one Anderson—General Robert Anderson of Fort Sumter fame—survives in historians' memory, but his kinsmen and kinswomen were notable as well for what they achieved on the early American frontier of Kentucky and Ohio. Together the letters and diaries tell a crucial but largely untold personal story of the making of the early American republic's social, political, and economic infrastructure from national origins through the Civil War.

Neither the Andersons nor their more storied associates were aristocrats enjoying inherited power, wealth, and status. The men were hardworking, ambitious people who believed passionately in the promise of America and in cashing in socially, politically, economically, and culturally on their privilege as free white men. It is not the story of nineteenth-century titans like John Jacob Astor or Marshall Field but rather of a forgotten family who came to be part of the nation's financial elite. They lived at the intersection of the traditional and the modern, where people still interacted in local, face-to-face networks, knew each other, and identified themselves and other local families in hierarchies of property and authority. In many ways Washington, DC, itself—a city of eight thousand people in 1800 that grew to seventy-five thousand by 1860—was a place where longtime inhabitants knew each other. Leaders, including Congressman Richard Clough Anderson Jr., General Robert Anderson, and attorney Larz Anderson, dwelled in a select world of intertwined elites.

While this book is not a microhistory of "ordinary" characters who stand in for a larger set of "ordinary" people about whom little information survives, neither is it an elite history of powerful public figures whose papers are scrupulously preserved and exhaustively edited in the multivolume critical editions reserved for heads of state, courts, and commerce. The Andersons represent a broad swath of movers and shakers who substantially played the central role in determining what the American experiment in republican capitalism would look like.[1]

As forgotten elites they necessarily left gaps in the information surviving for each Anderson family member. To some extent these lacunae dictated the organization of this book. Rather than present a collective biography of more or less complete histories, I have chosen a chronological narrative that follows different family members at moments when their careers blossomed and the trove of information is richest.

Collectively, the Andersons were part of a network of first-wave territorial leaders whose stories suggest revisions to our sense of the frontier and what it meant to be a "pioneer." Their frontier, in contrast to Frederick Jackson Turner's imagined frontier, was not atomistic and radical. It craved organization and civilization and a corporate ethos that would come to be embodied by the Anderson family. Americans ironically fancy themselves as rugged individuals resistant to outsiders' rules, but in fact in the early days of the republic they were rugged organizers, resistant to insiders' disorder.

In the Andersons we see a keen sense of loyalty to kin and extended family. In their lives we see that families are not genealogical charts that can be untangled and laid out in separate lines. The Anderson extended family was a web, impossible to touch at one point without setting the rest vibrating; impossible to understand as one story without recognizing the contributions of each individual to the whole. The Andersons were politically informed and active. Many served in key offices in Congress and the Electoral College and as state governors, as well as held diplomatic assignments to Latin America. Some were career military officers and generals. Though living on or one step removed from the frontier, the women were highly literate and the men well educated at colleges: William and Mary, Harvard, West Point, Transylvania, and Miami of Ohio. Most important, all were consumed with and consumers of land, and most were actively involved in land speculation, not unlike members of the renowned pantheon of Founding Fathers, particularly Washington, Jefferson, and Franklin.

Not surprisingly, information on the Anderson women is less complete than that on the men, though there are enough letters to confirm that they occupied largely traditional roles in their families. What were the customs and activities of women in a patriarchal society? Instead of simply assuming a patriarchy that ignores women's role, the Anderson women call attention to just what that meant in the lives of Anderson families. When placed in the historiographical context of a generation's work on women and families, it is possible to flesh out women's significant contributions to the family business.

As liberal, educated American citizens, the Anderson men and women followed the rule book of the bourgeoisie. The men occupied the public sphere, serving in multiple public capacities. The Anderson women—though actively involved on their private lands and farms and inheriting land of their own or property held with their husbands—embodied the "cult of domesticity." There apparently were no proto-feminists among the women, nor do risqué affairs or child abuse appear in the record. There were two instances of marital consanguinity—first-cousin marriage—between Anderson men and women, but in nineteenth-century Kentucky this was accepted. So, too, was their reckless land speculation and shameless exploitation of enslaved African Americans and native inhabitants of the land they usurped. Clergy and reformers insisted that the survival of the republic depended on a virtuous citizenry and that the central schools for virtue were the churches and homes; the Anderson families modeled those values.[2]

Like the Founding Fathers, the Andersons were fervent patriots who fought for and believed passionately in the American experiment. Their love of the new nation was profound even as they detested those whose views ran contrary to their own. They engaged in politics naturally and sound remarkably modern in their reverence for democracy and capitalism. They also shared with their contemporaries a hatred of politicians (from the wrong party) and banks (that they didn't control). They could simultaneously embrace democracy, represent it in the halls of power, and be profoundly disillusioned with it.

The avidity with which they pursued land was perhaps the greatest surprise of my research and provides an important clue to the evolving meaning of America. Ever since Frederick Jackson Turner's remarkable "frontier thesis," historians have recognized the frontier and cross-border encounters on the continent as key environmental factors—perhaps *the* key environmental factors—in the evolution of American history. But in invoking land as my main protagonist, I mean more than the American frontier and borderlands. I mean the mass acquisition of land everywhere in the pursuit of accumulation that likely stands as the greatest middle-class land grab in world history. At a profound level, the promise of personal property surfaces as the driving engine of American history.[3]

Americans' great land grab was not only massive in scale but also relatively democratic in execution, opening up land ownership to masses of individuals who were closed out of European property. Of course, elite politicians and speculators were able to game the distribution of public lands, and this history tells that story. But *relative* to virtually all other Western societies, the new American republic would stand as the most egalitarian landed society yet seen. With no monarchy or inherited aristocracy claiming ultimate ownership and Native Americans uniformly discounted and progressively displaced, the land was available to all who were white and male. That many Americans never attained ownership (most notably enslaved persons and industrial workers, native and immigrant) demonstrates the limits of the promise. But millions did, whether on sprawling plantations, extensive farms, or yeoman holdings. Real estate ownership is so taken for granted today that it is difficult to imagine the novelty it represented on a continental basis. The idea that land might be commodified as private property required a Copernican revolution in thinking about property and private ownership. What began haltingly and piecemeal in Tudor England became in colonial America nothing less than a radical new economic orthodoxy whose promise would draw millions of immigrants to American shores. The acquisition of land became the magical elixir that would transform western lands from "wilderness into property."[4]

Early Americans on an unprecedented scale embraced private ownership of land, and with it the greatest freedom and power of any population of common people on earth. And therein lies the rub as well. Native Americans, who had never believed that they "owned" the land, were now driven from their ancestral agrarian and hunting grounds by these alien Euro-Americans who brought with them equally foreign European conceptions of land ownership.

These new Americans were promised not only personal-property ownership but protection of their ownership by the full might of American government. In fact, the legitimacy of the state depended on its ability to preserve the absolute sanctity of personal property—especially land—from seizure or surrender. For land ownership to work it had to be perceived as irrevocable and inheritable. Far from being beyond the law, Americans moving to the frontiers depended on the inviolable rule of law in order to grow and prosper. Houses required titles, farm lands required deeds, businesses and banks required statutes of incorporation, and boundaries required defense. All of these markers of individual ownership are taken for granted in modern, non-communist societies, but even today the majority of world populations lack any property guarantees. In contemporary China, the world's most populous nation, there is no such thing as private property. From colonial origins to the present real estate bubble, land has constituted one powerful magnet that draws ordinary immigrants hoping to realize their own dream, grounded in the trinity of entrepreneurship, property rights, and capital markets.[5]

More than any other commercial medium, land became the conduit for many (though by no means all) to realize their own economic dream in the new nation. The Prussian immigrant Francis Lieber (later of Civil War fame) observed that in America everywhere he looked he saw a "striving and driving onward . . . a diseased anxiety to be equal to the wealthiest, the craving for wealth and consequent disappointment, which ruins the intellect of many." Land acquisition drove the "diseased anxiety" more fully than anything else in the early republic. It was a universal commodity distinguished mainly by its abundance and easy access. The Andersons exemplified this striving for wealth and rode its waves of profit and anxiety in a ceaseless circle of emotional extremes.[6]

Along with the acquisition of land inevitably came intense levels of anxiety about holding on to it. What one can acquire, one can also lose. There is a large and still-growing body of psychological, sociological, and medical literature on anxiety in modern American culture. But absent from much of this modern literature is attention to anxiety as a historical phenomenon. Puritan anxiety over salvation is a well-worn path of historical analysis. Anxieties over political independence grew aplenty in the aftermath of independence. And in the early republic, no one knew where America's experiment in democracy and capitalism might go. Federalists and Jeffersonians worried that victory of the other would be catastrophic. Anxiety was not a function of disproportionate material needs but arose out of soaring expectations. Told they were a "redeemer nation" and "the last best hope of earth," Americans perceived apocalyptic stakes in what it meant to be an American.[7]

By invoking anxiety as the controlling interpretive theme in this book, I do not mean to employ it in the clinical sense of the term as a nervous disorder characterized by excessive apprehension, typically with compulsive behavior or panic attacks. Rather, I have in mind a particular (and rational) concern over heightened expectations and fears surrounding one's material well-being. Anxiety stands as a marker for understanding the worries of families like the Andersons about class and status, and also as a means of understanding how it actually felt to have such incredible opportunities for speculation. Anxiety captures both the sense of possibilities and the dangers inherent in the great land grabs of the late eighteenth and early nineteenth centuries.

Beyond national apprehensions about the meaning of America, anxiety was especially pronounced where opportunities and failures were the greatest: on the unsettled frontier. Stories of incredible wealth and success were more than offset by stories of loss and failure. The causes, moreover, appeared to result from luck as much as character. Good and decent people went bust while charlatans and gamblers could profit wildly at others' expense.

It was precisely the luck factor that could make anyone anxious. What if drought follows the season when I acquire my farm? What if Indian attacks destroy what I worked so hard to build? What if ubiquitous but unpredictable banking panics devalue all I have struggled to achieve by a factor of ten? All of these calamities struck people who settled the often-isolated homesteads in the nation's unstable frontier communities.

The intimate association of Andersons with land, property, and anxiety was profound but not exceptional for their time. Our story begins with the patriarch, Colonel Richard Clough Anderson Sr., a twice-wounded Revolutionary War hero. With America's independence, his fellow Virginia officers elected him to the critically important lifetime position of surveyor general of the Virginia Military District—a vast tract of land in what is now Kentucky and Ohio that was set aside by Congress to pay Virginia veterans for their service in the Revolution. In this position Anderson was responsible for surveying and distributing millions of acres of land. In the process, he acquired a fortune in land for himself and his children. We also look at his two wives. Elizabeth (Betsy), sister of Revolutionary War hero George Rogers Clark and William Clark of Lewis and Clark fame, bore four children— Richard Jr., Ann, Cecelia, and Elizabeth—before dying in 1795. Richard Sr.'s second wife, Sarah (Sally), second cousin of Chief Justice John Marshall, bore twelve children, eight of whom survived to adulthood: Maria, Larz, Robert, William, Mary, John, Charles, and Sarah. In all, there were twelve surviving children.

From the patriarch, I turn to his distinguished children and chart their careers and families, both individually and collectively, as a close-knit family that functioned, in effect, like a family business, in which different members contributed different skills and achievements but all worked to encourage family well-being. In one way or another, all were centered on public service and land acquisition. While different children come to the fore at different points in time, I aim to weave their stories into a single narrative. Although I begin with the patriarch, Richard Clough Anderson Sr., and introduce some of his more famous grandchildren, most attention is given to his children—the first generation of men and women born under the stars and stripes.

As founding elites, the Andersons were actively complicit in two of America's greatest shames: slavery and Indian removal. Anderson Sr. and all of his sons were at some time slave owners (they believed slaves to be essential to the development of land assets), and all possessed the common white racial attitudes toward African Americans. All were also eager to procure Indian lands in Ohio and Kentucky that lay within the Virginia Military District, through force when necessary. Anderson Sr. served as a militia commander in his frontier community. His brother-in-law William Clark also became inextricably involved with Indian removal as superintendent of Indian Affairs, overseeing treaties that removed Indians from their traditional lands and opened up over four hundred million acres of land for sale to farmers and speculators. Through Robert Anderson, who fought and was badly wounded in the Seminole campaigns to remove the Indians from Florida and in the war with Mexico, we get a graphic sense that the frontier was not in fact free and open but instead a space of conquest.

But this story is bigger than the shames, tragic as they are. What binds the narrative together is the history of land in the American West. Lots of land. In his classic book *People of Plenty*, historian David Potter made the provocative case that successful democracies required "plenty" of resources to marry political democracy with emergent capitalist markets to create an "American Dream." The Andersons personified this thesis. Whether in Kentucky or Ohio, the Trans-Mississippi West or Mexico, wherever the Andersons went land acquisition followed. Like other early Americans caught up with land, they participated in a roller coaster of emotion that exacted great costs, from speculative frenzies to sensational panics. Landowners were especially afflicted by the boom-and-bust business cycle. Every depression year in the span of this study—1819, 1837, 1857, and 1873—was followed by a sharp decline in land sales and valuations. Most—but not all—Andersons fell victim to the financial panics. "Plenty" could be transformed into crushing debt overnight and then back to plenty, leaving Andersons ever wealth-anxious for their futures. This was the world the Andersons inherited, and, in their engagement, this was the America they and their compatriots would do so much to shape.[8]

This book takes advantage of the Andersons' numerous links to American luminaries to connect their narrative with the larger political, social, economic, and cultural history of the new nation. Local themes and events in the Andersons' lives are woven into the larger tapestry of national politics, wars, diplomacy, banks, and religion. Through their lives we witness the ideological explosion of the American Revolution and the birth of patriotism as a civil religion. We see the emergence of democratic rule around a two-party system and the revolutions wrought by Jefferson, Jackson, and Lincoln. Richard Clough Anderson Jr., the first American diplomat to Colombia, championed the Monroe

Doctrine and the doctrine of Manifest Destiny, even though they were later decried by his brothers General Robert Anderson and Governor Charles Anderson. In the Anderson families we trace the rise of a landed middle class. Always in the picture is what scholars label the "Market Revolution" and, with it, the outlines of an emergent laissez-faire capitalist system that observed few restraints and that was, perhaps, the greatest source of anxiety. Finally, as the Andersons were slave owners, we see the emergence of sectional tensions that would culminate in the third two-party system of Democrats and Republicans, with the American Civil War as the climax. Almost all of the Anderson sons and grandsons fought in the Civil War, most on the side of the Union.

Like many nineteenth-century families, the Andersons spanned many decades, and the children defy standard classifications of a generation. There was a roughly seventy-year spread from the first to the last son's death covered in this narrative. Some of this generation's wives lived into the twentieth century. What begins as a late-colonial story spans every decade of the nineteenth century. Genteel Virginians evolve into revolutionaries and frontiersmen, who, in turn, become professionals, wealthy landowners, and major politicians. The wives and children leave behind lonely and isolated lives on the edge of American civilization to become the toast of western society.

In the final analysis, this project aspires to tell the big story of the growth of the American republic through particular stories of the Andersons and the acquisition of the territory that would become the United States. After they and their peers broke the chains of an inherited colonial past, they stood ready to invent their future as citizens of a great experiment. They offer examples of how many would face the difficulties and opportunities of their time. Through their stories we see how daily decisions in league with continental aspirations expressed assumptions that shaped the fundamental character and structure of the United States then and now.

1

Richard Clough Anderson, the Patriarch

1750–1787

A fter an ocean voyage of several weeks, supercargo Richard Clough Anderson arrived in Boston's harbor in late November 1773. The young man had been at sea since he was sixteen, visiting many ports of call. Now, age twenty-three, he was in charge of overseeing the loading and delivery of trade goods from his employer, Richmond merchant Patrick Coots.

He arrived in Boston to a scene of chaos. The citizens of Boston were outraged by a modest tax on tea, proclaiming that they would not pay taxes to an institution (Parliament) in which they were not represented. The word they used most often to describe this arbitrary exercise of power was "tyranny." In their perceived world, history was determined not by impersonal forces of economics or demography but by good and evil men. In this contest between tyranny and liberty, tyranny would always win unless arrested by lovers of liberty.[1]

A new world of thought and action blossomed before Anderson's eyes. Led by the brewer and activist Samuel Adams, a number of Sons of Liberty assembled at Boston's Old South Church on December 16, loudly denouncing the act of Parliament and pressuring the captains of three ships carrying tea to return to England with their cargo still on board. Most of these protestors were tradesmen, young merchants and craftsmen who worked with their hands and knew how to use their fists. The tea was owned by the East India Company and was considered essential to preserving the company's declining fortunes.[2]

In early December, tea consignees in Charleston and Philadelphia had been forced by protesting mobs to resign, and the tea ships had returned to England with their cargo. But Massachusetts governor Thomas Hutchinson was determined to stand firm and unload the tea, along the way receiving substantial tax revenue. Meanwhile, Samuel Adams had prepared a set of resolutions, modeled on an earlier successful boycott in Philadelphia, urging the captain of the *Dartmouth* to return the tea without paying the import duty, which Bostonians claimed was a tax.

Following the December 16 protest meeting, inflamed members of the Sons of Liberty famously streamed out of the church into the streets, bent on mayhem. That evening, over the course of three hours, they dumped all 342 chests of tea on the three ships into the harbor. The following evening, Sam Adams's cousin, John Adams, described the "magnificent" action in his diary and concluded, "This Destruction of the Tea is so bold, so daring, so firm, intrepid and inflexible, and it must have so important Consequences, and so lasting, that I cant but consider it as an Epocha in History."[3]

The events of the day radicalized Anderson, turning him into a patriot willing to sacrifice all to the "Sacred cause of liberty." The sight of a hundred determined colonists tossing 342 chests of tea overboard thrilled him and drove him to be one of the first Virginians to enlist in the American cause when resistance morphed into outright rebellion and revolution. Many Loyalists, including Anderson's employer, Coots, did not endorse this course and labeled it "anarchy." But Anderson chose to view it as disciplined, calculated resistance in a just cause.[4]

By 1776, Anderson's career had come a long way in a short time. His familial roots were formed in soil receptive to the cause of independence. Anderson's ancestral record finds its American progenitor in Robert Anderson of New Kent County, Virginia (1644–1718). Anderson's great-grandfather was born shortly after the Andersons arrived from England. The name is Scandinavian, but most of the ancestry is British, including English and Welsh. Robert Anderson is referenced by Bishop William Meade, the third bishop of Virginia, and served as a vestryman of his Anglican parish. His descendants would follow his denominational lead. He married, in succession, Mary Overton and Elizabeth Waters, and left two sons on his death. The older, Robert Jr. (1712–1792), moved with his wife, Cecelia, to a prosperous plantation at the aptly named Goldmines plantation alongside the Gold Mine Creek in Hanover County, Virginia. They had two sons, David Anderson, the older, and Robert Anderson III (1712–1792). Robert Jr. had a land grant in 1683, which he allowed to lapse but which was subsequently taken up by Robert Anderson III.

Robert Anderson III married Elizabeth Clough (1722–1779) in 1739. She was the daughter of Richard Clough and Ann Poindexter. Robert and Elizabeth's children, born between 1741 and 1762, included seven boys and four girls. Our patriarch, Richard Clough Anderson, was born in 1750, the sixth of these eleven children.

Of Richard's childhood and youth, little is known. But what is known is significant. First is place: Virginia. By the time of independence, Virginia had emerged as a prosperous, settled colony whose total number of inhabitants far exceeded those of any other of the twelve colonies. His county, Hanover, was located just north of Richmond and had evolved into a settled community of farmers and traders, free whites and slaves. Hanover County was at this time part of the Virginia backcountry, located in the east-central Piedmont and Coastal Plain areas of Virginia, between the Chickahominy and Pamunkey Rivers. Although only twelve miles from Richmond, it sat at a distance from the seat of government in Williamsburg. Two Hanover County politicians destined to play leading roles on the national stage were Patrick Henry (1736–1799) and Henry Clay (1777–1852). Young Richard knew Patrick well, and several of his sons would grow up to be major political allies of Henry Clay.

Richard lacked Henry's and Clay's college education and always regretted it. Whereas his older brother studied in England in preparation to run the family's Virginia plantation, Richard was entrusted to his mother and a tutor. He briefly attended a common school in Richmond but would later insist that all of his children be educated at the finest institutions of higher education. In the meantime, he traded learning for an abiding love of outdoors and adventure. The world of hunting and living in the bush appealed to him. He spent youthful days hunting with his father and a neighbor, John Findley, who owned a pack of dogs. This preoccupation became the locus of Richard's real education, and he acquired a proficiency with a gun and the chase. Though clearly literate, Anderson soon acquired physical capabilities that equipped him well as he traveled miles throughout the country in search of game. Though only of medium height, he was considered remarkable for his strength and agility—qualities that counted heavily in his raw New World environment.

Richard's ancestral home of Goldmines was an imposing structure with massive timbers and large outside chimneys that he would later emulate when he built a fortress house in Kentucky. His grandson Edward Lowell Anderson would later purchase Goldmines and live in it for fifty years. Next to Richard's home was the imposing plantation of the Dabney family, in particular William Dabney (1718–1776). The planter family intermarried with the Andersons and would play a major role in both the Revolutionary War and the Civil War. Like other large plantations, the Dabneys' was both a home and a business enterprise for its white masters, who participated eagerly in the evolution of a national market economy with staple crops of tobacco, cotton, sugar, rice, and hemp. William Dabney was a merchant who dealt with English markets for tobacco and with Bristol shippers.

Slavery was a central part of Richard Anderson's world and would remain such until his death. As part of the largest human-trafficking tragedy in the sixteenth to the nineteenth centuries more than twelve million Africans were captured and shipped against their wills to ports throughout the Western world. Many of these slaves died of disease or murder or suicide along the way. Throughout this period slavery was the straw that stirred the drink of Western economic growth and intersected with virtually every dimension of economic and cultural life, from trans-Atlantic trade to technology, religion, and medicine.[5]

Virginia, with more slaves than any other American colony, participated heavily in the "spiritual holocaust" of enslavement. Hanover County resident Patrick Henry purchased up to 78 slaves for his estates. By the first federal census in 1790, Virginia's black population totaled nearly 300,000. In the second quarter of the eighteenth century, native-born slaves occupied a growing percentage of the slave population. Like his neighbors, Anderson's father owned slaves, and Anderson would as well.[6]

Most of the slave population originated in West Africa, dubbed "Guinea," which included the Ivory Coast, Gold Coast, and Slave Coast. Upon debarkation on American shores, the majority of slaves lived and worked on tobacco plantations and large farms. They were chiefly responsible for transforming raw land, taken from the neighboring Indian tribes, into vast plantations like those found in Europe.[7]

The sea also called to enterprising tidewater Virginians. Their colony was a vital part of a larger trans-Atlantic economy that heavily depended on trade in slaves, agricultural produce, and textiles. By contrast, New England had no plantations and relatively few slaves but benefitted greatly from the trade in slaves and rum. New England merchant ships routinely sailed between Virginia and Massachusetts. In cities such as Boston and Newport, merchants made fortunes directly or indirectly rewarded from the trade in slaves.[8]

Virginia merchants fared equally well, including Patrick Coots, who became a leading elite of Virginia society and benefactor to Anderson. Recognizing the young man's physical strength and evident courage, he took Anderson into his employ. Against the wishes of his father, the sixteen-year-old chose not to stay at home with his favorite brother, Matthew, but instead sailed for distant ports on two continents. At age twenty, Anderson was promoted to supercargo, supervisor of the ship's cargo. In this important post, Anderson's duties included managing the buying and selling of Coots's trade goods at every port the vessel visited. Given the international dimensions of trade, Anderson had to master French as well as seamanship; the ports he visited frequently included Martinique, Barbados, and England. And, of course, in 1773 Coots's vessel also made a stop in Boston harbor, where Anderson's world was turned upside down.

When colonial protest and resistance morphed into armed rebellion, the young Anderson fought to create a new, independent republic. His choice could have been different. Many options were open to colonists, and independence was by no means a foregone conclusion, as Anderson's employer Patrick Coots insisted.

Volunteers like Anderson have been largely lost to history, but they were the soul of what later became the American Revolution. The names of Washington and other Founding Fathers loom large in the retelling of the Revolution. But lost in the star turns of biographers and constitutional scholars is the simple fact that congressional deliberators and many heroic leaders were not soldiers and would have been summarily executed by British authorities were it not for the thousands of young men (and some women) who donned uniforms to fight for independence. To privilege only the voices of the prominent white men is to miss the people outside the starlight. Late in life, Private Joseph Martin, veteran of the Revolution, recorded this thought: "Great men get great praise; little men, nothing."[9]

In speaking of the Revolution, historians underscore its ideological origins and the power of patriotism as its underlying and sustaining causes on a macro level. But such broad strokes rest firmly on the idiosyncratic drivers that propelled ordinary soldiers into harm's way.[10]

We can infer a love for "the cause" from Anderson's willingness to sacrifice all, as well as from local circumstances. Family legend had it that Anderson brought news of the Boston Tea Party to his older friend Patrick Henry. Both attended the church of Henry's uncle, St. Paul's, and grew up in a portion of Virginia destined to stand, with Boston, as a pillar of radical resistance. We can assume that Anderson shared Henry's frothy enthusiasm for liberty and probably found inspiration in his stirring oratory. With the onset of war, he could have sought a safe assignment behind the lines of battle—Henry sought to place him in the position of paymaster general for the Virginia army. But Anderson's preference was active duty on the Continental line. He quickly raised a company of volunteers from Hanover County and was commissioned as captain of the Fifth Battalion, Regiment of the Continental Line (later he would be promoted to lieutenant colonel). His commission was signed by John Hancock, president of the Continental Congress, and dated March 7, 1776.[11]

Once commissioned, he never looked back. Unlike many volunteers, who were frustrated with harsh conditions and poor pay, Anderson stayed the course, fighting from Trenton (1776) to Yorktown (1781) and, in the process, winning higher rank and the respect of his fellow soldiers. Anderson's heroic participation in the battles of the Revolution is important because it forged relationships that would largely shape the later appointments that would enable him to oversee and obtain land and realize the American Dream.[12]

In general, each state organized its own militia as well as Continental soldiers to serve the regular army under General Washington's command. Company officers tended to be local elites, reflecting all the hallmarks of a traditional, deferential social order in which people identified as superiors or inferiors on a finely graded hierarchy.[13]

At the same time that Anderson enlisted, another Virginia patriot, nineteen-year-old James Monroe, mustered into the Third Virginia Infantry as a newly commissioned first lieutenant. The two would come to share a storied revolutionary legacy, though only one would be remembered in history.

Captain Anderson's regiment fought alongside Monroe's with General Washington at the battle of White Plains, New York, on October 28, 1776, a devastating defeat for the patriots. Anderson was assigned to General Charles Lee's detachment of seven thousand at White Plains, while Lieutenant Monroe remained with Washington's three thousand men moving into New Jersey. Washington assumed that Lee's inexperienced force would augment his forces, but in the confusion that ensued after Washington crossed the Hudson, Lee failed to arrive on time. A furious Washington marched through New Jersey for three weeks with no Lee in sight. Anderson, no doubt, shared in that frustration.[14]

By December, Washington's badly depleted army reached the Delaware with only a third of its original strength. Of seventeen officers, only Monroe, Anderson, and four others were with Anderson's regiment at Christmas. The weather was horrendous as poorly fed and clothed soldiers marched through unending rains in a bitter November chill that extended into December. General Washington feared the game was about up unless something happened. Fortunately for him and the cause, something did, indeed, happen—a Christmas Day crossing of the Delaware River followed by a stunning victory at Trenton on December 26.

On January 2, 1777, the Second Battle of Trenton was fought at the Assunpink Creek bridge, resulting in another victory for the Continentals. In the course of battle, Captain Anderson received a wound in the hip. He was transported on a gun carriage to Philadelphia for recovery. While in the hospital he fell victim to a severe case of smallpox, which left him disfigured and, according to one account, "one of the three ugliest men in the army."[15]

On February 10, 1778, Anderson was promoted to major in the First Virginia, then encamped at Valley Forge, where they endured one of the bitterest winters on record. For the poorly supplied American soldiers the main challenge was simply survival. Starvation, disease, and exposure killed nearly 2,500 Americans. But their location in dense forests was eminently defensible and supplied lumber to construct log huts. Throughout the winter, raw troops gained valuable training from the Prussian drillmaster Baron Friedrich von Steuben. His "Blue Book" manual served as the official American military training guide until the War of 1812.[16]

After Valley Forge, Anderson fought at Monmouth, New Jersey, in June 1778 in a standoff that confirmed the value of von Steuben's training and discipline. In autumn 1779, the Americans, allied with five hundred white, free black, and slave soldiers from the French colony Saint-Domingue, sought to recapture the port of Savannah. The American commander, General Benjamin Lincoln, ordered Anderson and the First Virginia to join the expedition and assault the British defenders at the Spring Hill redoubt—an imposing embrasure sixteen to eighteen feet high. Anderson took the lead in the attack, and he was among the first to reach the top. No sooner had he arrived, however, than a British soldier stabbed him with a sword through his shoulder, sending him tumbling over the edge. He hit the ground with such force that he ruptured his spleen, an injury from which he would never fully recover. The assault was repulsed, and on the march to camp Anderson gave comfort to yet another foreign ally, his former messmate and Polish nobleman Casimir Pulaski, who was mortally wounded and died in Anderson's arms. Before dying, Pulaski presented the American with his ornate sword, which remained in the Anderson family as a poignant reminder of the costs of war.[17]

With the Savannah campaign in tatters, the Continentals retreated to Charleston, where Anderson was again hospitalized. When General Lincoln surrendered his army on May 12, 1780, the still-recuperating Anderson was thrown into the prison at Fort Moultrie (which his son, General Robert Anderson, would command eighty years later). Freed on exchange after nine months, Anderson was promoted to lieutenant colonel of the Third Regiment, Continental Line.

As the course of war moved to Virginia, Washington appointed Anderson as the aide-de-camp to the "boy" French commander the

Marquis de Lafayette, who was placed in command of the Continental troops in Virginia. Anderson's intimate knowledge of the country made him a natural for this command and indispensable to General Lafayette. No sooner did Anderson arrive than a desperate Lafayette wrote to Washington on May 24, 1781: "Were I to fight a battle I should be cut to pieces, the militia dispersed, and the arms lost. Were I to decline fighting, the country would think itself given up. I am therefore determined to skirmish, but not to engage too far." He added that of special concern was the British cavalry riding Virginia's finest horses, "whom the militia fear as they would so many wild beasts." To save his army, Lafayette marched on June 3 and 4 in Virginia through dense Spotsylvania thickets known as the "Wilderness," where he was protected by overgrown terrain and torrential rains.[18]

Already outnumbered, Lafayette's situation became even worse when General William Phillips's force was augmented by another seven thousand British troops led by General Lord Cornwallis. To counter the move, General Washington had General "Mad" Anthony Wayne divert his army's movement from Pennsylvania to the Carolinas to come to Lafayette's aid. A relieved Lafayette, already in retreat from Richmond, gave Wayne the route his army would follow, expecting to intersect with Wayne's Pennsylvania troops. A confident Cornwallis, sensing the destruction of the Continental Army in Virginia, wrote a note exulting that "the boy" Lafayette (he was then twenty-four) would soon be routed. Lafayette was derided by the British and resented by the Americans, none more than General Wayne, for his youth and high rank.

Wayne deliberately failed to meet up with his superior Lafayette on schedule, and the marquis ordered Major Anderson to intercept him and hasten him along. According to Anderson's grandson, Major Anderson visited Wayne twice. On the second visit, frustrated by Wayne's petulance and slow progress, Anderson entered his quarters with pen, ink, and paper and asked him what he should write to General Lafayette. An incredulous Wayne stared at Anderson and asked in a menacing tone, "Do you mean to insult me?" Anderson denied any desire to insult the general, only to confirm that Wayne answered to the commands of a superior officer, to which Wayne thundered in reply: "Superior! Superior! Do you dare call any damned foreigner, and a boy, too, my superior?"

Eventually Wayne ran out of energy and returned to a more reasonable mind. When asked about the prospects of victory, Anderson replied to Wayne that in seeing the example of a highly ranked officer refusing to obey the orders of a superior, he didn't have much hope for victory. Then, taking Wayne's measure, he spoke to the prickly commander: "General Wayne, I look to you to remove these apprehensions." Though jealous and proud and quick-tempered, Wayne was also a loyal patriot and replied to Anderson, "Tell him I'll jine him! Tell him I'll jine him! By God! Tell him I'll jine him to-morrow!"[19]

But it would not be easy. Wayne's army, long plagued by disgruntled soldiers unhappy with their pay and supplies, balked at the march, to which the intrepid Wayne responded by immediately court-martialing and executing seven malcontents on the spot, quelling the disturbance and freeing him to continue at a forced-march pace to keep his word.

Finally, on June 10, five days later, Wayne united with Lafayette and marched on his adversary, then forty-eight hours away. Major Anderson, who knew the terrain intimately, directed Lafayette through unused and unknown roads in heavily wooded areas to place his army between Cornwallis and the magazines they were ordered to defend. Without ever confronting the superior forces of the British head-on, Lafayette played a cat-and-mouse game of limited skirmishing with constant surveillance from a distance of twenty miles.

Failing to engage in a climactic battle with Lafayette and unable to turn north due to a French blockade, Cornwallis harbored his entire army in Yorktown, whence he would leave only as a prisoner. Upon seeing Cornwallis trapped in Yorktown with the French navy cutting off his escape, an enraptured Lafayette reported to Washington, "It is the most beautiful sight which I may ever behold." For his central if largely unremembered role in the defeat of Cornwallis, Anderson was promoted to lieutenant colonel on the Continental line and was coterminously promoted to brigadier general of the Virginia militia.[20]

WITH AMERICA'S VICTORY AND independence, Anderson entered the next phase of his career, which would define the abiding passions of his family in years to come. He was a celebrated war hero, and for his loyal service his fellow officers in the Society of the Cincinnati in December

1783 selected him to be the surveyor general of the Virginia Military District—an area of more than four million acres in what is now Kentucky and Ohio set aside for Virginia veterans of the Revolutionary War as payment for their service. The Commonwealth of Virginia had made grants of land ("script") available to the officers and men of the line in lieu of money. To give the script value, the land had to be surveyed and segregated into specified geographical districts. Levels of compensation were determined by rank. For the remainder of his life, Lieutenant Colonel Anderson oversaw the distribution of land and in the process acquired thousands of prime acres for himself and his family. The cost for the natives inhabiting the district would be horrific.

Anderson's election as surveyor general of the Virginia Military District marks a decisive moment in the future of North America. Thus far, his story agrees perfectly with well-loved tales of Revolutionary idealism and bravery. Liberty was a goal worth fighting—and dying—for, and republicanism represented a novel experiment in self-government that transformed the new nation into a laboratory testing whether it could survive without a monarchy, aristocracy, or established church.

But Anderson's election as surveyor general signaled that republican government was not the only experiment in the new nation. Capitalism would also be tested as the overarching economic system. The origins of American capitalism can be fairly traced to the colonial era, but its triumph waited on the conquest of the continent. Capitalism appeared most dramatically in two forms. First was middle-class land acquisition on a massive scale, which represented something new on the face of the earth. Private property would henceforth be considered the right of ordinary men and women. Second was the enduring existence of slave labor—or, what was the same, slave property. Andersons would actively invest in both.[21]

Anderson's appointment as surveyor general, replicated in similar appointments in other states and territories throughout the new republic, signaled the end of autonomy for native inhabitants. In what stands as one of the greatest ironies of the American Revolution, Indians and African Americans belatedly realized that, as far as they were concerned, the wrong side won. Britain would free its slaves in 1833, a full generation before Americans would fight a brutal war to force slavery's end. Indians fared no better in the new republic. As long as Great Britain governed the colonies, the Proclamation of 1763 prevailed, forbidding, at least in theory, expansion into "Indian country" west of the Appalachians. Of course, this did not prevent streams of hunters and squatters from moving west, but it was still a stream then, not the flood that came with independence. Surveyor General Anderson and his family and associates played a central role in that post-Revolution land grab.

Beginning in December 1783, Anderson oversaw the future state of Kentucky (then part of Virginia) between the Green and Cumberland Rivers and what would become Ohio's Northwest Territory between the Little Miami and Scioto Rivers. Soon after signing his land contracts, Anderson moved to Kentucky with his inherited fortune, three slaves, and his belongings, on seven pack horses. He promptly built a log house at a spring on the headwaters of Beargrass Creek on a grant of five hundred acres and named it "Soldier's Retreat." The naming was deliberate, as Anderson would spend a lifetime welcoming soldiers and veterans to his home. In 1787 he served on the first Electoral College for the presidency, voting as a Federalist for George Washington.

In actions that would be replicated across the early national American frontier, Anderson immediately set about imposing traditional order and institutions on the unsettled territory. In 1784 he founded the first Masonic Lodge west of the Alleghenies. As well, he set out into the Kentucky wilderness prepared to survey heavily forested and difficult-to-map land for veterans, their heirs, or purchasers.[22]

In 1787, four years after his appointment as surveyor general of the Virginia Military District and shortly after the United States achieved independence, Anderson married Elizabeth (Betsy) Clark (1767–1795), the daughter of John Clark and Ann Rogers. Her brothers and sisters included Jonathan, John, Anderson's hunting friend George Rogers, William, Edmund, Mrs. William Croghan, Mrs. Owen Gwathmey, and Mrs. James O'Fallon of St. Louis. The tie with the Clarks brought two Virginia—and later Kentucky—families together in one bloodline, sharing a life often defined by the frontier, agriculture, and war with Indians, the French, and the English.

Like Anderson, the Clarks were legendary warriors. One of Betsy's brothers, the highly decorated General George Rogers Clark, was a near contemporary and acquaintance of Richard Clough Anderson Sr.—he was born two years after Richard, in 1752, and died eight years sooner, in 1818. George was one of four Clark brothers who fought as officers during the Revolution. The youngest brother, William, was too young to enlist in the Revolution but later achieved fame with the Lewis and Clark expedition and later as superintendent of Indian Affairs and governor of the Missouri Territory.[23]

We know relatively little about Betsy Clark, but something can be gleaned from the relatively small corpus of letters that survive in her hand. The hand itself is unsteady and the grammar unrefined, reflecting a woman of minimal education and a writing style much like her husband's. Punctuation was minimal, lending her words a stream-of-consciousness effect born of necessity rather than literary creativity.

In a letter to her sister Anna Gwathmey dated April 25, 1788, she announced her marriage: "On the 14th of August [1787] I resigned the single life with a man who, was you acquainted with. I think sister you would approve of my choice. I have no reason to think he was disagreeable [to] the Family who was acquainted with him which is certainly a happiness." Women were lonelier than men on the frontier and depended heavily on family for emotional support. Betsy went on to inform Anna, "I am yet at Ampthill, [in Virginia] which is some months longer than we expected. I am very desirous to go to House keeping and flatter my self we shall have it in our power to accomplish it, in a month or six weeks. [date by a later descendant in pencil: '16 Sept 1788!']" Later in the same letter, Betsy implored her sister to join her: "I learned the other day by a letter sister Lucy received from you, that you was in great hopes of coming to this Country, very pleasing news to me sister, having it now in my power to form a better idea of the place, or near it of my residence probable for life which makes me wish more ardantly than ever, you was living heare, or could I see you, the satisfaction it would give me would be unparalleled." That said, "the risk of life at present is enough to banish every thought of the kind, but this will not be the case always, and I may yet go to see them. Mr. Anderson joines me in love to you, and in obligations to you both for your kind congratulations on our nuptuals." Betsy's letter left no doubt that "the risk of life" was great but also that danger would recede with time, to be replaced by other opportunities and dangers.[24]

With Anderson's short-lived marriage to Betsy (she would die only eight years after they married), his role shifted from war hero to patriarch. Their children would all receive the education he had craved for himself. As well, they would receive land and move into the upper ranks of community leadership and wealth. In time they would marry and parent children of their own who would inherit the colonel's values and patriotism. But his immediate task, as he and Betsy settled into life on the frontier, was to measure and distribute land in the Virginia Military District.

2

Measuring the Land

1787–1796

W hen Richard Clough Anderson Sr. began his new career as surveyor general he was, at the same time, assuming a major role of leadership in a brand-new nation, born in a revolution he fought for and dedicated to a new proposition: that in this republic, the people would be sovereign, "the people" of course being adult white men. Surveyor generals like Anderson were every bit as important to America's evolution as the military generals. They, more than anyone else, were instrumental in measuring the vast space of the public domain and replacing boundless frontiers with organized, commodified boundaries. Anderson and his deputies spread throughout American territories and served as the foot soldiers of an emerging nation premised on the idea that every man was a potential landowner and stakeholder in the new republic. In measuring, marking, and distributing parcels of land, Anderson and his peers made possible the dream of America. They were literally measuring America inch by inch and rod by rod to impose order on the land and make possible prosperity for its ambitious citizens.

Most accounts of the first constitution of the United States, known as the Articles of Confederation, adopted in November 1777, begin by pointing out the weakness of the federal government it brought into being. But this misses the government's control over land. As owner and regulator of the public domain, the federal government assumed enormous potential strength—the ability to employ fiscal and military powers—to acquire land through treaty or war and to regulate its sale and distribution.[1]

In distributing land, Congress turned first to the western territory north of the Ohio that had been ceded by Massachusetts, Connecticut, New York, and Virginia. In the Land Ordinance of 1785, the Northwest Territory was surveyed and laid out in townships six miles square. Each of these townships was subdivided into thirty-six sections, with each section containing one square mile, or 640 acres. Congress mandated that the land be sold for not less than a dollar an acre in lots of at least one square mile. One section in each township was to be set aside for schools.

The Land Ordinance of 1785 set the stage for a final, comprehensive law for the territorial and political organization of the Northwest. In what became known as the Northwest Ordinance, passed on July 13, 1787, the newly surveyed land was organized into territories, each governed by an appointed governor and three judges. When the number of adult free white males in a territory reached five thousand, the territory was permitted to elect a local legislature and send to Congress a delegate, who might speak there but could not vote. Once the adult free white male population numbered sixty thousand, the territory was eligible to be admitted as a state, on equal footing with the original thirteen states. The ordinance stipulated that no less than three or more than five states were to be created in the Northwest. To encourage settlement, the ordinance further provided full protection of private property and encouraged the establishment of schools, but also, in theory, fair treatment of the Indians. Finally, and controversially, slavery was prohibited in the Northwest Territory. With the exception of the slavery prohibition, never agreed to in southern territories like Kentucky or Tennessee, the Northwest Ordinance established the pattern for the organization and government of the substantial lands already owned and those later acquired by the US government. In sum, it made it possible for the new territories of the expanding Union to grow into fully equal states.[2]

Far from being hostile to governments and institutional structures, frontier settlers and speculators depended on the government and its laws to preserve their right to property. Upon settlement, their first act was to register their land and claim private ownership. Their claim to the land—and the full support of the state—was grounded in the fact that they paid taxes. They did not seek out open spaces with fluid boundaries but measured grids marking the exact location of the property they owned in perpetuity.[3]

American ideas of landownership differed radically from European ones. As newly independent Americans contemplated the distribution of huge tracts of land, they hit upon a novel concept that would democratize land distribution and landownership. Land in England was collectively titled "crown lands," implying that all land was ultimately owned by the crown. A very different meaning evolved in America, where unsold and unsettled lands were grouped together into the "public domain" and owned ultimately by the people.[4] In place of crown ownership, the American government installed allodial tenure, a form of absolute private ownership independent of any superior landlord. Ultimately this signaled a new relationship between the individual and land—a landowner's inalienable right to private ownership that could not be superseded and that required the full enforcement power of the state in perpetuity.

In 1787 a new national government was ratified, signaling that the nation was transitioning from a "confederation" of thirteen more or less independent states under the Articles of Confederation to a united collection of states under a strong and central federal government that was empowered to act directly on its citizenry in such all-important matters as taxation, the regulation of commerce, and the disposition of lands in the public domain. The new Constitution laid the groundwork for a functioning nation-state, and its creation of the public domain also pointed to the means by which it could be encouraged and maintained. By wresting the vast western lands from the claims of the original thirteen states and expelling resident Indians, the federal government acquired the means to create a coherent nation-state made up of states and territories. In time, the profits generated by land and mineral wealth would flow to the federal and state governments and to emerging new states that coveted a portion of western land for their own schools, roads, canals, and railroads.

From the start, the Founding Fathers who drafted the Constitution recognized that democratic forms of government alone would not be enough to sustain their republic and constrain their citizens. There would have to be rewards and incentives comprehensive enough to allow a significant number of citizens to participate directly in the spoils of independence. Men and women did not fight and die to be reduced to economic servitude. Successful democracies do not exist by fiat. The experiment in liberty required a substantial material promise and vast abundance. Democratic and constitutional principles are necessary but not sufficient to anchor a successful republic, which is why American foreign policies that attempt to export democracy so often end in failure. Alongside philosophy, there has to be vast, centrally controlled material wealth that can be made available to the populace as shared inheritors of the dream. In contrast to Frederick Jackson Turner's frontier thesis, which argues that American democracy was formed by the American frontier, the frontier was merely one arena in which this abundance was found. In fact, other forms of abundance—by sea, land, and minerals—existed before settlement on the American frontier. This all but limitless bounty, rather than the frontier alone, collectively produced what Turner collapsed into "the frontier aspect of American culture."[5]

Chief among the rewards of independence were the great unclaimed expanses of land. What was once only a dream for many immigrants and citizen soldiers—owning land—would materialize under their feet, with the proviso that they submit to the nation that would grant and guarantee their right to private property. For Virginia veterans, this meant substantial land grants in the Virginia Military District.

The promise of abundance in the nascent republic did not come without great costs. Capitalist mechanisms put in place to exploit the plenty ensured both winners *and* losers in a highly competitive sweepstakes. The anxiety attendant on relentless growth imposed restraints on neighbor-love and Christian brotherhood that could not be reconciled with the insatiable desire for material goods and property, which sat in uneasy tension with traditional communal values. In the necessary trade-off between security and opportunity, the promise of potential abundance all too easily tempted Americans to trade security for excessive risk—until the costs of insecurity became so steep that anxieties set in that could prove crushing.

As surveyor general of the Virginia Military District—an appointment that, like those of Supreme Court justices, carried lifetime tenure—Richard Clough Anderson was tasked with overseeing the measuring and demarcating of this vast treasure. He also stood poised to gain personally from this bounty. Anderson did not have to purchase land to acquire his reward (though he eventually did). His government intended to give it away to him and his friends as the coveted prize for their brave military service. In return for this gift of private property, the new central government asked for unquestioned loyalty. There could be no more local revolts against the national government like Shays' Rebellion in Massachusetts (1786–1787) or the Whiskey Rebellion in western Pennsylvania, which began in 1791. The new government imposed its authority through a system of sticks and carrots that obviated the anarchy and rebellion that many had feared under the Articles of Confederation.

OF COURSE MEASURING AND then distributing the land to an acquisitive citizenry necessitated first its acquisition. To free up the land, the native inhabitants had to be uprooted from their tribal lands and removed to reservations west of the Mississippi, presumably in Spanish territory. The new government aimed to acquire lands through treaties but, failing that, employed forced removal and war. Treaties were drawn up by which Indians virtually gave away expanses of native lands for token payments. This process stood in contrast to that of land acquisition in the colonial period, when British colonists purchased lands from the Indians, either privately in the seventeenth century or through government purchase in the eighteenth. Indian tribes and European governments alike recognized that once the new Americans had finally removed England from the picture, no Indian tribe or competing nation could prevent them from literally overrunning the land and claiming it as their own. The process had already begun with a trickle of pioneers into Kentucky in the colonial era and grew to a steady stream as citizens of the new nation flooded through the Cumberland Gap and squatted on land west of the Alleghenies. The question for the US government was how to control the distribution of land, once acquired, in ways that would contribute to the wealth and cohesion of the nation as well as to the prosperity of its grasping citizens.[6]

The dispossession of the Indians required a legal and moral rationale. Most simply conceived, their land was the spoils of victory. Since so many Indian tribes had allied with the British in the Revolution, they were now obligated to make extensive cessions. Furthermore, Americans claimed that the terms of peace with Great Britain allotted them British lands that Indians occupied but never owned.[7]

But not all Indians had sided with the British. Many on the banks of the Mississippi did not even know a revolution had taken place, nor did they understand the implications of American victory for their lands. So in addition to asserting punitive claims, the Americans had to invent normative moral and religious arguments for Indian removal. America being a nation professing Christian (primarily Protestant) values, its statesmen could not rationalize simply stealing the land from the Indians. To placate their consciences they had to ground their theft in Christian theology and Enlightenment philosophy. Richard Anderson did not have to worry himself through this thorny issue as long as his commanders did. But he did have to fight and defend what he came to believe was his own private property. And he had to convince his neighbors, relatives, and children to do the same.

In looking for the rationale for confiscatory Indian treaties and removal, two concepts were primary: "improvement" and "discovery." Enlightenment theorists, most notably John Locke, had perfected the idea of improvement as the basis for private ownership of land. Americans, like Europeans, claimed the Indians forfeited their rights to the land because they did not improve it according to European standards of farming. John Locke famously proposed "that people could, by adding labour to things found in a state of nature, exercise a maker's right that entitled them to articles, including fields." Because of this supposed Indian deficiency, Americans claimed the right of preemption, asserting that the Indians had lost any right of ownership. In all likelihood, if he had encountered this argument, Locke would have realized that the Indians did engage in farming and that his argument was specious. This does not mean that it was not invoked. Preemption was the lever used to dispossess the Indians of their land and replace them with white property owners throughout the British Empire.[8]

Ultimately, the doctrine of improvement as a grounds for removal did not hold up. American land grabbers conveniently rationalized away the fact that Ohio Indians had occupied and improved their lands, not unlike the Cherokees to the south. But there were differences between

Indians' and squatters' claims to improvement and ownership that doomed the Indian claims. First of all, in Indian societies women typically farmed while the men hunted and warred. For Europeans and Americans, proper farming was men's work, and patriarchy legitimated them even as it discredited Indian female farmers. Second, and even more important, Indians claimed collective ownership of their tribal lands but not private ownership and personal property. Indians, in other words, had no concept of private property, where land was a commodity to be bought and sold like a horse or a plow—or a slave. In a remarkably short time, private ownership would prevail everywhere on the American continent, and with it the perpetual struggle—and anxiety—to own and retain as much land as possible, regardless of one's ability to improve it.[9]

The second moral and legal justification for removal drew on the medieval theological concept of "discovery." Based on a series of sixteenth-century papal bulls, European (and later American) theologians agreed on the right of Christian nations to own the lands they "discovered" if those lands were inhabited by uncivilized "savages." Ultimately, they looked to ancient Israel's conquest of Canaan as the model and archetype for this doctrine. Closely related to the Catholic concept of discovery was the Protestant concept of America as a "New Israel" and of Americans as a chosen people. Undergirding federal Indian law, and the cornerstone of private-property law, was the principle that God commissioned a Christian people to take dominion over all lands on the model of ancient Israel. The foundation of American property law was not only the secular Constitution but also the biblical model of a righteous conqueror acting in God's name to possess the "promised land" for a "chosen people." In this theological logic, chosen peoples were not held to the same standard of defensive wars that defined classic just war theory, nor were they obliged to take prisoners. They could seize the offensive and destroy "hostile" populations just as ancient Israel destroyed entire Canaanite populations. In both cases the rationale was divine exceptionalism. Some American Protestants denounced the argument of discovery as "papist," but not the courts.[10]

As Christian conquerors, European discoverers claimed the right to seize "pagan" lands on the North American continent and to apportion them among themselves. The French, Spanish, English, Russians, and Americans all made claims to North American lands. Again the model was ancient Israel. In commanding the Israelites to inherit their promised land in Canaan, Yahweh at the same time made clear that no natives would be allowed a coexistence. All would be put to the sword. In Deuteronomy 20:16–17, Yahweh commanded the Israelites to commit what in modern parlance would be termed genocide: "But of the cities of these people, which the Lord thy God doth give thee for an inheritance, thou shalt save alive nothing that breatheth: but thou shalt utterly destroy them; namely, the Hittites, and the Amorites, the Canaanites, and the Perizzites, the Hivites, and the Jebusites; as the Lord thy God commanded thee." However harsh these sentiments ring to modern ears, they were what justified early Americans in their audacious land grab. Backed by biblical precedent and America's resurrected identity as the New Israel, the process of Indian removal made perfect sense to them. When secularized, the logic continued to hold, positing superior and inferior peoples. But this should not obscure the Judeo-Christian origins of American Indian policy and the right to private landownership.

Armed with the moral rationales of improvement and discovery and a strong dose of racism, Americans began their relentless march westward. They had imbibed the intoxicating prospect of private landownership for the ordinary man and embraced it to the full. In a remarkably brief period of time they would conquer, measure, and distribute the North American continent, and in the process overthrow Old World models for who got to own land that were grounded in feudal tenets of primogeniture and entail.

KENTUCKY FELL FIRST TO the new American land hunters. Through a series of deceptive treaties and token payments, American citizens steadily eroded Indian territory and surveyed it for private American ownership. Between the lives of frontiersman Daniel Boone (1734–1820) and the powerful Kentucky senator and presidential candidate Henry Clay (1777–1852), a new world of landownership imposed itself on the landscape. This transformation encompassed the initial American conquest of the Trans-Appalachian West (the New West) and marked the onset of the westward expansion of the United States.[11]

While Anderson's stone mansion on the Kentucky frontier, Soldier's Retreat, proved an ideal fortress when Indians sought redress, other early settlers were not so secure. In July 1789, in Anderson's sparsely populated neighborhood north of Middletown, Kentucky, the Chenoweth family was hosting a dinner party when Indians attacked, killing six and wounding seven. Hearing of the raid, Anderson and his brother-in-law William Clark raced to the Chenoweths' house only to find it burnt to the ground. A four-year-old girl who'd survived the Indian raid said, "We are all dead here, Colonel Anderson." The bodies of three of her brothers and a servant lay before her. Her mother, Peggy Chenoweth, survived a scalping and covered her bare head with a knitted cap until her death in 1825. Anderson immediately assumed command and with Clark and a party of six searched for the Indians through the bluegrass country and down the Kentucky River to the Ohio but failed to find them. He brought the Chenoweth survivors back to Soldier's Retreat.[12]

Because of the difficulties and dangers of the Kentucky wilderness, few people embarking on the four-week trek from the East Coast to Kentucky traveled alone. The great migration of squatters, speculators, and veterans began in the late eighteenth century with pioneers coming chiefly from Virginia, Pennsylvania, and North Carolina. They began clearing land and establishing farms only to learn that unoccupied land was no longer free for squatters. They were "free" to bear the brunt of Indian raids and act as a buffer for the populated coast, but not to acquire their own private property unless distributed by the federal government.[13]

In the first years of post-Revolution settlement, the threat of Indian attacks like that on the Chenoweth family was constant. Roaming Indian tribes coming from Ohio raided at will. They ranged through impenetrable woods in small parties and struck without warning in Jefferson County, where the Andersons settled. In 1781, Indians—chiefly Shawnees—killed or took prisoner 131 people, roughly 13 percent of the total population. The isolated nature of the settlements made them especially vulnerable to surprise attacks. If the pioneers managed to survive, their cattle and livestock did not, subjecting them to malnutrition and starvation rations. For many, the only alternative was staying in forts or fortresses like Soldier's Retreat.[14]

The dire straits would not last. The sheer number of clamoring pioneers served notice to the Indians that they could not hunt in Kentucky indefinitely. With America's independence, the Indians could no longer play the British off against the Americans. Instead the Americans were given a free hand in destruction. They burned and plundered Indian villages and cornfields with devastating effects and left Indians solely dependent on hunting for food. Compounding the Indians' problems was the willingness of American pioneers to sell them alcohol in ruinous quantities. The result was that many natives remained in the safer environs of Ohio, where they were a clear majority. By the mid 1780s, native and backcountry hunters had largely left the disappearing forests of Kentucky for Illinois and Missouri. Years of overhunting in Kentucky by Indians and whites alike depleted herds of buffalo, deer, and bears. In their place streamed tens of thousands of men, women, and children, following in the footsteps of families like the Andersons. All were pursuing land—as much of it as they could beg, borrow, or steal.

In Ohio, the other primary site of the Virginia Military District, the triumph of white landowners would not come easily. With independence and the burgeoning of capitalism, four large land companies hoped to accumulate millions of acres of public land on credit, to be parceled and sold for profit. But when a financial panic hit in 1792, the gentlemen speculators were ruined.[15]

The failure of the land companies did not end speculation. A new, second wave of gentlemen speculators emerged for whom military bounty claims and federal lands created competitive alternatives to the land companies. This new breed of speculator played a crucial role in transferring land from public to private ownership in a fairly democratic evolution. The new speculators were, in effect, competitive middlemen who brokered land to the masses, fueling a race for acquisition and spurring the development of the country's economy and western settlement.[16]

In the period prior to 1794, however, it was not clear who would preside over the Ohio Valley. In November 1791, a confederation of Ohio Shawnee and Delaware warriors defeated an American force of 1,400 led by Arthur St. Clair, killing more than 600 men. Not until General Mad Anthony Wayne's defeat of allied Indian tribes at Fallen Timbers near present-day Maumee, Ohio, on August 20, 1794, was the way paved for measurement and settlement. In the ensuing Treaty of Greenville (1795) the United States gained control of the Northwest Territory, an area north of the Ohio River, east of the Mississippi River, and southwest of the Great Lakes, encompassing all of present-day Ohio and southeastern Indiana.[17]

After the Treaty of Greenville, eastern speculators seeking to purchase massive land grants from the government had to compete with other, smaller, private speculators offering land options at lower prices. Initially the government land sales were hampered by elevated land prices. But that did not last as federal prices dropped and migrants poured into Ohio in unprecedented numbers. This vast movement of peoples west was the greatest single fact of nineteenth-century American history. All told, millions of people moved repeatedly, contributing to one of the largest and fastest population shifts in the history of the world. In Ohio alone the population nearly quadrupled, from 223,760 in 1810 to 937,903 in 1830.[18]

For many veterans, the first option was the Virginia Military District. For their service they were awarded bounty land warrants to parcels of land that could also be claimed by their heirs. These awards could feed further speculation when subsequent laws allowed for the sale or exchange of warrants to investors or speculators. The uncertainty of the frontier and the long waiting periods before the final acquisition of land encouraged many veterans to sell their bounty land warrants at cents on the dollar. Surveyor-speculators led by Anderson and his deputy surveyors spotted the best lands and collected the military bounty land warrants to buy them from veterans for their private gain. Sometimes they sought them for themselves, other times for eastern warrant holders whom they charged anywhere from one-quarter to one-half of the land. Nathaniel Massie, for example, surveyed 708 tracts containing more than 750,000 acres either for himself or in partnership with a Richmond firm that collected bounty warrants. In the process he founded the towns of Manchester and Chillicothe.[19]

With Indian removal accomplished through treaty or conquest, the process of survey and settlement took off. Surveyor General Anderson played the lead role, along with his trusted deputy surveyors. Once the Indian threat was suppressed, the surveying began in earnest as the veterans or their warrant purchasers flooded Anderson's office with applications. Besides processing land bounties, Anderson received many inquiries from surveyors interested in working with him in Kentucky and Ohio (and getting more land for themselves).[20]

In order for a veteran to receive a bounty land warrant he first had to get a certificate from his commanding officer stating his years of faithful service and rank. These would determine the size of land he was entitled to. At first, the Continental Congress assumed that the states would provide bounty lands, but with independence the ownership of land beyond the original thirteen states passed to the federal government, which then assumed responsibility for the land's distribution.

After acquiring a certificate that would secure a warrant, the veteran then had to present the certificate to a Virginia court of record, swear an oath to its authenticity that was signed by a clerk of the court, and present the signed oath to the Virginia land office in Richmond. Upon receipt of a warrant, the veteran secured entitlement to claim lands in the Virginia Military District. Unlike nonmilitary warrants, the military bounty warrants specified no particular location for the claim. This lack of specificity would be the source of unending confusion and litigation, rendering Kentucky unique even by frontier standards. Overlapping ("shingled") and competing claims overwhelmed the Kentucky courts. Other issues included competing state and federal courts, with state courts siding with resident landowners and federal courts more open to recognizing absentee owners who had paid for their claims. To further complicate the process, claims had to be settled in a limited amount of time or face foreclosure; if left unsettled, the land would be designated "waste and unappreciated" (i.e., unimproved), allowing others to claim it. Clearly, for veterans lacking basic literacy and legal skills, the roadblocks to actual ownership were formidable. In this sense, land-ownership "by the people" was not as democratic as it appeared on the surface.[21]

Included in Anderson's business records were many land transactions. Unlike the rectangular system of surveying employed in the Northwest Territory, the Virginia Military District continued the colonial and British system of metes and bounds. Lots were divided based on topography, using local markers such as prominent landscape features or notches in trees. By modern standards the boundary descriptions on many warrants, both in Kentucky and Ohio, were extremely vague and impermanent, making it virtually impossible to avoid shingled claims. Typical of these descriptions in Anderson's records was an entry for ten thousand acres from John King. The area encompassed "the upper end of the first yellow banks on the Ohio River." It lay below the mouth of Sabt [Green] River about fifty-five miles and extended up the river. On July 30, 1784, Anderson entered a land claim below the mouth of the Sabt River, a "military warrant No. 165 forty two thousand six hundred 66 acres to be laid in the lands given by law to the officers and soldiers of the Virginia line." Clearly the borders were vague and subject to change over time as the topography changed. But in the race for ownership, precision was not required.[22]

The state of disorder prevalent in early-nineteenth-century land distribution was not the result of neglect or irresponsibility. Quite the opposite. The new government was simply overwhelmed by the challenges it faced on all sides, and ambitious land seekers could easily exploit the lack of deep institutional structures. Answers to myriad questions had to be resolved on the spot. Enforcement mechanisms were inadequate. Boundaries meant nothing. Ultimately the only boundaries that mattered were the Atlantic and Pacific Oceans. Surveyors like Anderson tried to keep up with insatiable demands, but without hope. There were simply too many land-crazed citizens—all on the take—to possibly control and manage far-flung affairs. The government could set policies and establish institutions, but implementation would require a full generation and more. This was the golden age for exploiting weaknesses in the emerging nation.[23]

How did surveying proceed in the Virginia Military District? Given the primary role that land would play in raising government revenue, Congress authorized the secretary of the treasury to assume responsibility for surveying public lands. The Public Land Act of 1796 provided detailed instructions for establishing land offices to sell land and issuing patents to maintain records. In place of the geographer of the confederation, an office that had been established under the Articles of Confederation, the new act appointed surveyor generals and gave them instructions to survey as many meridian ranges as needed. In addition, deputy surveyors were authorized to "run the lines," using marked trees to establish boundaries in each corner of a township and to indicate mines, salt licks and springs, water courses, and, most importantly, the quality of the lands based on soil type. Using the deputy surveyors' notes, the surveyor general was to make a fair "plat" for each township. Plats were cadastral maps consisting of discrete units, each of

which represented a single registered plot of land drawn to scale, show-
ing divisions of a piece of land. They were available at the surveyor general's office and at the place of sale. Eventually, millions of Americans
seeking land would pour over the plats in the thirty public-land states.
Beyond that the surveyor general had few specific instructions. In 1812
the administration of land sales was handed over from the secretary of
the treasury to the General Land Office, which was headed by a commissioner. This included lands in the Virginia Military District, which
earlier had fallen under the purview of the secretary of war. In all, the
thirty public-land states, totaling close to a billion and a half acres, fell
under the administrative machinery of the commissioner.[24]

Anderson's Virginia Military District augured well for the veterans or those who purchased their warrants. Virginia had some of the
most generous veteran land warrants, growing from 100 acres to 400
acres for NCOs and from 1,100 acres to 15,000 acres for major generals. Soldiers who fought with Anderson's future brother-in-law General
George Rogers Clark in the Illinois country received bounties of two
hundred acres. As enlistments waned during the Revolution, incentives
were added, including "a healthy sound negro between the ages of ten
and thirty years, or sixty pounds in gold or silver."[25]

The earliest surveys found Anderson along the rich soil by the
Cumberland River running through Kentucky and Tennessee. The
Anderson-supervised surveying began almost immediately following
the Revolution, and the opportunities for public and private gain were
quickly apparent. In the course of surveying the vast expanse of government lands, surveyors were in a perfect position to identify and chart
the choicest parcels of arable soil for themselves and create a substantial
business that could generate a fortune. Lands that would be surveyed
on the Cumberland River included, for example, 1,666 acres for James
Pendleton's military warrant number 113; 1,666 acres for Nathaniel
Burwell on warrant number 2133; and 500 acres for John Dandrige "as
part of a military warrant no. 77 near Cumberland river, beginning at
James Pendleton's upper corner on the dividing line between the continental and state troops lands, runs with Pendleton's and Burwell's lines
700 poles." Owing to the severity of Anderson's injury when he fell
from the parapet in Savannah, he appointed a number of young assis-
tants to work chiefly in Ohio, far from his office at Soldier's Retreat

along Beargrass Creek in Kentucky. By virtue of their appointment, many of these deputies were destined to play leading roles in Ohio political, military, and economic history. Later, Anderson's sons and son-in-law Allen Latham would also play active roles and often ran the office.[26]

Besides serving veterans and those who purchased veterans' warrants, Anderson's surveying business brought prosperity and substantial land-ownership to him and his family. In all, he acquired twenty-eight thousand acres of land in Kentucky and Ohio, in addition to his homestead at Soldier's Retreat and town lots in Louisville. His career as surveyor general afforded him a comfortable life at Soldier's Retreat, though not the fortune that some of his deputy surveyors and family relations made by speculating in frontier/western lands. He refused to leave Soldier's Retreat, which distanced him from much of the Ohio land.

For Nathaniel Massie, one of Anderson's ambitious deputies and the founder of Chillicothe and several other Ohio towns, land survey-ing led to the eventual ownership of 75,825 acres in the Virginia Mili-tary District in the Scioto Valley. Massie began as a clerk for Anderson and soon became a deputy surveyor. As early as 1788, when the Indian threat still loomed large, he disregarded the dangers and traversed the wilderness, surveying over seven hundred tracts of land spreading over 750,000 acres. When not surveying, Massie partnered with eastern moneyed connections to purchase veterans' warrants at cents on the dol-lar. Other big winners in Anderson's employ included Duncan McAr-thur, future governor of Ohio (90,947 acres), and Thomas Worthington (18,273 acres). Of the 3,900,000 acres in the Virginia Military Dis-trict, seventy-five owners (individuals or companies) eventually claimed 3,320,247 acres, with twenty-two men claiming 1,035,408 acres. And this did not include the lands in what is now Kentucky that were farmed by Anderson. To modern eyes such acquisitions smell of insider trading, and in fact they were. But they were not illegal. In a new nation with no real conflict-of-interest principles, the temptations to profit proved irresistible.[27]

Lawmakers were as avid in their pursuit of property as ordinary cit-izens. The gainers—not nameless thieves operating on the margins—could be found at the very heart of the new republican governments, with names like Washington, Jefferson, Henry, and Morris. In his classic work *Western Lands and the American Revolution*, Thomas Perkins Abernethy traced the often greedy pursuit of land before and after the Revolution and concluded, "It matters not that men speculated in lands, but it does matter that men in high places should have used their official position to fasten their claim on the greatest asset the nation possessed."[28]

Military land warrants were exempt from the Northwest Ordinance, which stipulated survey according to the rectangular or rectilinear New England model and required survey before settlement. And because the Virginia Military District was reserved by the state of Virginia for its veterans, it was not bound to the rectangular survey system of the Land Ordinance of 1785, nor to the requirement of predetermined boundaries. Rather, it followed the method Anderson learned in Virginia of "indiscriminate" (non-rectangular) location of metes and bounds with subsequent survey. Squatters, of course, represented the extreme form of indiscriminate location, but purchasers in the Virginia Military District enjoyed the same freedom, in contrast to the survey-before-settlement mandated by the Land Ordinance of 1785 and the Northwest Ordinance. Competition in the district kept prices low and within the range of ordinary purchasers, thereby, in relative terms, democratizing the whole process. Indiscriminate location enabled the surveyors to act with speed in surveying and acquiring tens of thousands of acres of land. Of course, it also set the stage for multiple claims and inevitable litigation as sometimes two or three "owners" claimed the same land.

Indiscriminate location opened up opportunities for far more abuses and confusion than occurred with the rectilinear, pre-settlement survey. But it also allowed for greater flexibility and speed of acquisition at a time when speed was paramount. An alarmed Northwest Territory governor, Arthur St. Clair, warned Congress in 1801 of a vast number of squatters invading the Ohio territory, stating, "If they are not disposed of soon, such numbers of people will take possession of them, as may not easily be removed." In response, the secretary of war, Timothy Pickering, issued warrants to all eligible veterans upon application. At first, the land warrant was not transferable, though this would soon change. When the lands were ready for distribution, the veteran delivered his warrant to the General Land Office, indicating in it the territory where he wished to locate his tract, which was then drawn by lot. Eventually the warrantee received a patent for his bounty.[29]

After choosing their land, demonstrating that it had not been previously claimed by someone else, and entering it in the General Land Office, the holders turned over their rough drawings or plats to the official surveyor, who, as a federal (not Virginia) employee, then ran the lines with compass and chain, marking the boundaries with blazes or notches on trees.

The basic technology of surveying was simple. The first and primary surveyor's tool was a compass to establish what direction his line was running. A standard-sized Gunter's chain was then employed to measure distance. Each chain was divided into one hundred links, with each link measuring a fraction less than eight inches. The full length was sixty-six feet. An acre measured ten square chains in Gunter's system. The surveying process, while relatively simple, was time-consuming. Land surveys were worked with small-enough units of scale so that surveyors could assume the earth was flat, allowing them to employ only a sextant and a compass for measuring direction and the Gunter's chain for measuring distance. The surveying methods employed by Anderson and his deputies were used consistently during the nineteenth century and beyond, until the entire continent had been measured, mapped, and graded for quality.[30]

Once the land was surveyed, plats were entered in the survey book of the Virginia Military District and a copy with the warrant was sent to the secretary of war or, after 1812, the General Land Office. There the patents were enumerated and sent to the state office in Richmond for delivery to the grantees or their legal representative. Prospective purchasers paid the cost of the survey to the surveyor, estimated at thirty-six dollars for the township. Upon payment, the Land Office commissioner issued a deed for a specified tract.[31]

After the Harrison Land Act of 1800, people were enabled to purchase land in the Northwest Territory directly from the federal government. Soon federal land offices were opened in Marietta, Steubenville, Cincinnati, and Chillicothe. To encourage federal sales the government gave purchasers four-year credit to pay off their land and state governments provided a five-year exemption from state taxes. Ohio's Republican leaders aimed at least in part to attract sufficient immigrants for Ohio to attain statehood. In this they were strikingly successful as eager immigrant purchasers flooded the state looking to procure the

American Dream of substantial landownership. By November 1801, public-lands offices had sold 398,646 acres in a trend that would continue over the next twenty years, making Ohio the fastest-growing state in the nation and enabling it to attain statehood in 1803.

In the event that strapped purchasers did not have cash available, Congress passed several relief acts between 1806 and 1820 to help them hold on to their land. The older gentlemen speculators seeking to corner the market could not compete. Their moment had passed and they were left out of business. Public-land sales transformed land speculation in Ohio by making more and more land available to more and more people. Easy credit terms from western banks helped solve Ohio's chronic currency shortage, allowing public-land sales to reach new heights when immigration peaked after 1815. Rampant speculation by more people fed further speculation. The public-land markets in Ohio, offering access to anyone, made widespread speculation a defining feature of democracy in early Ohio. Of course there were losers as well as winners in this land sweepstakes, but either way, the thirst for land and private property fueled a rapidly expanding economy and would be replicated in other frontiers across the nation. These new speculators, unlike their aristocratic gentlemen predecessors, made speculation morally acceptable as long as it took place on a relatively level playing field, in a competitive market open to all.[32]

Public land represented the future of America's emerging capitalism. But private ownership did not come without costs, beyond the initial warrant or purchase. It was well and good to plot the land and secure private boundaries. Throughout the Anderson family correspondence, we will see that the words *anxious* and *anxiety* appear regularly. Anxiety would be the cost of private landownership. After an individual secured a land stake, the stage was set for conflicts and litigation. First, as we have seen, were wars with Indians, who contested the violent seizure of their ancestral lands on a vast scale. For them, a Gunter's chain represented the shackling of Native American freedom. Then there were competing claims with overlapping boundaries, to say nothing of outright squatters who refused to leave their land after it was surveyed for sale. Then there was the irresistible urge to "trade up" and speculate on vast bodies of land available sometimes for cents on the dollar. The problem with speculation lay in devastations wrought by regular financial panics. Bank closures led to dried-up credit and ensuing anxiety as land assets were massively devalued, reversing the sequence, from dollars to cents, and leading often to bankruptcy—and then, if serious enough, leading to debtor's prison. Add to these man-made catastrophes shortened life expectancies, epidemics, drought, and blight, and many of the pieces of an anxious republic fall into place.

One additional piece loomed large: problems with other European land claimants. With independence, America was not left alone with the Indians. Other European powers—notably Spain, France, Russia, and Great Britain—maintained claims on North American lands that would have to be wrested away. In frontier Kentucky, frustrations with the "East" festered, leading many to openly contemplate a declaration of independence of their own from the United States and/or alliances with competing European powers. Presidents and legislators from Washington through Jefferson realized that they were far from secure in their western claims. Only time and demography would multiply the American population so dramatically that it would dwarf all other claimants and simply overrun them.

The most dramatic instance of threatened secession centered on a dynamic provocateur named James Wilkinson, who schemed to pull Kentucky (not yet a state) out of the Union and into Spain. At the time Kentucky was still seeking statehood and frustrated by perceived slights from the East Coast establishment. On July 2, 1787, the flamboyant Wilkinson arrived in New Orleans and boldly informed the local Spanish authorities that disillusionment with the neglect of eastern power-brokers in Congress was placing Kentucky "on the eve of establishing herself a free and independent state." Wilkinson went on to claim, disingenuously, that Kentucky's legislature had commissioned him "to develop if possible the disposition of Spain towards their Country, and to discover, if practicable, whether she would be willing to open a negociation for our admission to her protection as subjects." Wilkinson's promise to provide access to the Mississippi and to New Orleans ports offered angry Kentuckians an alternative to shipping east, and for a time, he was the toast of the town. With the ratification of a new constitution the next year, however, Wilkinson's hopes floundered, but not before offering powerful testimony that Kentuckians were more than willing to sacrifice membership in the Union if their economic wishes (chiefly cheap land) were not met. Republican ideology would only go so far to placate acquisitive citizens, but Anderson was not among Wilkinson's allies. At a 1787 meeting of the Danville constitutional convention, he was offered a $1,000 bribe to support Kentucky's secession from both Virginia and the United States in order to become a ward of Spain. He turned the offer down immediately.[33]

With a more powerful federal constitution, the East would no longer be able to play the role of Great Britain to the West's humiliated American colonies. There would be representation and their voices would be heard when it came to navigating the Mississippi and, in 1802, formal Kentucky statehood in the Union.

COLONEL ANDERSON'S WORK AS surveyor general was substantial, but it did not constitute his only economic interest. Beyond surveying for veterans he pursued his own private investments, including the purchase of land in the downtown Louisville district. He also drew on his supercargo experience, building the 450-ton *Caroline*, the first schooner to sail the Ohio River. Fortunes could be made quickly with successful voyages, and Anderson made one such voyage to London. But then his luck ran out. On the next voyage to London the ship was wrecked in the West Indies, and with it, Anderson's dream of mercantile wealth.[34]

Anderson also experienced disappointment with a hemp factory he built at Soldier's Retreat. In December 1810 he wrote his sixteen-year-old daughter Elizabeth (also called Betsy) at the Domestic Academy, a finishing school for girls located in Frankfort, that "I am under the disagreeable duty of informing you of my misfortune. The factory was yesterday consumed by fire, with the hemp and everything appertaining thereto. I shall endeavor to rebuild as soon as the season and circumstances will admit. . . . Heavy as the loss is, I am and shall be satisfied while you my dear girle and the other children continue to act with propriety." Thenceforth all his ambitions would be connected to land.[35]

With independence, Anderson's civic and social engagements included membership in the Electoral College that elected Washington president and service as the first Masonic Lodge master west of the Appalachians. As well, he was elected a member of the Society of Cincinnati, a fraternal order limited to officers who had served at least three years in the Continental Army or Navy. Included in the order were such luminaries as President Washington, Alexander Hamilton, Major General Baron von Steuben, South Carolina statesman Thomas Pinckney, and Revolutionary War veteran Henry Lee. Three generations along, a fabulously wealthy great-grandson of Anderson, Larz Anderson III, would donate his luxurious winter residence in the Dupont Circle neighborhood of Washington, DC, to the Society. Ever since, the Anderson House has stood as the national headquarters of the Society of Cincinnati.

At home, the Anderson family thrived. One year after marriage, Richard and Betsy had their first child, a son named Richard Clough Anderson Jr., who would spend the first ten years of his life at Soldier's Retreat. Along the way three sisters would join him: Elizabeth, who died young; Ann (1790–1863), who later married another frontiersman, John Logan (d. 1826); Cecelia, who remained unmarried and died in 1862; and Elizabeth (1794–1870), who married Isaac Gwathmey (dates unknown).

Betsy soon fell into a mother's frontier existence. Like other women on the frontier, she was often left alone in a hostile and dangerous environment and missed her parents and siblings mightily. In fact, the women depended upon their families more than on their husbands, whose work often took them out of the house. In a letter to her brother, General George Rogers Clark, written from their childhood home in Urbana, Ohio, the still-young Betsy (age twenty) sounded a surprisingly wise (and prophetic) note on the shortness of life on the frontier for the women no less than the men. After a difficult childbirth with her daughter Elizabeth, from which she would never recover, she wrote: "There comes a time in life, when instead of looking forward with hopeful longings, dreaming dreams, and building castles, one begins to look back, and find pleasure rather in the past, and wonder how hope let on so long. I believe I am getting old, and perhaps beginning to discover as Solomon did, that all is vanity."[36]

In 1789 Betsy reiterated her desire to be reunited with her sister Anna. After announcing her housekeeping duties at Soldier's Retreat, she wrote that they were "six or seven miles from daddayes [sic] and in an exalant [sic] neighbourhood. I fear it is yourself Sister, to wish you was, one of our neighbours."[37]

In 1794, Betsy wrote what would turn out to be her last surviving letter to Richard, who was away surveying. After noting that she had just received his letter, she wrote:

> Our little children rejoice with me, at the happy news of your safe arrival thro' the wilderness. . . . Dick and Nancy (Ann) often ask how long it is before Papa will come home, and Cecelia replyes Papa is gone to bring her red shoe . . . thus am I entertained by the children, they are the most of my company. I see no one, but those who come to the House, except one week at my father's. I have never dined from home since we dined together. Daddys family appears to be well except Fannys children, Benjamin they expect will die.

She closed on a somber note: "[I] am left to every reflection, the approach of the end of my travails." She then charged her husband to care for their children: "But remember mr. Anderson, you would be their only guide, their only protector, and live for me and them, and be assured, I shall fulfill the promise I made you when we parted, of taking care of my self, for your sake, and for our dear, our helpless childrens."[38]

By the time Richard got home, Betsy had died. In a letter from Soldier's Retreat to friend and neighbor Owen Gwathmey, a distraught Anderson wrote, "Great God, and am I to be the messenger of the most disagreeable and tragic news to all my friends. I got home here on the eighth of December," and here the page is discolored and unreadable, but its meaning is clear.[39]

Many were quick to offer condolences and help. In May 1795, Anderson's friend Thomas Parker wrote, "It was with the most unfeigned sorrow that I heard of the death of your amiable wife by Mr. Ware; But I trust that the reflection that she now enjoys a more compleat happiness than she could do on earth together with your natural strength of mind and good sense will support you under so heavy a loss." More concrete assistance came from fellow soldier and neighbor William Croghan, who had fought with Anderson and married Betsy's sister. He lived next to Anderson in a mansion of his own and was a fellow surveyor of the Virginia state line. In November 1795 he wrote to an absent Anderson that he was happy to help with the surveying and the children: "I am happy in having it in my power to inform you that your children are all well, as are my and Mr. Clark's family, except Mrs. Clark who is recovering from a fever. . . . The applications were so frequent to your office by different people that I was under the necessity of bringing your books of entry and record to my house otherwise I could not do the business without moving to your house."[40]

By 1795, after Betsy died, the modest Soldier's Retreat mansion-fortress was rebuilt of stone, with walls so thick that the sills of the windows afforded ample space for sitting. The sixteen-room house was constructed of local gray limestone, which would not withstand the test of time, but in its day it was a destination stop for friends and fellow veterans. Anderson's surveyor office was located to the rear of the mansion, together with the "servants' quarters," which eventually housed twenty slaves.

Richard administered discipline among his children and his slaves with seeming equity—or at least as much equity as could occur in the vicious system that was slavery. If his sons instigated fights with slaves, they were punished (unless the slave administered sufficient punishment on his own defending himself). However, Anderson shared the thoroughgoing racism of his time and place and sought to minimize contact between his children and slaves. As throughout the slaveholding populace, hard labor was performed almost exclusively by slaves in a system premised on the violence of the lash and terror.[41]

Horsemanship was taken for granted in Kentucky, and most landowners were experts in judging and breeding horses. The Andersons proved no exception. Frontier society also highly prized dancing, and one's status was reflected in the types of dancing performed. Members of the Anderson household learned to dance the minuet, reels, and country dances. Anderson-sponsored dances in the second-floor ballroom of Soldier's Retreat were regular occurrences. In addition to slaves who played the fiddle, other members of the Anderson family also played, including Anderson (who did not dance).

Anderson depended on crops of sweet potatoes, peas, corn, and nuts. In addition to the quail, venison, bear, and other game available in the surrounding woods, the household at Soldier's Retreat provided ducks, milk, and home-brewed beer. Of all the animals, pigs were by far the most important in Kentucky, and the Andersons enjoyed their ample share of ham.

However, in contrast to Europeans', Americans' appetites ultimately focused insatiably on land. Precisely because it was so abundant, they wantonly used up the land and its resources. They gave little or no thought to fertilization or crop rotation, and all sought maximum acreage. The preferred crop of tobacco took an inordinate toll on the soil.

With the measuring of the land and the removal of the native nations, land speculators threw open the gates of expansion to an infant nation. Richard Sr.'s children, the first generation to be born under the stars and stripes, would inherit the rewards. They would also inherit the perils.

3

A New Generation

1797–1812

Colonel Richard Clough Anderson would live until 1826. Meanwhile, the family's history would steadily expand as the extended network of children and in-laws matured and assumed center stage. The children would inherit the fruits of their parents' revolution and represent the face of the new republic. Of Richard's four children with Betsy Clark, few traces of information exist for the girls. Not surprising for this era, the eldest son, Richard Clough Anderson Jr., appears frequently in the historical record.

It did not take long for Anderson to remarry after the death of Elizabeth. His second wife, Sarah Marshall, brought yet another storied name into the Anderson web of associations. Sarah, born in 1779—and twenty-nine years younger than her husband—was a second cousin of Chief Justice John Marshall of the illustrious Marshall family of Virginia and Kentucky. Together, Richard Sr. and Sarah produced twelve children. Typically, frontier families were large, with an average of seven children born to white women and nine to enslaved black women. The latter statistic has relevance to the Anderson family life because, in addition to her own brood, Sarah eventually oversaw forty slaves and spent a great deal of time providing basic needs for both her own children and slaves.[1]

In his genealogy of the Andersons, Clarks, Marshalls, and McArthurs, General Thomas Anderson recalled his grandmother, Sarah

Marshall, talking about famous visitors to Soldier's Retreat, including Henry Clay, Andrew Jackson, James Madison, Aaron Burr, and the Marquis de Lafayette, but the most memorable to her was Little Turtle, chief of the Miamis, who visited often. On one occasion he was presented with a pair of pistols, and on another he met George Rogers Clark: "To her, Little Turtle was a great man. She remarked on his dignity and fondness for children."[2]

Richard Anderson Sr. proved to be an attentive father to both the girls and boys of his large family. Making good on Elizabeth's plea, he strove to ensure that their daughters and Richard Anderson Jr. were well taken care of and directed into meaningful lives. Although not well educated himself, he clearly favored education as a path to success for both the girls and the boys from his two marriages.

Anderson Sr. took particular care with Elizabeth (Betsy) and Maria, two of his daughters with Sarah. In a typical letter to Betsy, who was then a student at the Domestic Academy with her sister Maria, he enjoined her to work hard and brought her up to date on the family, including his children with Sarah: "Robert, William and Sophia have all bad colds, Robert has a fever with it, your mama is a little unwell also; the rest of the family are well. I am much pleased to see that you have attended a little more to your writing. . . . I would wish you to practice a little more frequently in writing to us, the letter you mentioned that you had written to Cecelia has not come to hand. . . . You may expect to see me at the vacation." Two months later Anderson Sr. again entreated Betsy to "continue your attention to your studies."[3]

In June 1810, Betsy received news from her father of a visit from her cousin John O'Fallan; he also queried her about her classmates: "My dear Betsy Will you when you write again tell me what number of pupils are at the academy if any newcomers and if any of the pupils has not retained? Maria has written to your mama, she is now answering her letter. I have just returned from Louisville it is near night I cannot write to Maria, you will let her know the reason of my not writing." In July he asked about upcoming examinations: "It is probable that you may have given me information when the examination will take place. Should that be the case and I receive them in time you may calculate on seeing me there. . . . Continue your diligence dear girl, for if you did but know the violence it is doing my feelings to part with my children you would endeavor to shorten the time of our absence on account of your loving and affectionate father."[4]

Obviously frustrated by the lack of prompt response, he followed up with another letter to Betsy the same day to "inform you that it was my intention to be up in August at the examination, which I shall now decline, unless I am informed what time the examination will commence. . . . You my dear Betsy will continue to deserve the praise she [Maria] is pleased to bestow on you." Again, on the same day, Betsy's stepmother Sarah also wrote a pleasant, if awkward, note asking for "your drawing which I prize highly." "Eliza Samuell says will you please to draw her a flower she is soon here going to school and is a very good child for learning her book. . . . I send you a few open work stitches Sister Samuell done when she was down."[5]

Meanwhile, Anderson's surveying business was thriving, bringing prosperity and substantial landownership. Anderson's career as surveyor general afforded him a comfortable life, though not the fortune that some of his deputy surveyors and family relations made by speculating in frontier/western lands. Part of the explanation for Anderson's lesser (though still substantial) fortune was the sheer rigor of the work on his war-weakened constitution—at least in the early years, when most of the land was distributed. As well, his refusal to leave Soldier's Retreat for Ohio left him distant from much of the Ohio land distribution, for which he relied on his deputy surveyors, who secured larger claims. Finally, his private fortune was limited by his own active disposition. Office life was not for him. The outdoors constantly beckoned, and nothing afforded him greater pleasure than long hunting trips with his neighbors and brother-in-law General Clark, before the latter's removal to the Illinois territory. When not hunting or surveying, Anderson shared with Sarah the responsibilities of farming and managing a growing staff of slaves.

In a patriarchal society, the sons were privileged with preparation to lead the rising generation, even as the daughters played equally important, if less noticed, roles on the farm and in the household. For Anderson Sr., this meant that special hope was invested in his first son, Anderson Jr.

Richard Clough Anderson Jr. began his childhood in the family home in Louisville and two years later moved to Soldier's Retreat, soon after which his mother, Elizabeth, succumbed to complications from the birth of his sister Elizabeth. As the eldest son and firstborn, he occupied a unique place in his father's eyes. Already, Anderson Sr. enjoyed some fame, and the same was expected of his son.

Following the death of his mother, Richard divided his time between his father, who traveled frequently to Louisville and the survey sites, and his grandfather, John Clark. His education began at Soldier's Retreat with his cousin, a private tutor named Charles Anderson, who was brought into the home by his father. In his diary, begun in 1814 at age twenty-six, Richard notes his birth and the death of his mother and then proceeds to bring the story up to date.

The tutoring with Charles Anderson lasted until November 1800, after which young Richard moved to the ancestral homeland in Albemarle, Virginia, where he studied with the Reverend James Maury (who earlier had tutored Thomas Jefferson) and T. L. Elliott. Of Elliott, Richard recalled, "He was a good teacher. The neighborhood was most kind polite and hospitable—hospitable beyond any I have ever known." He made a good friend there, Lucy Hill Walker, "and became as much attached to her as a boy could be to a fine and handsome and good girl." He remained there until the fall of 1802, when he moved again, to Gloucester, Virginia. There he completed preparation for college with his uncle, Matthew Anderson. Apparently Anderson Sr. was gone so often surveying (and adventuring) in Richard's early years that he left the education of his children to other friends and family members. Of his experience with Matthew Anderson, Richard recalled: "My uncle tho eccentric, was most kind and affectionate to me for more than four years during which time I was under his Control and management. I will revere his memory as long as I can remember that he lived. He was a proud, independent and most honest man."[6]

In 1802, while under Matthew Anderson's "management," the fourteen-year-old Richard entered the College of William and Mary in the same class with the future general Winfield Scott and two years before his close friend John Jordan Crittenden, who was destined for political greatness in the new republic. College attendance was rare at that time, particularly on the frontier, but Anderson Sr. was determined that his children would receive the education he never enjoyed. Anderson Jr. blazed a trail that all his brothers would eventually follow, an achievement that would position them well to participate in the burgeoning nation's leadership at a most critical moment.

THE ELECTION OF THOMAS Jefferson as president in 1800 signaled the era of yeomen farmers and austerity, and Jefferson won immediate approval from western farmers when he eliminated the hated tax on whiskey. Other federal taxes were also reduced. This had a critical impact on the designs for the nation's emerging capital city, and it effectively slashed general federal budgets as well. Army and navy expenditures shrank despite ongoing threats from the British and the Barbary pirates.

Washington, DC's unfinished and dilapidated buildings during Jefferson's presidency underscored how far the Jeffersonians moved from the Federalists' more regal bearings under George Washington. Republican lawmakers approved no new monies for the nation's capital and refused to provide a decent salary for the president. Aspiring legislators gravitated to state governments rather than a national government that did little besides maintain a postal system, run occasional federal courts, and maintain one national road and a few lighthouses. The entire federal civil service amounted to 153 people when Jefferson assumed office.[7]

But all was not lost with diminished tax revenues. Land would come to the rescue in unrivaled munificence. Instead of a grandiose capital, as planned by designer Pierre L'Enfant and Major Andrew Ellicott, Jefferson promoted his Louisiana Purchase in 1803—his "empire of liberty"—as a perpetual guarantor of the yeoman republic. This acquisition—though technically incompatible with Jefferson's philosophy of minimal government—together with low taxes and simple style, would characterize the new party's orientation.[8]

Although the Constitution made no provision for federal acquisition of new lands, Jefferson was willing to overlook the possibility of federal overreach when the opportunity to acquire the vast Louisiana territory from Napoleon arose in 1803. He aimed both to remove France's and other European nations' presence from the region and to address Americans' insatiable appetite for land.

Rival land claims by Spain, England, France, Russia, and the United States had led to a breakneck race to acquire more Indian lands and claim them for national colonial purposes. But the contest was never equal. Hundreds of thousands of American settlers crashed through borders everywhere, and no European nation could maintain a force in North America sufficient to contain them.[9]

On January 11, 1803, Jefferson announced the retrocession of Louisiana to the United States and his nomination of Richard Anderson Sr.'s friend and presidential hopeful James Monroe to join Robert Livingston in bargaining with France, with a congressional appropriation of $2 million. Monroe's mission was to gain an exact sense of the boundaries of the retrocession and to acquire as much of New Orleans and the Floridas as possible. As well, the agents were to make plain that neither France nor Britain would be welcome at the mouth of the Mississippi. Monroe did not know that Livingston had encouraged the United States to assume claims against France and permit speculators to profit by buying up claims in advance of the formal purchase—another instance of insider trading.[10]

Many supposed that negotiations with France would be long and protracted, but within two days of Monroe's arrival in Paris, Napoleon clinched the sale of the entire Louisiana province based on his knowledge of Congress's appropriation. In what stands as the largest territorial gain in American history, the Louisiana Purchase stretched from the Mississippi River to the Rocky Mountains. In all, the purchase expanded US territory by 828,000 square miles, totaling 529,920,000 acres. In one fell swoop Jefferson's purchase increased American territory by 140 percent, with no major tax hike. All of this for the grand total of $11,250,000 in cash and $3,750,000 in debt forgiveness (far above the congressional appropriation), for a total purchase price of roughly four cents per acre. Although it was not entirely clear at the time, this would mark the single greatest achievement of Jefferson's presidency.[11]

Whatever opposition Jefferson faced from Federalist New Englanders quickly disappeared with the realization that hundreds of millions of acres had been added to the American land grab. In like manner, criticisms of Jefferson's constitutional right to annex land disappeared in the euphoria of America's rapidly expanding "empire of liberty." If "liberty" did not encompass the Indians' horror of the new purchase, the "empire" stood crystal clear. With ratification of the purchase, the United States became the second-largest nation in total land area in the world (after Russia) and the first nation in amount of tillable soil. Equally important to the promise of land and agriculture was the commercial promise made available by control of the Mississippi.

One year after the purchase, Jefferson followed up his coup with an expedition to determine exactly what he had acquired and what stood between his purchase and the Pacific Ocean. In casting about for a commander he settled on his secretary, Meriwether Lewis, who shared his residence at Monticello and participated in all of Jefferson's activities. The two hoped to find a route to the Pacific via the Missouri River. Equally important, they sought on-the-ground intelligence of the vast acquisition. Was the land arable? Were there subsidiary rivers that could support trade and travel from the East Coast to the West? Besides land, was there mineral wealth to be acquired? Lewis combined the talents of soldier and scientist and was the ideal leader for such a venture.

In the course of planning, Jefferson and Lewis realized that one commander would not be enough for such a complex and dangerous mission into the unknown, with its natural threats and ubiquitous Indian tribes. For Lewis's partner, Jefferson chose Anderson Sr.'s younger brother-in-law William Clark. Clark was born in Caroline County, Virginia, in 1770, but grew up in pre-statehood Kentucky, where his home neighbored the Andersons'. Of all the extended Anderson family members in the new republic, Clark played by far the most important role in the exploration of the western territories, Indian removal, and Indian treaties ceding vast tracts of land to the national domain. Like the Andersons, he was also a planter and slaveholder. And, like the Andersons, he was going to be an Indian fighter.[12]

Skirmishes between the Americans and Indians had remained inconclusive until the Battle of Fallen Timbers near present-day Toledo, Ohio, in August 1794. At a grand council at Greenville, Ohio, in June 1795, Indians from the Miami, Shawnee, Wyandot, and Delaware from the Ohio country joined the Ojibwa, Potawatomi, and Ottawa from the north and the Wea, Piankeshaw, Kickapoo, and Kaskaskia from the Wabash and Illinois country. With the tribes assembled, all pretense of negotiations was dropped and the Treaty of Greenville signed, bringing an end to thirty years of vicious fighting. Between 1795 and 1810 the number of Ohio settlers exploded from 5,000 to 230,000, including many veterans claiming or selling land warrants in the farm-rich Ohio Valley.

During the Battle of Fallen Timbers, twenty-four-year-old Clark made the acquaintance of young Ensign Meriwether Lewis, four years Clark's junior and an experienced soldier. Before Clark left the army in July 1796, Lewis learned all he needed to know about Clark's skills as a fighter, savvy appraiser of land, and freehand mapmaker.

As plans for the journey solidified with congressional approval, Jefferson agreed with Lewis that Clark would make an ideal co-commander. In May 1803, Lewis wrote to Clark proposing partnering in an irresistible project, namely, a journey of exploration designed to reach the Pacific. After describing the adventure, Lewis closed: "If therefore there is anything under these circumstances, in this enterprise, which would induce you to participate with me in it's fatiegues, it's dangers and it's honors, believe me there is no man on earth with whom I should feel equal pleasure in sharing them as with yourself." Clark received Lewis's letter of invitation on July 17 and immediately responded: "The enterprise etc. is Such as I have long anticipated and am much pleased with—and as my situation in life will admit of my absence the length of time necessary to accomplish such an undertaking I will cheerfully join you."[13]

Such an ambitious expedition could not be launched overnight, and it was many months before the explorers were adequately prepared. But finally, after numerous agonizing delays in acquiring all the necessary supplies, the "Corps of Discovery" was ready to embark. With little fanfare Lewis and Clark, with a company of nearly fifty men and one woman, started westward from the mouth of the Missouri River on May 14, 1804.

The expedition to the Pacific Coast would take three years. Clark's duties included managing the expedition's supplies, dealing with the Indians they encountered, and leading hunting expeditions. More important was his charge to survey and draw maps of the land they traversed. The maps and surveys were critical to American interests. While furs drew the French and British, the main attraction of the West to Americans was land.

As it traveled west, the expedition continued to be drilled as a military unit and the men practiced their marksmanship. Clark led hunting parties and became their most prolific hunter, often killing multiple bison, deer, and elk in one outing. As well, he handled much of the navigation while Lewis explored the flora and fauna and made celestial observations. When it came to dealing with the Indians, Clark was at ease, having adopted many of their patterns of dress and hunting. His facility with Indian languages and sign language, while more limited than that of a formal translator, could still serve.

The most relied-upon translator was the only woman on the journey, an "interpretress" named Sacagawea. She was seven months pregnant when Clark engaged her in November 1804 with her undependable and sometimes abusive French husband, Toussaint Charbonneau. In February 1805 she bore a son, Jean-Baptiste. At one point on the journey she almost died of fever but survived. Several years after the expedition returned, when Sacagawea died, Clark would adopt her child. Jean-Baptiste went on to be educated in Germany, and on his return to America followed in his mother's footsteps, earning a reputation as a trusted mountain guide for expeditions.[14]

One black man participated in the expedition, a slave of Clark's named York, a large man adept at dancing and hunting. Wherever they traveled the Indians sought to acquire his—and other soldiers'—power by offering the sexual favors of their young women. Tribes like the Nez Perce and Shoshone perceived no difference between York and the white men. In Clark's words, white or black "made no difference" to them.[15]

The first leg of the journey led to a winter campsite, Fort Mandan, near today's Bismarck, North Dakota. The fort was not, strictly speaking, a discovery. French, American, and Spanish traders had traversed the ground and gained valuable information from the Indians. Still, Lewis and Clark sent a remarkable trove of information back to Jefferson. Clark provided key maps and "An Estimate of the Eastern Indians," describing seventy-two different tribes based either on personal observation and interaction or word of mouth. He met many tribal leaders, which would serve him well in his later career as superintendent of Indian Affairs.

The real mission of the Corps of Discovery only began after the winter camp was broken up in April 1805 and the journey commenced into unknown terrain.[16] On April 15 they passed the furthest point upstream on the Missouri known by Lewis and Clark to have been reached by white men. From there on they encountered uncharted territory nearly half a continent wide. Danger, beauty, wonder, and the unknown lurked at every bend of the journey. Here at last was Jefferson's New World. In classic discovery mode, Lewis and Clark asserted their mastery of the unknown by measuring the terrain and naming its key features. Measuring and naming also proclaimed ownership of the vast territories. At first they chose names from nature, but soon the politically astute pair realized they would gain a lot more traction back home by naming the places for major political and military leaders. Jefferson, Madison, Albert Gallatin, and Henry Dearborn would soon find their names attached to rivers and plains along the route.

On May 26, 1805, the members of the expedition became the first Americans to view the Rocky Mountains, behemoths in comparison to the Appalachians, their sole reference point. Clark's maps of the Rocky Mountains would revolutionize Americans' understanding of this decisive barrier to westward movement. This was no single range of mountains but rather a massive chain of ridges and valleys stretching in depth from the Black Hills in North Dakota to the Columbia Plateau. The expedition would find no short overland passage or "northwest passage" across the Continental Divide to the Pacific.

Not until November 1805, after traveling the Snake and Columbia Rivers, did the expedition reach the Pacific, where Clark carved into a tree: "By Land from the U. States in 1804 & 5." They rested through the winter, then returned by land, with Lewis traveling the Missouri and Clark the Yellowstone. They reunited on the Missouri on August 12 in North Dakota. In September 1806 the triumphant expedition arrived at St. Louis. The total cost to the expedition was far more than originally requested, $22,393.51, but the payoff dwarfed the investment. A land-crazed republic received word that in the West, fertile soil, game, and fruit were so plentiful that herds numbered in the tens of thousands, huge flocks of birds blocked the sun, and rich topsoil measured deep into the ground. What was more, the mountains abounded in fur-bearing creatures, among them the most terrifying animal Lewis and Clark had ever encountered: the grizzly bear.[17]

AT ROUGHLY THE SAME time that Richard's uncle-by-marriage, William Clark, was map-making his way into history, Richard was pursuing the education his father insisted he get. A college degree in 1806 virtually guaranteed membership in Kentucky's natural aristocracy. The College of William and Mary was thriving under the presidency of Bishop James Madison, inaugurated while Richard was a student. Richard boarded at Parson Brackers, where he shared accommodations with Anthony Lawson and John Page, grandson of Governor John Page. His curriculum, shaped by Bishop Madison, was evolving from a classical orientation to a more Jeffersonian enchantment with deism and the Enlightenment. Not surprisingly, the political atmosphere was virulently anti-Federalist and robustly Republican. Locke, Descartes, and the French Encyclopedists led by Denis Diderot displaced Plato and Aristotle, while Shakespeare remained as popular as ever. Although the curriculum was modern, Kentucky was still a frontier society, and Richard did not return home once in his time at William and Mary. Like many of his classmates, he studied law and conceived a consuming interest in government and politics. William and Mary alumni would compose an interlocking political elite in Virginia and Kentucky, giving Richard a network of associations distinct from that of his citizen-soldier father. They formed the leadership of the "court party" in Kentucky, an offshoot of the "old articulate center," with strong loyalties to Jefferson and Madison.[18]

After four years at William and Mary, Richard returned to Kentucky in 1806 and entered this plaintive note in his diary: "On the 11th July 1806 I left Williamsburg and arrived at my fathers on the 1st September. None of the family knew me." He remained at his father's until late February 1807 and then proceeded to Frankfort, Kentucky, for a year to read law. In September 1808 he returned to William and Mary by way of Washington, "where I witnessed the inauguration of President [James] Madison." He concluded his legal training at William and Mary in 1809, age twenty. By then his younger half sisters were studying at the Domestic Academy. His siblings were growing rapidly but had little to do with Richard.[19]

Relatively few letters survive from father to son. With Richard in Williamsburg and Anderson Sr. building prosperity as surveyor general, there was little opportunity for a sustained personal relationship. More correspondence would appear between the two only as Richard's political career evolved. The first surviving letter was written in November 1808 from Anderson Sr. to Richard in Williamsburg and describes money transfers needed to complete his education. In a second letter dated December 1808, Anderson Sr. informed his son, "Since my last I have received a letter from are [sic] kinsman Benjamin Anderson in which he informs me that it will be quite convenient for him to furnish you with money during your stay at Williamsburg." In January 1809, Richard received a letter from family friend Richard Gamble in Richmond noting that he was "in expectation of finding some safe opportunity to forward you the two hundred dollars you request me to advance you (with an assurance of its being rapidly replaced by a remittance from your father)." At the same time, Gamble noted that he was facing financial shortfalls of his own: "At this difficult time—from the Embargo and other causes—I am unable to make collections. . . . I mention the circumstances as such a matter in more prosperous times—would have been no inconvenience."[20]

The embargo Gamble referenced grew out of policies enacted by Thomas Jefferson and his fellow Republicans in a deliberate attempt to roll back the perceived aristocratic pretensions of the Federalists. In many respects, the Jeffersonian Republicans set about redefining a simplified government that would glorify the yeoman farmer. In the process, the Jeffersonians overturned Pierre L'Enfant's (and President Washington's) ostentatious vision for the national capital. As a result, the capital rapidly devolved into a sorry mess, prompting one traveler to observe, "Some half starved cattle browsing among the bushes present a melancholy spectacle to a stranger whose expectation has been wound up by the illusive description of speculative writers. . . . So very thinly is the city peopled, and so little is it frequented, that quails and other birds are constantly shot within a hundred yards of the capital."[21]

In this context the Embargo Act of 1807, preempting all foreign trade, anticipated the War of 1812. Jefferson ignored the warnings of his treasury secretary, Albert Gallatin, that such an act was unnecessary, given that the warring nations of France and England would recognize American neutrality and stop seizing American shipping. By going forward, the embargo imposed great economic hardships on the young republic as trade froze and commerce disappeared. Western farmers had no international markets, while the French and British simply shifted their trade to South America. After Federalists made decided gains in the 1808 elections, Jefferson repealed the embargo in 1809. But by then the damage to the American economy was done. Many in the Anderson circle would not emerge unscathed.[22]

On March 15, 1807, thirty-six-year-old William Clark was formally engaged to fifteen-year-old Julia Hancock. On January 5, 1808, they married, and by mid-April they were in Louisville, where they met Clark's niece Ann Clark Anderson (Nancy), the daughter of his late sister Elizabeth and Anderson Sr. The eighteen-year-old Nancy and Julia became fast friends and traveling companions in the coming months as they crossed the Mississippi into St. Louis with slaves and supplies. In October the newlyweds stopped in Louisville and visited William's ailing brother George Rogers Clark, who had suffered a stroke and whose leg had recently been amputated. In a festive antidote to the visit to George Rogers, they also visited Soldier's Retreat, the home of George's friend and fellow veteran Richard Clough Anderson Sr. As the couple continued west they discovered from a news report in Shelbyville that Meriwether Lewis had cut his own throat with a knife. Actually, the report was right about the suicide but wrong about the method. Lewis shot himself twice. The news was devastating, but apparently not entirely a surprise. Lewis had been depressed and anxious for some time over land losses and had resorted to heavy drinking.[23]

The news of Lewis and Clark's expedition, once made public, had a far more optimistic result, and settlers began streaming west. Fur merchants like John Jacob Astor, who plotted a line of forts from the Missouri to the Pacific, joined the migration. In a letter to his daughter Elizabeth in 1810, Anderson Sr. referenced the expedition of "Uncle William" and informed her that his slave James would "deliver you the map that your uncle William drew" while on his expedition, adding, "This will give you some idea of that country." In 1834, Anderson Sr.'s son William Marshall Anderson would retrace many of the steps of his uncle and record the journey in a journal of his own.[24]

With the onslaught of American speculators and pioneers streaming west, Indian removal continued its relentless pace. Tribes that had been moved west of the Mississippi were once again removed through forced treaties. They faced futures far worse under the Americans than under the French and British. Despite token efforts to teach the Indians European methods of agriculture, few citizens cared about anything except securing their lands and turning them into private property under the constitutional treaty clause empowering the president to negotiate treaties with other nations, subject to Senate confirmation. In all, Presidents Jefferson and Madison negotiated fifty-three cession treaties, downgrading the tribes from protectorates to wards while acquiring tens of millions of acres, for which the so-called sovereign nations received pitifully small annuities, relegating them to abject poverty. Behavior did not matter: peaceable Indians received no more mercy than warring Indians.[25]

The land grab continued as public domain land sold for $1.64 per acre and state lands went for between six and sixty cents an acre. States were steadily carved out of the territories, with Congress admitting Ohio and Indiana in 1803, Illinois in 1809, and Missouri and Louisiana in 1812. The United States population increased from 5.3 million in 1800 to 8.5 million in 1815. Many of the new citizens gravitated westward.[26]

With obvious land abundance, the problem of management soon loomed large. How do you oversee a vast public domain that you own but do not control? Here the sheer size of the continent represented a huge problem and threatened to choke the nation. The task of superintending would be left to William Clark.

BACK IN KENTUCKY, ON the fourth of July, 1808, Richard delivered an oration on the patriots in the Revolution. A compelling public speaker, his oration was well received, leading the chair of the occasion, William O. Allen, to write: "Permit me in the name of the committee of arrangement to thank you for the politeness with which you have complied with their request in preparing the oration they had the pleasure of hearing yesterday and to express their high sense of its merit. If you have no objection they would be much pleased in procuring a copy for the press." The word *politeness*, a carryover from the colonial era, signaled a superiority that demanded deference from the masses.[27]

Shortly after the oration, Richard received a letter from a classmate, Benjamin Watkins, praising his speech and waxing nostalgic about college days: "It remains for you Clough, a genuine old Revolutionist, to recall to my mind with peculiar force, the scenes of former joys." For many young men in the early republic, adolescence was unknown. There were few options save to remain on a farm or in a shop and work like one's father. But college students came closer to modern adolescence and clearly relished the associations of their youth in college, maintaining correspondence well into adulthood.[28]

While traveling to Virginia, Richard wrote a long letter to his eighteen-year-old sister Nancy, in which he outlined his interests in land speculation and laid out a planned trip to be undertaken in August. He was uncertain "in what part of the creation my destinies will then fix me" and asked her opinion of "the advantages and disadvantages resulting to a young lawyer, from a settlement on the western water." Nancy had just finished at the Domestic Academy, and he encouraged her to participate in the growing cadre of female writers unleashed by the Revolution. Women's journals and magazines proliferated, featuring fiction and nonfiction writing together with a large corpus of children's literature. Publications like *The Ladies Magazine, Godey's Lady's Book,* and *The Mirror of Life* all featured women writers. Writing was one of the few outlets available to women outside of the household, and Richard saw in his sister the ability to succeed. In suggesting possible topics, Richard referenced her recent trips on the Ohio and Mississippi rivers with William and Julia Clark: "Perhaps you have some idea of publishing your observation on the navigation of the Ohio and Mississippi as your voyage on these rivers must doubtless have put you in possession of extensive information on this subject. . . . Be good enough to send me your perspectives possibly I may be able to procure subscribers for so valuable a work." Another possible topic, Richard suggested, was the Louisiana Purchase. He closed with a note on deportment, with a focus on dignity: "Dignity is that charm which commands respect."[29]

Besides familial advice and looming travel plans, romance was in the air now both for Richard and his friend Richard Brown, who had developed an attachment to Nancy that he mistakenly assumed was reciprocated. Nancy turned him down twice, leading Brown to write angry replies to Richard and Nancy. Apparently Richard wrote a reply (not preserved) that led Brown to apologize: "Your letter has produced an entire revolution in my thoughts. I feel the utmost remorse for having ever said any thing to your sister or to you, that could bear the construction of a charge of cruelty to her." Brown's interest in Nancy was more than a romantic impulse. There were concrete economic gains to be secured through the "right" marriage to elite partners. In early nineteenth-century America (as later), courtship had ramifications far beyond an incident of heartbreak. It involved life-defining themes of wealth and land acquisition. As young people sought out partners, they were acutely aware of status and property. Courtship brokered delicate negotiations that were an intrinsic and essential aspect of the westward movement.[30]

Richard Brown's was not the only heart Nancy broke before she married. Richard's college friend and fellow Kentuckian John J. Crittenden also felt the sting of her denial. After receiving her rejection, Crittenden noted with mock bravado, "Even the name of Nancy can not excite me. It does not in the least ruffle my stagnant feelings. To me she is dead and buried and her name is as cold as the grave."[31]

Richard Brown and John J. Crittenden felt rejected, but John Logan, future state representative, was more fortunate, and he and Nancy were wed in 1808. Apparently their marriage did not sit well with her father. In a letter to a friend, Alexander Bullitt, first lieutenant governor of Kentucky, wrote: "Your old friend and acquaintance Nancy Anderson is to be married on next Thursday fortnight to Mr. John Logan of Shelbyville very much against the inclination of Col. Anderson who it seems has told them that they have little to expect from him. His objections to Logan I believe proceed entirely from his want of fortune, but is not that a very great objection, has Miss Nancy ever been accustomed to struggle with difficulties, or does she know any thing about what Poverty is?"[32]

Upon receiving his law degree, Richard rapidly entered the adult world of elite leadership. There would be no apprenticeship, no long climb up the corporate ladder. Men and women grew up early and often died young in the early republic. With that reality, unrelenting work and rapid advancement were required, along with all the important connections acquired through a college education and an accomplished father. Among these connections was membership in the Freemasons, which Richard inherited from his father.

College graduation also meant a season of love and marriage and the making of a family. In October 1809, Richard moved to Louisville and began his law practice. At the same time he pursued a romance of his own with Elizabeth Gwathmey (another Betsy). The couple had fallen madly in love. The problem was that they were first cousins, children of the Clark sisters, Betsy and Ann, respectively. As of 2010, thirty American states prohibited marriage between first cousins ("consanguinity to the fourth degree"), but in Richard's Kentucky no civil laws prohibited such marriages. Some moral ambiguity existed, though, and the practice was condemned by the Roman Catholic Church, but not by Richard's Episcopal Church. Cousin marriages in the early republic were not common, but neither were they rare. Indeed, Betsy's brother Isaac Gwathmey married Richard's half sister Elizabeth in yet another instance of consanguinity.[33]

Clearly Richard worried about the propriety of pursuing Betsy, but equally clearly, he could not resist. Recognizing this, his friend and William and Mary classmate Benjamin Watkins encouraged him: "She is the only woman I have ever seen, who unites total beauty with modesty and diffidence. You have so often described her to me that I fancy I know her well; certain I am, that I admired the picture of your painting and equally certain . . . that I should rejoice at your possessing the original." Then he followed with some advice: "Tell her you are *not* her cousin, but her lover and wish her hand. I could tell how richly you deserve it. Some one has said that a wife, is the 'last best gift of God to man,' may she one day, prove so to you." In a follow-up letter to Benjamin Watkins, Richard confided his intention to marry Betsy.[34]

Despite the well wishes from friends and classmates, Richard continued to fret over his intention to marry Betsy—and for good reason. After Betsy visited his parents at Soldier's Retreat in March 1810, Richard wrote to his father seeking his approval. In contrast to many sons in the Revolutionary era who perceived their fathers as material failures, Richard and his siblings entertained the highest regard and admiration for their father, and he, in return, reciprocated with loving attention and full support, moral and material.[35] The formal prose of Richard's letter to his father characterizes all of their correspondence, generally beginning with "Dear Sir," but it also registers deep respect and a desire to assure him he was not seeking material support. In fact, stilted language in letters to intimates was common in the early nineteenth century. After greeting his father, Richard got right to the point: "When I see you again, you will be pleased to communicate the result of your sentiments on the subject. With regard to this letter your reflexion will suggest the propriety of making such a disposal of it, as well prevent its publicity from possibly causing Betsy's feelings, to become the subject of sportive conversation. I shall proceed to Shepherdsville in a short time, though a violent cold makes me very unwell."[36]

There is no record of the patriarch's response, but he clearly blessed the union, and on December 1, 1810, Richard and Betsy were married. The ceremony was small but convivial. In a mark of the time, step-mother Sarah's daughters Betsy and Maria were absent from the wedding, as they were boarding at the Domestic Academy. Sarah wrote briefly: "My dear daughters I suppose you have heard we were at your Brother Richard wedding there were only a small party we returned Sunday. . . . I expect Richard and Lady [Betsy] here tomorrow. . . . Papa and the girls send their love to you he is as usual busy he will write soon that is whenever you write to him." Again we are reminded that the early-nineteenth-century sense of distance was very different from today's intimacy among family members, and trips, especially in the winter, were undertaken only for the most essential matters. Family members were distant but not forgotten. Writing almost like a father, Richard penned a note to half sister Betsy in which he announced, "I shall give myself the pleasure of visiting the Academy immediately on my return from the springs. Present my compliments to Mrs. Keets. Maria always has my love. Most affectionately."[37]

Initially, the newlyweds lived in the Louisville home of Betsy's brother John Gwathmey. Within months the couple moved to a house of their own on Walnut Street and, in typical fashion, started a family. On Christmas Eve, 1811, Richard recorded in his diary, "my daughter Elizabeth Clough Anderson was born." Alongside this announcement, he noted, "My prospect of practice was good but hardly furnished me with money for the necessary marketing"—a term that referred to his interest in land speculation. Like his father, Richard was obsessed with speculation, ranging from an investment to a form of gambling that he would later regret deeply.[38]

In a letter to Richard, a London friend and classmate, Thomas Boswell, expressed his equal disillusionment with love and England but most especially bemoaned his personal money woes. The economy continued to spiral downward with the embargo and looming war with England, and with it, Boswell's own finances were deeply imperiled. When seeking to withdraw some money, he exclaimed, "Horrible! Horrible! I found there was not enough left to discharge the expences I had already incurred." The solution was land. In a p.s., Boswell reminded Richard that he had power of attorney and directed him "to dispose of my land in Kentucky. . . . By selling it now I shall make a sacrifice still as money is of more value to me at present than possibly it will ever be I am anxious it should be disposed of."[39]

By July 1811 John Crittenden had clearly gotten over Nancy and announced to Richard that he too had gotten married, to Sarah Lee, descendant of the famed Lee family of the Old Dominion. As well, he announced his candidacy for the Kentucky House of Representatives: "Do you know that I am a candidate at the election of representatives for this county [Logan]? I do not know what my fate will be, nor do I much care. If you were a candidate I should feel more concern about my own election." In fact, Richard was also contemplating a run for the Kentucky House in another district.[40]

As the "War Congress" met in Washington, DC, in November 1811 with clear Jeffersonian majorities in both houses, there emerged a group of young "War Hawks" led by Speaker of the House Henry Clay—impassioned patriots too young to remember the horrors of the last war with Britain and aching for a fight. This group of southerners and westerners included Richard and his fellow Kentucky representatives John and Thomas Crittenden and Richard Johnson. Under Clay's leadership, the War Hawks pressed relentlessly for war. With the added support of Secretary of State James Monroe, President Madison agreed to declare war if American complaints over British impressments of American merchant sailors and a British naval blockade were not resolved by May 1812. College friend Benjamin Watkins did not share Richard's ardor. He asked Richard whether, if war was declared, he would enlist, and then registered his own reservations: "A man who continues in the military only sacrifices the time and opportunity given him for better purposes. With this sentiment I have not been among the innumerable applicants for commissions." Unlike Anderson Sr., the young father would not enlist, but his friends John Crittenden and Richard Johnson did and fought with General Isaac Shelby in Ohio and Michigan.[41]

Tensions with England were growing strong. Stephen Ormsby, a congressman from Kentucky and brigadier general in Indian Wars, and later president of the Kentucky Bank of the United States, wrote from Washington, DC, on Christmas Eve 1811 in solidarity with the War Hawks: "For my own part I think our character as a nation requires we should no longer tamely submit to British insolence and shall be decidedly for the strongest measures unless Britain shall cease her system of plunder."[42]

In March 1812 Speaker Clay persuaded Congress to adopt a ninety-day embargo as a prelude to war. Unknown to him, Britain had already rescinded the system of blockades in June, but word did not arrive in America until August, by which time the war had begun. On June 17, the Senate approved a bill authorizing a declaration of war, and Madison signed the measure into law the following day. On June 18, the War of 1812 began.

By 1812, Richard had resolved all questions of achievement. His father could not have hoped for a better eldest son. Educated, articulate, happily married, and a successful politician, Richard had assumed the mantle of leadership his father bequeathed. But in this period and thereafter, father and son would both discover unpleasant anxieties of their own making. Stress was the cost of success and would play itself out in many ways, not least in the relentless pursuit of land and the wealth that flowed from it.

4

Richard the Sage

1812–1817

A ndersons were reared to serve as a form of noblesse oblige. If service in the army was not an option, service in the public sphere
would suffice. Richard Jr. was a popular young lawyer with a golden
tongue and a famed warrior father, and he ran on a plank supporting
the War of 1812. The extent to which the hardships of serving the public made demands on a marriage can be inferred from correspondence
between Richard and his wife. On April 23, 1812, Betsy wrote Richard
to say that "Papa [Owen Gwathmey] being obliged to be in Louisville
to day, will prevent my going home on Sunday unless you can come for
me." They had been separated for some time, leading her to close, "I
wish very much to see you, and every thing at our little cottage, but if
your coming the last of this week, will interfere with any arrangements
you have made, an anticipation of that pleasure, shall satisfy me until
an opportunity occurs." There was, in the meantime, an election to win
and a war to back, and Richard rose to the occasion of both.[1]

As the election approached, Anderson's father-in-law, Owen Gwathmey, warned him to distance himself from the powerful senator John
Pope of Kentucky, who had voted against war with England. Gwathmey went on to express confidence in Anderson's powers of persuasion,
knowing he could distance himself from Pope "in a moment" and remain solidly in the Henry Clay War Hawks group. Anderson heeded
the advice. In a letter to the press he left little doubt that he stood in

opposition to Senator Pope, with whom he had done some private business. On the question of Pope's opposition to war, he wrote, "I think he was wrong. I believe our country had been insulted and injured too much for longer tolerance. . . . I entirely disapprove his conduct in opposing a declaration of war against England; a nation which has heaped on insult and injury until war or disgrace stared us in the face."[2]

Anderson won the election in November with "a greater vote than any man had ever gotten in the County." His charismatic skills and public speaking prowess put him in a league with his senior congressman (and potential rival) Henry Clay. For the next decade Anderson devoted himself to public service as a Jeffersonian Republican (unlike his Federalist father) and allied his policies closely with those of Clay and John Crittenden. He would serve in the Kentucky House of Representatives during the 1812–13, 1814–15, and 1815–16 sessions. He then served as a Kentucky congressman in the 15th and 16th US Congresses, from March 4, 1817, through March 3, 1821. In the 16th Congress, he served as the chairman of the powerful House Committee on Public Lands. He declined to run for Congress in 1820 and returned to run the Kentucky House of Representatives in 1821 and 1822, serving as Speaker of the House there in 1822.[3]

Anderson's entry on the Kentucky political scene coincided with the War of 1812, which consumed much of his correspondence and attention. Anderson's friend and fellow state legislator Thomas Crittenden (John Crittenden's brother) wrote him in November 1812 to say, "The time is approaching when you are to meet in council as one of the legislators of your country." In this context, Crittenden wanted to introduce him to Republican congressman Joseph Hawkins and warn him about Congressman Sam South: "Do you know Sam South? I know him well. He is ignorant, stupid and sycophantic. . . . It is indeed a truth that this man has too much influence in the house already. . . . Hawkins is a man of intelligence, study and a perfect gentleman. . . . You will admire, you will love him when you know him."[4]

In a letter from Congressman Stephen Ormsby, Anderson learned about recent events in the war: "It is said that [Major General Henry] Dearborn has gone into winter quarters and abandoned his intended campaign. . . . I trust he will not attempt to cross [the Niagara River] unless he sees his way clear, another defeat would be unfortunate in the extreme." Better news emerged from the navy: "Our navy seems to carry all before it on the 25th of October off the western Isles. Commodore [Stephen] Decateur in the Frigate USS *United States* after a close engagement of 17 minutes captured the British frigate Macedonia commanded by Captain [John] Carden mounting 49 guns and carrying 306 men." Of these, the report continued, 106 British sailors were killed, compared to 5 Americans.[5]

On the home front, a lonely Betsy wrote again from Louisville to Richard in Frankfort to assure him of her loyalty:

> You left me everything to procure comfort, and I make myself as contented as you can wish me. When I tell you that I had seventeen visters [sic] the day after you left me I expect you will begin to grieve a little for the smoke-house and, that I was at party at Brother Johns dressed so gaily that no stranger could have thought me a wife and the mother of a suckling yearling, you will think a little of your cash or credit. But laying aside all jests you have nothing to make you uneasy.

Betsy also assured him that all was well at home with their newborn daughter, Elizabeth Clough Anderson, but the same could not be said of her neighbor: "Poor Mrs. Dunn lost her daughter and only child two days after she heard of the death of her unfortunate son Isaac."[6]

A week later Betsy sent another letter to Frankfort, most likely in part as a hedge against ongoing separation and loneliness:

> You have such easy times at Frankfort this winter, I am fearful you will have an itching to spend your next in the same way. All this cold weather you and Mr. Crittenden (except two hours in each day) have been in a comfortable room twisting your sides about, before warm fire and your wives, sleeping cold at night, and nursing your squalling brats all day, and you forsooth writing to me about your balls, bells and what not. I wrote you that I was at a party and look'd very handsome but say not a word about the house, or say that I was not thinking of you every minute that I was in the room. When you read this nonsense I expect you will think my health is better than when I commenced writing. Indeed I believe it is for I never feel as happy in your absence, my dear Richard, as when writing to you or reading

your letters. Let me again entreat you not to be uneasy about home, believe me I am as comfortable as I could be were you here.

Little Betty stands very well, but is too much of a coward to walk. My love to you, and Mr. Crittenden.[7]

In Richard's defense, travel in 1812 was difficult and time-consuming, and he, like most of his colleagues, did not travel home for the holidays. Another letter arrived from Betsy reporting a trip to her family with nurse in hand, and the good news that "little Betty" was no longer a coward: "My dear Rick, I betook myself, my little one and nurse to this place the day on which you left home where I remain possessed of every comfort that can be afforded by hospitality and affection. I sleep in Sisters room where there is a good fire day and night. . . . Little Betty will be able to meet you when you come home, as she can now walk about the floor."[8]

Writing to Richard on a weekly basis, Betsy moved from the subject of children and trips to pork—a side business that she engaged in with great energy and enthusiasm. On January 12 she reported receiving 1,020 pounds of pork, which she sold to "brother Temple." Pork had emerged as the leading meat in the Ohio Valley, and pigs proved to be well suited to the backcountry, assuming more prominence there than they did in Europe or the East. Thanks in no small measure to pork, backcountry settlers were less dependent on hunting than their Indian coinhabitants. For the Andersons, pork was an essential component of their domestic economy. Year in and year out, it offered a steady stream of meat and profit.[9]

In 1813, Richard took a brief detour from politics and Frankfort, veering instead "more to the prudent appropriation of the money I had than to its acquisition by my practice." Apparently he was "appropriating" money from his land, perhaps acquired from his father. But in 1814, he again ran successfully for the Kentucky House of Representatives, where "until the present time politics and speculation [in land] have engaged more of my time and attention than the law."[10]

In February 1814, as he was preparing his candidacy, Richard wrote a long letter to his father contemplating his future course of action. Most immediately, he expressed a desire to move away from the town of Louisville to "the country." Of course, professional considerations had to play a role in such a move, and that meant sorting out a preference for politics, law, or farming. Since politics did not really provide an adequate living, this meant "weighing the relative pleasure of agriculture and the bar." If he was to pursue land, one obvious farming option would be a choice property that Anderson Sr. had offered him earlier from his substantial land holdings: "Some years ago you made to me the offer of Watt's place provided I deemed it a proper situation for residence, but I would now very gladly make it the seat of my permanent abode. . . . My own opinion always has been that if it could be enlarged by the purchase of some adjoining land on the East . . . it would be one of the most desirable seats I ever saw."[11]

If the option were still available, Richard wrote, he wanted to move immediately because "in its cultivation I should delight." But realizing he had business to wrap up in Louisville and that Anderson Sr. had rented the property out, he was prepared to wait. In the meantime, "I should not make it known before the period arrived. It might have effect on my situation in town." By August 1814, Richard was able to enter in his diary: "My father and his wife came down. They gave me a deed for Wells." This whetted his appetite for more speculation away from Kentucky, to the Indiana Territory, where prices had risen. In particular, he wrote in his diary, "I have a great inclination to buy up the interests of Genl. George Rogers Clarks heirs to two fractions in Indiana."[12]

Speculation mania in Indiana followed closely on a graduated program of Indian removal. Like Kentucky earlier, Indiana laid claim to the Indian territory through wars and imposed treaties. Earlier, in November 1811, the territory's governor, William Henry Harrison, had launched a preemptive expedition against the Shawnee chief, Tecumseh, and his prophet-brother, Tenskwatawa, at the Battle of Tippecanoe. For some time the brothers had expended mighty efforts in bringing Indian tribes together in a last-ditch effort to drive the Americans out of their lands. A year later, in October 1813, Tecumseh was killed at the Battle of the Thames, effectively ending armed resistance and freeing the land for treaty and plunder. Most of the defeated tribes were removed west of the Mississippi River, where they would subsist for only so long as it took American settlers to begin coveting those lands as well.[13]

Acquisition of Indian lands did not mean financial security for all Americans. At the same time that Richard was pursuing the prospect of land in Indiana, he received a series of letters from Mary Anderson, his uncle's recent widow. Apparently people had taken advantage of her husband's goodwill, leading to a lawsuit that threatened to bankrupt her. She hoped that Anderson Sr. would help her sell back a loan that was owed her to pay off debts, but apparently Anderson Sr. had never responded to her: she wrote to Richard, "I hope you will exert yourself in my behalf and urge your father to do so." Her deprivation included her slaves: "I have had great loses [sic] among my negroes there are but very few that belong to the estate."[14]

By late July 1814 Richard was virtually assured of reelection in the Kentucky House of Representatives. Still, he visited the counties in his district, suffered through innumerable barbecues, and republished "a short address to the People," a speech he had first delivered in 1808. In the midst of stumping, land again precipitated a family crisis. Richard's brother-in-law John Gwathmey was hurt by bad speculation and, being "a good deal alarmed," was forced to sell some prime land at bargain prices. This would not be the last time that Richard would observe Gwathmey's bad speculations. On August 3, one day before his twenty-sixth birthday, Anderson was reelected. His opponent, James Hunter, had attempted to discredit him because his father was a Federalist, but to no avail. Anderson Sr., meanwhile, voted for his old deputy surveyor Henry Massie over congressman and later judge Stephen Ormsby, even though Ormsby had supported Richard.[15]

War with England continued to play in the press but did not directly impinge on Richard's day-to-day life. In September 1814 he received "the report of the Enemy's taking Washington," the nadir of the war for Americans. London officials had ordered British warships and troops to the coasts of American cities as a diversionary tactic to protect their army in Upper and Lower Canada. In a stunning display of miscalculation, American commanders failed to erect defenses for the nation's capital, assuming that Baltimore represented a more strategic target in need of defense. The American commander, General William Winder, had only five hundred regulars to defend Washington and no worthy defenses. Only after the British landed 4,500 soldiers at Benedict, Maryland, did the Americans understand their dire straits. By then it was too late.

As worrying as the defeats were, Richard's preoccupations remained closer to home. Sadly, "little Betty" Anderson, like far too many children of the early republic, did not survive beyond toddlerhood. On May 31, 1814, Richard made a plaintive entry in his diary: "My little daughter Elizabeth C. died." She was two years and five months old when she died of "fever." Though Anderson doesn't specify what kind of fever, yellow fever was prevalent in the region and persisted in his neighborhood through June. Not surprisingly, mosquitos thrived. In a diary entry for October 2, 1814, Anderson noted: "Musquetoes [sic] have been troublesome for several nights. I am told this is the first summer since 1802 in which they have been so." It was not solely in rural regions like Kentucky that the toll from little-understood diseases was devastating. The health of the entire nation suffered badly. Between 1815 and 1845, the average height of native-born white males fell from 173 centimeters to 171.6, while life expectancy at age ten fell from fifty-two to forty-seven years. Economic development outran medical science, and those who lived through this era paid a hefty physical price. Tragically, death from fever in the Anderson family would not stop with little Betty. In little more than one decade it would also claim both her parents.[16]

NOT SURPRISINGLY, LAND CONTINUED to be at the center of Anderson Jr.'s legislative activities and interests. Of particular concern in the Kentucky legislature was the maldistribution of land. The new republic might have offered unprecedented opportunities for landownership, but many remained closed out of those opportunities. Kentucky lawmakers altered the rules of property and the rights of landowners by quietly eliminating those "rights of the woods" that had designated uncultivated lands as a hunting and herding common. "Indian country" or "hunting commons" were relics of the past destined to cough up their acres to the insatiable cravings of American citizens. Henry Clay's "American System" emphasizing protective tariffs, internal improvements at federal expense, and a national bank was a white man's system funded by federal dollars gleaned ultimately from land. Private property would destroy the Kentucky of Daniel Boone and transform uncultivated lands into cultivated private property.[17]

In 1814, financial chaos incurred in part by excessive speculation in public lands and ensuing anxiety over plunging land prices loomed, inserting state representative Anderson into a steady period of hard times. In November 1814 William Booth, Richard's brother-in-law, wrote Anderson to say he would collect money from two who owed him (including Richard) "and then pay [John] Crittenden." A month later Richard's father wrote a brief note regarding land bills due: "Dear Sir I am very sorry to send this due to the United States . . ."[18]

On December 13 Richard received the first hint of a larger financial crunch from another brother-in-law, George Gwathmey. After enclosing a note for $500 and apologies for the delayed repayment, Gwathmey wrote, "Our friends in the neighbourhood are generally well. . . . The citizens begin to complain of hard times, and not without a cause but I trust that there will be but few instances of a sacrifice either of credit or property."[19]

Despite ominous clouds on the financial horizon, Anderson was back in the land business, noting in his diary on September 8, 1814: "Sold five acre lot to [Walter] Pearson [sic for Pierson]." Reflecting on the ups and downs of land speculation, he added: "Not much pleased with the sale." Money was always tight, and in a letter to Peter Funk of Middletown, Kentucky, he wrote, "An unexpected call last evening presses me for money. Can you lend me about $400? It will be a favour. That is the sum I want but if you could spare a smaller sum, it would be an accommodation. If you will be so good as to inform me by the by, I will ride over immediately. I can return it in ten days." Funk was happy to help his friend: "As soon as it quits raining I will call on you as it is likely I can assist you some. Mr. Head is coming to me and if he has any I can get it from him." Thomas Crittenden was also hard-pressed and sought money owed to him from Charles Todd. In November 1814 he wrote to Anderson: "The times are hard here and the little money which [Charles] Todd owes me would be some relief. . . . He tells me that he will pay it whenever requested by you. I must beg of you to get it and bring it with you to Frankfurt [sic]. Do not fail. I rely on you."[20]

Todd would later intersect with Richard more directly when Richard succeeded him as diplomatic minister to Colombia. But in 1814, Todd had grave financial concerns at home brought about by the failure of a Frankfort warehouse that collapsed, killing his partner and leaving him deeply in debt. Foreign service proved to be a way out for Todd, as it would later for Anderson. Ever mindful of frontier opportunities for land, Richard closed the September 8, 1814, entry observing, "For several days have had a serious idea of moving to Indiana at some period— viz in a year or two."[21]

Competing land claims were worse in Kentucky than in any other state. Shingled land claims plagued every corner of the state and threatened to impose chaos on the states' property holders. Andersons were invariably affected, and land claim issues grew painfully close to home. On September 21, 1814, Anderson noted in his diary: "D. Carneal as agent of W. Lytle entered into a Contract with my father relating to the Copy of his books. I fear the misunderstanding will not be closed by the contract." Other problems emerged. A note that "old John Brooks told me that he purchased 10 or 12 claims to the land he lives on" highlights the tangled legal condition of overlapping and conflicting claims in Kentucky's land system.[22]

Membership in the Kentucky House continued to keep Anderson away from home, with correspondence his only link. Friends and relations gave birth and died with little notice. In a letter dated November 1814, Betsy wrote: "I hope you will write frequently to me, and never think of sending a short letter. Have you an agreeable room-mate, and a pleasantly situated room? Papa is well and in good spirits, Mama desires me to tell you, that she has been a little drooping since you left her, she think she could laugh a little if you were here." She closed with a p.s.: "I wish you to bring me some knitting cotton." While land was central to Richard's speculation, Betsy's involvement in pork and knitting contributed to Kentucky's domestic economy, and Betsy was determined to play her part in the family business. In fact, no Andersons in the next generation would inherit land without women's labor supporting the venture.[23]

In December 1814, John Crittenden wrote to Anderson complimenting him on his rise in politics and urging him to take an active role in the state legislature's deliberations regarding money and banking: "You are just in the centre of the political body—At the seat of intelligence, and of course will have many of the general things of this world to communicate. . . . You will have to take a forward active part in the proceedings of the house—I am not sure that you are inclined to do so, but I think you will be forced into it."[24]

A week later Crittenden again wrote Anderson from Russellsville, Kentucky, where he was serving as a state representative, again on the subject of money—this time for Thomas Prather, who was soliciting funds for a meeting house: "I enclose you twelve hundred dollars for Mr. Thomas Prather one of your constituents. It is money which I have collected for him, and which I think it safer to transmit by private conveyance." As for Anderson's work in the state House of Representatives, Crittenden added, "Through various ways I have lately heard of you and your standing in the legislature. I congratulate you upon your high and rising reputation—This is no flattery—I am above flattering even you—I love to witness the prosperity of my friends—more particularly the friends of almost my whole life—I feel a pride in their exaltations. I claim some credit to myself from the reputation of my friends. Believe me to be very sincerely your friend."[25]

Anderson's rising reputation followed closely that of his senior Kentucky mentor Henry Clay, who was taking advantage of his powerful position in Washington as Speaker of the House to challenge President James Madison in ways calculated to advance his own intense ambitions to win the presidency. Clay's favored line of attack was the failure of Madison and Congress to recognize the newly established Latin American democracies in their bid for independence from Spain. By focusing on Latin American recognition, Clay indirectly set the stage for Richard's brief but historic rise to diplomatic prominence. Richard, no less than his mentor, harbored high political ambitions, perhaps including the presidency itself.

President Madison did not fully share Clay's (and Anderson's) enthusiasm for Latin American independence. He spoke instead of neutrality, unwilling to commit to being drawn into a European quagmire with Spain. But Clay would not be deterred. As early as 1813, Clay had denounced the perils of neutrality and boasted of the economic and ideological gains to be made through diplomatic alliances with fledgling democracies. In opposition to a bill that would prohibit the arming of foreign ships in American ports and waters, Clay took to the floor and asserted, "It would undoubtedly be a good policy to take part with the patriots of South America. . . . We have a right to take part with them, that it is our interest to take part with them, and that our interposition in their favor would be effectual." Clay's hostility to his own party would continue into the Monroe presidency. Much of this was simply positioning himself for a subsequent run for the presidency.[26]

For Richard, Clay's maneuvering offered the possibility of a diplomatic assignment in Latin America, made attractive by his increasing, speculation-driven financial duress. As money woes crept into his immediate family setting, Richard was feeling the pinch. Several entries in his diary for October 1814 reveal a mounting wave of problems: "October 13, 1814 Great distress prevails among the relations of Mrs. B[oothe]. I received several suggestions from A[lexander] Pope of the approaching pressure for money." Then on October 20: "The banks curtail their discounts." This effectively made it more difficult to borrow money, which proceeded to wreak havoc on Anderson's speculative endeavors. On October 24, he confided in his diary: "I am fearful of a call on my paper. I see no means of preventing a protest, but the sale of Hardyman." Hardyman was property Richard owned about a mile from Soldier's Retreat on Beargrass Creek. Anderson and other investors/speculators had hoped to profit from a rise in land values and had leveraged their purchases with money borrowed from banks, hoping to sell the properties at a profit before the loan payments were due. But as land values began to decline, the speculator had no way to pay off his loans without selling off valuable assets at bargain prices.[27]

By November 1814, Anderson's financial affairs were so tight that he feared being unable to even buy the necessities for the coming winter: "Have been endeavouring to collect a little money. I have to borrow money to buy wood and to go to market." The ebullience of a year earlier had given way to another painful round of anxiety that increasingly darkened his world. Not everyone was suffering. On November 18, Anderson noted that Denis Fitzhugh, third husband of his aunt Francis Eleanor Clark, bought a choice lot at the discounted price of seventy-five dollars. Apparently Anderson had alerted him to the property, and he added, with telling italics: "*Another* instance of *others* benefit arising from *my* information."[28]

The new year dawned ominously. From Louisville, Betsy wrote her husband on her pork business and other news that made her anxious: "I wish my dear Richard you were at home for in spite of all my efforts to prevent it my situation keeps me awake the half of each night. . . . The people in this place complain so much of the times, that I have carefully wrapped up the money you left me nor have I purchased the articles I want." Instead of closing with her usual enjoinder to resist temptations that might arise with his single life, she closed, "As you have but a short time to remain in Frankfort I now give you leave to participate in the amusements of the place, convinced you know that you will not receive pleasure from an improper source."[29]

Domestic concerns did not monopolize the Andersons' attention to the exclusion of all else. On January 8, 1815, in parts far from home, General Andrew Jackson staged his dramatic, if ironic, defeat of the British at New Orleans after the signing of a peace treaty of which neither army was aware. Word of the victory had not yet reached Louisville, leading Betsy to note: "Every person here are alarmed for the fate of New Orleans, particularly the messers [sic] Bullitts who have $4000 worth of cotton there. Couch is totally unable to smile." In her own household, she lamented, "Denison delivered 189 lbs of pork, which he swears is all he can let us have."[30]

Meanwhile, the superfluous victory at New Orleans elevated "Old Hickory" as the military hero of the new generation and a person of immediate mythic celebrity. With that victory, Jackson became the embodiment of values that Americans craved for themselves. He was a self-made man of iron will destined by Providence to lead the new nation even as he led its army.[31]

On February 16, 1815, Anderson received a confidential note from fellow William and Mary graduate and US senator William Taylor Barry announcing a pending treaty with England. While Barry could not reveal the details, he wanted Anderson to know that life would now go forward without war: "The Senate of the United States on to day gave their assent unanimously to the Treaty of Peace—signed by the British and American governments. We were labouring with difficulty to find the ways and means to get along with the war. We have now a more agreeable duty to perform—that of reducing the military establishment and curtailing the terrible expenditures."[32]

A week later the news had spread, and with it a renewal of hope. On February 28, Anderson heard from his brother-in-law Isaac Gwathmey what he already knew: "All the town is rejoicing at the news of peace, which I think is well confirmed. . . . Goods have fallen [in price] already in this place and the merchants seem willing to sell them off. . . . Sugar speculators are at an end. . . . The town is to be illuminated this evening."[33]

OVER THE WINTER, WHILE Anderson was away for much of the season, Betsy stayed in her father's home. During this time she had another daughter, with Richard again absent from the happy event. All he could do was note in his diary on March 15, "A daughter born called Elizabeth C[lark]. All well." But equally engaging to Anderson was the improved land market that ensued with peace. With unrestrained enthusiasm, he exulted that a lot adjoining his was sold for eighty dollars per foot, assuring him a handsome profit of $3,000 "on the purchase [I made] from D[enis]Fitzhugh." Over the next two years prices would continue rising spectacularly in Louisville, from $80 a foot in 1815 to $300 per foot in 1817. Clearly these prices were inflated, but few (including Anderson) could see it. Speculators (then and now) were not stupid. They just made the classic mistake of assuming that an ever-expanding population would overspread the continent and ensure the ever-rising value of western land.[34]

Most likely, the roller coaster of property speculation played a significant part in Richard's ongoing career choices. Though pleasing to his father and estimable to his friends, politics failed to reward him financially. On April 15, he confided in his diary that he would likely be nominated as a candidate for the US Congress, but more attractive to him was the thought of "a small farm, excellent orchards, vineyards, meadow and butter, cheese in abundance." The reason was simple: money. Congress simply could not support a career. The idea of a well-paid professional politician on a national scale awaited the rise of Jacksonian democracy. A congressional salary was emphatically inadequate, paid out over a six-month period and paltry. Anderson could augment that with his law practice, but the distances were forbidding and, in the end, unfeasible. In that same entry he noted, "I have rented the house and lot on M[ain] Street to N[icholas] Clarke," adding, "very pressed for money." Two weeks later matters had not improved: "I have been more pressed for money since I returned from Frankfort than ever. I have been dunned for small accounts three or four weeks ago and still they are unpaid."[35]

The Andersons' significant financial obligations included their other primary form of property: slaves. In fact, slaves make regular appearances in Anderson's diary and correspondence. On May 6, 1815, he noted, "Meany buys a negro man from a Spaniard for $100. They come here [to court], the Spaniard is drunk, I wrote a bill of sale but would not attest it. However I apprehend the Spaniard is a *knave* and the negro not his own. I am sure Meany is [making a mistake]." A week later, at Whitsunday (Pentecost) dinner, Anderson's brother-in-law Samuel Gwathmey told a harrowing story of an attempted murder by a slave of family friend Major Edmund Taylor's wife: "Negro woman giving arsenic to her Mistress. She made several attempts. Succeeded in one. She was detected and has confessed. Mrs. Taylor is living but it is feared will not [ever] be well." This set Anderson to thinking of the legal question of punishment for "administering poison" when death did not ensue, and the different status that slaves occupied in the penal code. His conclusion was harsh: "Upon examining the code I find it is punished by death under a law of 1811—where the person administering is a *slave*."[36]

What Anderson did not appear to question was a slave's motive for attempting to murder her mistress. As an economic system, slavery was grounded in violence, which made it not only immoral but risky. If Richard recorded no instances of personally whipping his slaves in his journal, it is certain he "disciplined" them as needed, just as had his father and, more notoriously, his uncle William Clark. Any debates over slavery that accompanied Kentucky's entry into the Union were largely resolved in favor of the "peculiar institution." For those truly disaffected with slavery, migration to the other frontier society of Ohio was always a possibility, though economic losses were likely to ensue. There, slavery was outlawed by the terms of the Northwest Ordinance, and continued to be so after Ohio attained statehood.[37]

One such disaffected friend was Richard's classmate Brooke Hill, who, in a letter to Richard, described the work of editing his Virginia newspaper, the *Lexington Reporter* and commended Anderson as someone who would make an outstanding editor. He then moved to the sensitive subject of slavery, in which all of the Andersons were heavily invested. He acknowledged he would like to leave Virginia and move closer to Kentucky (which he eventually did), but the practice of slavery goaded his conscience: "The same causes which make me desire to remove from Virginia, would prevent my settling to the S. of the Ohio. I mean the use of African *slaves*." He was particularly offended by the cruelty: "When he is compelled daily, to behold and to practice the cruelties, which are necessary for our own safety, on the poor unresisting slaves.

Really, I long to leave Virginia, that I may wash my hands of this iniquitous practice—and should prefer the state of Ohio on that account."[38]

When contemplating politics—including the nearing election for state legislators, for which Richard was the strongest candidate—Richard's thoughts never strayed far from money. For a time he considered entering into a mercantile partnership with Denis Fitzhugh. Such a move would require capital, and land was his most fungible asset, leading him to conclude in his diary entry for May 24, 1815: "Although I dislike placing my property at hazard, so sanguine I am that money must be made if prudently managed that I entertain an intention that a year or two hence if I can get a partner perfectly safe I will convert a part of my property into a mercantile capital."[39]

Anderson also considered more land speculation and reflected on land purchases in free states. Again his attention turned to Indiana: "Money judiciously laid out in the purchase of land in the Indiana (new purchase) would be very prudent and safe. The land in that country populated by poor persons (divided into small tracks [sic for 'tracts']) and worked by freemen instead of slaves, will be highly cultivated and become more valuable than any Country settled by Virginians held in large parcels and cultivated by slaves." Like many planters in a slave-holding state, Anderson understood the liabilities of slavery, though he neither uprooted it in his own household nor campaigned for its eradication.[40]

Anderson also understood the importance of slaves to land in Kentucky. On November 3, 1815, he traveled to Shelby "for the purpose of [buying] Nelson, a negro man." Ten days later he "bought Rose, a daughter of Daphne, belonging to the Estate of Edmund M. Clark [accepted] $291. High price." He would have to fund the slave purchases, along with inevitable new land deals, with debt: "By the purchase of some negroes, repairs and other unavoidable expenses, (including however some purchases of lots) I have been compelled to increase my loan in Bank to near $5000." This generated some anxiety when a bill to create the Second Bank of the United States was passed in April 1816, virtually guaranteeing the resumption of payments in gold by state banks and the contraction of the nation's money supply. Anderson and others like him, who were deeply leveraged in bank debt, had little but paper to cover the loans.[41]

At home, Anderson property was under heightened threat of disease, in particular during the warm weather, which polluted the water: "The aspects of the ponds is dreadful," Anderson recorded. One victim was his father's slave, Timothy: "Timothy was taken very ill and continues so. I ascribe the disease to the fatal sickliness of the place which must continue until the ponds are drained of the stagnant water, which by inattention is daily increasing." By October 1815, the problem had not passed: "There is now and continues to be great and unusual unhealthiness in the town and country, particularly Country. . . . The Musquetoes [sic] still continue. They have been here in greater numbers this season than ever were before."[42]

In the up-and-down world of personal finances, Anderson happily reported, "My father proposed to lend me several hundred dollars this day which he lately received and has no immediate use for." Unfortunately, that happy news quickly dimmed as the elder Anderson himself suffered land speculation losses. Equally promising was the prospect of making money on speculation with his sister-in-law Ann Gwathmey's husband William Booth: "Booth is filled with the mania for buying lots. We have agreed to buy No. 93 and 107, if practicable." The fact that he would go in with Booth, given his ongoing money troubles, confirmed that the "mania" was his as well.[43]

Recognizing that land in Kentucky would never realize its full potential without adequate sources of money, Anderson volunteered to serve as director of the local branch of the Bank of Kentucky, then the only source for currency in Kentucky besides the Bank of the United States. He wrote: "I deem the establishment of an independent Bank at this place as a circumstance which would tend more to enhance the value of property than any single occurrence which could take place."[44]

On October 11, 1815, Anderson noted that he had qualified as a director of the Bank of Kentucky in Louisville, with a capital of $100,000. He joined his senior colleague Henry Clay, who had been appointed director in 1808. The legislature appointed bank directors and the state owned a fifth of the bank's stock. Not surprisingly, the news of Anderson's appointment brought immediate attention from friends and family members. No sooner was he appointed than his brother-in-law John Gwathmey asked him to secure a $5,000 loan to hold off a flood of creditors. Conceding that Gwathmey was a very genial and helpful friend, Anderson nevertheless refused: "I am so thoroughly convinced that not only all his property will be swallowed by his debts but that his friends who are assisting him must eventually be materially injured in the Shipwreck . . . I cannot agree to the request of the man who has hardly refused any man in his life."[45]

When not ruminating over land, debts, and disease, Anderson focused on looming elections in Kentucky and national politics. On August 7, 1815, he recorded the congenial news of a landslide victory in the Kentucky House of Representatives: "Final vote Anderson: 1472 James Hunter 11!" On a national level, Anderson predicted that his father's friend James Monroe would win the presidency, although his Virginia roots might hurt him. Other contenders included John Calhoun, William Harris Crawford, and William Bibb. In an afterthought Anderson added, "Henry Clay will not permit himself to be overlooked. However, I think he is hardly ripe yet." Anderson correctly gauged both Clay's raging presidential ambitions, which he observed firsthand, and his lack of "ripeness." Much of 1815 Clay spent in Ghent, Belgium, as one of five American commissioners negotiating a peace treaty with Great Britain. In September, he was again elected to the US House and in December reelected Speaker of the House. As before, Clay viewed the speakership less as an end in itself than a rostrum for bringing national attention to his policies, with a particular emphasis on South America.[46]

Alongside Clay, John Crittenden also began an ascent to political fame that would span fifty years. In a letter to Anderson, Crittenden noted that some friends had urged him to run for Speaker of the Kentucky House. Despite hesitations and "alarms," he was leaning toward running, but he wanted Anderson's frank appraisal of his chances for success: "I appeal to you not to be flattered, to be advised . . . I have a right to expect from you the true and open councils of a friend. . . . I must require you to consider all this as confidential."[47]

A week later Anderson wrote in his diary that he "received a letter from John J Crittenden stating his intention of being a candidate [for US Congress]. I have advised him to offer. I think his prospect of success very fair." Again Anderson was correct. With the US Senate not yet a possibility on account of Crittenden's youth, he remained in the Kentucky House and faced John Rowan for election as Speaker. Despite being Rowan's junior, Crittenden's support from the friends of Clay won him the election. He would be reelected Speaker the following year with no opposition.[48]

In early December 1815, Anderson traveled to Frankfort to meet with the legislature. Like most members, he lived in a boardinghouse, sharing a room with fellow representative Daniel Weiseger. He was happy to support John Crittenden's successful bid for House Speaker. Meanwhile, banking issues dominated the session. Too many "wildcat" banks were emerging with little more capital than the printing presses they used to print notes. To control this, Anderson favored the creation of "a Farmers Bank of Kentucky." But the Kentucky bank whose board he sat on with Henry Clay resisted by reversing its former practice of resisting branches and establishing branch banks at Winchester, Shelbyville, Richmond, and Hopkinsville. His financially strapped brother-in-law John Gwathmey reluctantly agreed. Although he preferred independent banks, Gwathmey believed the branch banks were inevitable and each would be dependent for paper currency on the "mother bank" in Louisville.[49]

The first Bank of the United States, chartered by President Washington over the constitutional objections of Jefferson and Madison, had expired in 1811 when a Republican Congress refused to renew its charter. With war pressing in 1812, there was no safe currency, leaving many to rue Congress's failure to renew the national bank. In the void, state banks proliferated with no adequate capital controls and functioned, in effect, as wildcat banks chartered under state law and free of federal oversight, draining their own and other banks' precious specie. By 1814 every state bank in the West had been forced to suspend specie payment and rely exclusively on paper currency, which promptly lost all its value. The dire state of affairs persuaded earlier skeptics to promote a Second Bank of the United States, with power to create a uniform national currency.[50]

In response to mounting pressure, South Carolina senator John C. Calhoun's committee introduced legislation for a Second Bank of the United States in January 1816. Locating its headquarters in Philadelphia raised suspicions in the West, but the needs were too great to ignore. The bank was capitalized at $35 million, with one-fifth purchased by the US government and the remainder in public investments. Its notes would be accepted for all payments owed the United States, including, of course, land.

Henry Clay had earlier opposed a Second Bank of the United States in deference to the West, but with shifting circumstances he swung around because state banks, including the Bank of Kentucky, could no longer be counted on to assist the US Treasury in the collection and distribution of public revenue. Clay and other supporters prevailed, and the bank bill passed the House in March 1816, with the Senate following and Madison signing. Anderson had his doubts about the bank but realized that the banking crisis threatened landownership if specie payments could not be resumed. Accordingly he supported the Second Bank of the United States and the creation of branch banks in Lexington and Louisville.[51]

In this same period, Betsy became very ill with a liver ailment that required stimulated "salivation" (a supposed cure). Upon her recovery the family moved to Anderson's Myland estate near Soldier's Retreat, where they established a permanent presence better suited to Anderson's long absences from home. On August 7, 1816, Anderson won election to the US Congress with 2,578 votes to his opponents' 1569 and 394. Congress generally sat about three months a year and members served with minimal pay of five dollars a day. Clearly this required additional work in the off-season. With his election won, Anderson's venue changed from Frankfort to Washington, DC (known then as "the City"), where, he noted, "I received by my father a polite offer from Henry Clay to assist me in procuring pleasant lodging in the City during the session of Congress." Not entirely trusting Clay, Anderson viewed this offer as a ploy to gain his support in preparation for later favors. At the same time, Clay was Anderson's most powerful supporter in the Congress, leading Anderson to confide in his diary that two could play the same game: "I will write him [Clay]. He will think the bait is taken and that I am flattered by his attention and I will think that very idea will make him friendly and may be of use to me."[52]

Anderson's gambit paid off. From his home in the bluegrass country of Lexington, Henry Clay wrote to Anderson with advice intended to win his gratitude: "Dear Sir I find by your favor of the last that you intimate too highly the tender I made, through your father, of my services in selecting a situation [room], during the ensuing winter, in Washington. . . . Should I have it in my power, in any other respect, to render you service, I beg you to consider me as fully disposed to do so. I am, very respectfully and faithfully yours, H Clay."[53]

Soon into his term in the 15th Congress, Anderson's fellow legislators voted to raise their salary from $5 a day (about $900 a year) to $1,500 a year, retroactive. This was embarrassing for congressmen like Anderson and Clay, who had supported the bill but sought to downplay it. That, together with Clay's reversal and vote for the Second Bank of the United States, created tough waters for reelection.[54]

In a congratulatory note celebrating Anderson's victory, John Crittenden urged him to repeal the congressional raise and added his own interest in running for office. Like all "gentlemen," Crittenden posed himself a reluctant candidate who would serve not out of pride but duty only. Personally, he claimed, "I feel an entire unconcern about the matter." Then in a mock criticism of Anderson he closed by blaming Anderson for his decisions: "And that I have been brought to think of it [running for office] at all is altogether to be ascribed to the bad company I have kept, and the bad advice I have laid." Crittenden decided to run for the US Senate and was elected in 1817, the first of two extended terms.[55]

In January 1816, before Anderson moved to Washington, Betsy had written him from Louisville with hard news on her business: "I have as yet been unable to purchase any pork." In a follow-up letter she described a local tragedy and ongoing problems securing pork: "Little Julian Booth . . . expired at nine o'clock on Sunday night of a dropsy on the brain after suffering eight days. . . . I have no prospect of getting any pork at four dollars five and six have been given at market, you will let me know in your next if I shall give more than four. . . . My love and a kiss from [second daughter] little Betty."[56]

Eight days later the pork situation had not changed, leading Betsy to complain that the escalating cost of pork created artificial shortages, which, in turn, raised the prices even higher. Evidently in a good humor, she noted that although he had not written sooner she "was pleased with your excuse, you may visit that amiable family as often as you can, notwithstanding you telling me you would like to marry both the Miss Lees. There is not much hope of your getting rid of me as I have not felt more like living for twelve months than I do at present." To this Anderson responded in equally light tone: "I was at a Ball last evening—where I saw numbers of pretty women—but I only saw them for I did not speak to one—towards the close of the evening I began to think my money was being foolishly spent."[57]

In March, as planting time arrived, Betsy took over farming respon-sibilities on top of her multiple responsibilities with home and slaves. Owen Gwathmey, her father, provided seed and requested bags to trans-port them. On the home front Gwathmey complained, "I have seen no person since we came home and have not heard one sentence from town. . . . See you when you can make it convenient. Your mother's arm better or no alteration in it. I have got the rheumatism so bad in my shoulders, I can scarcely sleep."[58]

Religion did not generally figure in Anderson's correspondence or life, with the exception of family deaths. In time, two of his brothers, Robert and William, would embrace religion. To the extent that Rich-ard considered religion, it was less the evangelical religion of Methodists or Baptists, exemplified at the famous Cane Ridge revivals in Kentucky, than a more genteel Episcopal faith. In fact, the operative religion for Anderson and many of his congressional peers was the "civil religion" of American patriotism and faith in the divine mission of the new republic.[59]

A LONG GAP IN Anderson's journal ended in June 1817, when he again took up pen after election to the 15th and 16th Congresses as a Jef-fersonian Republican. Communications were the lifeblood of the new republic, in particular post offices and post roads. Mail delivery was by far the largest activity of the federal government, and one that it pur-sued with avidity. Between 1815 and 1830 the number of post offices grew from three thousand to eight thousand. Kentucky was a major beneficiary of this expansion. In June and July 1817, Anderson gleefully recorded two events that confirmed in his mind the rising power of the West in the new republic. The first was the completion of a road from Louisville to Wheeling and the commencement of mail delivery, "a new evidence of the wondrous improvement of the Western Country. . . . Those who come after me will wonder as much at my admiration as I do at this unparalleled improvement which it has received in my memory." A year later, mail was also being carried between Wheeling, Virginia, and Washington, DC, on the National Road (also called the Cumber-land Road). The second event was the employment of steamboats be-tween Louisville and New Orleans. "The course of trade," he noted, "has already changed." Kentucky had moved well beyond its frontier stage and was integrating with the larger national economy.[60]

Both the National Road and the steamboat represented internal improvements at federal expense—a central feature in Clay's American System. For many southerners, nervous about a powerful federal government, Clay' proposals were threatening. Others, including Anderson, supported his platform.[61]

Anderson's brother-in-law Isaac Gwathmey, who, in a letter to his sister Betsy, described Louisville as a "prison," offered a very different perception of the "western country" from Anderson's optimism as sickness and hard times prevailed: "Nothing affords enjoyment when such sorrow and alarm prevails as is every day with respect owing to number of complaints which desolate the town. With me it never was a place of great pleasure in its most lively periods, but now it is odious and in the highest sense disagreeable." By the end of June 1817, Anderson shared Gwathmey's discouragement in the face of "a great alarm about the Small pox—which is said by all . . . to prevail there." On July 9 he recorded, "The small pox is spreading—slowly I think." Two days later he noted, "The second death from Small pox occurred this morning." The deaths from smallpox would continue to mount, leading to the adjournment of the Kentucky court in July. Epidemics then—as now—were terrifying affairs, especially when there were no evident cures that could stem their advance.[62]

In August, Anderson again faced financial straits brought on by his obsessive speculation: "Pressed for money. I have borrowed of A. for a few days—then of B to pay A then of C. to pay B." A week later he complained, "Borrowed money of Samuel Arterburn at 15 pr. cent. The first time I ever gave usurious interest." Anderson was not alone. A few days later he wrote, "Brooke Hill has a great inclination to buy land and engage in Speculation. But I believe he has no money. He can only adventure on his credit." A year later, John Gwathmey's bets on land and a tavern were turning sour, leading a vindicated Anderson to speculate in his diary whether "his friends and relations will be very much injured by him. He has sold property in the last 3 weeks for 110 thousand dollars and I know he has other property to the amount of $30 or 40 thousand. Still his solvency is doubtful."[63]

Anderson was correct, and again we see the devastating cycles of boom-and-bust that characterized land speculation in the early republic. Between 1816 and 1818, Gwathmey was forced to sell much of his property in Louisville, including the Indian Queen Hotel.[64]

Despite financial stress, the speculative bug in Anderson could not be stifled. On October 10, 1817, he went to Jeffersonville and noted "more land has been entered in that office within 3. mos. than ever was in the same time." The great national land grab was in full gear, and Americans were on the move in their insatiable search for cheap land. Again his thoughts turned to Indiana: "The Emigration is now great to Missouri and Indiana," leaving Anderson determined "to invest some money in public lands. I know not where." Besides Indiana, Missouri interested him as a possible site for speculation. An even greater gamble would be Florida, still a Spanish territory but, in his view, soon to become a US territory. "In the Spanish dominions large concessions have been usually made to individuals. If they could now be bought they would become much more valuable immediately on the cession." In fact, the Floridas would be purchased from Spain by treaty on February 22, 1819.[65]

Though Indiana always interested Anderson as he noted in his diary, it came with that nasty corollary that occurred throughout the great land grab, namely, the removal of the native inhabitants:

> It is represented to me that a fine tract of Country is held in Indiana by the Delawares not more than 40 miles from the Ohio. If the Indian titles could be extinguished it would greatly increase the strength of that State—be an important acquisition to the Western Country—and be convenient to me if I desired to [in]vest money in public land. Would it not be well this winter to promote the idea of extinguishing it, to engage Gen. [William Henry] Harrison.[66]

Meanwhile, closer to home, panic shifted to jubilation as land profits began soaring, feeding the lust for speculation. Half-acre lots in Portland, near Louisville, rose in price from $200 in 1814 to $300 by 1817. This mania led Anderson to increase his purchases. On November 1, 1817, he noted: "I buy a lot of 5 acres at the extravagant price of $2000. I think it is prudent to invest some money where the public

attention is so highly excited." Two days later he wrote: "Go to Louisville and buy Holmes house and lot for $8000. I think I shall make
money but it is not so great a speculation as many have lately made."[67]

In early November Anderson met John Crittenden in Lexington
and together they traveled to Washington for the new session of Congress. The trip took twenty-two days by stage, which explains why there
were no trips back and forth when Congress was in session—including
at Christmas. The two took the old Wilderness Road from Louisville
to Maysville, the Maysville Pike to Wheeling, and then the National
Road. Along the way they stopped off at the homes of friends and relatives. In Ohio, Anderson made the surprising observation that in many
respects Ohio was better than Kentucky. The reason? "The rapid improvement of this Country shews the good policy of excluding slaves
and of the high benefits of dividing land into small parcels in the congress manner."[68]

On November 28, they arrived at last in Washington. "Mr. Crittenden and myself immediately waited on Mr. Clay who introduced us
to a Mess at Dowsons—where we engaged boarding at $15 pr. week."
This represented a two-thirds jump from the boarding prices Anderson
had paid in Frankfort as a Kentucky congressman. In addition, lodgers
were obliged to pay for their own liquor, which occasioned some angst
on Anderson's part: "We have Madeira, Claret, Cider and porter every
day—Champagne frequently." Anderson was no teetotaler, and he went
along with the costs so as not to appear impoverished. Within days they
were immersed in the gossip of the city: "It is surmised that before long
Mr. Clay may break with the president. I know nothing to authorize—
but I do think a new party will arise during the present or next session
of Congress."[69]

Anderson's rise in Congress presaged greatness. Like his friend
Crittenden and his mentor Clay, he was primed to play a major role on
the national scene. Friends and family speculated that he had presidential timber. But land was an ever-present issue, even in Washington, and
it would dictate behaviors and anxieties that worked tragically at cross
interests to his public ambitions.

5

"My Debts Must Be Paid!": Politics and Land in the Evolving West

1817–1822

The period 1817–1822 would prove to be one of contradictions in Congressman Anderson's life. Politically, he would rise to the heights in Congress and rub elbows with the most powerful figures in government. Financially, he would suffer the sharp swings of agony and ecstasy that characterized the new republic. And personally, he would experience separations from home and deaths that would render his life a searing disappointment.

When Anderson, age twenty-nine, began his term in Congress in 1817, all of his brothers and sisters, save the youngest, Sarah Jane, had been born. Anderson Sr. was sixty-seven and still surveyor general, though he had slowed down considerably. His wife, Sarah, was thirty-eight and would live until 1854.

Anderson began his term in Congress on December 1, 1817, with something akin to a prayer: "May the transactions of this Congress be as honourable to its Members and as glorious for their country, as the sun of this day is bright and splendid." As its first action, the House of Representatives elected Henry Clay as Speaker by a substantial margin. Clay wasted no time establishing his leadership of the movement to recognize the independence of new Latin American states—a policy that might distance him from President Monroe. This would prove to have great implications for Anderson in seeking a diplomatic assignment to the region.[1]

In a telling signal of the ambition for greatness that motivated most of the Andersons, Richard evaluated the fellow legislators in his mess and found them wanting. Philip Pendleton Barbour and Nathaniel Macon, he observed, "say some smart things, but I cannot think (as yet) either of them great men." Rather, they were "ordinary." Anderson's judgment was premature. Barbour would go on to be the only American to serve as both Speaker of the House from Virginia and, later, Supreme Court justice, while Macon would be elected twelve successive times to the House of Representatives from the state of North Carolina. Perhaps Anderson's prejudice came from Barbour and Macon's regional arrogance and denigration of the West. Anderson noticed that easterners like them underestimated the West and the political implications of its rapidly rising population. Representatives from the Carolinas and Georgia realized that settlement could reach the Pacific Ocean, "but they seem never to have supposed the possibility of the Seat of Gov[ernment] being removed or of any struggle or commotion arising on that subject." Anderson knew that expanded national boundaries and new states would have major political consequences: "I can assure them that if the ability is ever possessed [for new states to gain the ascendancy] the power will be exercised."[2]

On December 6, 1817, Anderson recorded in his diary, "I placed my brother Larz at Mr. Ironsides," a Washington prep school. Larz apparently possessed the qualities of greatness, which his family helped to nourish, and Anderson's influence as a congressman surely helped to bring him visibility.[3]

The same day that Anderson placed Larz in school, he described his introduction to President Monroe by US congressman William Henry Harrison: "On Wednesday last Mr. [John J.] Crittenden and myself were introduced by Genl. Harrison to the president. Surely he [Harrison] is awkward and dull and I thought there was an awkward attempt at pomp and style in our mode of introduction." That Anderson did not feel the least bit awkward in the president's presence testifies to the clubby nature of Washington politics in the early republic and to the friendship between Monroe and his father. Nor is it surprising that he could freely criticize Harrison as an equal, in the same way he would also disparage John Quincy Adams for his abolitionist views on slavery. The slight to Harrison was predictable in a family committed to speculation. As a congressman, Harrison had introduced the Land Act of 1800 (also called the Harrison Land Act), which prevented speculators from acquiring western lands already improved by settlers and made it possible for the settlers to eventually become owners. That Harrison, the "Hero of Tippecanoe," and Adams, the sixth US president, are remembered to history while Anderson's premature demise ensured that he would remain a forgotten elite cannot obscure the fact that all of his messmates were close to the highest offices in the country, even as arbitrary circumstances would pick one for fame and not the other. Surely if Anderson was asked who he thought would be president, himself or Harrison, he would not have hesitated to pick himself. The next day, Anderson noted in his diary, "Genl. [William Henry] Harrison has talked himself very low here," apparently in reference to an investigation of Harrison's financial dealings as governor of the Northwest Territory. As well, Harrison did not measure up to Anderson's standards of a gentleman: "Harrison is very low I think in the estimation of the house. He certainly is in mine. He is vain, little and intriguing."[4]

That sense of self-importance came through loud and clear the next week, when Anderson announced: "This day I made my first speech in Congress on the bill for commuting the Soldiers bounty land into money." This was a subject he knew well, and he took the moral high ground. Essentially, Anderson and Clay favored the government's buying unused soldiers' warrants rather than speculators (like himself and his father), in order to reduce the influence of speculators—in particular, absentee speculators. Anderson and Clay were not successful, the bill was defeated, and speculators continued to profit in land. A week later, Anderson wrote in self-congratulation, "Dined with Mr. Clay—most of the Kentucky representation was with me." The following day was Christmas, with Anderson again away from his family and "engaged in writing letters."[5]

Meanwhile, the boom of rising land prices was rapidly deflating. On January 3, 1818, Samuel Gwathmey wrote Anderson of approaching bad times in Kentucky: "We have nothing very new in this country—hard times seems to be the universal cry, and I believe now prevails to an extent much greater than has ever been known at in this country, particularly with those persons who are purchasers of public lands."[6]

In service to his family, Anderson had occasion while in Washington to visit with his younger half brother Larz. Though lonely, Larz seemed to be doing well and appreciated Richard's closeness. In a letter to his sister Betsy, Larz wrote, "I am now in the school where I generally stay except when I go to see brother Richard. It is the only place I like to stay in for unless I have books to amuse me I begin to think of home." It seems clear that Richard was monitoring his younger brother's progress, for in a follow-up letter to his father, he wrote, "Larz is very well." That said, he was concerned that "dull or idle" students were retarding the progress of bright students like Larz. Already thinking ahead, Richard addressed the question of college for Larz: "The Eastern members [of Congress] give such varying and contradictory reports about the merits of their respective colleges that I have not decided which I shall recommend to you." In the end, it would be Harvard that drew Larz's interest in what would mark the start of a multigenerational family commitment.[7]

In other news, Anderson notified his father that his fellow soldier and friend, and now president, James Monroe would be in Kentucky upon his return from Missouri, adding, "He never fails to surprise of all his acquaintances when I see him and I will certainly present your respects to him. He has lately sent a message to Congress [attacking Andrew Jackson] which I believe his friends here are generally sorry for; not indeed that the country can receive much. . . . Remember me affectionately to my mother [and] the girls and boys."[8]

Anderson's congressional days included personal time with Crittenden, Clay, and Monroe. In ruminating about Clay's ambitions for political advancement in advocating United States recognition of South American revolutions (which Monroe resisted), Anderson confided to his diary, "Henry Clay may be an ambitious man, may be a bad man, but he is apparently the most frank politician I ever saw. He avows in all his companies his views of the administration and of the course which he means to take as to the South Americas. He intends to have the question tried in the House: ought we to recognize the Government of Buenos Ayres and probably some others?"[9]

From the time he was passed over for a cabinet position—preferably secretary of state—the fiercely proud Clay had put himself on a collision course with President Monroe, a fellow Republican. His focal point of attack, as Anderson's diary reveals, was the question of American neutrality toward Spain and the recognition of democratic insurgents in Latin America. Another major mission of Clay's was the promotion of internal improvements at federal expense. Contrary to many southern politicians' preferences, Clay's American System encouraged lavish federal spending to promote the welfare of western states. In direct criticism of President Monroe, Speaker Clay placed his fellow Kentucky Republicans in a quandary by ridiculing Monroe's "irregular and unconstitutional" interference with Congress on the subject of internal improvements. No one, including Anderson, expected such a personal attack on Monroe's presidential integrity and fidelity to the Constitution.[10]

Earlier, on January 14, Anderson had noted, "I was at the Presidents drawing room." Only a week later, Anderson again noted, "I dined with the President." He doesn't record the subject matter, but the very next words provide a hint of what may have been discussed: "Luxury is increasing in this Country as fast as our wealth or population. The same love of style, etiquette etc. prevails here, which does among the aristocrats of Europe." Here we see Anderson's self-perception as less a rugged American frontiersman in the stamp of Daniel Boone or Davy Crockett than a self-made American aristocrat with American democratic rather than inherited aristocratic sensibilities.[11]

Talk of luxury took Anderson's mind again to land. "At my request Mr. S. Sergeant has promised to ascertain where the contract entered into between Genl. [George Rogers] Clark and [Humphrey] Marshall now is. I have thought it possible that some thing might be made by purchasing it." Like Anderson the patriarch and Kentucky frontiersman Daniel Boone, General Clark was very involved with land speculation and military warrants and eventually emerged bankrupt and embittered. Perhaps Anderson hoped to work something out with Clark's substantial land claims. On February 8, 1818, he dined with Clark and learned that he intended to run for governor in the new state of Missouri when it joined the union in 1820. Upon his return to quarters, Anderson wrote his brother-in-law and business assistant George Gwathmey "to borrow for me $1500 with which to buy Soldiers bounty land." Having lost the congressional battle to require land warrants to be sold to the government rather than speculators, he made the most of it by again speculating in land.[12]

On June 12, 1818, an obviously frustrated Anderson wrote from his home in Myland, "Three months have elapsed since I wrote one word in this diary. I mention this to show the indolence of Man." He then went on to describe his return trip from Washington in April, including a leg by steamboat, "a most pleasant mode of traveling." In reflecting on his term in Congress, the thirty-one-year-old Anderson reproached his "injudicious expectations" that things would get done but, again, found the antidote: "During the Session I purchased 15 soldiers patents in Illinois for which I gave an average of $96." He then added, "I left Larz [then sixteen years old] with Mr. Clay to go to Boston [Harvard] with his son Theodore." In a letter to Anderson, Clay noted that in addition to dropping Larz and Theodore at the stage coach, "I gave to Mr. Shasbee $300, one hundred and fifty for each of the boys, and particular instructions in relation to them both. They left here in good spirits and I hope their affection for each other will continue."[13]

Four months later, the verdict on Larz was in. He loved Harvard, primarily for the intellectual challenge that it offered. In a letter to his older half brother, who was so instrumental in his matriculation, he wrote, "We [he and Theodore Clay] both like Mr. Gilman, our teacher, very well and he is very attentive to us. I have learned more here in three weeks than in all the time at Mr. Ironside's and as well for there was a continual noise, but here we have no persons to disturb us. I am very glad that I have come here, and indeed could desire no better place to learn." He then closed on a financial note: "I saw Mr. Shasbee last week he said nothing to me about the funds. I suppose he will inform you if they are insufficient." Larz received favorable receptions from his fellow students, most of whom were northerners whom he referred to as "Easterners."[14]

Once home, Anderson found somewhat to his surprise that he was again a candidate for Congress. In response to the announcement of his candidacy, John Crittenden wrote, "This is rather more than I could have hoped for, knowing how much you were in love with your wife last mention. How much you were disgusted with your place, and how bitterly you denounced Congress—I must attribute it altogether to an excess of your patriotism. . . . Are you like to have any opposition to your decision?" Later, following Anderson's reelection, Crittenden wrote a note of congratulations, adding, "I hope however that your folly, as you call it, will do me some good." In any case, Crittenden concluded, he hoped to "have the pleasure of seeing you this fall on your way to your theater of glory."[15]

In September, Anderson received a note from Henry Clay enclosing letters relating to Larz and Theodore and inviting him to join him for a trip north to see the boys at Harvard: "I have some thought of visiting Cambridge next month, and in that case I shall set out from this place about the 5th. Can you not go? I should like very much to have the satisfaction of your company. I offer you, most sincerely, my congratulations on the occasion of your recent honorable reelection. Do me the favor to present my respects to your father [a recurrent theme] and believe me, cordially and faithfully yours, H. Clay."[16]

BUT POLITICAL OFFICE-HOLDING AND Larz's schooling were not Anderson's chief concerns. Land preoccupied him: "What concerns most of [my] thoughts now, is a desired speculation in the Missouri lands. The sale comes in Sept. I fear I shall not be able to raise money to go." At that time Missouri was selling land under the Harrison Land Act of 1800 for the legal minimum of two dollars per acre. There was plenty of room for speculation as potential purchasers like Anderson could take up to four years to complete their payments, by which time, they bet, the value of the land would have increased greatly. Of course, if land prices moved in the opposite direction, speculators would face dire consequences. But that did not worry Anderson because, at the time in Louisville, town property sales were still rising "to an extent truly astonishing." Besides his own investments, Anderson encouraged relatives to join him in speculating: "By my advice Isaac Gwathmey has bought a lot . . . for $7000. This is entirely speculation as he is not worth one tenth of the money for which he has bound himself."[17]

Troubles with Indians and Spaniards in the Floridas also occupied much of Anderson's attention. Again, land considerations were paramount. When General Andrew Jackson invaded the Floridas in 1817, with questionable authorization from President Monroe, he immediately marched on the Seminoles, attacking and destroying village after village, marking the start of the First Seminole War. A decisive victory eluded Jackson as the Indians melted into the forest, from which they could launch what amounted to guerrilla attacks. In response, Jackson destroyed their homes and fields. Again, without a clear authorization, Jackson took the fight to the Spanish, seizing Spanish forts at St. Marks and Pensacola in May 1818, serving notice to the Spanish that if they could not control their lands they should sell them to the United States. From the start, Anderson recognized the undeclared war Jackson had launched and correctly assessed the outcome: "Genl Jackson has lately taken Pensacola—I believe without particular orders [from President Monroe]. But if it is ascertained that the public sentiment will bear it he will be justified and the taking avowed. . . . Spain would surely go to War, if she had anything to war with—but she is miserably poor."[18]

Later, Anderson determined that Jackson had misstepped but predicted that his popularity as "Old Hickory" would ultimately keep him out of trouble: "The majority of the newspapers is I think against him. Certainly his conduct has been violent and unauthorized. I have no doubt the President thinks so and would be glad to get rid of him but fears that his [war] services have made him too popular to put down." Again the relentless appetite for land stopped at nothing, including war, to gain satisfaction. Anderson was party to it, and in a speech to Congress he strenuously defended Jackson's actions in executing the British trader Alexander Arbuthnot and the soldier of fortune Robert Ambrister for supplying his Spanish enemies.[19]

Virtually everyone in Monroe's cabinet loathed Jackson and recognized his actions as an unjust and unwarranted attack on Spanish territory. But at the same time, many saw in Jackson's actions unparalleled opportunity. Secretary of State John Quincy Adams brilliantly used Jackson's de facto occupation of Florida as a powerful bargaining chip to force a purchase of the land. Anderson judged aright Spain's weakness, witnessing the stunning unraveling of its American empire in North and South America. Arguing that Spain should cede Florida and territory west to the United States in compensation for properties lost to Indian raids by Florida Seminoles in Georgia and the Mississippi Territory, Adams demanded reimbursement. With no war chest, Spain reluctantly agreed to the Adams-Onís Treaty in 1819, ceding Florida and the Gulf Coast on either side of the Mississippi. Equally important, the treaty fixed the new western boundary of the United States at the Pacific Ocean, a boundary that Jefferson had not imagined. In the relentless American appetite for expansion, Adams could look with pride at his role in transforming Jackson's illegal raid into a massive acquisition of western territory. For the first time, the United States ran from coast to coast. In the process, the wheels were set in motion for the Oregon Trail and the settlement of the far West.[20]

The concrete and mythic consequences of acquiring the Floridas were immense. Adams's treaty ensured that Americans could travel and own property throughout the continent, giving added life to the burgeoning frontier myth later romanticized by Frederick Jackson Turner. Unlike many others, Adams recognized early the potential of Manifest Destiny to conquer—and own—a continent. Indeed, if he'd had his way, American expansion would have extended even further, to Canada and Cuba.[21]

In addition to the acquisition of the Floridas, Adams also articulated what would come to be called the Monroe Doctrine, declaring the Americas off-limits to European meddling or settlement. Again, Adams grounded his argument in a prevailing sense of American Manifest Destiny to "overspread" the West with democratic (and Protestant) values at odds with the monarchies in Europe. Only as events unfolded did Adams come to bitterly regret his stupendous achievements, as he saw a nation overspreading the continent indeed, but with the cancer of slavery, a disease that would threaten the nation's existence. With unalloyed disappointment, Adams later questioned whether the Union could survive half slave and presciently concluded that "slavery is precisely the question upon which it ought to break."[22]

Accompanying America's relentless expansionism was a powerful strain of Protestant exceptionalism that realized expression in a series of urban and frontier revivals known as the Second Great Awakening. While Richard Anderson Jr. and his family remained largely immune to the cadences of Methodist exhorters and Disciples of Christ, many on the frontier embraced the new, highly emotive religion. Besides making unprecedented numbers of converts on the Kentucky and Ohio frontiers, the Second Great Awakening served the nonreligious purpose of organizing the potentially lawless fringes of the frontier with social reform movements and voluntary associations.[23]

The highly individualized, optimistic, and voluntaristic organization of the Second Great Awakening in the West was of a piece with the democratic ethos of the West and was, unsurprisingly, reflected in land policy. Unlike the East, where there were restrictive franchise requirements for significant landownership, western states immediately enacted far more inclusive legislation abolishing property requirements for voting that greatly expanded the pool of potential male voters. Inevitably this would lead to the removal of all voting restrictions for white males.[24]

While the franchise remained crucial in distributing power throughout the West, land distribution was an even more powerful democratizing agent. More than any other measure, the Public Land Survey System, ordaining rectangular surveys and public sales and opening up landownership to potential millions of ordinary Americans, came to define the West. In 1820, the smallest parcel of land, known as the half-quarter section (eighty acres), could be secured on loan at a minimal price of $1.25 per acre. The consequences had no equivalency in the Old World as the dispersal of wealth through the Public Land Survey encouraged the growth of a society of landowners without precedent. The survey not only fostered a sense of independence that came with property but also encouraged the qualities of self-sufficiency and enterprise, which historians would associate with the frontier.[25]

The close connection between Anderson and the Gwathmeys continued when, in September 1818, Anderson learned that his sister Betsy was engaged to Isaac Gwathmey. This was another Anderson marriage of first cousins, but at this point in Kentucky's history, it broke no laws, and in a much smaller population such instances of consanguinity were almost commonplace.[26]

In July, Anderson received a letter from John Crittenden with the welcome news that "I have at last succeeded in procuring for you the loan of twelve hundred dollars. Mr. Clay and myself endorsing the note. From the condition of our banks, I had some difficulty in doing it and I assure you I am now not a little happy in having accomplished it. . . . I herein enclose [it] to you by Mr. Steele." Then, on a lighter note, Crittenden announced his plans to run for Congress and praised Anderson for his achievements: "You stand like Caesar, peerless and have nothing to do but to pass with acclamation the triumphal arch but I pray you no more of your waggery upon us little folk that bustle in the shade beneath you, or I bid you remember that you too may find your ides of march. Tis too hot to write—So, good by. I am your friend."[27]

Anderson's finances continued bouncing up and down, though the trending pattern was down. The year 1818 witnessed a manic bout of land speculation on borrowed money. One interesting offer came to Anderson in August from one of his father's deputy surveyors: "H[enry] Massie yesterday offered me twenty two hundred acres of land in Indiana for Myland and agreed to warrant (as far as Myland could support the warrant) that the land he let [me] have should be worth $40,000 at the expiration of 10 years." But on second thought Anderson refused, despite it being "a great offer." The reason was simple: "Nothing but a love of ease and an unwillingness to part with a farm when another could not easily be gotten prevents me from taking what is I think greatly more than it is worth." While Anderson's finances were precarious, his abilities and connections would, he was confident, see him through, especially if he got a foreign appointment that paid far more than congressional salaries.[28]

This did not mean, however, that all was going well, and Anderson might have had a different response to Massie if the offer had appeared in September. By then, he was hard up for cash and the economy was on a downward spiral, leading Anderson to lament, "I have been more severely pressed for money this fall than I ever was. I must sell some town property and am now endeavouring to effect [it]. It is for me to sell in time for the payments which I am to make the next year." Though Anderson routinely referred to "my" money, the Anderson economy was not simply the work of one person but of a whole family system incorporating husband, wife, children, extended kin, and slaves. The creation of the "self-made man" was in fact a complex process involving many parts all working together to ensure the family's survival. And now that survival was threatened.[29]

October brought no economic relief, and he conceded the follies of excessive speculation: "The pressure for money generally is very great—on me is severe. I fear that I must sacrifice a part of my property. I have done what thousands have done before me and but few will fail to do after me, purchase more than I can conveniently pay for." The tone in Anderson's diary entry is revealing, suggesting that speculation was more an addiction than a calculated risk: the withdrawal was painful and the anxiety intense. Like compulsive gambling, obsessive land speculation thrives on intermittent gratification, leading Anderson to hope, "If the sacrifice that I make is not very great, my property will still be very much enhanced by my adventures."[30]

Perhaps as a consequence of his mounting financial woes, Anderson began addressing the big questions of life and searching his own ambitions. First, he looked at his father in old age, observing how he spent his senior years "amused with hobbies," including horses, sheep, hogs, and, most recently, Freemasonry. There was a lesson here. While many might "ridicule" such non-moneymaking activities, "I think it's very fortunate when avarice, ambition or other passions which rule man have ceased to act their part, that others can be found however trivial to give employment to the mind and to prevent the tediousness of doing nothing." Unbeknownst to Anderson, all this time his father was also very much in the land speculation business and would end his life virtually ruined.[31]

As for himself, Anderson was again uncertain of which direction to pursue. As he saw it in 1818, the choice was stark: either make money to be inherited by his children or spend it on his own self-contentment. This had him "agitated between two opposing inclinations." The first was to live sparingly and "devote myself and the money I can raise to the increase of my property by purchasing land." The other inclination was "to live for myself by building a good house, improving the farm and every way devoting my money for the comfort and pleasure of myself." Sensing that his children would no doubt inherit (and read his diary), he noted, "My children, should they ever see this will wonder that I felt any doubt and will feel vexation that I did not lay out every thing for their benefit." In the end, he hoped to do both.[32]

Money was not the only crisis in Louisville. In autumn 1818 and into the next year, Anderson reported "great sickness and mortality in Louisville and the country generally." Close to home, his uncle Jonathan Clark's widow died, and even closer, "my little daughter Elizabeth is now sick with a fever and cold." But on the positive side for all those living in the West, he rejoiced at the news of a federal effort to carry mail on the Ohio and Mississippi Rivers by steamboat. The year prior, the steamboat *Enterprise* had made a record run from New Orleans to Louisville in twenty-five days. Steam, he was sure, would transform the region: "Surely no invention in any art or science is likely to produce such beneficial consequences to the Western Country as the invention of the new one of Steam—no nor all put together!"[33]

Anderson's land speculation continued to range throughout the western territories and states. In 1818, he received a property tax bill from Illinois for "224 acres of second rate and 160 acres of first rate land the sum of eighteen dollars and forty cents." But signs of trouble were looming, both for Anderson and the nation, as a full-fledged financial panic marched ominously throughout the country. The causes were foreclosed mortgages and failed banks that led, in turn, to falling prices. In late November Anderson received a letter from George Gwathmey that proved prescient. The Bank of Kentucky had suspended specie payment as the state sat on a crippling real estate panic generating "insurmountable debts": "I do not conceive it requires much wisdom to predict the entire ruin of a great number of persons, particularly our high handed speculators, who have purchased property on credit at a dear rate to be paid for when in my opinion, money will be much dearer that it is at present." Gwathmey went on to declare that the banks were no better. Indeed, the two were interconnected: "Town property is now literally forgotten nothing talked of but Banks and Bankrupsies."[34]

Happily for Anderson, one source of revenue was Betsy's pigs. It is not clear from Anderson's diary or correspondence how Betsy and Richard understood the relationship between her labor and his, but the subject came up often enough to confirm that there was a real financial partnership between the two that made Anderson's political and speculative enterprises a viable option. On December 2, 1818, Betsy reported: "For the want of salt I did not kill our pork until Monday. I then killed twenty, I gave $16.50 a barrel for the salt I have, and shall be very much engaged this week." The average 250-pound hog yielded about 144 pounds of meat. Multiplied by twenty, the labor involved in slaughtering and dressing pigs was prodigious. Generally, the ideal time for butchering was late fall, when Betsy did her slaughtering. After killing, hanging, and bleeding the pig, the butchering proceeded; the blood, meanwhile, was used for sausage and the skin for bacon. Ribs had to be separated and meat placed in large buckets of boiling water. The profit, as pork remained the staple meat in Kentucky, made the demanding labor worthwhile.[35]

Despite Betsy's contributions, Anderson did not think he could escape financial damage. On Christmas Day, 1818, he recorded in his diary, from Washington, DC: "Real property and indeed all other I think must undergo a depression (temporary). I fear its effect on me will be troublesome. I have purchased property at a high price and I cannot now sell it. I have no fear (if I can meet the payment) of its ultimate value." Of course the anxiety centered on the "if," the magical elixir of risk and speculation. It drove every investment and characterized American capitalism at the macro and individual level. Providence no longer governed human destiny in the American economy. Risk and chance were the new "freaks of fortune," and neither provided any guarantees or peace of mind. American capitalism feasted on fear and greed, leading to the sorts of behavior that threatened to undo Anderson and millions like him. Fortunately for the Andersons, none ended up truly destitute. The family network was too strong. But the fear of ruin was ever present.[36]

In 1818, reacting to intense pressure from small businessmen for credit, Kentucky chartered forty-six banks—soon reviled as the "forty thieves"—with a total capitalization of $9 million, all in paper notes not backed by specie or accepted by the Bank of the United States. With no backing, the notes were soon rendered worthless. The manic land speculation of 1818 ended in disaster as the land bubble burst in 1819, leaving chaos and broken lives in its wake. For Kentucky, the label "Panic of 1819" could not have been more literally true. The legislature promptly annulled the "forty thieves" charters of state banks, leaving gross debts due all banks at an estimated total of $10 million. Much of the debt was owned by the same small farmers and businessmen who had been most vocal in calling for new banks and currency.[37]

As Richard and Betsy worked to stay afloat in the fall of 1818, the Panic of 1819 loomed ever nearer. A letter from Betsy on November 20, 1818, sounded a note of frustration: "No letter from you since you left home although you promised to write from Lexington and, I think, some other place on your way in. Your Fathers family is well he is very much confined by business, I have only seen him three times. . . . Do write if you are well enough and if not get Mr. Crittenden. Elizabeth Anderson."[38]

Anderson may have written infrequently because he had so little good news to announce. Finally, he could no longer hide his financial distress from Betsy and shared it in a letter that has not survived. It was news she did not wish to receive. In response to his letter she offered frightened words of criticism rather than support: "[It] gives me less pleasure than they usually do as you appear to be a little low spirited you must not write to me in that way any more you must tell me about all the fine things and people you see, how they look, and what they say, and who treats you best. . . . I asked Elizabeth what I should tell you, she say I must tell you that Uncle Isaac and Aunt Betsy am married and you must bring her a red baby and scissors for telling you."[39]

On December 20, Betsy wrote again: "Today I have been cutting out the negroes cloaths. Except for my tongue and hands I have been very lazy since you left home." As for her business, she was pleased to report, "Last week we had 65 pigs, we have lost none that I know of. I have not had time to kill the balance of our hogs." She then closed on a humorous note: "I am knitting your summer socks, if I dye in Feb. I wish to leave you as many as will last you while you remain single, you must let me know how many will do, will one?"[40]

Christmas 1818 again found the couple apart. And, once again, Anderson spent the day alone in his room. For diversion he turned to his diary, lamenting that "the finances of the country generally (I do not mean the government) were never in such a deranged and distressed state. The immense and improper issues from hundreds of Banks . . . have produced the embarrassment. The great premium offered for specie, causes the notes to be pushed on the Banks in great quantities and the Banks either call on their debtors or stop payment."[41]

For her part, Betsy wrote, "My dear Richard I hope you will have a merry Christmas and many many happy new years. I was alone but we are all well and I cannot complain. Louis has had no return of fever, I say I am alone. Isaac [named for Isaac Gwathmey] and Betsy are in their room. I can find no more papers. I did not get a letter from you yesterday write often and take care of your health. Yours forever." A letter from Isaac Gwathmey, in contrast, focused on the ever-present fear: "I have had no offer for my lot, which I am very anxious to sell as the day of payment is fast approaching." *Anxious* became the word of the day.[42]

This dire economic situation stayed in Anderson's mind and, together with his deteriorating finances, determined him to bring the family with him to Washington the next year or he would not go to Washington for the session of Congress. On the same Christmas Day he wrote in his diary, "I have several thousand dollars to pay during the next summer and I do not know where one thousand is to come from. I hear that my friend at home cannot sell my property. The next summer must be one of unpayment to me and I fear of some embarrassment." He then turned to his unhappy wife and family: "The course of things is so precarious. . . . I now think that unless my wife and children can come with me I shall not return [to Congress] next winter. My personal wish is to come with them; I wish Betsy to see what might be seen in a visit to this country." Betsy, of course, had her own preoccupations with home and business: "My pigs grow finely, I have lost very few, I have two calves both of which Elizabeth calls Mr. Anderson, as she thinks it the prittyest name in the world she often talks of you, I can get her to say her book at any time, by telling her I will not write to you unless she does, did you tell her to make me write to you?"[43]

In the same month Anderson heard from his uncle William Crogham, who had surveyed earlier for Anderson Sr. and was hoping to survey yet more land that Andrew Jackson had extracted from the hapless Chickasaw. In that context, he played on family connections to receive advance word of when the surveys might begin: "I am in hopes that it will be in my power to have the land entered on military warrants surveyed during the course of this year. Should the treaty be ratified you will very much oblige me by giving me early information of it that I may prepare for having the surveys made." As for the military warrants, he wrote, "There will be considerable difficulty in establishing a number of the military entries, the owners of them had better give part of the land (say about one fifth) to a person capable of doing the business, who should have the land survey and patented to the owner clear of expense."[44]

Four days after receiving Crogham's letter, Anderson heard from William Clark, who had moved from superintendent of Indian Affairs to governor of the Missouri Territory. Like Crogham, his concern was

Indian lands and how the tribes should be administered, noting the problems with unjust agents, "illicit trade," and unending "disputes which may arise between the whites and Indians and between the Indians themselves." Clark recommended creating a western superintendent of Indian Affairs for all tribes west of the Mississippi, who would oversee trade and intertribal relations. As for St. Louis: "Suitable agents should be placed for the Indians immediately within our neighborhood."[45]

As for himself, Clark noted that he did not intend to remain governor after Missouri attained statehood but would return to land and trade. His interests lay chiefly in land—lots of land. In particular, he wished to secure claims his recently deceased brother, George Rogers Clark, had to Chickasaw lands, as the new boundaries would make their settlement secure. As compensation for his leadership in the Revolution, George Rogers Clark had received seventy-four thousand acres in western Kentucky, which he had turned over to William in payment for his services in settling his considerable debts. To that end, William Clark hoped "that the Superintendent be vested with power to adjust and settle all claims, both of the citizens and Indians for property taken. My opinion is that the U.S. should pay their citizens for all the property proved to be taken by the Indians . . . and oblige the Indians to accord to the U.S. and property proven to be taken by citizens in any part of the country it should be made the duty of the Superintendent or agent to prosecute."[46]

In fact, Clark's wishes had already come true. By 1818 Jackson had negotiated a treaty with the Chickasaw that eliminated all their claims to the land. With that, Clark participated in the utter devastation of the natives whose interests he was supposedly upholding. He played a major role in their dislocation. On instructions from Secretary of War John Calhoun, Clark acted to stop the warring among the Cherokee, Osage, and Quapaw tribes and secured their lands for white settlement. In return, Clark was authorized to spend up to $3,000 to reward the tribes for moving west of the Mississippi. Clarke succeeded on all fronts and won the enthusiastic approval of his president and secretary of war. With cash in hand, Clark was able to extinguish most of the Indian titles in two future states—Missouri and Arkansas—totaling over fifty-one million acres. "The once-powerful tribes north of the

Ohio—the Delaware, Miami, Wea, Potawatomi, Shawnee, and Wyandot—could be relocated across the Mississippi. In all, Clark's Indian removal would extinguish Indian titles to 419 million acres of land."[47]

There was no panic in Missouri. In 1819, the *St. Louis Enquirer* reported that five hundred families were crossing the Mississippi every day to occupy lands freed by Clark's treaties with the Osage. With a population of over forty-five thousand, the territory qualified for statehood. This meant Clark could retire to tend to his vast lands taken from the Indians.[48]

But money issues continued to plague Anderson. In a January 25, 1819, letter to Isaac Gwathmey, who was managing his financial affairs, Anderson confessed, "I am mortified to be under the necessity of putting you to so much trouble but when we change situations I will pay the debt." Then a thought occurred to him. He could borrow funds from the bank once it received a $200,000 payment for loans on February 8: "I cannot suppose that they can confine their discounts to only what is actually paid in—if so no one has a stronger case than myself. I have not borrowed and do not propose to borrow a dollar more than I pay in—this as a stock holder I can certainly demand, but I think I have claims under this idea if it be necessary."[49]

Even Anderson's father was not spared blowback from the Panic. In a letter to his son, he noted that he had to sell some land and was presently working "to prevent the sale of a negro of mine." In addition, Anderson Sr. noted that his son John Roy "came here Thursday evening and just before we were going to bed he informed me that John Gwathmey's property was to be sold the next day. I inquired what property he said he believed all his property, the negroes, and his part of my slip of land." Congressman Anderson was right to suspect that John Gwathmey had dug himself a financial hole from which he could never escape. The hope was that other family members would not be brought into the disaster.[50]

Besides facing mounting financial issues, Anderson Sr. was fighting to protect his appointment as surveyor general. For forty years he had been responsible for land office transactions extending over ten million acres to satisfy bounty claims estimated at six million. As the center of those operations moved from Kentucky to Ohio (with Anderson remaining in Kentucky), oversight became minimal. In 1819, Anderson

Sr. refused to obey instructions from Virginia's state legislature to relocate his office from Louisville, Kentucky, to Chillicothe, Ohio. In response, the governor of Virginia fired Anderson, only to see Anderson sue on the grounds that his authority (for life) derived from the federal government and not the state of Virginia. Eventually the US Supreme Court, under the guidance of Chief Justice John Marshall, declared that Anderson could not be removed. Despite his poor oversight, an aging and increasingly weakened Anderson would remain surveyor general until his death.[51]

By February 1819, Anderson Jr.'s eyes were on the US Supreme Court as its members debated the right of Maryland to tax a branch of the Bank of the United States out of existence. The case of *McCullouch v. Maryland* was presided over by Chief Justice Marshall and argued by Daniel Webster. "I think the Court will decide against the state right," Anderson correctly predicted of what was arguably the greatest case decided in his term as congressman. Marshall delivered an opinion that the state had no right to impede the national bank by taxation. With this decision, the hand of the federal government was strengthened immeasurably over the states. This landmark case in constitutional history took place at the same time the House was debating whether to repeal the charter of the Second Bank of the United States. Anderson voted against repeal and, in the process, alienated many of his constituents who blamed the "Eastern money power" for their mounting financial woes. Anderson conceded, "It is probable that a great majority of my constituents are the other way and some will probably be wrathful—<u>but I care little enough about a seat here to do as I think</u> right." Anderson's use of underlining is revealing, suggesting that the financial pressures were becoming so extreme as to close off the possibility of his returning to Congress the next year.[52]

Closer to home, Anderson learned from Owen Gwathmey that in early February Anderson Sr. had bought the "slice" of land they owned in common for $10,000. This, Owen complained, was only half of "what it would have brought if the commissioners had laid it off in lots as many people think." But Owen had no choice. Anderson's seldom-heard-from brother John Roy was also in great distress and forced to sell his slaves: "One or two went low but others went high." Throughout the state, property values fell between 30 and 50 percent, leaving many unprepared to pay their debts. Owen closed his letter by noting that if he continued to live, "my life would be very little comfort for me." The local distress was rendered worse by the realization that "there appears to be a good deal of money in circulation but very little of it receivable for anything."[53]

Even as Anderson was determining to leave Congress and renew his law practice, John Crittenden was contemplating a similar action. In a letter to Anderson, Crittenden noted his intention to resign his seat in the Senate and return to his law practice in Frankfort. He then asked for Anderson's advice: "And now what think you of this? Am I doing right or wrong?" He then offered Anderson some advice, urging him to seek "a fat office. You have strong claims. Your 'lean and hungry looks' have always so moved my compassion, that I could not but be pleased to see you put up to fatten upon some good office. All business men, I think, must agree on this sentiment."[54]

Anderson's reply has not survived, but he clearly advised Crittenden against resigning. In reply Crittenden conceded, "You advise correctly." He then closed, noting he "visited with the President on horseback accompanying him for several miles."[55]

In a June 1819 letter, Anderson's brother-in-law George Gwathmey briskly summarized the disastrous state of affairs unleashed by the financial panic hitting close to home: "Hard times and worse coming seems to be felt and calculated on by the good people of the West. In this recalculation I am sorry to add that Louisville [can]not be excluded. I fear the devil will be to pay." Once George's lament began the palpable fears spilled over into what amounted to a short treatise outlining the inflated and unrealistic valuations of property. When combined with the inability to procure money, the effect was devastating. "Extravagant estimates of valuations" led to "enormous debts," such that "a day of payment is expected—this day of payment will be a day of judgment to many indeed—add to their misfortunes the impractability of getting produce to market during the whole of last fall on accdt of the low stage of water. . . . The major part of independent banks must discontinue."[56]

In a December letter to Isaac Gwathmey, Anderson summarized affairs in Washington: "We have as yet hardly touched the surface of the important subjects which are before us. I think it very doubtful whether any law will pass on the subject of the Missouri Territory. . . . The vice president (it is said) will be elected governor of New York."[57]

For once, Anderson was wrong in his speculations. The vice president, Daniel Tompkins, did not seek to recover the governorship he'd held from 1807 to 1817 but remained Monroe's vice president for both terms. And a law was indeed passed on the Missouri Territory the next year when Henry Clay introduced legislation that resolved the issue of statehood with the Missouri Compromise, which regulated the status of slavery in the western territories. At first blush, the "Missouri question," dividing pro- and antislavery forces, seemed unresolvable. If Missouri was the only state considering entry into the Union, the loser of the pro- and antislavery factions would be unconstrained in condemning the Compromise. But Clay sensed a solution. If Maine could be separated from Massachusetts and admitted as a free state, then a slave state and a free state could both enter the Union—preserving the balance of pro- and antislavery states. With Speaker Clay's forceful backing, the Compromise passed with an additional amendment prohibiting the extension of slavery in the territory of the Louisiana Purchase north of 36°30'—with the exception of Missouri.[58]

Through the years surrounding the Panic of 1819, Kentucky was virtually bankrupted. The same land that had promised easy profits and limitless wealth soon produced the opposite—shattered land values—and hyperanxiety. In Kentucky, the Panic of 1819 was really the panic of 1818–1820 and more than lived up to its name. Businesses and branch banks of the United States refused to accept Kentucky bank currency. Banks that were easily chartered in 1817–1818 were forced to close their doors and forfeit their charters. Real estate values dropped to one-sixth of their boom values and homes foreclosed. Anderson was caught in the vortex of speculation. With land debts reaching $20,000, it was all he could do to pay the interest on his loans. On January 14, 1821, he was dunned by the state of Kentucky. In a letter from the Kentucky treasurer, E. C. Berry, Anderson learned that he was delinquent on taxes for 1820 and 1821. Despite his sympathies, Berry had hard news to offer: "It is still time to make payment without any additional cost, save interest. . . . Your tax and interest for the years 1820 and 1821 on 159 sections of land will be $75. . . . I am always ready to serve a distinguished native Kentuckyian. Neither Missouri nor Kentucky paper is received into our treasury. Illinois paper is good for all debts due the state."[59]

Anderson was clearly in a bad situation. His law practice bored him, but his options were limited. He would have to secure "an appointment" (what his friend John Crittenden called a "fat office") through the government that would pay more than his paltry congressman's salary. He had already decided against running for reelection in 1820, but as he wrote in his diary, "A return to my profession is not my first view, I have an expectation of receiving some public employment, which will supersede the necessity of resuming the labours [of law] which I look to with apprehension. . . . My debts occupy my whole time and if I practise law, or obtain an appointment, it is with the object of liquidating them."[60]

Anderson's financial and familial woes with his father precluded his return to Congress in the fall of 1820, but he returned to the Kentucky House in 1821 and sat on the Public Lands Committee, tasked with the sale and settlement of public lands. While serving on the committee, he delivered a speech opposing the prohibition of slaves in Missouri on the charge that it would deprive Missouri of its sovereignty. This aligned him with Henry Clay. As well, he moved his family to Louisville to revive his law practice and rented out his farm at Myland to generate some badly needed income. It was a choice he saw as all but unavoidable: "I have purchased much faster than I have paid. I have partaken, as the preceding part of these notes will shew, largely of that spirit of speculation which was produced by the great and increasing prices of property, resulting from prodigious issues of paper money. I purchased when the circulating medium was .10 and must pay when it is 3!" A letter from his friend Edward Coles confirmed that lands in the Virginia Military District were virtually impossible to sell: "The land mania has been so completely arrested by the change of times from an excess of money to a comparative deficiency of it, and the consequent depression in the price of every thing, that it is exceedingly difficult, if not impracticable, to effect a sale in this country, at this time, of remote and unimproved lands at any thing like their value."[61]

As if his own financial distress was not enough, Anderson realized by 1821 that his father had not escaped damage wrought by his own speculations. In a letter to Isaac Gwathmey, Anderson Sr. noted he would have to sell lands he had surveyed to pay his taxes. This was only one of many problems leading Anderson Jr. to lament, "To that uneasiness which my <u>own</u> debts give me there is added my father's unpleasant situation. In a few days executions to the amount of several thousand dollars will be issued against him and he has no provision to satisfy them." There was a "valuable lesson" in this: "I never knew within my recollection that he suffered the slightest inconvenience for the want of money, until lately. Now he is distressed. At the age of 70 he has become distressed by the consequences of an attempt to <u>increase</u> his fortune."[62]

That, in a nutshell, was the problem of land. Once someone was addicted, the speculative urge never waned, and the consequences were devastating. In the capitalist vortex of America, enough was never enough. The addiction to land wealth could not be kicked. In a country lacking aristocracies and titles, cash was literally king and bespoke status. Conversely, the absence of cash spelled ruin. Anderson Sr.'s children were not about to let him go bankrupt, but the whole affair offered a stunning confirmation of the power of land to generate both euphoric highs and crushing lows. Nothing in the new republic was secure from panic, least of all land, which represented the one fungible asset that debt holders could seize.

In another letter to Isaac Gwathmey, a concerned Anderson summarized his father's business with the trustees of the bank that Anderson Sr. had borrowed from. On July 2, in less than an hour, $6,000 in expenses would come due. In a desperate effort to avoid the call, "I offered to Prather the whole instead of the parcel of land which my father bought for $10,000 the other day, but he would not touch it. It is not so easy now to give security on bonds and then on appeals, even if that be the best way." Another family member reading this correspondence in retrospect wrote in pencil at the top of the letter, "Hard times at Soldier's Retreat." Hard times indeed.[63]

IN APRIL 1821, THE prospects of a fat foreign-office appointment at last appeared to bear fruit. Anderson was apprised by his friends in Washington of rumors that President Monroe was considering him for a post in Brazil. But that country's independence would not be secured until 1823, making an immediate appointment impossible. With that information, Anderson knew that the law work must continue, though not indefinitely: "The Presdts [sic] intentions toward me are very favorable. I have, however, resumed my profession, not as my first object—but to give me employment for a time and may be for life."[64]

In the same diary entry, Anderson noted an earlier "incident" with President Monroe that confirmed "the weakness of men—even the best." Anderson referred to a letter he received from Monroe in 1820 marked "confidential" in which Monroe asked for his support for a bill before the House making an appropriation for American fortifications. Acting on news that the federal deficit was larger than expected, Congress recommended substantial cuts in the budget for the army and funds for fortifications. This Monroe perceived as a betrayal of the national trust in America's defenses. He immediately sought to influence as many congressmen as possible to support the fortifications and honor contracts already signed. To help his case, Monroe asked Anderson to immediately appeal to the secretary of war, John Calhoun: "I would be glad that you would press Calhoun on the subject today."[65]

An obviously concerned Anderson confided, "It was highly improper. He was the chief Executive officer and I was a member of Congress—but it manifested great weakness. The bill was comparatively unimportant yet so far were his feelings interested, that he risked his reputation and placed his fame on the prudence and honesty of a man, whom he considered as his friend, but of whose friendship he had never had the opportunity of receiving any remarkable proofs." Clearly Monroe expected favors in return for his friendship. Equally clearly, Anderson was prepared to dispense any favors that might further his ambition. He might have judged Monroe privately, but politics and self-interest dictated that he not do so publicly.

Anderson Jr. understood the game he was playing with Monroe and wrote an obsequious letter in April 1821 praising his inauguration speech: "Your speech at the inauguration has been the common theme of conversation and (I speak truly) of universal praise." Then he turned to the sine qua non, assuring his support for fortifications: "But that part of it which has been most spoken of is that relating to the defence of the coast of the States; and on this subject I do not believe that there is one man in this district nor one hundred in Kentucky who will not support you in the most ample manner to execute the system which you have commenced. . . . I think that you will soon see that it was peculiarly fortunate that you introduced the subject in a manner so emphatic in your speech."[66]

In September 1821, Anderson received the assurances from Monroe in a long, confidential letter that offered hopeful words both for himself and for his brother Robert, who hoped to attend West Point. For Richard Jr., Monroe promised, "I can assure you that it will afford me singular satisfaction, to have it in my power, which in this trust, to place you in some situation in which you may render valuable service to your country, in a manner agreeably and honorably to your self." As for Anderson Sr.'s invitation to visit Soldier's Retreat, Monroe regretted, "My time is not at my command. . . . I hope to see you in the approaching session, and it will give Mrs. Monroe and my daughters great pleasure to see Mrs. Anderson, to whom present their best regards."

For Robert, Monroe added welcome news: "I received some time since a letter from your father intimating his willingness that one of your brother's should enter the military academy which I communicated immediately to Mr. [John] Calhoun with a request that a warrant be sent him." Monroe then closed with praise for his friend and fellow soldier: "I will attend to this of which inform your father and his circles of friends near you, I have always felt the warmest regard. Most of them I have seen in difficult and perilous circumstances, I have shared with them the greatest hardships. I never think of them but with utmost appreciation. Remember me to them in the kindest manner." Despite the colonel's financial straits, he enjoyed the enduring friendship of a revolutionary comrade in arms who did not forget his friends.[67]

In terms of his financial life, Anderson was approaching a breaking point. On April 29, 1821, he wrote in his diary that Monroe had implied a fat federal post for him, but "if the expectations raised by the President's conversations and positive declarations are not realized, I shall be injured—seriously injured. I <u>cannot</u> devote my mind to my profession." Even properties that were unencumbered could not be sold. There were simply no buyers, and despite his owning the land, the taxes and upkeep put additional strains on a small fortune that was diminished by $40,000. With rising desperation Anderson concluded his entry, "My debts must be paid. My debts must be paid!"[68]

In July 1821, with no federal post secured, Anderson again ran for the Kentucky legislature and, with the support of his friends, won both in his election and his selection as the next Speaker of the House. But his financial woes continued, and on the home front, loneliness and sickness prevailed. Childhood mortality raged in his home and family. His sister Betsy and her husband, Isaac Gwathmey, lost their only child in July. October 6, 1821, he recorded in his diary, was "the day of the greatest unhappiness I ever felt." Having already seen three of his children die, Anderson was devastated to come to his father's house and find his daughter Elizabeth apparently at death's door, though she did eventually recover from her illness. For reasons he did not understand, her brush with death affected him more than the actual deaths of other children. In a letter from his wife, Betsy, on October 21, Anderson learned that his worst fears for his daughter were past, but his wife's spirits were low, dragged down by the burdens of single motherhood with no help in sight: "Mother is so unwell as to be entirely confined to her room, and Maria consequently to the management of the house. Elizabeth will not allow me to leave her a minute. I have not had my foot on the ground since Thursday, but I am very well as are the two boys [Louis and Arthur]. . . . I wish you would write something to raise my spirits for they are at a very low ebb. Take care of your health."[69]

But the dying had not stopped. On July 31, 1822, Richard and Betsy's young son Louis died of fever, leaving Richard to lament: "He was a most lovely child and I never think of him but with misery. He is buried at his grandfather's [at Soldier's Retreat] near his two sisters and a brother who have gone before him." Other relatives also lost young children, making it "the most afflicting season that ever came over this Country." The cause, he rightly suspected, was excessive rain: a "wet season produces great ill health." Still, he concluded, in terms of finance, "it is not believed that any material effect is produced on the improvement or business of the town. Surely sickness and death are forgotten sooner than any thing in the world." Anderson concluded that this forgetting was an act of Providence to help the living get on with their lives when the alternative was devastation. But still he betrayed a certain callousness to death that families facing high mortalities had to impose for the sake of survival. Others suffered similar fates. Of Clay's eleven children, only four survived him.[70]

Despite local tragedies, Anderson fell badly behind in his familial correspondence. An obviously agitated Betsy wrote her husband in session in Frankfort:

> My dear Richard, It would seem by your silence that you cared very little for us, yet I cannot think that you are so busy as not to be pleased to hear that elizabeth is quite well, and recovering her flesh very fast. . . . I hear that you are the greate beaux in Frankfort, for you must understand, old man, that although I have heard from you but once, I hear of you every day or two. Mr. [William] Wallace shewed me a pocket full of letters from you and not one for me and this will be four to your one. I will not tell you when I will write again.[71]

In January 1822, Anderson received a letter from the Senate chamber written by Virginia senator Jesse Burgess Thomas. In part, it read: "There will not be a minister sent to Rio Dijinara [sic for 'Rio de Janiero'], but missions will be sent to Colombia. . . . [I] would advise against your accepting either should it be tendered to you. Come to the Senate, as Crittenden of Cincinnati says you can without doubt if you wish it." Knowing how Colombia would end for Anderson, a later reader of this letter (perhaps his younger brother Charles) penciled at the top: "Excellent advice not taken!"[72]

Writing to Richard from Washington in February 1822, Henry Clay confided his sense of politics and his own optimistic calculations of his chances in the upcoming presidential election with a divided cabinet and multiple contenders: "My name has not been thrust upon the public, and my friends here have generally deported themselves with great prudence. Their confidence and my own is strong. And I think the signal will prove that all our expectations will be realized. On this subject I cannot enter into details, what I will as soon as I have the pleasure of seeing you."[73]

Clay's optimism would prove ungrounded. Clay had been badly burned by the Panic of 1819 and, like Anderson, had officially "retired" from politics in 1821. The retirement, of course, was temporary, but it was not so short as to prevent him from accepting a lucrative position with the Second Bank of the United States, serving as "standing counsel" in Kentucky and Ohio. Through this office he expected to recover his land losses and gain a powerful financial ally for his reentry into politics and bid for the presidency. Clay assumed his chief rival in the 1824 election would be John Quincy Adams, completely underestimating Andrew Jackson as a serious contender. In preparation, Clay was returned as Speaker of the House on December 1, 1823, from which he would launch his campaign for the presidency. For Richard, waiting for a diplomatic mission continued as his life was put on hold.[74]

6

An Ill-Fated Mission

1822–1824

Richard Jr.'s anxieties over land and money coincided with a central galvanizing moment in the overlapping histories of racial Manifest Destiny and the Monroe Doctrine in the early republic. Anderson would be deeply implicated in both.[1]

As American statesmen viewed the Latin American revolutions of 1808–1822, they saw both great potential and grave threat. The exploits of Latin American leaders such as Simón Bolívar in Venezuela, José de San Martín of Argentina, and Bernardo O'Higgins of Chile brought to mind the patriots of 1776 and confirmed the promise of democracy they held. The potential came in the form of a major expansion of the boundaries of American Manifest Destiny from within the continental US to the broader Latin American world. Closely intertwined with destiny was, of course, the issue of land. Most Americans believed that unending territorial expansion was America's God-given destiny. With expansion came land and, ultimately, empire, first in the Western Hemisphere and then, in the twentieth century, throughout the globe. In effect, Manifest Destiny would represent a corollary of the Monroe Doctrine because expansion was necessary to help enforce it. It is in this broader context that Anderson's part was a logical piece of the "land issue"—it was not just about buying land (although that was obviously crucial) but also about protecting it by keeping European powers out of the hemisphere.

The threat came from the meddling of Europeans in Latin America and the vexed questions of whether they would be permitted to meddle and whether the United States would extend formal recognition to the new governments of La Plata (Argentina), Chile, Peru, Colombia, and Mexico. President Monroe and Secretary of State John Quincy Adams proceeded cautiously with recognition, fearing that it might ignite a costly war with European colonizers. But others, notably Henry Clay, were enthusiastic about recognizing the nascent democracies and bringing them under the sphere of American influence. Not until the rebels expelled the Spanish armies from the New World in 1822 did Monroe move to extend formal recognition to the newly independent Latin American countries.

With some pressure from John Quincy Adams, Monroe came to the conclusion that the United States needed to send an ambassador to South America. Secretary of War John Calhoun was in no hurry, but when the Colombian government sent a chargé d'affaires to Washington, the way was clear for a reciprocal appointment. In late December 1822, Anderson got the long-awaited offer of a diplomatic post from President Monroe:

> It has been my intention when an appointment should be made to the republick of Colombia to nominate you as minister plenipotentiary. . . . The time is approaching and at hand, when it is thought that it will be proper to make such nominations. My object is to nominate you, provided it is your wish to accept the mission. . . . I had spoken of my intention in your favor, to several of our common friends, who I thought it probable had made your acquaintance. . . . If you are willing to act be so kind to inform me, because in that case, I shall proceed as I originally intended. . . . At what time would it suit you to sail?[2]

Immediately Anderson saw in this offer both a deliverance from his own financial affairs and an opportunity to shape American foreign policy.

ANDERSON WAS MORE THAN willing to begin a new life and quickly accepted the offer. In his diary he explained his motives. Not surprisingly, getting out of land debt was paramount: "In a pecuniary point of view it was very convenient [to accept]. This memo: shews that I am [in] debt and this mission shall pay these debts whatever may be the deprivations necessary to make it accomplish that end." Among the "deprivations" that could be anticipated was a mostly unhealthy climate—not only for himself but also for his family, three slaves, and a nephew, who would accompany him. Anderson knew his decision was not without risks, and family members urged him to reconsider. Many hoped he would run for governor of Kentucky instead. Anderson himself considered a run for the Senate. But neither position paid as well, and in the end economics prevailed and he determined to take his remaining family with him—"my wife, my daughter Elizabeth, my son Arthur and my daughter Nancy my only remaining children go with me." Left unmentioned were his three slaves. He then added ominously, "I am not without apprehension as to my health and that of the family—but I must go." Anderson well understood the dangers of disease from periods of contagion in Kentucky that took friends and family. But he had no real experience with the far more lethal fevers that proliferated in tropical climates. As for how long he would stay in Colombia, that "depends on the climate, our health, the expenses of living and many other things. If all these things are agreeable I shall certainly remain 3 or 4 years—perhaps longer."[3]

Fraught decisions to move to promising but dangerous destinations—be they along the Oregon Trail or in South America—were virtually always made by the men. There is no record of Betsy providing any input into Richard's decision to accept a diplomatic post in Colombia. It is clear that family members registered strong reservations, and no doubt Betsy did as well. But Richard's debt and heightened anxiety rendered any debate moot.[4]

Anderson also recognized that with death so constant a presence in his native Kentucky, he could be seeing many friends and family members for the last time, including especially his father: "The idea of never again seeing a father, from whom since the hour of my birth I never recd. any thing but kindness and affection is afflicting." Then, in a nod to the ultimate intended reader of his diary, he closed the entry, "I hope that my son [Arthur] may have virtue enough to look at me with the feelings with which I now look at my father!" With that, Anderson sealed his Kentucky papers and diary with instructions they be delivered to his son in the event that he did not return. He would continue his diary after departing for Colombia.[5]

The national election of 1824 would coincide with Anderson's estimated departure, and he took note of the leading candidates for president. In the same entry where he sealed his diary, he concluded that "without having any strong feeling on the subject I have avowed my sentiments for [Henry] Clay. . . . I think that in honesty and talents he is equal to his competitors and he is a Kentuckian." At the same time, he added, "My own opinion is, that his prospect is not very bright." Clay did not agree. In a letter to Anderson written from Columbus, Ohio, on January 5, 1823, Clay sounded a confident note, asserting that the members of the Ohio legislature clearly favored him. Of the fifty-seven who voted, fifty voted for him. Thirty-three members did not vote, but Clay added, "In fact, I am well assured that a majority of that thirty three, almost amounting to entire unanimity were in my favor. I hasten to give you the above in letter. It happened extremely well that the event took place prior to my arrival." While knowing that he could discount New England, solidly in John Quincy Adams's camp, Clay's optimism was further buoyed by the hope of winning support in the middle states. In the end, that would prove illusory.[6]

To prepare for departure to Colombia, Anderson sent ahead through Ohio two of his slaves, Spencer Hite, forty-two years old, and Denis Hite, a "dark mulatto" sixteen years old, along with horses and supplies. At least one female slave, Mary, a "light mulatto woman about 44 born in Kentucky," would travel with the family and attend to domestic chores. The presence of mulattos attests to the miscegenation that was rampant in slave societies. The slaves, Anderson noted, were "by the laws of Kentucky, slaves for life." This was important because it meant that residence in any free territories could not free them. His nephew Ferdinand Bullitt also accompanied him, serving as his personal secretary, thus including (and endangering) more family members. Information on the diplomatic front was advanced from "confidential agent" Charles Stewart Todd to Secretary of State Adams in the form of a memo confirming that Colombia very much wanted diplomatic relations with the United States. A meeting with the Colombian secretary of state "assured me that Colombia entertained the most friendly feelings towards the U. States, and was anxious to establish and maintain the most cordial relations. . . . In a few years it would be in the power of this Government to draw much closer the bonds of Union with the U. States."[7]

In early February 1823 Anderson received formal notification of his appointment as "minister plenipotentiary" to the Republic of Colombia from Secretary of State Adams, who promised a fuller briefing would be forthcoming. This was followed by a letter advising Anderson of his generous salary and living accommodations.[8]

In March, with presidential aspirations burning brightly, Henry Clay sought to make his name in South American politics. Having already pushed for a diplomatic presence in Colombia and recommended Anderson in particular, he gave Anderson a letter to be handed to the Mexican democrats, protesting the appointment of the Mexican emperor, Agustín de Iturbide. In introducing Anderson, Clay wrote that he "is among the most highly esteemed of our fellow citizens, has been the friend of South America, and a particular friend of your esteemed servant."

In May 1823, shortly before his departure, Anderson received an extensive briefing in the form of a personal letter from John Quincy Adams concerning the independence of Latin American nations, with particular reference to Colombia. The letter is preserved at the Huntington Library in California and contains a remarkably cogent rendering of foreign affairs that amounts to nothing less than a primer in diplomatic history. At the center of the letter is a thorough explication of American identity and Anderson's mission to the emerging democratic states in Latin America. From America's revolution emerged "the doctrine that voluntary agreement is the only legitimate source of authority among men." This revolutionary idea was, in Adams's opinion, irresistible. It would only be a matter of time before the Spanish colonies followed suit. America's—and Anderson's—mission was to prepare them for such independence.[9]

Because the United States was not at war with Spain, it had to consider "the struggles of the colonies for independence as a case of civil war, to which their national obligations prescribed to them to remain neutral." That said, America could never be "indifferent" to governments "involving the whole theory of Government on the emphatically

American foundation of the sovereignty of the people and the unalienable rights of man." This moral approbation entitled the United States to exert a "moral influence" on the course of events without acting in any way belligerent toward Spain.

When Spain failed to win early battles against rebels in Cartagena and New Granada, the United States was freed from the burden of neutrality and able to recognize the popular governments "both in a moral and political view." In recognizing the former Spanish colonies, the United States had "taken the lead of the whole civilized world." In so doing, it established an important difference between itself and the emperors and kings of Europe. European royalty, Adams wrote, "have assumed as the foundation of human society, the doctrine of unalienable <u>allegiance</u>. Our doctrine is founded upon the principle of unalienable *right*. The European allies, therefore, have viewed the cause of the South Americans as a rebellion against their lawful sovereign. We have considered it as the assertion of natural rights." These founding principles "will serve to mark the boundaries of the rights which we may justly claim in our future relations with them." Sooner or later the Europeans would have to follow America's example, "that is, to recognize without condition and without equivalent" the democratic states in Latin America.

Anderson's responsibility would be to iron out a reciprocal relationship between the two republics in ways beneficial to both. Adams closed his briefing with a reflection on European greed: "Our own recognition [of Colombia] undoubtedly opened all the ports of Europe to the Colombian flag, and your mission to Colombia . . . cannot fail to stimulate the cabinets of maritime Europe, if not by the liberal motives which influenced us, at least by selfish impulses, to a direct, simple, and unconditional recognition." Left unmentioned by Adams were America's "selfish impulses" in expropriating native lands and, in time, meddling in Latin American affairs. Anderson's challenge was severe. The stakes were huge: "It involves all that is precious in hope, and all this is desirable in existence, to the countless millions of our fellow creatures, which, in the progressive revolution of time, this hemisphere is destined to rear and to maintain."

The rewards would be commensurate with the stakes. Northern and Southern Hemispheres would unite in liberty "with the magnificence of

the means placed by Providence in our power" to introduce "principles of politics and of morals new and distasteful to the thrones and
dominations of the elder world, but co-extensive with the surface of the
globe, and lasting as the changes of time." Obviously Adams had no
inclination to witness the persistence of "thrones" in his hemisphere.
There, in a nutshell, lay the basis for American Manifest Destiny and
the accompanying Monroe Doctrine, which was, in fact, more the prod-
uct of Adams's vision than that of his president. With this glorious
vision of a democratic Latin America linked equally to America, Anderson would depart for a world he knew far too little about, which spoke
a language he was only beginning to understand.

AS ANDERSON PREPARED TO travel to a distant and unknown land, he had
much to be proud of. As colleague and confidante to senators, congressmen, presidents, and cabinet members he was at the center of America's
burgeoning national enterprise. He had a loyal and dedicated wife and
mother to his children, who was also adept at the business of pig raising, agriculture, and supervising slaves. His two younger half brothers,
Larz and Robert, were at Harvard and West Point, respectively. The
diplomatic posting could be seen not only as a prestigious appointment
in its own right but also as a stepping stone to further political offices,
including the Senate and, with his friends Crittenden and Clay in mind,
perhaps the presidency itself.

Steep debts determined Anderson's move to Colombia rather than
to the United States Senate. It was as risky a bet as the land speculation
that bedeviled him in the first place, and indeed in his mind was its
unavoidable culmination. Tropical diseases besieged countries like Colombia, especially in the Magdalena Valley, where he was headed with
his family. The combination of high temperatures and high humidity
rendered it a literal breeding ground for mosquito-borne diseases, including malaria, yellow fever, and bilious fever. The threat of disease
was doubly dangerous to Europeans and Americans because they had
no immunity to these lethal illnesses.

In making preparations for the journey, care had to be taken with
lands and slaves. While some slaves accompanied the Andersons to
Colombia, others were sold or loaned. In May 1823, prior to his June

departure, Anderson's brother-in-law and sometime business manager George Gwathmey wrote to update Anderson on his accounts and discuss a slave named Preston, whom he wanted attached to a more humane owner: "Keats wants Preston for which I object to, I shall I think hire him today to a man by the name of Fisher Livingston [known] for humanity honesty and I will agree that he shall have him." Keats would "instruct him in the gardening business which should be as Preston will work something next year, and much prefer the country for young negroes, particularly Sam is with Lucy Rupell at Oakland."[10]

On May 4, George Gwathmey wrote Anderson with some disturbing news regarding Hercules, another slave left behind. As soon as Anderson departed, Hercules ran away with some stolen pistols, with the intention of boarding a ship for South America. Clearly Hercules was running for freedom and deemed South America his best bet. He would have been part of the Maroons, fugitive slaves seeking an independent settlement. They appeared everywhere from Florida, Louisiana, and Mexico to the Caribbean islands, especially Jamaica and Haiti, to South American redoubts in French Guiana, Brazil, Colombia, and Ecuador. Some joined indigenous peoples, others carved out a living on their own. Perhaps Hercules first learned of South America from Anderson's preparations.[11]

In any case, Hercules never made it. Once he was apprehended, Gwathmey sent him to Anderson Sr. with the promise he would behave. But again he sought to escape, claiming to a ship's captain that he was from South America but betraying himself with his good English. Evidencing no sympathy or essential understanding, Gwathmey wrote that the slave Spencer "took great pains with him," but he proved incorrigible: "This is an extraordinary rascal of his age—this I regret on many accounts. . . . I forgot to mention that Gov Tompkins had hired him to work with Mr. Aulen in his factory but he would not go—indeed—under all the circumstances, selling seems to be the only alternative. . . . Please advise me what you think best to be done; before you leave the U. States if practicable."[12]

Money remained on Anderson's mind. On May 12 he received an update from his brother-in-law Allen Latham on his attempts to raise money for his father-in-law's debts. With cash spare and land not moving, selling some slaves appeared the best option: "Maria tells me he has

23 negroes big and little. It strikes me as being the most ready mode of raising money to part with some of them. . . . If you have leisure I wish you would write him on this subject."[13]

At the time of his departure, Anderson's brother Robert, seventeen years his junior, had recovered from an illness and hoped to join Richard on the voyage to Colombia. Upon learning that Larz also would travel to Colombia as Anderson's envoy to bring a treaty back to Washington, Robert wrote: "I am glad that Larz will go with you if his health permits, as the trip will be I hope advantageous to him both on account of the recovery of his health and the improvement he will derive from traveling." He closed with the hope of ending his two years of remaining active service in the army and returning to "the bosom of my family and friends, where none I can assure you will feel happier than I will."[14]

On May 20 Anderson was still in Washington, DC, awaiting final orders and was learning some "terrible" things about the voyage. John Quincy Adams warned him that the civil war had devastated the country. Beyond preparing for decimated plantations, many advised Anderson not to leave Caracas for Bogotá until December, "when the dry season sets in" and the danger of disease is reduced. In cavalier fashion, Anderson wrote to Ferdinand's father, Thomas Bullitt, that despite the advice "I shall judge for myself in every way when I get to the Country."[15]

Finally, on May 22, President Monroe and Secretary of State Adams wrote a formal letter of introduction for Anderson as designated plenipotentiary of the United States to bring with him to Colombia. President Monroe wrote: "I have invested him with full and all manner of power and authority, for and in the name of the United States to meet and confer with any person or persons duly authorized by the Government of Colombia . . . and to conclude and sign a treaty or treaties convention or conventions touching the premises, transmitting the same to the President of the United States for his final ratification by and with the advice and consent of the Senate of the United States."[16]

As his departure drew nearer, Anderson still had no word from Larz on his anticipated arrival in Colombia, prompting him to write their father, "I fear that I shall not see Larz. If I could have foreseen that I should have been detained so long, I could no doubt have given him ample time to reach me. But I have constantly expected to have been off in ten or fifteen days."[17]

The uncertainty of communications would only grow worse for letters to and from South America. Despite an expanding post office and networks of post roads paid for by the federal government, communications could be weeks in transit, forcing writers to speculate into the future regarding everything they wrote.

The most important news for Anderson reached him in late May in the form of a letter of authorization from Secretary of State Adams to the London financial firm Baring Brothers and Co. In it, Adams stipulated the financial information that drove Anderson to undertake his uncertain journey: "Richard Anderson is authorized to draw upon you for his salary, counting from the first day of July, to which period he has been paid here, at the rate of nine thousand dollars a year, and the contingent expenses of the Legation; and I have to request you to honor his drafts, accordingly, and to charge them to the Diplomatic account of the United States on your books."[18]

This was a substantial amount of money (about $205,000 in 2015 dollars), and multiplied by the three to four years Anderson anticipated being in Colombia, it would solve all his financial problems with plenty to spare.

On June 17, 1823, the Andersons' ship, the USS *John Adams*, weighed anchor at Norfolk and went to sea, bound for Venezuela's port of La Guaira. To prepare for his mission, Anderson studied Spanish every day, though he never achieved more than a modest ability to read and write it. He took meals with officers of the ship in the wardroom. By the second week the seas had become heavy and rolling, leaving Betsy very seasick and everyone uncomfortable. Some relief appeared when crewmen from the ship *Visitor* boarded the *John Adams* bearing pineapples, oranges, and limes.

On July 2, the ship arrived at the northern coast of Puerto Rico and docked at San Juan. Obviously relieved, Anderson recorded the harbor as deep and "said to be one of [the] healthiest places in the W. Indies." He found the country one where "everything . . . seemed to declare a state of intellectual night." Everything, that is, except the fortifications, which bespoke "terrible strength." Despite the fact that Puerto Rico remained Spanish and technically at war with Colombian "rebels," Anderson went ashore and was not molested. An officer of the Colombian army named Colonel Brooke Young was traveling with Anderson, but because he remained on board, he remained on American territory and so could not be arrested.[19]

On July 10, with Betsy still seasick, the ship arrived at La Guaira, a Venezuelan fishing town of about 4,500 residents. As this was the rainy season, Anderson pushed on overland to Caracas, the largest city in Venezuela, journeying along a winding mountain road on mules, with the children Elizabeth and Arthur seated in wicker baskets called "panniers." Immediately upon arrival, Anderson's party was feted by all the local dignitaries, including Madame Juana Bolívar, sister of the president. Apparently Anderson's meager attempts to learn Spanish met with a humiliating failure: "My ignorance of the language makes me feel an insignificance I never felt before." Besides the liability of political conversations, Anderson's ineptness with Spanish meant his social associations would be minimal, requiring as they did an interpreter.[20]

En route, Anderson received another update from George Gwathmey noting that he had to sell some of Anderson's certificates at a loss due to an unfavorable exchange rate with the banks in Kentucky. More positively, he informed Anderson that his houses and lots were all occupied by reliable tenants.

In a follow-up letter written in August, Gwathmey noted: "Your negroes remain as when I wrote last, except Sam for whom I have gotten a good home, if his services will be worth his keeping. Hercules is still with [Benjamin] Bridges although I get nothing for him, I am afraid to take him away until towards new year, least he might again set out for S. America." With land prices underwater, slaves remained the most valuable property to rent or settle debts. While the price of slaves varied with the state of the economy and with region, age, and skills, the average value of $400 per slave would yield a value of just under $10,000 per slave in today's dollars.[21]

On July 12, Anderson wrote his father from La Guaira describing the voyage and its stops and sicknesses. Plans to settle down were imminent: "Tomorrow we go to Caracas about 15 miles hence over a tremendous mountain along which a wheel has *never* passed. The only conveyance is on Mules or Jacks." He closed the letter registering his deep ignorance of place and manners: "I have not been here long enough to form any opinion on the political situation of the country."[22]

Most of the entertaining Anderson enjoyed came through private dinners, as public state dinners did not yet exist. In one celebration, they attended the christening of Venezuela general Carlos Sublettes's daughter on Sunday, July 20. To Anderson's surprise the christening was followed by a ball, "the first occasion on which I had ever seen joy manifested by dancing on Sunday." With the Second Great Awakening at full throttle in the United States, the Puritans' shadow loomed large in America and Sunday dancing was taboo.[23]

Anderson and his family set out from Caracas for Bogotá on October 19, 1823, with a caravan of eight horses and five baggage mules. They made the long journey without major incident and, according to his diary, "had the good fortune to preserve our health." On December 10 they arrived in Bogotá, and Anderson had his first appointment with the secretary of foreign relations, Pedro Gaul. Gaul desired a commercial treaty with the United States and perhaps all of the republican governments of the Americas.[24]

Like Anderson, Charles Todd had strong connections with John Crittenden and President Monroe, and in 1820 he had been appointed agent to Colombia for commerce and seamen. Also like Anderson, his salary was fixed at $9,000 a year. Unlike Anderson, however, Todd was designated a "confidential agent" and thus lacked the legal authority to negotiate treaties. And in Pedro Gaul, he encountered a man without scruples for whom the ends justified the means. In response to the capture of the American ship *Caravan* in 1824 by cruisers of Colombia, Gaul returned the ship but not the cargo, intended for Spain. Gaul justified his action by stating that US treaties did not cover the new republic and the law of nations did not apply because Colombia was at war with Spain. Todd replied that since the United States was neutral, it could trade with Spain, and "free ships make free goods." Todd complained repeatedly about the illiteracy of Colombian rebels and the "imbecility of Gaul."[25]

When Anderson arrived in December 1823, Todd had not communicated with Gaul in months. Earlier he had written Anderson complaining about the country generally and Gaul in particular. In Todd's view Gaul vilified America and "tilted" toward Britain. Todd recommended signing no treaty with Colombia. In a staunchly isolationist spirit he asserted, "We have every thing to lose and nothing to gain by a political connexion with any power." With the opening of Anderson's conversations with Gaul, Charles Todd "left this country embittered" by his personal enmity with Gaul, leaving Anderson to conclude that "Todd has as little common sense as any man whom I ever knew."[26]

By New Year's Anderson realized Colombia was as difficult—and dangerous—as Adams had intimated, but "the necessity of saving some money" compelled him to plan on remaining there for at least two years. Were it not for the money and the experience of his children learning to speak Castilian fluently, "I would not stay two months." A little later Anderson made an entry in his diary directed to his son. The subject was debt: "My son, Never permit yourself to be in debt." He then went on to confess his own "imprudence" that had led to his present insolvency. Without his diplomatic appointment "many more years would have passed before he would have been extricated—perhaps never." Instead of leading to "peace and tranquility," greed for land had led only to anxious uncertainty.[27]

Anderson followed with yet another enjoinder to his son urging "prudence": "But it may be of service to beseech you to be prudent. Do not go in debt. It will make you unhappy. If it did not—it destroys your independence. Every debtor is the slave of his creditor." Here, in a nutshell, was the dilemma of the Revolution: when independence was yoked to private land ownership, "slavery" was as likely the outcome as independence.[28]

Soon after arriving in Bogotá in December, Anderson received a disquieting letter his father had written in October 1823, not on the subject of money but on health: "This has been as sickly a season as has been known throughout the country. . . . Larz went to my brother Sam by way of Washington, Fredericksberg, and Richmond while at his uncle he was ill." The same week Anderson Sr. received a letter from his brother Sam informing him of Larz's illness and adding a more evangelical note than Anderson Sr. would write. In the course of quoting scripture to his brother, Sam wrote that Christ "will add to our happiness in the world of smiles, if we are prepared to meet our God, and this I think ought to be the most important part of our concerns particularly as we have both lost relatives." Larz himself soon wrote to Richard Jr. explaining that his illness had prevented him from joining up for the trip to Colombia. Instead he went on a horse journey of recuperation.

Eventually he hoped to join Anderson in Colombia. In the meantime, "I shall do what I can to dispose of some of my father's lands in Ohio. He seems rather unwilling to let me undertake his business or any part of it—otherwise I should have no hesitation in devoting myself entirely [to make money]. . . . I must do as much as I can for myself and as much as he will allow for him.[29]

The subject of Anderson Sr.'s finances did come up in another letter, from Isaac Gwathmey: "His debts I understand remain the same as when you left here with the exception of some money my brother George paid with which transaction you have been apprised. He is in good spirits, and if it could be so arranged as to keep the sheriff from him during his life I would not much care for the result afterwards."[30]

Soon after Anderson's arrival, a departing Charles Todd wrote to Anderson apprising him of the availability of his house and closing with praise for Betsy and the trip she endured: "Allow me to congratulate Mrs. Anderson on her intrepidity." Intrepid she certainly was, but it was an "intrepidity" necessitated by her husband's reckless striving. While Anderson met with Gaul in Bogotá he was separated from Betsy and the children, who remained in the village of Zipaquirá. In a letter to Betsy he explained that they could not yet reunite because he and his secretary Ferdinand Bullitt could not move into a house in Bogotá until they were formally received by the Colombian government. As for housing, he informed Betsy that her "fears are realized." Todd was offering them his house, which Anderson knew he had to sell before returning to the States. Todd, Anderson continued with obvious frustration, "speaks as if he was indifferent, advises me to look at other houses, says he will dispose of what furniture I do not wish. But I know that unless I take a part he cannot go home." The house was good but not great. "No doubt there are houses better, but this is good enough."[31]

While Anderson was waiting to settle his appointments and housing, he received instructions from the State Department in response to a resolution of the House of Representatives on the subject of the "effectual abolition of the slave trade." Colombia had not yet abolished slavery or the slave trade. Most Colombian slaves passed through the port at Cartagena, and slavery and the slave trade would not be abolished there until 1852 and 1851, respectively. Anderson was ordered to show the Colombian government "several acts of our Congress for the suppression of the slave trade . . . pointing their attention particularly to the 4th and 5th sections of the last, which subject to the law of piracy, every citizen of the United States guilty of active participation in the African slave trade."[32]

In a letter written in September 1823, which Anderson did not receive until 1824, Samuel Gwathmey wrote that finances in Kentucky were still shockingly harsh: "The pecuniary situation of this country is much the same as when you left us, every day develops new Bankruptsies in individuals who are considered in affluence until an execution aspires against their estate when to the astonishment of every body they are found to be completely insolvent." Gwathmey went on to note that even marriages were affected by the economy: "Tell Betsy that there have been many births, and not many deaths, and but few weddings since I wrote last. The times are so hard that the men are all afraid of extravagant wives, and the girls of broken husbands; however there are many marriages spoken of as soon as the times get better."[33]

THE NEW YEAR OPENED with a new president. John Quincy Adams defeated Andrew Jackson, even though Jackson received more popular votes. Soon, word of a "corrupt bargain" surged through Democratic circles. The election was thrown into the House. A late-night meeting between the Adams and Clay camps led to an agreement by which Clay would withdraw from the presidential race and throw his support to Adams in return for an appointment as secretary of state. From that station, Clay would be able to promote his Latin American agenda, including the establishment of a Congress of the Americas in Panama, where the United States would be represented by Anderson.[34]

While presidential contestants were screaming, George Gwathmey informed Anderson that only his letters were getting through—Ferdinand Bullitt's were not. He enclosed a letter for Ferdinand, "and poor fellow what a letter it will be to him, for it is true indeed my dear sir, that it will tell him he has no Father." Gwathmey went on to note again that while Anderson's father had plenty of land, there were no buyers. Gwathmey assured Anderson he would do all he could to avoid the patriarch's bankruptcy: "I will go so far as to sell valuable property in this state, even my own at ½ its value to discharge the debts. . . . If any indulgence can be had, the creditors may rely on having abundant security for the payment of their debts within a reasonable time." The problem was that the "security" creditors sought was not in land or paper but specie, which was in scarce supply.[35]

With mounting concern, Anderson realized that the loss of Ferdinand's father was not his only problem. On January 22, 1824, Anderson sent word to George Gwathmey that Ferdinand Bullitt "just begins to walk about after a very severe attack of fever." Tragically, that would not be the end of Bullitt's illness. On February 7 Anderson wrote in his diary, "We are uneasy about the situation of Ferdinand Bullitt. He was taken sick on the 6th Jan. And although he has been both walking and riding since, he is now in bed and I fear dangerously sick." Because of mail delays, Bullitt would never learn of the death of his father. On February 19 tragedy struck, as Anderson wrote to Ferdinand's father, Thomas Bullitt—who, unbeknownst to Anderson, was already dead—"I hope that you will have a mind prepared to receive the distressing intelligence, which I must give you; the most distressing which a father can receive. It is to tell you that your son is no more. He is gone where we all must go." Anderson went on to note that Bullitt's death followed a seven-week illness. "I will only say that Ferdinand was in every respect a most affectionate, kind and dutiful child. May God bless you. I am sincerely yours . . ."[36]

In reply, Isaac Gwathmey wrote that Ferdinand's mother was devastated, having lost her husband and son in two months. Fearing (correctly) that Ferdinand would not be the last to suffer the fever, he closed his letter to Anderson with the desperate plea that the family "wish you make as short a stay in that country as possible."[37]

Throughout this period, Anderson was in negotiations with Gaul regarding a treaty with the United States, and Gaul was using another treaty with Great Britain as leverage to entice the United States to likewise grant exclusive trading rights to Colombia. In particular Gaul implied "that the Gov: would grant to England any Exclusive privileges." Anderson found Gaul as devious and untrustworthy as Todd had declared. Nor was he surprised at British arrogance: "The English have so long felt their power and are so inflated with the notions it inspires, that they do not think that equal treatment is fair treatment."[38]

The Monroe Doctrine was, at least in part, a response to British imperialism. In President Monroe's seventh State of the Union message, delivered on December 2, 1823, he had clarified American foreign policy regarding Latin American countries, stating that further efforts by European nations to colonize land or interfere with states in North or South America would be viewed as an act of aggression, requiring US intervention. Monroe further stipulated that the United States would not seek to upset existing European colonies nor interfere with events and nations in Europe. Many of the newly independent Latin Americans applauded the Monroe Doctrine, but European reactions were harsh. One French editorial opined: "Mr. Monroe, who is not a sovereign, has assumed in his message the tone of a powerful monarch . . . armed with the right of suzerainty over the entire New World." While it was true that Monroe was not royalty, he did enjoy the executive privilege of recognizing nations. In Anderson's opinion, Monroe's response was "superior to that which a like document has ever excited before."[39]

By 1825, a disappointed and frustrated Anderson was planning to return home early. Nothing about Colombia had won his admiration or desire to remain. By his calculation, he would have achieved his mission: "I shall have about $10,000 in cash and my property—as my Estate." A short while later he wrote graphically on the anxiety of debt and its debilitating quality: "[Debt] prevents you from any of the enjoyments of family and of this life, it destroys y[our] independence, it ruins your temper. It so fills all your thoughts as to prevent you from excelling in anything or exerting to any useful purpose your faculties." There it was, in stark relief. Such was the angst of debt connected to land that even family paled in comparison. What use were the "enjoyments of family" if one was preoccupied with debt?[40]

For those Americans unfamiliar with the harsh reality, curiosity about Latin America grew greatly with the rise of the new South American republics. On March 31, Secretary of State John Quincy Adams wrote Anderson to ask him to correspond with the renowned Unitarian minister and Harvard professor Jared Sparks, editor of the *North American Review* and "Father of American History," to discuss contributing an article on the state of affairs in Colombia. This comported well with Anderson's own intention "of procuring and preserving facts with regard to the situation of this Country for the purpose of preparing and publishing 'notes on Columbia.'" Because of the time-consuming nature of back-and-forth correspondence, Sparks did not write to Anderson until July 1824 with an all-inclusive documentary request. For some time Sparks had been seeking to acquire "authentic materials" on the South American republics, but he found it extremely difficult: "Our newspapers are treacherous guides, and often relate things without good authority." Sparks hoped that Anderson "might be willing to procure such materials of this description, relating of Colombia, as come readily within your reach, and forward them to the United States. It is desirable for me to have every public document, or other work pertaining to the revolution, which had appeared since the contest commenced." Sparks closed noting that he would be happy to pay for them.[41]

For Anderson, remuneration made the request irresistible: "I thought of [writing something] again with as much a view to profit as any thing else." If land could not produce wealth, maybe South American history could. By October, he was writing a chapter on "the population and slavery of Colombia," a strategic topic relevant not only to South America but also to the United States.[42]

In a follow-up letter from Gwathmey, Anderson was undoubtedly relieved to learn that he had just received a check from London and that Gwathmey, John Logan, and Allen Latham had assumed some of his father's debt, "which is sufficient and a little more than the Trustee debt." So, in the same year, both father and son saw their debts relieved, though not without tremendous pressure for the entire family. In Richard Sr.'s case, his financial problems were postponed but not eliminated. Debt from speculation would pursue his estate past the grave.[43]

In the space of two days, Owen Gwathmey wrote two letters to his daughter Betsy and son-in-law Anderson. In the first he speculated that he would probably not live to see them again, but his hopes for the future were bright, and "so long as I live, my prayers will be that heaven may guide and conduct in your life in such a manner as to give you an assurance of meeting in Heaven where we shall never shed a tear again." The next day he received a letter from Anderson that put him and Anderson Sr. in better spirits: "I took the letter up to your old Father yesterday. The old man cheered up immediately saying Richard will come back. . . . Indeed you might be the old man's soul sparkle in his eyes."[44]

Gwathmey closed his letter by noting, "Your father as well as the rest here are surprised at your not receiving letters." The reference to unreceived mail is a recurrent theme and no doubt added to Anderson's malcontent in Colombia. Letters could take as many as seventy days to arrive after mailing. On April 27, 1824, Anderson Sr. wrote to inform his son that he had written "three or four" letters to Colombia. He went on to note that Larz was in Chillicothe and doing well: "I received a letter from Robert by the last mail, he is in good health." More than any other primary source, letters underscore the preoccupation of nineteenth-century Americans with the question of health. Illness remained an existential threat to peace and well-being and, like speculation, could undo a person or family with no advance notice. The high rates of mortality experienced in most American families give bitter testimony to the lack of medical practice. In matters of health, like matters of transportation and communication, there had been hardly any advances over the past millennium, though in the latter two domains that would soon change with the appearance of railroads and telegraphs in addition to steamboats.[45]

In his diary, Anderson noted he had to miss a dinner with Vice President Francisco de Paula Santander and British emissaries due to illness. In his place, the American-born merchant and arms trader William Robinson attended, and wrote that he gave the finest toast: "I gave a toast to 'the union of north and south America';—as the Republic of the U.S. was the first to recognize the independence of Colombia, may she be the first to support it with all her strength, and as she was likewise the first nation that unfurld the standard of liberty in the new world, may she be the last to abandon it." In a matter of months Robinson would die of fever in Caracas.[46]

Apparently restored to health himself and reunited with his family, on April 30 Richard took Betsy and the children for a walk to Venezuela liberator Simón Bolívar's Colombia villa, which impressed him greatly. Bolívar's home and the surrounding houses were beautiful and included an average of fifteen to twenty rooms in each. Later, on June 22, Anderson confided in his diary, "I do think that if Bolivar resigns his dictatorship, leaves the Country in tranquility and returns to Colombia and becomes a private citizen he will be one of the most renowned men in modern history. . . . Buonaparte and Washington being dead Bolivar will be the most renowned man living."[47]

Despite George Gwathmey's best efforts, Anderson Sr.'s financial health was not good. In an effort to satisfy his father's creditors, Anderson Jr. wrote on November 29, 1824, that "an Ex[ecution] has been levied on my property as security for my father." He added, "This [is] vexatious and mortifying and may produce injury to me." He hoped to avoid a loss but in any event had no regrets because "my father has been to me too affectionate, too indulgent, too devoted to all his children for me to hesitate to incur any responsibility wh[ich] w[oul]d not ruin my own family." It does not require much imagination to realize just how galling it was to the Anderson family to see their elderly father in financial distress.[48]

But Anderson had more on his mind than family finances. His interactions with Colombian legislators left him cynical about their competence. He was particularly distressed by the utterly unqualified Roman Catholic priests who constituted nearly half of the legislature. Reflecting an anti-Catholic bias common to most American Protestants of that time, he found little to admire. Writing of a meeting with several legislators and the vice president, he observed, "Their looks and the looks of the House (in a most dirty and wretched state) declared that they had been gambling and drinking all night. I am told that most of the officers of Govt. and others of distinction here, gamble at a most extravagant rate almost every night—and that [American merchant William D.] Robinson has been fleeced by them."[49]

Ironically, despite all his animadversions against his speculation, Anderson could not see the hypocrisy of judging Colombian legislators' gambling as somehow different from his own. A dinner party also elicited his criticism when the host "gave us evidence how ridiculous an Entertainer can make himself by railing at his servants, complaining of his fare and making apologies." Then, with some satisfaction, he added that in America, "it is rarely or never done by any one who is much used to entertaining genteel company."[50]

To add to his woes, Anderson found the weather disagreeable. In May, he wrote to Isaac Gwathmey, "The climate of this city I can only say, it is too cool for me. . . . It rains a part of almost every day. . . . The only true North Americans here leave the country in a few days and understandably go to the UStates." These various concerns, all part of the risky deal Anderson had made to relieve his speculation losses, would soon be overshadowed by the greatest loss of all.[51]

7

A Tragic End

1824–1826

With Ferdinand's death, the ever-resourceful Betsy temporarily assumed the duties of Anderson's secretary. Anderson certainly needed her, for in May 1824 he received authorization from Gaul to pursue a commercial treaty with Colombia. As before, he questioned Gaul's commitment to a treaty, as the United States, Great Britain, and Colombia all had their own interests in mind and sought exclusive agreements. He ruefully concluded that "protraction and not the formation of a treaty immed[iately] is desired by the Govt."[1]

By August 12, Anderson was ready to share with Gaul an extract from his instructions relating to a proposed "Confederation of American States," which Gaul dearly desired. In preparation for the confederation, Gaul invited the United States to a meeting in Panama. Anderson would be one of two American delegates. As August moved into September, there was still no treaty, leaving a frustrated Anderson to complain, "I think I shall conclude a treaty with him—but I am not confident."[2]

August 4 was Anderson's thirty-sixth birthday. His reflections read in the twenty-first century like those of someone twice his age. He contrasted the "joy" he felt on his eighteenth birthday with the "melancholy" he felt at thirty-six: "Whatever change the body may sustain must be for the worse. Many flattering illusions have gone—and if any still remain they are such only as are necessary to make life comfortable. The anticipation of great bliss and happiness in this life is gone."[3]

By June, half brother Larz (fifteen years younger than Richard) had finalized plans to join Richard in Bogotá as secretary of legation and hopefully return with a treaty. Larz blithely assumed he would "arrive at Bogota nearly as soon as this letter. . . . It will be unnecessary to communicate the news of the country at present." He would also bring letters from their father and brother Robert. Larz could not have been more wrong in his estimated date of arrival, and the journey would prove far longer and more difficult than in his (or Richard's) wildest imaginations. August 5 found him still lingering in Kingston, Jamaica, almost two months after his departure, and seeking a steamboat to Cartagena.[4]

Not until September 30 did Anderson receive a letter from Larz saying that he had finally made it to Cartagena. The letter was written on September 1 and described Larz's miserable stay in Jamaica enduring the "dreadful heat, and danger of either dying by sickness or murder and the boredom of having nothing at all to do and nobody to kill time with." His situation was so desperate that "I was strongly tempted to return in despair to the U. States—and between the motive to go out and the motive to go back scarce any thing but my father's earnest desire that I should join you, could have prevailed in disposing me to persist."[5]

Upon reading the letter, Anderson was dismissive: "All young travellers think that they have suffered more than ever was suffered before and [know] perfectly that every man after his adventures are over, is glad that they were perilous and strange. It increases his importance." Perhaps, but in Larz's case the misery would only continue. In a letter written on September 20, Larz complained of the "extraordinary delay" that was costing him dearly in time and money. Added to this, "almost every vessel from the U. States that comes here now is either chased or boarded and plundered by pirates on the passage." This left Larz "heartily sick of piracie" and desperately hoping the perpetrators would soon receive their "due punishment."[6]

While Larz languished in Cartagena, Anderson received a letter from Robert, who was in his fourth and final year at West Point. Robert waxed eloquent about the academy, believing it "superior, to any in the U. States and perhaps equal to any similar institution in Europe." This heady endorsement stood in some contrast with his opinion as a plebe when he complained that southerners were generally discriminated against. Robert went on to describe a furlough to Soldier's

Retreat in July: "Papa was not very well when I was there, as he had to get bled twice during my stay, he looked very badly when I went home but I think that he looked much better when I came away." The practice of bloodletting to balance "humors" was by then two thousand years old, though it is now understood to be harmful to patients in virtually all instances. Without knowing of his father's grave financial situation, Robert added, "I wish he would give the office [of surveyor general] up and ride about the farm."[7]

On another subject, Robert noted his father's excitement at the prospect of General Lafayette's return to the States, including a possible visit to Soldier's Retreat. He then closed, "My love to Larz and tell him that the Ky girls frequently speak of him," little realizing that Larz's problems would persist for an agonizingly long time.[8]

In fact, Lafayette did not visit Soldier's Retreat on his triumphant tour of the new republic. But he did connect with his former aide de camp. With Lafayette's visit to Louisville looming, Governor Joseph Desha named Colonel Anderson to be the official state host. Anderson would be the first person to greet Lafayette when he arrived by steamboat. As crowds roared their welcome in the rain, the sixty-nine-year-old French general limped across the wharf to be warmly greeted by his old compatriot. General Lafayette and Colonel Anderson rode into the city in a carriage to the ovation of ten thousand adoring Kentuckians. The visit lasted for two days and closed with a reception at the Masonic Lodge, which Anderson had founded. The attendees included Revolutionary War veterans whom Lafayette had led, and each was greeted by name.[9]

Anderson Sr.'s joy was matched by Anderson Jr.'s in Colombia on October 3. Anderson Jr.'s diary entry for that day proclaimed: "Sunday! . . . I have *this* day signed with Doctor Gaul Commissioner for Columbia a Treaty of Amity, Commerce and Navigation between the United States and the Republic of Colombia." He then went on to gloat: "It cannot fail to excite some *emotion in me*. It is the first Treaty between the UStates and any Republic. It is with a State now free, which for 300 years was an oppressed colony of Spain. That I shd. be the person who signed that treaty cannot fail to produce a strong emotion."[10]

The signing of the treaty immediately validated Monroe's and Adams's good judgment in appointing Anderson and affirmed Anderson's self-confidence as well. At the time, the emotional boost accompanying the treaty also led him to see Colombia in a new light. In a letter to his father written on October 8, he chose not to focus on "bad roads and bad accommodations" but on the future of Colombia's republic. "In the republic of Colombia everything is as tranquil as in the U States and more so than in Kentucky." Speaking as though he himself were the representative of a long-standing republic, Anderson conceded that, of course, Colombia was a "new republic" and "another generation will probably be necessary before they can come to the full enjoyment of all the blessings of a free Government," but now the foundation had been emphatically put in place. As Anderson's American generation enjoyed freedom and prosperity, so, he thought, would Colombia's. He did not reckon with Colombia's comparative lack of material abundance, without which freedom for all could not ultimately succeed.[11]

Anderson was so enlivened by his treaty that he even changed his mind on the weather, claiming, "I have seen nothing to make me believe that this is a sickly country." He assigned Ferdinand's death to an "unsound liver." This message was repeated in a letter to Thomas Bullitt when Anderson wrote, "We are all well. Everything induces me to believe that this place is as healthy as any on earth. There is but one plague—the fleas are abominable."[12]

This would prove to be a tragic miscalculation, but in the immediate aftermath of the treaty all was aglow. He informed his father that Larz was expected imminently and "we shall of course detain Larz with us as long as possible. However he cannot remain long, as I shall wish him to be in Washington in the month of January" in order to present the signed treaty to Congress.[13]

OCTOBER 19 ARRIVED AND there was still no Larz, but the bright time continued for Anderson. It marked the anniversary of the family's departure from Caracas to Bogotá and gave Anderson occasion to pause and reflect on the difficulty of the journey from a different perspective. He did not make the trip alone but with his family, and it was long and dangerous. They could travel only on mules or on foot, and the journey exceeded a thousand miles in length: "None of us could speak the language. . . . It was not known that we [were in danger] from robbers." But, after all, the journey was made, all arrived safely, and history was being made. A new revolution was being born and Anderson was at its center. Perhaps only because of his precipitous demise does this event—like Anderson's family—barely appear in the historical record.

News from home cited the nasty national commentary that had reached a crescendo as the presidential elections loomed, the primary candidates being Secretary of State Adams, House Speaker Clay, Senator Andrew Jackson, and Secretary of the Treasury William H. Crawford. William Robinson, who had earlier stood as Anderson's toastmaster, would soon die of fever, but not before conveying in a letter to Anderson his thoughts on their native land and its politics: "Here we are all politically mad, or commercially insane, and I am heartily sick of every thing that I hear and see around me. . . . Our newspapers are going on with a system of vituperation and defamation shameful in the highest degree, and much exhibit our character in a contemptible light among foreign nations."[14]

Whatever joy Anderson took from his treaty was of scant concern to Larz, who lurched from mishap to mishap in his efforts to reach his brother. On October 20, he was still in Cartagena, broke and beyond unhappy: "Were it not that we are just about starting I should absolutely be ashamed to write again from this place. I cannot tell the vexation I have suffered from these eternal disappointments that have beset me from the time I left home, which is five months since, to the present."[15]

A month later, Larz had made it to Mompox, Colombia, with the happy prospect of reaching his brother on November 20. On the third day of the journey to Bogotá, he "had to sleep on the bank at the best place we could see. . . . We had scarcely fallen asleep before a heavy shower came on which soon drenched us to our hearts content but this was not all for the wind was so violent that away went some of the cots into the mud and all the party scrambled into the boat with much expectation and I was left alone with a few boys . . . the whole night in the rain."[16]

On December 1, 1824, Anderson entered a reflection on his four-teenth wedding anniversary. The conflicting emotions he recorded expressed well the dilemmas of life in the early republic and abroad. These included both his family and his debts: "I have certainly had many happy days during that time, but I have had also much unhappiness; I have seen four children die. I have suffered uneasiness from debt, but it seems impious to consider that an unhappiness when others so much greater strike a father's heart from the death of his children. My children are in Heaven, but, Oh, it is the most terrible [thing for a father] to see his children die—and I believe that the suffering of a mother is greater."[17]

November had come and gone, and still no Larz. On December 12, Larz wrote his brother while still en route. There would be no November rendezvous. He had lost any and all affection for Colombia: "For as to comfort I believe that word never has applied to Colombian traveling. . . . But the most vexatious of all the vexations we have encountered has been the tardiness of the navigation." By this point Anderson realized Larz's situation was genuinely urgent. On December 6 he wrote in his diary: "The delay of Larz in getting here begins to give me some uneasiness about his returning to Washington with the treaty. There has been seldom a more vexatious and expensive trip than he has had." Anderson seemed more concerned with the delivery of his treaty than the well-being of his younger brother.[18]

Finally, on December 23, Anderson noted in his diary, "This day about 4 oCL [o'clock] Larz came. Of course we had much talk about people and things in Jefferson [County, Kentucky]." Larz had to leave five days later if the treaty was to arrive in Washington in time to present the treaty to Congress. Again, Anderson's chief concern was the treaty: "I shall of course be uneasy until I hear of his safe arrival in the US. As the time is so short that with a little bad luck . . . he might not reach Washington until Congress has re-cessed."[19]

On Christmas Eve, Robert wrote his brother from West Point that "the news of a treaty's having been signed by you has reached this country and is hailed with joy by all as they think (indeed know) that it will unite the two republics more closely together. The substance of the treaty is not yet known as the President has not yet recd the original of the treaty." Soon after, John J. Crittenden wrote to express praise for the treaty: "Mr. Monroe told me and others, and has frequently said, you have done your self great honor in your negotiations, and that you have even transcended his most sanguine predictions. In short, and in truth, it is very frequently said by the members of Congress, our Ky minister is the ablest now employed abroad by the government. This bye the bye is no great compliment."[20]

Whatever joy Anderson felt was quickly dashed when, on December 31, Betsy delivered a son five weeks prematurely, leaving her critically weakened and attended to by her doctor and Mary, her slave. On January 9, 1825, Betsy died. Just as Anderson had lost his mother to childbirth, so he now lost his wife. In a poignant entry Anderson made plain the depth of his loss and the heavy questions of evil it raised: "My Betsy, my beloved, my virtuous, my amiable wife left me for Heaven. . . . Her sufferings had been beyond any thing I ever saw. Her God has received her. What was her offence I do not know. I have thought a thousand times, what offence can she have committed to deserve such punishment from her maker. . . . Never was there a more loving, kind, wife, mother and woman. . . . Oh God have mercy on me and my children. . . . Whatever may happen I can never forget her." What he could not admit was the devastating fact that her "offense" was not hers at all but his own decision to move to a country with poor medical treatment. First Ferdinand, and now Betsy.[21]

With the loss of Betsy, domestic arrangements consumed Anderson's attentions. She had been the mainstay of the family enterprise, and with her death a multitude of duties now fell to him. First and foremost was determining where the three children might live and go to school in the States, without mother or father. Anderson evidenced no real quandary over whether to return to Kentucky with them or not. His finances required that he remain for at least one more year in his Colombian post. While contemplating the fate of his children, no family members came immediately to mind to look after them. Nor could any family members offer immediate assistance, as it would be two months before they would even learn of Betsy's death. By February, Anderson was narrowing his choices for the children even as his American relations remained ignorant of the need. He determined that Elizabeth was old enough to be sent to a boarding school. The two younger children would live with relatives. Arthur could reside with his grandparents, either Andersons or Gwathmeys. Ann (Nancy) could reside with her aunt Diana Bullitt. But all of this presupposed that the interested parties would accede to the arrangements.

As Anderson grieved, Larz was again languishing in Cartagena, but he hoped to be on his way back to the United States shortly. Even in Cartagena he remained ignorant of Betsy's fate, closing his letter, "I am sorry I have not been able to hear any accounts of my sister's health: do endeavour to let me know as soon as possible."[22]

George Gwathmey continued to monitor Anderson's Kentucky assets, and slaves continued to occupy much of his time. In February he wrote about the slaves: "Hercules time with Phillips will not expire until 17 May next, Prestons time with Fisher is up on 14 April next year. Each of the boys seem well pleased with their respective situation and I will add that I believe they have comfortable homes." But a new problem arose with the slave Obadiah: "I have had a great deal of trouble in collecting Obadiah from himself, about which I had no trouble for the first six months after you left us, he was at that time as remarkable for punctuality, as he was faithless and the cause of this is I fear chargeable to intemperance a vicious habit produced by a control of his own time."[23]

A month later, Gwathmey wrote another report, again in complete ignorance of Betsy's demise. He happily reported that in the matter of Anderson Sr.'s finances, there was hope: "I have however now the pleasure to inform you that I am under no apprehension of a serious difficulty for several months to come at least. You are released [from property attachments] in all the cases that I know of or that have come into court except the Buckner Case."[24]

On a more poignant note, George Gwathmey's next letter, written the same day (February 5), was addressed to Anderson but directed to his deceased sister Betsy: "My dear Elizabeth You will be much surprised on your return to us to meet with so many little cousins whom you never have seen. In answer to this letter I shall expect a long epistle, you must give me all the news; describe the country in which you live, the manners of the people, their dress."[25]

On February 22, 1825, Larz was able to write from Washington of his meeting with the president-elect, John Quincy Adams: "Yesterday morning I reached this place and immediately presented myself to Mr. Adams with treaties letter as desired. I arrived before the opening of the House and was obliged to seek Mr. Adams at his own house. He appeared very much pleased that they had arrived at last, it seems they have been long looked for." The following day, an exhausted Larz visited President Monroe: "He was very communicative and talked much of your conversation and declared his unqualified approbation. He said he was very glad that I brought them and that I had made such exertions to bring this during his administration. He seemed to flatter himself much upon his good fortune and in having witnessed this great revolution brought during his incumbency, to a happy issue. He appeared much flattered at my presentation of matters."[26]

Larz found Adams more circumspect but not opposed to Anderson's request for a leave of absence to look after home affairs. Still without knowledge of Betsy's death, Larz reported, "Today I ascertained from Mr. Adams himself that 'there would be no difficulty I suppose, provided Mr. Anderson's presence in Colombia be not necessary to arrange some matter not agreed to by the Senate which necessity I do not apprehend.'"[27]

Anderson dreaded the thought of returning home with the tragic news of Betsy's death: "Oh God, how different will be my return from what I expected two months ago." By March 26, he could write in his diary: "I expect in a short time to leave Bogota with the children. All are now engaged in fixing the baggage. My God, is it possible that my Betsy does not go with me." As it turned out, Richard would not have to break the terrible news. In early March word reached Kentucky about Betsy's death.[28]

In a letter of condolence written on March 6, Larz wrote, "I need say nothing of my feelings upon receiving or upon having to communicate the melancholy intelligence to our friends. The sympathy for your loss is universal and sincere. . . . I can scarcely withdraw my thoughts to any other topic." He closed with a note in regard to Anderson's slaves: "I must caution you if you go to Jamaica against taking your slaves with you to that island as they are adamant in their prohibition."[29]

At the same time, Anderson's brother-in-law Allen Latham took over Anderson Sr.'s surveying work. In a letter to Isaac Gwathmey, he celebrated younger son William Anderson's help for his father. He added this word of advice: "You ought one and all to prevent [Anderson Sr.] from writing if necessary by force—as his health and comfort depends so essentially on his habits [of not writing] in that respect." An analysis of Anderson Sr.'s handwriting confirms it had deteriorated badly. Once clearly written, his letters could no longer be easily deciphered. Latham's letter does not reference Betsy's demise. Given that Larz knew of her death by his March 6 letter to Richard, it is probable that Anderson Sr. had learned the news from Latham or Larz. Latham closed the letter to Gwathmey with some financial advice—on land, of course. Learning that a canal was in process, he wrote, "I have no doubt but it will increase the wealth of this country almost incalculably. Men who have lands any where near it had better wait till the work is considerably advanced before they sell." Another letter of condolence from George Gwathmey to Anderson Jr. summed up his attitude to Colombia: "It does certainly seem to me as a matter settled that I am to hear nothing good from S. America and my solicitude will not abate until I shall hear of your arrival in the UStates."[30]

In April, Richard Jr. was disappointed to report that as of the twelfth, there was still "no appearance of getting off." The children were fine, but Mary "the nurse" (and slave) was sick. As he waited, he had second thoughts about ever returning to Colombia, "but when I cool again and feel well and a little forget what now perplexes me, it is probable that my courage will again return."[31]

Finally, on April 16, Anderson arranged for passage to New York. That same day he learned the details of the election of John Quincy Adams, and despite family connections and friendships with Clay, he could not escape the feeling of a corrupt bargain being behind it: "I see their [Jacksonian] enemies are handling them severely. It is a strange thing. They dislike each other, I know. But it is certain that Clay's influence elected Adams. *I do suspect corruption in them*, not an express bargain, *but moral corruption*."[32]

On May 11, Anderson could finally report in his diary that the family was off the North Carolina coast, headed for New York. Still uncertain about returning to Colombia, he wrote, "Will not return unless prudence shall direct it." With Betsy's death and the "moral corruption" he suspected in Adams and Clay, he could not help but note, "How different are my feelings on approaching the shore of my Country from those I once expected to feel on reaching it." And, surprisingly, he added, "It is most likely I should have voted for Jackson agt. Adams." In addition to the corrupt bargain, Anderson disliked Adams for his aggressive opposition to slavery.[33]

But these were private grievances. Publicly, Anderson reported a follow-up meeting with the president in June 1825, when Adams persuaded Anderson to return to Colombia by expressing "his opinion of the importance of the Mission to Colombia at this time and of the necessity of my not being long absent." That evening he had dinner with the president and his family. In addition to the Colombia mission, Adams also mentioned the upcoming Panama Congress in 1826, at which Anderson would represent the interests of the United States. Adams's decision to send representation to Panama, at Clay's urging, had been in the works for a long time. Later that year, in his December 1825 message to Congress, Adams proposed a Panama Congress of Republics, including the United States, and met with the immediate and strident opposition of the Jacksonians. But Adams was not deterred. If completed, the Panama Congress would become, in effect, the first Pan-American Congress. He followed his address up by forwarding the names of Albert Gallatin and Richard Anderson Jr. to the Senate for confirmation as representatives to the Panama Congress. When Gallatin turned the nomination down, Adams replaced him with John Sergeant of Pennsylvania. Both were friends of Clay and accepted the nomination.[34]

The Senate approvals would take time. Congress was again up in arms—literally. In 1826, John Randolph of Roanoke called Clay a "blackleg" and a "corrupt bargain" on the floor of the Senate in obvious reference to the presidential election. Clay then foolishly challenged Randolph to a duel in a formal summons to a field of honor, noting, "Your unprovoked attack of my character, in the Senate of the U. States yesterday allows me no other alternative than that of demanding personal satisfaction." Randolph accepted the challenge. Both missed their shots (Randolph deliberately) and called off the duel and shook hands. Writing on May 10, John Macpherson, United States consul to Cartagena, noted, "[The duel] is to be most deeply lamented; it excited party spirit and bad feelings throughout the country."[35]

When Anderson read about the duel in Colombia on June 4, 1826, he agreed: "I consider it the most outrageous act of folly I ever knew a man to commit." It was precisely these fights and political hatreds that delayed a final decision on the mission to Panama. For that decision, Anderson believed, there had to be "a coalition between the friends of Crawford and Jackson." It worked, for on May 15, Anderson wrote in his diary that "the Senate had approved the Panama mission by a vote of 24 to 19." The House grudgingly followed in April. The approval marked a victory for Adams and Clay and yet another historic moment for Anderson.[36]

Clay drafted the instructions for Anderson and Sergeant, which in effect amounted to what Clay labeled a "good neighbor" initiative, committing the United States and the new Latin American republics to an alliance opposing any further European colonization. Clay instructed Anderson and Sergeant to reject any propositions founded on "the principle of a concession of perpetual commercial privileges to any foreign power." Finally, Clay instructed his ministers plenipotentiary to support a canal in Panama that would be constructed—and shared—by many countries, alongside support for religious toleration. In the end, Clay's remarkably enlightened vision would not come to pass, because neither American would make it to Panama. It would be more than a century before President Franklin Roosevelt would officially endorse the Good Neighbor Policy.[37]

BY JULY 1825, ANDERSON and his children and slaves were back in Louisville, staying for the time at Soldier's Retreat with Anderson Sr. The homecoming was far from pleasant: "Such a meeting can never happen to me again. That is impossible. It was the day to which I had once most fondly looked—but it was a day of wretchedness. . . . The name of my Betsy has never been mentioned by one of the family." If that was not enough, "I find nothing done in my fathers [land] business. My responsibilities still continue for him—and I see no way of clearing myself soon." Nor was he alone. "My friends generally are but little relieved from their pecuniary difficulties." In August, he took his seventy-five-year-old father to Virginia for a last visit with his relations and the place of his youth. While riding in the carriage with his father, Anderson noted, "I have observed a decay in his memory and judgement beyond what I before knew or supposed." On August 5, Anderson participated in a family reunion with all eleven of his father's surviving children.[38]

Given his new assignment, Anderson determined to leave Kentucky in August and depart for South America in October. As for the children, Elizabeth would attend a Catholic school near Bardstown, Kentucky, with Eloise Bullitt, daughter of Anderson's sister-in-law Diana

Bullitt. It was not easy on father or daughter, leading Anderson to despair: "I shall never forget the distress of my dear child at being left—
far from her father. May God bless and protect her." The two younger
children, Arthur and Nancy, stayed with his sister-in-law Diana Moore
Gwathmey. This was the last time Anderson saw his children.[39]

Older sister Elizabeth may have fared better than Anderson feared
in her new school, but she did not hesitate to paint a graphic picture of
her immediate woes. In a 1825 letter to her father, she updated him on
her new situation. The food was terrible, and that was just the start: "At
night it is impossible to sleep for the bugs and flees that race over us
like so many horses. We eat in the cellar which is as hot as a stove, and
the bead room has about twenty five beds in it and with dirt and heat
we almost melt. Tell Aunt Diana I miss her good clean bead and vitels
very much." The next letter from Elizabeth was even less enthusiastic:
"I received your very affectionate letter the other day and I do assure
you I will try to follow the good examples which has ever bin set me.
The sisters are all very kinde but they are not very nice. They pay no
attention to their dress nor that of the scholars either. The mother came
in church the other day barefooted. . . . You need not be afraid of my
following their example."[40]

The younger children adapted well, according to a report from
Larz: "I have been twice in town to see the children. . . . Arthur says
he intends coming out to stay with me and he'll be dogged if he goes
to town any how. The little fellow is much better contented than I
could have supposed possible being so young." But by the end of August, George Gwathmey had worse news on Elizabeth. He enclosed an
unhappy letter from Elizabeth and went on to talk about both of the
girls and a visit he planned to make: "I shall be better able to judge
when I get up what influence Louisa's discontent has on Elizabeth's
feelings. I have very little hope that Louisa will remain even a quarter.
Elizabeth may be so much opposed to a separation that I may be compelled to withdraw her also notwithstanding." Again the time delays
rendered letters a mishmash of miscommunications. Not knowing Elizabeth's situation, Anderson wrote her in September from Washington,
DC, to say, "I hope to hear that my daughter is well and is doing well;
that she is improving daily in every thing that is good and praisewor-
thy. . . . Be a good girl, learn well, and remember well what I have told

you of cleanness and neatness. I am my dear Elizabeth your affectionate father."[41]

In early September, Anderson was in Baltimore when he wrote to his sister-in-law Diana Moore: "My dear Cousin and Sister I am as well as a dyspeptic man can ever expect to be. . . . About my children I have but little to say. You know what I feel and what I wish. My thanks you have, and the thanks of the children, you will have—but you do not need them. God will be kind to those who are kind to the motherless."[42]

On September 16, President Adams wrote to Anderson granting him authority to conclude a navigation treaty with Colombia, with instructions to transmit it to the president "for the final ratification by and with the advice and consent of the Senate of the United States." While waiting for passage to Cartagena from Baltimore, Anderson traveled to Boston, where, in the land of Puritans, he recorded going to church on October 2: "This is the first sermon I have heard delivered since May 1823 at Baltimore." While in Boston he also met with major political figures. The list of luminaries he entered into his diary was impressive and reflected his high standing in the halls of power:

> Dined with Mr [Daniel] Webster on the last of Sept.; was at the house of Mr. [George] Ticknor. Saw [Josiah] Quincy, [Harrison Gray] Otis, [Israel] Thorndike, Eli W[hitney] Blake. . . . I went to Quincy to visit the Presidents, Father and Son [John Adams and John Quincy Adams]. The day was delightful and the ride fine. The old man [John Adams] will be 90 years of age the 30 of this month. His face looks full and his intellect strong—but his eyes, legs and hands have failed him. . . . Saw Judge [Joseph] Story—Waited on Timothy Pickering.[43]

Even a well-connected man of destiny, however, was not immune to the dangers inherent in his next appointment abroad.

Daughter Elizabeth, meanwhile, continued to be homesick and became afflicted with an enlarged spleen. The Gwathmeys decided to remove her from the boarding school and reunite her with her brother and sister. She would go to Mrs. Shane's school near the Gwathmeys'. In response, Anderson wrote a letter of encouragement coupled with forthright admonition to behave and study: "I expect that as soon as you are well, you will resume your studies and make such progress as I very well know you can. Even if you were not quite well enough to go to school, you might still read and write every day. It would be an amusement I think." He closed the letter with an admonition: "I observe several words in your letter spelled wrong. I do not at all blame you, my dear. I only mention it that you may tell your Uncle George to buy a small dictionary for you. You can soon learn to find the words. . . . Your father loves you most dearly and hopes and believes that you will be every thing which he could wish. Write to me very frequently. I shall set sail in a few days for Cartagena."[44]

Anderson's words and behavior reveal the conflicting loyalties inherent in public service—love for family but also dedication to duty. It is not surprising that he earned the respect of most who came in contact with him. That he was driven to face the dangers and separations in equal parts by loyalty to his nation and financial exigency (including the buying and selling of human beings) does not offset his major responsibilities and achievements in the nation's service.

On October 16, 1825, Anderson set sail for Colombia in the company of his brother Robert and slave Denis Hite. Robert had just graduated from West Point and was on furlough. Richard reached Cartagena on November 6 and wrote presciently, "If I am to go to Panama I wished I had my authority [instructions] here, it would save me a most troublesome and terrible journey to Bogota." On November 26, on board the steamship for Panama, he noted ominously, "There is much sickness all through this Country, the land is low, flat and now covered with water." As if that was not enough, on December 13 he wrote, "It is very hot. The musquitoes [are] intolerably bad." It was a perfect formula for disease. By December 26 the constant swarms of mosquitoes displayed their virulence when one Colonel Hamilton had a "most violent attack, whether typhus or yellow fever I know not." All of Hamilton's cups and saucers were thrown overboard, but by day's end two or three additional cases appeared on board and "produced much alarm." They disembarked from the boat with Anderson complaining, "I do not feel quite so well as I did a few days ago." Robert was faring little better, with "the head ache almost every day. It is a pain in the back part of his head."[45]

Though staying clear of land speculation in Colombia, Anderson was sorely tempted by another speculative investment in government paper at a steep discount. Ever the deal seeker, he wrote in late November, "A great deal of money has within the last two or three years been made here [in Colombia] with very little, and sometimes with, no trouble. It would be quite convenient to me to make ten or 20,000 dols. By a turn over. it wd. give certainly what I require, some employment to a mind that requires it." In February 1826 Anderson would still be tempted: "I have great inclination to buy some of the 'deuda domestica' of Colombia. . . . I think much money might be made."[46]

New Year's Day 1826 was spent again in rumination: "It seems to me that few men at my time of life can have run their race more completely than I have. I have no great hopes to be accomplished." Instead, he resolved to take satisfaction from his children. Of course, his determination to serve in Colombia apart from his children belied his reflections. And upon their arrival in Bogotá on January 28, 1826, he, Robert, and Denis were all quite ill, though not yet mortally so.

In late November 1825, Henry Clay had written to Anderson to inform him that President Adams had accepted the invitation from Colombia and other American republics to attend a congress in Panama. Anderson was to travel there from Bogotá with John Sergeant. Given the slow delivery of mail, Anderson probably received this letter in January, when he began the preparations for his ill-fated journey.

On December 7, 1825, Elizabeth wrote her father from Shelbyville, Kentucky. From both spelling and grammar, it was clear she had matured greatly in a year with her new teacher: "My dear Father I am now under the care of Mrs. Tevis in Shelbyville. I am very much pleased with my situation, and I have learned to play one tune on the piano. I am learning the English grammar, and I read, and write a great deal." She went on in the letter to note, not surprisingly, her unease in not hearing from her only and absent parent: "I have not heard from you since you left the United States. . . . I pray you dear Father to send me a letter as soon as possible."[47]

Reading this correspondence today, it is important to remember the delays between sending and receiving mail (assuming it even arrived at its destination). Writing from Bogotá on January 28, 1826, Anderson noted, "I have heard nothing from my children since 20. Sep." Since the children did indeed write in that interval, it meant that four months had passed since correspondence caught up with Anderson in Bogotá.

Anderson would repeat his complaint in May, noting, "It is now nearly five months since I have even heard that they were living."[48]

Meanwhile, for much of February in Bogotá, Richard, Robert, and Denis Hite were all sick with stomach disorders and fever. The worst off was Robert. In a letter to his stepmother, Richard first noted the lack of any mail from Kentucky since his arrival in Colombia. He then went on to tell her that Robert suffered from "ague," a malarial fever with sweating and shivering. On March 10, Richard recorded in his diary, "Robert is very sick. I am uneasy about him." The effects of the malaria would dog Robert throughout his storied military career.[49]

As the Panama mission prepared to depart, Anderson rationalized his reasons for undertaking the journey. He made no mention of climate and disease, even as his brother Robert lay ailing. The main reason, not surprisingly, was financial. All his expenses would be paid in Panama: "I wish to get to Panama 1st because I can save some money in it. . . . I do not like the expense of preparing myself [in Bogotá]."[50]

In March, Anderson finally received word from home, and with it news of another death, this time his brother-in-law John Logan. He wrote: "How uncertain is life! How dreadful has been the visitation of death upon our family in the last three years! I never knew a better man. He and my old father-in-law [Owen Gwathmey] I have frequently thought of as the purest of men. . . . I fear that his affairs are disordered." Anderson's fears would be confirmed when his recently widowed sister Ann wrote late that year describing the financial plight generated by her deceased husband's errant speculation: "I feare I shall have to make some sacrifice the immediate demands are so heavy. The estate by the calculation of Mr. Wolfolk and myself is about 6000 dollars in debt 3000. I expect to git with my hogs and horses if I can be indulged three years I think I can pay all if not the estate is gone. . . . Oh dear brother, if you were only here to give me advice my father is my security."[51]

On March 19, Anderson penned a long letter to Henry Clay on the subject of Latin America, Cuba, and Puerto Rico. Clay feared an attempt by the new republics—Mexico, the Central American Federation, Colombia, Peru, Chile, the United Provinces of the Rio de la Plata—to invade and annex the Spanish colonies of Cuba and Puerto Rico. Such a war "of conquest" (Clay's words) would upend the balance of power in the West Indies and quite possibly draw the United States into a war it would regret. Of particular concern was the prospect of Mexico and Colombia seizing the two nations in their ongoing war with Spain. Any such attempt would all but guarantee European intervention and threaten US interests. In his diary Anderson stated: "I think our Govt. has assumed great responsibility in urging this country to suspend its operation on Cuba under the hope that Spain can be induced to make [them a] people. I do not believe Spain will. . . . I think the US has incurred a very great and unnecessary responsibility of which they will hear hereafter."[52]

On June 12, Anderson set off for Cartagena on his way to Panama with Robert and Denis. On June 19, he reported very hot weather (103 degrees), but happily "no musquetos yet." On July 4, he triumphantly recorded in italics, "*This day my Country has existed one half Century.*" Three days later he wrote, "Passed a miserable night on account of the Musquetoes."[53]

On July 12, four leagues (13.8 miles) from Cartagena, Anderson complained of ill health: "I was taken with a fever and head ache." Other signs of yellow fever appeared with dire announcements. Half brother Robert observed that "the fever was brought in the last frigate which came from the U.S. There are four unfortunate citizens of the US who . . . have fallen victim to the disease, which of all others is most dread that is the yellow fever." The same day, the American consul in Cartagena, John M. Macpherson, wrote to Anderson "advising me to remain here, as that place was very sickly." Anderson did not heed the warnings, instead directing Denis to bring the baggage to Cartagena and get further intelligence. Hite returned, "bringing the information that Mr. Berrien the nephew of the Consul [Macpherson] was dead, that the town was dreadfully sickly and the advice of Doctor Byrne that no one come to it who could avoid it." If this was not enough, the British colonel Brooke Young wrote Anderson from Cartagena: "My dear Sir, I am sorry to inform you that this place is decidedly unhealthy—a fever is raging which has already carried off many, and every day adds to the sick list. I should therefore think it advisable for you to remain where you are until an opportunity offers for your embarking from this without delay." Written above Young's letter in pencil by one of the Anderson brothers are the words, "A warning! Neglected."[54]

Once again, Anderson chose to ignore the warnings. On July 11, he was "taken with a fever and head ache," but after taking calomel [mercury] pills he felt better "but not quite relieved." He decided to go forward: "In a state of much difficulty and indeed of some distress of mind I have detd. [determined] to take passage in the Vessel of Saturday for Chagres [Panama] if my health or some other cause does not forbid it." But even ill health did not sway him. On July 12 he entered the last words in his diary: "I am far from being well today. I fear the medicine has not relieved me."[55]

On July 24, Richard Clough Anderson Jr. died. In announcing his death to Henry Clay, Consul Macpherson wrote that on July 14 Anderson had arrived in Cartagena "suffering with fever and ague." He briefly improved, but then "the fever . . . returned but without the chills, and his disease assumed a character, that left little hopes of recovery. Every moment he became weaker until nature was completely exhausted."[56]

What drove Anderson to ignore so many warnings? He had already lost a nephew to fever and witnessed Robert's dreadful fevers. He gave no evidence of a death wish. What did appear, time and again, was his determination to pay his debts and acquire wealth, either in land or currency. Americans elites, Richard among them, may have been dedicated and courageous, but many were also pulled by avarice to gamble with their lives and the lives of their loved ones. Everyone knew how deadly yellow fever was and how easily caught in South American climates. In Anderson's case, the inescapable conclusion is that the allure of wealth blinded him to the threat of death.

Anderson was buried with full military honors in Cartagena. Macpherson concluded his announcement to Clay: "I am happy to say that young Mr. [Robert] Anderson and Captain Wharton continue well. The former has in charge his brothers papers and effects."[57]

By September, word of Anderson's demise reached the States. His sister Maria immediately went to be with her parents at Soldier's Retreat, and three days later her husband, Allen Latham, wrote to Maria perhaps reflecting his own thoughts on her brother's death. After providing his universal remedy for ills of "riding every day," he closed with a philosophical reflection: "Our object in life is happiness—we have travelled abroad in pursuit of it and found it not. We have ever found it at home and let us seek for in future a pleasant little valley in an elevated country with a gushing stream of water—plenty of fruit trees, a cottage with about 3 rooms, two horses, two cows, a few sheep—dog and gun a good library of books, one or two domestics attached to us otherwise. . . . Does this picture please you?"[58]

A week later, Latham extended his attempt at consolation with a warning against excessive risk—the sort that did Richard in. He remarked, "Ah methinks of what avail is all this life and all of its pomp and grandeur. One interchange of congenial souls is worth a world of noise parade and clatter. If I have you not present thought carries me back to the past and hope leads forward to the future. We have seen much happiness and to a degree been prosperous and on the contrary have suffered a great many misfortunes and lapses. It is a life of Hazard and the fewer risques we run the fewer losses will be felt."[59]

In a letter of condolence to Colonel Anderson, Allen Trimble, governor of Ohio, wrote, "I considered his early demise as a national calamity, and at this particular time perhaps more than any other that has or may happen his services were considered of the greatest importance to his country—but he is gone, and we must submit yet it must be a consolation to his aged parent and affectionate uncle of relatives, that the nation joins in their sorrows and participates in their grief."[60]

Soon thereafter, on October 16, Richard Clough Anderson Sr. died from complications from his war wound. In a matter of months, family patriarch and firstborn were cut down, and the Anderson family was left once again to mourn its losses.

8

The New Patriarch

1826–1834

R ichard Anderson Jr. never lived to replace his father as the family patriarch. Apart from Larz—who saw much of Richard in Washington, DC, and briefly in Colombia in 1825—and Robert, who was with Richard in Colombia in 1826, none of Richard's half brothers and sisters had much to do with him. By virtue of his time in Virginia, Frankfort, Washington, DC, and Colombia, he spent very little time at Soldier's Retreat. But his name lived on gloriously in the extended Anderson family, where he was remembered as "the sage." With patriarch and eldest son gone so precipitously, it was left to the younger brothers and sisters—children of Richard Sr. and his second wife, Sarah Marshall—to carry on the family business and establish themselves as first-generation elites of Kentucky and Ohio.

By 1826, most of the younger children had migrated to Anderson lands in the rapidly growing free state of Ohio. Politically, most Andersons were Whigs. Nationwide, however, memories of the Whigs' "corrupt bargain" between John Quincy Adams and Henry Clay festered and set the stage for Andrew Jackson's stunning victory in the 1828 presidential election. Though much would change in the age of Jackson, including the appropriation of yet more Indian lands, Jacksonian democracy did not transform the inhabitants of the vast interior lands of America into lawless frontiersmen, as claimed by earlier historians. Rather, these early US citizens replicated patterns of community—and institution-building—they had left behind. The rule of law did not stop in the eastern foothills of the Alleghenies; it generally restrained the more anarchic inclinations of a frontier society. The land grants evolved in time into the purchase of mortgages. Even speculators made positive contributions to the national enterprise by paying taxes and issuing mortgages for which cash-strapped settlers could apply to acquire private property.[1]

Andersons continued to be deeply involved in both farming and speculation as both the population and land values soared. Shortly after consoling Maria on the death of her brother Richard, her husband, Allen Latham, wrote to her at Soldier's Retreat, where she was helping her grieving parents. Latham was a New England transplant and perhaps the most talented lawyer-businessman of the family. The couple lived in Chillicothe, Ohio, and Latham wrote to Maria with information on his land dealings. They were substantial. He had just settled one land purchase, noting, "I have at length cleared my business with messers Sawyer and Greene which gives me about 17,000 acres of land for labour and vexation. It is the last I hope I shall have to do with them except to recover of him a few 100 acres he still owes me." He followed this by another purchase: "I have procured a tract of about 5000 acres of elegant hill land 14 miles south of this place well calibrated for a sheep range if you have any fancy to turn shepherdess."[2]

By the 1820s, land and its products had become commodities that could transform small, self-sufficient farms into participants in a more modern commercial capitalism, integrated tightly with national and international markets. As a center of commercial agriculture, Ohio exported grains, especially corn and wheat, and animal products, especially pork. Betsy Anderson's pigs were an example of this agricultural commerce. Although living individual lives on their own farms, the Andersons functioned as a "corporate family economy" united by webs of interdependency and mutual support.[3]

Large families like the Andersons predominated in both the North and South, but clear regional differences distinguished those in free states from those in the slaveholding South, playing out on a national scale. In the North, and among non-slaveholding southerners like the Mennonites, large families constituted the family labor supply. They provided the wherewithal, in an overwhelmingly agricultural society, to sustain the farm economy, provision the family, and create market profits for the patriarch. In time, their members would assume the same family leadership and replicate the large families, contributing to the explosive population growth in the United States. In the South, the landowners were not, strictly speaking, "farmers." Those tasks were delegated to the slaves, freeing landowners' sons for public service and daughters for domestic management. Some form of public service was expected of all southern planters. As well, many who did not have to engage directly in farming could pursue professional careers in the law, the military, medicine, or business and banking.[4]

Yet even as slave labor freed white owners to pursue other vocations and avocations, it also had the potential to erode a strong work ethic. In writing a memoir of growing up at Soldier's Retreat, younger son Charles would count what he perceived as the steep costs of slavery, not only to the slaves but also to the owners. From earliest childhood each Anderson son was assigned a slave as his personal servant, in Charles's case, a slave named Edom. Charles knew nothing of "menial" labor and could not be brought "to catch, bridle, and saddle our own horse; or to chop a stick of wood, or to bring in a handful of chips . . . or to grease or black our own shoes. Our whole Southern People have been and even are yet under the sway of this irrational half-barbaric influence."[5]

IN 1826, LARZ ANDERSON, age twenty-three, the second-born son of Anderson Sr. and the firstborn son of Anderson Sr. and Sarah Marshall, was the eldest surviving son. He and third son Robert, age twenty-one, had spent time with Anderson Jr. in Colombia, and they felt his death most acutely. The fourth son, William Marshall Anderson, age nineteen, was with the bereaved and indebted colonel at the time of his death, and later helped to run the office. Youngest brothers John Roy Anderson (age fifteen) and Charles (age thirteen) were living at the family homestead at Soldier's Retreat. Ann, the oldest daughter of Anderson Sr. and his first wife, Elizabeth, was thirty-six and married to John Logan, Kentucky representative from 1815 to 1818 and first superintendent of the Louisville and Nashville Railroad, until his death in 1826. The remaining two daughters of Elizabeth were Cecelia, age thirty-four and never married, and Elizabeth, age thirty, married to her cousin,

Isaac Gwathmey. Of the female children of Richard Sr. and Sarah, Maria (age twenty-eight) was married to Allen Latham. Mary Louisa, who would later marry the renowned author and judge James Hall, was seventeen and living with her brothers at Soldier's Retreat, along with youngest sibling Sarah, age four.

The sons and daughters of Richard Clough Anderson Sr. were a successful lot. All those who married chose successful spouses who expanded the family business from their bases in Kentucky and Ohio. By 1826, most of those home bases were in Ohio, in contrast to Andersons Sr. and Jr., who remained in Kentucky. It would appear that romantic love did not displace a larger interest in marrying well.

Larz assumed family leadership in 1826; William eventually worked in Larz's law firm, and Charles graduated from Miami University of Ohio in 1833 and married Elizabeth Brown. Charles would move to Dayton and attempt, with only limited success, to open a law practice there. According to family correspondence on the matter, his heart was not in it—nor, for that matter, in any other work. He favored travel and long hunts as an alternative.

Larz, however, suffered none of this ennui and was well prepared to assume his place as the new patriarch in family affairs. As a graduate of Harvard College and Harvard Law School, it would fall to him to settle the estates of father and son Anderson. Unlike Richard Jr. and William, Larz left no diary of his inner world and never served significant time in public office, with all the correspondence and documentation that entailed. But enough correspondence survives to paint a picture of his world.

One of Larz's more intriguing letters, received from a Harvard classmate and close friend, Edward Jackson Lowell, goes back to 1824, when he was en route to Colombia. Lowell was a scion of the mercantile giant Francis Cabot Lowell and part of a Brahmin elite that epitomized the New England establishment. Larz and Edward's class of '22 included an Adams, Ames, Endicott, Holmes, Lincoln, Tyng, and Wigglesworth, all prominent names in New England society. As a rule, "southerns" like Larz remained outside the inner circle, but Edward clearly took an interest in Larz that was reciprocated.

In the letter to Larz, written on August 22, 1824, Lowell apparently responded to word of Larz's woes in traveling to South America by inviting him to live with him: "The longer you are absent the more instead of less painful does separation become and often have I indulged my imagination in devising some scheme which would terminate it. . . . Are there no possible events which may induce you to take refuge from the rest of the world with me and become one of my family consisting at first at least of myself loved as—nothing else, and loving as nobody else?" Anticipating Larz's familial objection, Lowell continued: "But say you writing what's to become of all the young A's and L's if we are wedded to each other only? Oh the A and L must be of the same blood or *never* be. Then (grinnest thou) the world will lose the blood!! These ideas are in fact too delightful not to excite a smile too affecting not to draw a tear and both are always present to me when my reveries take that direction." He then closed on a hopeful note: "I should <u>feel</u> it the greatest boon that Heaven could bestow upon my prayers to have you with me at my home and your home, for my home shall always be yours when you will make it so. But I must tear myself away from this subject which only serves to display the poverty of words but I trust that sympathy of feeling will supply the place of language."[6]

No reply letter survives, but Larz did not travel to Cambridge to live with Lowell, choosing the Anderson family path of marriage, children, and the accumulation of wealth. Lowell died unmarried in 1830 at age thirty while on a book-purchasing mission to Europe. But it's clear that a very strong emotional bond existed between the two. Virtually every child born to the Anderson clan bore the name of a close relative, but Larz named his second son Edward Lowell Anderson after his Harvard classmate. And Larz would evidence a lifelong commitment to Harvard, echoed by the children produced by his two marriages. Over time, the Andersons would forge strong bonds of friendship with the Lowells.[7]

Larz would become by far the wealthiest of the Anderson children, and indeed was one of the wealthiest citizens in Ohio, both from his own work with law and banking and from the fortune inherited by his second wife, Catherine Longworth, daughter of Nicholas Longworth, who made his fortune in land and native wine. All Larz and Catherine's sons would marry Cincinnati heiresses, laying the foundation for a family fortune that would extend into the twentieth century. Many would go on to Harvard and found a dynasty of their own. Though not in the public limelight as a politician (like Anderson Jr. and Charles) or a famous general (like Robert), Larz served as the family patriarch until his death in 1878—a period of fifty-two years. But these prosperous outcomes lay still unknown in 1826.

That year proved a momentous year for Larz. In addition to having the responsibility for handling the estates of his older brother and, after October, his father, he had to look after his mother. That was also the year that he became engaged to Cynthia Ann Pope, known to the Andersons as "Ann," daughter of the wealthy farmer Miner Pope and relative of General John Pope of later Civil War fame. By her he would have one child, Richard Clough Anderson II, named for his deceased brother and father.

Soon after bearing Richard, Ann became seriously ill. In a letter to Maria, Ann's mother-in-law Sarah noted that she "looks very badly; I think as much as anyone I ever saw." In a letter to Allen Latham, Larz noted that Ann was sufficiently ill that he took her south "with an idea that travelling would benefit her health—but the weather was most unfavorable—the roads bad and the accommodations miserable—so that we came back after an absence of three weeks with no improvement in her condition." He closed referencing their child: "She has been obliged to wean Richard and deliver him over to a black nurse." Ann would not survive the year.[8]

Upon reconsideration, Larz thought better of managing his brother's estate, preferring that George Gwathmey administer it while Larz worked in the background. This did not mean he would not help, but for the sake of expediency, it would be better for him to work behind the scenes.

Wealth lay in Larz's future, but in 1826 financial ruin threatened. The Panic of 1819 had passed, but land prices remained depressed. Larz abruptly canceled his plans to visit Europe as he faced a looming financial crisis. In a letter to Allen Latham on June 18, 1826, before his brother's death, Larz got right to the point: "In the first place for business! As to that I must say that I am despondent and sick. I can't sell any of our land—don't know how to raise money enough to pay the next discount—am harassed by the keeping of the Buckner Executives and in addition by the resumption of many other debts which had been suspended and to end all my grievances feel very much as if I should be sick through the whole summer." Most galling to Anderson was the inability

to use the family's vast landholdings to cover the debt: "I have been trying to compromise with him but what have I to offer? He wants money
or negroes or good bonds out of the state—but land wont serve. Such is
the state of things at present." Larz closed on a plaintive note that would
sound almost comic were it not so serious: "I have been unwell for some
time am so now and expect to be very sick before long." Land, anxiety,
and slaves were threatening to undo a very frightened Larz.[9]

In July, again before news of Richard's death arrived, Larz wrote
another extended letter to Latham on family finances. He was inconsol-
able: "I received your last letter which offered me more consolation than
comfort. However you may philosophize about the matter, I cannot feel
easy or rest contented, while my father's affairs are in their present situation." In language that registers the desperate anxiety he was experienc-
ing, Larz complained that Anderson lands in Ohio found no buyers. At
best he thought he might get fifteen dollars per acre for a 120-acre plot.
But that was better than nothing: "I will sell and upon the worst terms,
just for this reason! To have at least a prospect of getting <u>something at
some time</u>. The truth is that I am just desperate enough to . . . sacrifice
any and everything that is put in my power; and whatever I can do in
that way <u>I shall do</u>." Apparently, in an earlier letter Latham had sought
to dispel Larz's fears, but to no avail. Larz was having none of it: "You
appear to rely for our security for sales upon the empowerments of our
land. You think they can't harass us—they can't sell the equitable interest! You are mistaken—they can—and will." This, he continued,
was no mere trifle: "Tis ten times worse than the grumblings of G. G.
[George Gwathmey] that you mention so often. . . . Even suppose that
on the next court (in October) I shall be able to quash the Exec and the
proceedings under it will that relieve us from the mortification and loss
of having the slaves taken from the plantation at this season and kept
until then?"[10]

Clearly Larz's pride was on the line as well as his family's finances.
Equally clear is a high-strung personality prone to heightened anxiety.
In a rare sign of fraternal tension he lashed out at Latham's attempts to
soothe his fears: "These things I write to justify my solicitude and to
let you know that I need no other consolation than what will arise from
a riddance of these annoyances! . . . I know he will not be contented
with any thing but specie. . . . So your horses and bonds and judgments

would but make him smile. Why, sir, it is a perfect Shylock!" The reference to usury registers the deep depression Larz was feeling. Not willing to leave it there, he closed with a p.s.:

> I do not wish you to be more uneasy than you have been. You have a
> more comfortable temperament than I have. At any rate it is enough
> for one of us to be miserable and I am content to be the one. If
> you can do anything, do it at your leisure. I know your avocations
> will not permit much time devoted towards that dullest of all works,
> the sale of lands and I cannot expect much assistance. But if any
> thing . . . If you can procure a few good horses cheap for they sell
> here. You may send some 6 or 8.[11]

This was the emotional context in which the Andersons would receive
the death of their brother and father.

News of Richard's death reached the Andersons in September. The
first Anderson to receive word was Allen Latham. On September 5 he
wrote to Maria to say that he saw an obituary for Anderson Jr. in the *Baltimore Patriot*. In an effort to be reassuring he conjectured that the notice
was probably an unfounded rumor. But, he soberly added, "if true there
ends our poor brothers grief in ours and his country's loss. I know of
no man of his age whose reputation stands higher or whose loss would
be more sensibly felt, but I cannot bring my mind to believe the fact as
stated. . . . I pity you all and feel deeply for you. But do not grieve: it may
not be so and if so remember it is but the end of our journey."[12]

On October 24, 1826, a grieving Richard Sr. wrote what was possibly his last letter, to William Beasley. It was, fittingly, on the subject of
land: "Dear Sir, Your letter of the 16th instant as also your other letter
enclosing the survey with a five dollar bill, the survey has been recorded
but cannot be taken on account of the death of R.C. Anderson. There
will be another survey appointed when congress meet."[13]

That same month, William Marshall Anderson's senior year at
Transylvania University was interrupted by word that his father was
dying. With Robert teaching at West Point and Larz studying at Harvard Law School, it was left to William to rush home. He proceeded
immediately, riding a relay of three horses and arriving in time to hold
his father in his arms as he died.

William never returned to college. Although only nineteen, he was appointed executor of his father's estate when, for tactical reasons, Larz decided not to be the administrator but instead, as with his brother's estate, work closely behind the scenes. His now-widowed mother, Sarah, wanted to move into her daughter Maria's home in Chillicothe, so William and Larz eventually put Soldier's Retreat up for sale in 1828.[14]

Sarah's children supported her but could not fill the void left by the loss of a husband and son. On her birthday on November 20, 1826, she wrote to Allen Latham: "This is my birthday and instead of rejoicing I feel melancholy indeed to think of the change since my last but we must submit to the will of the almighty. I think I miss my dear Husband more everyday being a good deal alone, on so few that I have more time to reflect on my situation. Robert gone William Samuel left here Tuesday lasts that parting one after another that I have been very much depressed." But in the midst of her grief she continued to pursue the issue of her finances: "I shall not sign any papers to any in person without your advice any information you can give me will be acceptable and I shall esteem it a favor. I fear I shall be all patience before I get home again, so far as regards my funds. Let no uneasiness arise for besides that I have been sufficiently economical and still have enough to defray all expences onward."[15]

By Christmas things were not any better at Soldier's Retreat. William Anderson wrote to Allen Latham describing the empty house: "You would not knowing the cause be astonished at the silence which pervades this house. No halooing or laughing nor kicking or stomping is now to be heard. All is sadness all silence! . . . Christmas is coming on, and all things are out of order."[16]

As Larz was settling the family estate, brother Robert received a family overture that he resign the army and succeed his father as surveyor general. But he was not interested. The army was his home. In a letter to Allen Latham he affirmed, "My right hand belongs to 'my country and my country's cause.'" This was the patriotism that would sustain him through three wars, several wounds, bouts of malaria, and the ordeal at Fort Sumter. Later, in a letter to sister Maria, he wrote that army preoccupations had prevented him from marriage and surveying. Of women, he wrote, "I have not yet met with any lady who will court me. . . . I cannot think of it as it would interfere too much with my duties." And as for surveying: "I had rather Mr. Latham should have it, than to get it myself. . . . With the New Year I have renewed my resolution to take every thing easy; to let the wheel of fortune present me with thanks or praises as it may please her majesty." If marriage was not yet in his present, land was. "The arrangements he [Larz] mentions of having petitioned for the disposal of lands owned by the estate in Ohio and Kentucky, meet with my decided approbation."[17]

In addition to looking after Richard Jr.'s three youngest surviving children, Larz also had the care of his mother to mind. For her, he wrote in a letter to brother-in-law Isaac Gwathmey: "I contemplate making a radical change in our concerns. For instance I think of getting a house in town for the family—renting the farm if possible—hiring out the negroes and selling off all the stock. This strikes me as the most advisable plan and mother would consent to it, but I should like to have advice on the matter." He closed, "The sooner you come the better. You know we must make some negotiations with the Bank respecting the mortgaged property sale so I think you will not fail to come."[18]

Larz's own affairs were not being sufficiently addressed. In a March letter to brother-in-law and adviser Allen Latham, written from Louisville, he complained that his work with the bank was being neglected but added, "I think that I am growing into some sort of consideration and hope by return attention to secure a living." But that did not ease his frustration. After noting that George Gwathmey had offered to "advance" funds to pay the Buckner debt, accrued through a contested land claim, but that would still have left Larz on the hook to repay the advance. He was not happy: "I suppose I alone can suffer for it at least I hope no one else will. I confess however I don't fancy being exposed to all responsibility." As for his mother and her property in slaves, he wrote, "I still think it advisable to bring mother here. I can hire the negroes for much more than hiring in town will come to and we won't have to pay for keeping them as we have hitherto done."[19]

By July, things were no better for Larz. Again Latham bore the brunt of his frustrations: "I am in lack of funds. If the Lord had pleased to put me in this world without friends—without funds and without fortune I could have thanked him for the dispensation—but it does at times seem too hard for me to be placed in a situation when I can scarcely make an exertion for myself—and when perchance I do by good luck make that exertion and get some little profit by it—that the pittance is to go for expenses which I had no hand in incurring." He then continued his tale of woe: "I must confess I really begin to despair of ever being worth a copper. I have no more chance of making any thing now or hereafter than if I belonged to the moon and I really do not see how I am to support the family when they come to town or if they stay in the country how to support them there. It is out of all reason—but no matter! I am just in a melancholy humour now and shall be as merry in two hours perhaps as if I had no care on earth." Even marriage had waning appeal, causing Larz to lament that while he could think of marriage, "I find I have got too many of the womankind already to take care of." Not quite through with his lament, Larz closed with a plea to Allen for some money: "If you can help me to a few of your acres turned into specie say some $20 or 100 or such like you will get me out of the dumps for the time being."[20]

Finally, in late July 1827, Larz was "in better humour with myself and with the world in general" and focused more on his mother than himself. In a letter to Latham he argued that Soldier's Retreat had to go. There was no child willing to relocate to the family homestead, leaving Larz to conclude, "It is . . . under present circumstances the only advisable plan to sell the place to the best bidders—that is let the bank foreclose the mortgage and appoint me to sell! Consider these things and let me know your opinion."[21]

By September 1827, Allen Latham could write Isaac Gwathmey that Congress had authorized him to close the colonel's estate, noting, "I think there are about 6,000 acres of land belonging to the estate in Ohio some of it of good quality. There are some debts due the state which are in suit. . . . I have regularly paid the taxes on the lands and as soon as I have a little leisure will make a full description of them if you wish it." Sarah Anderson, he continued, was entitled to "8 or 10,000 acres of valuable lands sold by the col. in this state [Kentucky]. I think it would be proper to give her an equivalent out of the remaining part of the estate after the debts are paid as by the arrangements with the bank she is cut out of a home. I shall insist as one of the representatives, that this be done." Sarah remained connected to the family economy even as her sons and sons-in-law saw to the disposition of her property.[22]

As the difficult year of 1827 drew to a close, Larz wrote to Allen Latham from Frankfort, striking a familiar Anderson theme: he was sick of politics, especially the "Jackson men," and was resolved to "quit politics." Larz gauged the political climate aright. In the 1828 election, Ohio voters would support Jackson over John Quincy Adams.[23]

Politics was only part of Larz's agitation. He feared that Arthur Lee Campbell, their father's successor as surveyor general, was "making an attack upon the Records in the office" and, in the process, threatening the Andersons' titles to lands in Kentucky and Ohio. In a letter to Allen Latham he wrote, "I need the appointment of an authorized person in relation to our lands. I hope you will attend to it."[24]

By 1828 Latham was assuming major responsibilities in handling the Anderson estates. In February 1828 the Ohio legislature acted to appoint "Allen Latham agent for the heirs of Richard C. Anderson deceased to execute and make deeds in due form of law to any person or persons, for lands sold by the said Anderson himself or by attorney, to any person holding title bonds to said land." Soon thereafter Latham gained power-of-attorney sign-offs from his siblings-in-law and was working closely with Larz, who was authorized to sign "any bill or bills in chancery which may be entered in the circuit court of Jefferson County Kentucky by Larz Anderson administrator of the estate of Richard C. Anderson deceased."[25]

By August, Sarah had sufficiently recovered from her depression to look after her affairs and wrote to her daughter Maria on the need to sell Soldier's Retreat and pay off debts. But she complained, "Larz has not had an offer for this place since it was advertised; he has sold lots in the city between 5 and 6000 dollars I believe. I feel willing [to] give up anything to have the debts paid. I know we must all wish it the case."[26]

With the house still up for sale, Larz solicited advice from Latham in November 1828 and conveyed his desire "to see, or at least hear from you upon the subject of our finances. You must know that I have considerable confidence in your financial abilities. As Mr. Clay said to Mr. Adams—Once upon a time I may say to you 'You sir play a deep game at every thing.'" Three months later, Larz continued to seek Latham's help with some "loose ends in land" left by his deceased father. Several clients were seeking deeds for land sold by Anderson Sr., and Larz needed Latham's help because he was "unfortunately unable to make the deed or what is worse to receive the money except through your hands I hereby refer him to you for the objects."[27]

William was having money troubles of his own as he studied law with Larz and monitored the sale of Soldier's Retreat. In a letter to Maria written from Soldier's Retreat, Sarah described William's need for financial support and her desire to help, noting, "I wish he could be contented, but if he cannot, I would do anything to make my children happy." But Sarah was in no position to help, given her own finances. Above all else she wanted to get out of debt, "for the very word sounds awful."[28]

In addition to the sale of Soldier's Retreat, Larz had concerns about his brother-in-law Isaac Gwathmey (married to Elizabeth). As one who put the family interests front and center, he had a proposition for Isaac: that they become law partners. "What say you to the prospect of coming to Louisville to practice law with me? I should like very much if it suited your notions of convenience and interest. You have prospects then which it would not be impolitic to improve."[29]

In the end, Isaac chose not to partner with Larz. A similar proposition was put forward to William Anderson by brother-in-law Allen Latham. In a letter to Latham written in April 1829, William referred to the offer and commented, "I had never thought of engaging in any other business than the practice of the law, a proposal then of an undertaking of a different kind could not but require close reflection." This too did not materialize. But in the same letter, William noted that Soldier's Retreat had at last been sold: "Larz had at length sold our old home, Soldier's Retreat is now the property of Saul Burke. He gave $17 per acre for 373 or thereabouts including all that part of the survey from Bullitts line to the Buckner tracts." This was applied to "as much of the bank debt as his purchase will pay, which reduces it to about seven hundred dollars." At the same time, Larz rented a house in town for their mother.[30]

When Soldier's Retreat sold in April 1829, Sarah was living in Louisville and had picked up her correspondence apprising the women of what was happening on the domestic front. In a letter written to Maria on September 13, she was happy to report that "William and Louisa has been to Soldier's Retreat, I have not been I intend going." In December she sent Latham a fur-trimmed coat, "the most fashionable," and conveyed additional family information. Larz had received an invitation to visit Robert at camp in Baton Rouge, and Anderson Jr.'s children seemed well: "Elizabeth looks well the last account we had of her, and Arthur looks very well." If they did not write as well as their men, the Anderson women still played a critical role in maintaining the ties of information and affection on which the families depended.[31]

Nineteenth-century letters were more than simply polite conventions. They were the sinews of family bonding—really a sort of "domestic currency." In addition to their networking, Anderson women remained steadfast in supporting their spouses even at the expense of their own happiness. In a letter to Allen and her sister Maria Latham, Mary Louisa Alexander, whose first husband, Frederick Alexander, would pass away prematurely, reflected on her loyalty to Alexander, despite her loneliness: "But if Mr. Alexander can do better here [Chillicothe] than any where else I will try and be contented as much as I detest it, I will never say anything to him to induce him to leave here for fear I might regret it. . . . I hope my description will not keep you away."[32]

ON THE NATIONAL SCENE, in 1829 most Americans embraced their new president. Andrew Jackson is most remembered for the Battle of New Orleans, his war on the Second Bank of the United States, a spoils system of rewards for loyal party members, and a white-hot temper that knew no bounds. But Native Americans remember him for the murderous appropriation of their lands to feed unquenchable white demands for ever more property. Jacksonian democracy promised, above all else, the continuing availability of land at the Indians' expense.

The 1823 Supreme Court case of *Johnson & Graham Lessee v. M'Intosh* laid out the Christian principle of discovery whereby "pagan" lands discovered by Christian conquerors became the property of the Christian discoverers. The case itself had nothing directly to do with Indians, but rather with two rival land claims colluding to defraud the United States out of land. In making its decision, the court assumed "that the United States as a society has an unquestionable right to lay down rules of its own making regarding the purchasing and holding of property."[33]

The implications for Indian removal policy are obvious. In writing the unanimous opinion of the court, Chief Justice John Marshall reached back to royal colonial charters to argue that when "Christian people" had "discovered" the North American continent, they had, by virtue of their chosen faith, "dominion" and "absolute title" over the "heathen" lands. In other words, American expropriation of Indian lands was not only a case of "might makes right" but also of "Christ makes right." For Chief Justice Marshall, what clinched the case was not the fact that the Americans were enlightened "Europeans" (as modern jurisprudence would render them) but the fact that they were *Christian*. In 1830, the United States government used this case to pass the Indian Removal Act, uprooting the eastern tribes (the Cherokee, Choctaw, Chickasaw, Creek, and Seminole nations).

At the start of the *Johnson* opinion, Marshall asserted that "discovery gave title to government by whose subjects, or by whose authority it [discovery] was made." He then continued: "On the discovery of this immense continent, the great nations of Europe were eager to appropriate to themselves so much of it as they could respectively acquire . . . and the character and religion of its inhabitants afforded an apology for considering them [the Indians] as a people over whom the superior genius of Europe might claim ascendancy."[34]

While improvement and discovery marked the formal rationales for Indian removal, an underlying inner accelerator fueled removal—racism and the concept of Anglo-Saxon supremacy. By the age of Jackson, American expansion was viewed less as a victory for the principles of free democratic republicanism than a confirmation of the innate superiority of the American Anglo-Saxon branch of the Caucasian race over inferior tribes and nations. The seeds of this white supremacy were clearly planted in the early years of the republic, as reflected in Justice Marshall's landmark opinion. War with Mexico in 1846–1848 did not originate doctrines of white supremacy but simply crystallized a mentality already in the ascendance.[35]

In prying the lands from the Natives, most white westerners assumed the races could not live together and behaved accordingly. *Johnson v. M'Intosh* became the new orthodoxy, boldly proclaiming (wrongly) that the Indians never owned the land in the European sense of the term. With new orthodoxy in place, Indian claims to the land were radically—and devastatingly—redefined from ownership to occupancy in the form of tenancy that could be revoked by the American owners. Many white "owners," moreover, had acquired land claims in the form of state-delivered "preemptions" before the Indians ever removed. In a mark of the US government's enduring blindness to the fact that British and colonial governments both had recognized the Indians' right to ownership of land they inhabited, *Johnson v. M'Intosh* proceeded as if all of the country's land had always been owned by the federal government. Astonishingly, Justice Marshall had knowingly misstated the truth, and *Johnson v. M'Intosh* remains the foundational principle of American property law to the present.[36]

When presented with the new orthodoxy, Indians reacted to the plunder of their land violently. Wars with Indians invariably followed a scripted pattern. Small groups of white settlers would occupy Indian lands, leading to confrontations and Indian violence. Indian violence would invariably be interpreted as an act of war, inviting the retaliation of the US Army. Every war with the Indians had its origins in the white settlers' greed for land, and every treaty following US victories involved the transfer of ownership of land, to the tune of millions of acres. In Jefferson's presidency alone, thirty-two treaties extinguished Indian titles to most of the land east of the Mississippi.[37]

Prior to Jackson, Indian tribes were considered as sovereign entities. Jackson recognized neither their nationhood nor their personhood. Rather, they were deemed lawless hunters who deserved to be driven from the land. With the passage of the Indian Removal Act in 1830, federal and state agencies under the umbrella of the Bureau of Indian Affairs, headed by Anderson in-law William Clark, enforced policies that relocated Indians to land west of the Mississippi. Under Jacksonian Indian policy, the southern tribes had to be driven to the far side of the Mississippi. The sixty thousand Cherokees occupying a twenty-five-million-acre territory in Georgia faced removal or death. The flimsy rationale for removal called upon the sanctimonious language of "higher laws" of nature displacing the uncivilized with the civilized "according to the intentions of the creator."[38]

Shawnee, Delaware, and Wyandot tribal nations in the North would be moved west from the Lake Erie region to what would become the states of Nebraska and Kansas. Creek, Choctaw, Chickasaw, and Seminole tribal nations would suffer the same fate as the Cherokee, relocating to Arkansas and Oklahoma. To compound the tragedy, even these new locations—particularly Oklahoma—were considered fair game for whites as other lands ran out.[39]

Before Jackson, the United States had honored (in theory anyway) the Indians' sovereignty by negotiating treaties rather than dissolving their sovereignty and ruling them directly. But the Indian Removal Act confirmed that the Indians were subjects of the United States. In dissolving the sovereignty of Indian nations, Jackson was ahead of his time. By the close of the nineteenth century Congress effectively ended the practice of negotiating treaties with Indian tribes and began governing and regulating the tribes directly. While some white voices condemned the activities of their government, their voices were never really heard in the mania for land.[40]

No one was more central to implementing Jackson's harsh Indian removal project than Superintendent of Indian Affairs William Clark. Though vocally concerned over the plight of Indian peoples, he never wavered in supporting an expansionist national agenda in which he expected that Indians would give up their lands through treaty, if possible, rather than war. He shared Thomas Jefferson's early view of "civilizing" the Indians. He employed military force to arrest white outlaws violently seizing Indian lands. He sought to prevent hostilities between warring tribes and removed unauthorized squatters from Indian country. His responsibilities kept him in the forefront of constant Indian relocations. He personally negotiated thirty-seven treaties, turning over millions of acres to US ownership.[41]

Like most Americans, including his Anderson in-laws, Clark considered Indian removal a humane measure to protect Indians from encroaching white settlers who simply would not give up their mania for land and would kill to satisfy it. This patently false dichotomy—relocation or extinction, as opposed to coexistence—effectively marked the abandonment of US claims to "Christian" humanity in the face of land greed and white racism.[42]

Meanwhile, by late 1830, Larz was beyond his immediate financial and emotional crisis but restless for more opportunities and money beyond his present business. In a letter to Allen Latham, he wrote, "I wish you to take a general view of all sorts of business to which a man of my genius may betake himself (for I am growing sick of my profession) and give me when we meet your wisest counsels thereupon." He wrote again a week later, lamenting, "I have done nothing in the way of speculation since you left here."[43]

While Larz and Allen Latham were settling the family estate, Robert was stationed in Baton Rouge, awaiting his next leave. He evidenced no sense that President Jackson's Indian policy threatened to explode into outright war in the Floridas. In the meantime, Robert wrote to Maria describing a visit from William: "William has come down with me, and will, I expect, remain until I am relieved, which I hope will be in the spring. He will perfect himself in French, and for ought that I know may take a French wife. . . . During Carnival he will observe them in all the fashionable dissipations of a modern southern belle. . . . In Carnival all the world visit this city of strangers, to see, to make money, to spend it, and to be seen." In fact, Robert would not be relieved in Baton Rouge but would remain in the army, with many battles still ahead.[44]

ROBERT WOULD SEE HIS first combat experience as commander of the Illinois volunteers in the short-lived Blackhawk War (1832). Jackson's Indian removal policy led Sac and Fox tribal chief Black Hawk to take 1,500 warriors and women to attempt to retake their ancestral lands in northern Illinois. They were also fleeing their Sioux enemies, who were allied with the United States government. Illinois governor John Reynolds chose to interpret their incursion into Illinois as an act of war, leading Black Hawk to attempt to surrender, only to be fired on by inept state militiamen. In the battle that ensued, Black Hawk's enraged forces routed the militia.

In April 1832, Black Hawk led his band of five hundred warriors and one thousand women and children to the east bank of the Mississippi. An alarmed Governor Reynolds complained bitterly to William Clark about his inaction and proceeded to raise a mounted militia of six thousand. One of the first to volunteer was twenty-three-year-old Captain Abraham Lincoln, who was then reenlisted in the regular army by army regular Lieutenant Robert Anderson. Under orders from Clark to administer a "severe chastisement" to the Indians as "a warning to others," the battle was joined. Clark had expressed compassion for the Indians, but when they resisted, he ordered a "war of extermination" against Black Hawk's tribe. President Jackson agreed and ordered General Winfield Scott to march one thousand regular troops in pursuit of the Indians. A starving Black Hawk fled across Wisconsin with US troops, including Anderson, close behind.[45]

Scott's and Reynolds's combined forces quickly attacked Black Hawk's band at the Battle of Bad Axe on August 2, 1832. They proceeded to massacre several hundred men, women, and children. Those who made it across the Iowa River were killed by Sioux enemies, leaving only 150 survivors, including Black Hawk, who was exhibited around the country. The government hoped his exhibit would humiliate Indians, but the effect was the opposite, as Black Hawk's dignity won over many Americans.[46]

Robert attempted to honor the West Point code of "discrimination" (the protection of innocents). He offered protection to children insofar as he was able. Warrior or not, he deflected all hints of celebration after victory. After the battle, he rescued an infant Indian from a dying mother's arms. The child was wounded as well, and Robert delivered the child to a dressing station. Three days later, he wrote in disgust to his brother Larz that he had observed scenes of "misery exceeding any I ever expected to see in our happy land. Dead bodies, males and females, strewed along the road, left unburied, exposed—poor, emaciated beings." War had come to Robert in an especially brutal way, and he would never forget it.[47]

In a now-familiar pattern, the devastated Sauks were forced to cede six million acres of land in present-day Iowa. According to the terms of the treaty, the Indians were forbidden to ever enter their ancestral lands, and they saw their sacred graves desecrated. Thomas Forsyth, a former agent of Clark's, blamed the superintendent for an unnecessary war, labeling Clark "a perfect ignoramus." But he missed the point of six million acres added to the public trust. To Clark and his president, Jackson, that justified whatever means necessary.[48]

For Lieutenant Robert Anderson, Indian removal became intensely personal. Change was in the air, as troubles with Indians in the Floridas would require action. In a letter to brother Charles dated November 1832, he wrote: "I must go and remain South until the Indians are removed beyond the Mississippi. Then, after a few months garrison duty, I may be permitted to visit my brothers' homes."[49]

WHILE ROBERT WAS IMMERSED in the horrors of Indian removal in Illinois and Wisconsin, Larz blithely traveled to Washington to meet up with friends from Harvard. In a letter to William in April 1832 he described other meetings of worthies: "I have paid visits to the President [Jackson]. . . . The old Gent looks thin but well—was again busy and very polite. . . . Today I am sick or I should have gone with [Henry] Clay to a fish feast some 12 or 15 miles from the City."[50]

In the same letter Larz complained about the nullification crisis between President Jackson and South Carolina, which threatened to secede from the Union in responses to the unpopular federal tariffs of 1828 and 1832: "Politicks—confound politicks. I am sick to death of it since I got here—Tariffs and anti-Nullification have nearly bothered me to death. I have almost sworn-never-never-never-never to have any thing to do in Politicks for the balance of my days!" In contrast to these sentiments, throughout Ohio's antebellum period political participation remained at record highs, with Democrats and Whigs evenly divided. Along with high rates of participation, this highly competitive partisan rivalry led to political instability, as political officeholders came and went with each new election. These political turnovers, in turn, reflected the demographic turnovers incurred with constant migration and ever-increasing numbers of new arrivals, which constantly altered the political balance in the process.[51]

For Larz, law apparently had little appeal. He was still working on estate issues, reflecting the tortured process of landownership and title in the Virginia Military District. In a letter to Isaac Gwathmey, he wrote: "Dear Sir If you can come down [to Cincinnati] this week while Robert [Anderson] is here I should be very glad. I wish to address the business of the estate and at all events to get clear of the town property."[52]

By 1832, Larz was the director of the Citizens National Bank and living in Cincinnati. Two years later, now a successful lawyer-banker and a widower, the twenty-nine-year-old Larz married Catherine Longworth, age nineteen, who was set to receive the largest inheritance in Ohio from her father, Nicholas Longworth. Larz and Catherine would produce children who included the highly decorated Civil War Union veteran Brevet Brigadier General Nicholas Anderson and Edward Lowell Anderson, who served as a captain in the Civil War, was wounded at Jonesboro, and later joined General William T. Sherman's staff. Other sons included Dr. Frederick Anderson, Edward's twin, who also served in the army, and Dr. Joseph Anderson. Another son, Larz Anderson II, for reasons attributed in the obituaries to "melancholy," "cut his throat" at age fifty-seven in 1902 while at his brother Joseph's house. Charles, Larz's seventh son, would marry Jennie Herron, sister of President William Howard Taft. Other sons included David Carneal Anderson and George K. S. Anderson. Larz and Catherine's two daughters both died young.

In contrast, William's situation was not happy. His family had been supporting him and he wanted to be independent. In a letter to Allen Latham in Chillicothe on April 4, 1829, he wrote of his desire to move to Louisiana, but Larz opposed the move, so that William "did not really know what to do." Apparently Latham offered him work and William accepted, noting in a letter to Allen Latham, "I felt inclined to accept it for the purpose of avoiding that despicable thing of acting the gentleman, and feeding and clothing myself, from the proceeds of my father's labour." He was also bothered by the fact that he was single, complaining in the same letter that his lack of a wife-to-be did not signal "that I am callous and unsusceptible to female charms. No! for it is not the case. But as the predestinarians say, 'my time is not yet come.'" Little did William know that weeks after writing he would make the acquaintance of a thirteen-year-old brunette named Eliza McArthur, nicknamed the "Highland Beauty," who five years later would become his wife.[53]

While settling their father's estate, William studied law with his brother Larz in Louisville, and he received his license to practice law in Kentucky in 1832, when he was also awarded the title of colonel as aide-de-camp to Governor Edward Breathitt, who commanded the state militia. Very little survives from correspondence of these years, save a letter from William to Isaac Gwathmey in December 1832 to bring sorry, if familiar, news from sister Mary Louisa about a death: this time of her husband, Frederick Alexander. He was, William wrote, "a very very estimable man. . . . His dissolution has caused Louisa more painful grief than I could have imagined, far more than I ever can describe. . . . Poor fellow. . . . Death is a cruel butcher!"[54]

Another brother, John Roy Anderson, barely appears in the Anderson correspondence. But one letter to Allen Latham survives, written on

November 29, 1832. The subject was land and finances: "I have for a long time wished to talk to you about what little property I have in this state and as I am a little in debt here I would be willing to dispose of it to you on any reasonable terms if you could advance money enough to settle my case I will satisfy you by making over to you such property as I may in this state which shall secure you from any loss." John Roy's Ohio land came as an inheritance from his father, and he later sold it to Latham.[55]

Although only nineteen years old in 1832, brother Charles was determined to follow through on his original plan of becoming a farmer. After exploring several counties in Kentucky, he visited his older brother Robert near St. Louis and formed a partnership with him on Gravois Creek, near Jefferson Barracks. While there Robert made the acquaintance of Jefferson Davis, whom he first admired and later would denounce as a rank disunionist.

The partnership would not survive financial difficulties. The same financial panic that devastated so much of the frontier soon extended to Charles and Robert. With banks no longer solvent the brothers could not meet the land payments and were forced to abandon their pastoral dream of privacy on their own property. Instead, Robert remained in the military to become the hero of Sumter, and Charles returned to the study of law in Louisville, in the office of Pirtle and Anderson, from 1833 to 1835.

By September 1834, Robert was at Fort Constitution in New Hampshire and wrote to his mother. In New Hampshire, he noted, the new soldiers trained on Saturdays rather than Sundays, leading him to reflect on the more religiously observant North: "The easterners are, you know, strict church goers, whether they are much better than our sturdy sons of the west, who can not attend church oftener than once a month in consequence of the inconvenience of having to go so far from home, is not for mortals to decide." Robert then went on to talk about meeting Larz's Harvard friends in Boston, noting, "It makes me proud of my white head brother, to have to answer so many friendly questions as are propounded by his yankee friends. They are very fond of him and would be pleased to have a visit from him." As for John Roy: "I wish John was in business. He is disposed to do something good, I fear will relax his exertions, unless he can meet with success. I wish I had a fortune at my disposal, I think I could use it to good advantage."[56]

In early 1834, William visited Robert in Baton Rouge and contracted yellow fever, which left him severely weakened. In an effort to regain his health, William determined on a trip through the Rocky Mountains. Robert was certain that this would be beneficial to him. In a letter to his mother, Sarah, he commented, "The trip to the Rocky Mountains, although arduous and not without dangers, is, I am confident, the best thing, which could have been recommended for the restoration of William's health." As for land, he confessed: "I do not know what to do with the Ohio land; for the present it may be as well to have it in the hands of my agent, as he may have decided on making some disposition of it. If any interests of the family will be bettered by selling it, I have no objection in the world at having it disposed of. I presume, however, that my share of the lands in Ohio is at present worth but little."[57]

As the nascent nation tested its politics and pushed out its boundaries, so too did the Anderson clan—grandchildren of a colonial colonel, children of the new republic. Anxieties prevailed on all sides, whether attached to the uncertainty of survival, the heavy risks of speculation, or the dreadful costs of securing a continent. Like so many others, the Andersons looked ahead with only tentative hope.

9

Rocky Mountain Highs
and Real Estate Lows

1835–1838

Williamm Marshall Anderson, born in 1807 and named for his mother's cousin, Chief Justice John Marshall, was homeschooled at Soldier's Retreat until age fourteen. While there he studied with a tutor "of education and correct habits," who taught him the basics of literacy and math. In 1822, at age fifteen, he undertook his first over-land journey through the Ohio frontier to board with his sister Maria and her husband, Allen Latham, in Chillicothe. At that time Ohio was a boisterous outlier democracy flexing its muscles over Indians and eastern elites. The territory had come through a speculative frenzy in the 1810s and a major panic in 1819. Nevertheless, it grew at a phenomenal rate, becoming the fourth-largest state in the Union by 1825. One marker of its rise was a renewed emphasis on voluntary organizations to promote morality, led by local politician-entrepreneurs such as Duncan McArthur in Chillicothe. Increasingly, Whigs like McArthur saw the need for greater government controls, and for internal improvements at government expense. By the eve of the Civil War in 1860, less than 30 percent of heads of households in Ohio had been born in the state. Lying behind this massive demographic shift was the inexorable pursuit of property.[1]

While schooling at the Chillicothe Academy, William concentrated on the classics and the Bible. Later in life, after converting to

Catholicism, he recalled: "All my sources of knowledge & morality were Protestant. I drew Episcopalianism from my mother's breast. A Lutheran taught me my catechism. A Baptist taught me A B C and Latin grammar. Presbyterians taught me to parse glibly the galloping verse of Virgil." As well, William attended a nearby Lutheran school, where he distinguished himself by committing entire chapters of the New Testament to memory. Biblical and classical allusions would permeate his writings throughout his life, contributing to a heroic style in both his correspondence and his diaries.[2]

William hoped to be appointed to West Point like his older brother Robert but was denied admission. Upon learning the news, brother Larz wrote him an advisory note on April 18, 1825, (before their father's death) beginning: "I regret its failure however it is no greater matter, as it is to the hope that you will make the best of your present situation. All that remains to do is—in all cases—to avail yourself promptly and efficiently of all that fortune brings. Let no advantage escape you and by no means leave yourself room hereafter for self accusation, by neglecting the opportunities and misapplying the time that are now at your disposal." Larz went on to encourage him to attend Transylvania Academy and focus his studies on history and geography. Given the centrality of land to American culture, geography would have been a natural subject for William to choose. But Larz had also learned the importance of self-expression, and he reminded William to concentrate on his writing: "Not only use good words to express yourself but the <u>best</u>." Finally, Larz reminded him of their father's mounting land debts and the need to be frugal: "You are well enough acquainted with our circumstances at present to know that it is incumbent on every member of the family to be as economical as possible. Not only are the debts great—but the creditors pressing and much of our property is now under execution—some of it sold to satisfy judgments at a great sacrifice on our part! My father . . . can now scarcely collect money to pay the interest of his debts." Larz's reference to "'my" father rather than "our" father was common and perhaps reflected the more parental tone he invariably took when writing to his younger brothers, though he himself was only twenty-three at the time of writing.[3]

A month later, Robert wrote his younger brother a jesting letter from West Point: "Dear Billy . . . I was a little disappointed when, after hearing that there was a letter for me the price of which was 25 cents I went to the office and found it was from you, not that I was sorry that you had not paid the postage or that I did not wish to hear from you but because now methinks you are laughing in anticipation because I expected that it was from my sweet heart." Robert went on to celebrate his pending graduation from West Point and trip to Colombia to meet up with brothers Richard and Larz. There was no reference to William's denied entrance to West Point.[4]

Whatever his disappointment with West Point, William entered Transylvania University in 1825 and pursued a classical education. Transylvania University was founded in 1780 as an academy and Presbyterian seminary and became a college in 1797. It was the first college to be founded west of the Allegheny Mountains. William's class included the son of Henry Clay, and Clay himself taught law there for periods of time and served on the board of trustees.[5]

After a year in college, William returned to Soldier's Retreat to witness his father's death in 1826 and, following that, to help settle the estate. Following the sale of Soldier's Retreat in 1829 and the resettlement of his mother, William studied law with Larz in Louisville from 1829 to 1832, when he received his law license and began working with Larz. When Larz moved to Cincinnati that year, William delayed working to spend time with his sweetheart, Eliza McArthur, in Chillicothe, Ohio.

In 1833 William began working with the Ohio Importing Company in Ross County, but in 1834 he suffered an attack of yellow fever that left him weak and dangerously underweight. Determined to regain his strength, William planned to make an outdoor trip to regain fitness and self-confidence—perhaps as well to seek adventure and "all that fortune brings." At first, he thought he would accompany a regiment of mounted cavalry (dragoons) under the command of a relative, General Henry Atkinson, who had recently crushed the Black Hawk Indians in 1832 at the Battle of Bad Axe in Illinois. However, Atkinson, perhaps fearing William's stamina, recommended he choose a different adventure—a fortuitous decision given that Atkinson's dragoons would soon be decimated by disease. In particular, Atkinson recommended that William join the fur-trading party of "mountain men" traveling to the Rocky Mountains and "Oregon Country" under the Kentucky-born frontiersman William Lewis Sublette. By then, Sublette

had been exploring and trapping in the West for over a decade, including a stint of hunting and Indian fighting with the famed mountain
man Jedediah Smith.[6]

By 1834 Kentucky and Ohio could no longer be considered the
"frontier." If William wished to explore new boundaries he would have to
push westward to the plains and Rocky Mountains—precisely the areas
Sublette's party would visit to hunt buffalo and trade with the Indians.

William followed Atkinson's advice and, on April 20, 1834,
joined the thirty-seven-man Sublette party, a choice that would prove
life-changing for him. In moving from the relatively cosseted and polite
society of his family, he was literally entering a new world, not only geo-
graphically but socially and culturally. The party was made up of men
lacking a formal education, who depended on their physical strength
and their not-inconsiderable skills acquired by living on the frontier.
The work required courage and fortitude, and a strong commitment
to one another in life-and-death circumstances. In contrast, William's
world had centered around refined society and the life of the mind.
William would soon be adventuring with men not unlike his father
and Daniel Boone a generation earlier. Besides the mountain men, William would encounter a polyglot population of French-speaking traders,
Spaniards, Mexicans, Indians from many tribes, and British. Considerable intermarriage existed between traders and a mosaic of Native
communities, and multiple languages abounded. Most families were
of mixed race, and the Indians predominated. This was less the "middle ground" of equal cultural exchange than a borderline region where
Native peoples determined trade, diplomacy, and security until overwhelmed by the ever-expanding and voracious American settlers.[7]

ON MARCH 13, 1834, the Sublette party began its trek west from Louisville. Anderson would join them in St. Louis after the dragoons following a very brief association. Throughout the journey, William kept
a journal recounting his experiences, observations, and reflections—a
practice as atypical of the mountain men as was the person of William
Anderson.

Anderson's account, written in a pocket diary and subsequently expanded on upon his return to Kentucky, is the only known account of

Sublette's party en route to the Rocky Mountains. Portions of it were published in local newspapers and magazines, including *Waldies' Select Circulating Library* in 1835, which reprinted daily notes from the time the Sublette party reached the Blackfoot River in present-day Montana on July 10 until it arrived at Fort Vancouver in present-day Washington State in September 1834. William's account of a descent on the Missouri River by pirogue (small boat) is the only record of the adventure.

As he described the western trails he rode in 1834, Anderson was careful to include information on the fur trade and its distinctive institution, the rendezvous, a continuation of ancient intertribal trading fairs—a sort of business convention for fur traders. The rendezvous would last for weeks and involved trading goods from the United States and pelts from beaver trapped in the mountains. Rendezvous generally occurred in the valley of the Green River near the mouth of Horse Creek in Wyoming. But in 1834, when Anderson made his journey, the rendezvous was located at Hams Fork, Wyoming, where the most heavily represented Indian tribes were the Snakes and Blackfeet.

William's diary began simply: "March 13, 1834—left Louisville to accompany the dragoons on their escort of the traders to Santa Fe. Thinking better, or worse of the matter as time will show, I changed my mind and determined to accompany Mr. W. L. Sublette to the Rocky Mountains." Sublette's party left St. Louis on April 20 for its first rendezvous in Lexington, Missouri, which it reached in five days. Thus began an experience that would raise William to the stature of his father, brothers, and uncle William Clark for sheer adventure and discovery. Like them, he would be transformed by his experiences and, in the process, learn a lot about the land his new nation was amassing.

Much of Anderson's diary contains observations of the shifting terrain and the mountain men with whom he traveled. He endured a predictable early round of hazing from grizzled traders who saw the incongruity of this gentlemanly college boy and farmer in the rugged company of seasoned mountain men on a westward trek. But he also enjoyed the friendship and support of group leader William Sublette and, in time, would win the loyalty and respect of his fellows.

The company supplied itself with horses and mules in Lexington. On April 30, William wrote: "We are finally up and off for the west, the far west. Where is that? I had always believed I had been born in the

West; but no, here we go in search of it, farther on, farther on." At this point, Anderson left for another country, not part of the United States (although claimed as a US territory) but "Indian country."[8]

Upon reaching Independence, Missouri, the birth of American civilization in the West, Anderson wrote: "This is now the very verge of civilization, and what civilization? Here was the scene of bloodshed, of civil bloodshed. Here the Mormons and the Jacksonites [residents of Jackson County] met in deadly conflict in 1833." He referred to a brawl between Mormon and non-Mormon residents that had threatened to break out into an all-out war. In response, Joseph Smith, the Mormon leader, even raised an army, Zion's Camp. But increased hostilities were avoided when Smith returned to Ohio. Unlike most of his fellow mountain men, Anderson sided with the Mormons, likening the non-Mormon aggression to the recent Protestant attack on the Ursuline Convent in Charleston, Massachusetts, in 1834, "by the degenerate sons of patriots and heroes. Spirits of Warren, Hancock, and Putnam, look down with shame and sorrow on this atrocious act of the bastard sons of New England!"[9]

Already "out of the United States and in the territory of our good Uncle Sam," Anderson had to rethink his acculturated response to hostile Indians: "Shall I say to the redman, 'Take care what you do! If you strike me, I will sue you for assault and battery; if you steal my horse, I will send you to the penitentiary.'" As part of the first generation raised with the rights of US citizenship, Anderson realized he was now far from the laws and protections of his native Kentucky. On May 5, 1834, he reported in his diary: "We are encamped at the Sapling grove, about 20 miles from Independence. We are about 37 men strong—95 horses. I am now out of the US for the first time."[10]

Not surprisingly, land held the greatest fascination for Anderson. Having grown up on a farm, Anderson closely observed the land at every stop along the way to Fort Vancouver. He found the prairie novel and, "being forest-born," preferred the timbered land, though in time he would come to appreciate the prairies. After ascending a three-hundred-foot-high mound and surveying the landscape, he marveled at the potential before him to cultivate land "unimproved" by the Indians: "To the east . . . is seen a boundless extent of country—boundless at least to the sight—A waste of fertility—unused pastures, unenjoyed gardens. To the west, and towards the Kansas . . . rich bottoms covered with timber. I consider the spectacle from Wausaroosa [Shawnee territory] more beautiful and gratifying than that of Monticello near Chillicothe, O." It is clear that Anderson had imbibed the moral argument of "improvement" to justify expropriating Indian lands, a rationale that would carry Americans across the continent in their unquenchable thirst for private property. On May 10, gazing upon one particular "glorious grazing region," he commented that "if our country should purchase it of the Indians, what a glorious grand state it would make."[11]

That evening the company left the Shawnee country behind and entered the land of the Kansa Indians of Siouan stock. Anderson found the tribe "a dirty, lousy-looking set of rogues." However, in their company he entered the first Indian lodge he ever visited, a round-topped tent about ten feet high in the center. He made no further commentary than to say, "The inmates, though savages, were kind, natural and hospitable."[12]

No matter how far from home, Anderson frequently encountered family friends on the trails and in the villages, either from his own circle of acquaintances or from his father's generation. On May 8, 1834, in Kansas, he met up with his famous uncle William Clark, who was serving as superintendent of Indian Affairs at St. Louis. Clark took him up the Kansas River and, after going some distance, turned to Anderson and said, "'Now, kinsman, I will show you how I used to drink, out of your father's spring on Beargrass;' and extending himself on the pebbles, quenched his thirst from the waters of the Kaw."[13]

As the Sublette party continued across Kansas, Anderson observed the wildlife closely as it ran "dashing over the prairies." He proudly reported killing his first rattlesnake in florid prose echoing the biblical account of the Fall: "He and I met as representatives of our first great ancestors [Adam and Eve], and I bruised his head. This is a token of regard for mother Eve. Hereafter, when I war with that sly, old apple thief, it shall be out of reverence for father Adam, whose innocent sweet-heart had been deceived in the garden, by his flattering tongue, and caudal castanets [the rattle]."[14]

Another party, led by rival trader Nathaniel Wyeth, raced past them in a contest to be first to the rendezvous, where they might enjoy trading advantages with the Indians. Anderson lamented their failure to pay respects but realized that when dealing with rivals, "all strategems are deemed allowable when interest is concerned." "Interest" would define Americans' actions whether in searching for furs or acquiring Indian lands. The lack of any moral inquiry on Anderson's part is revealing. America meant opportunity, and opportunity dictated that "all strategems are deemed allowable."[15]

Anderson's first encounter with possibly hostile Indians came on May 16 when a party of one hundred Pawnees appeared in a cloud of dust from the horses' feet before them. After making primitive efforts to construct defenses, the outnumbered Americans sought to negotiate. Four representatives from the tribe entered their camp and made plain their desire for "tobacco, powder, balls, paint, beads, etc.," which were quickly assembled and placed in a pile before them. After asking for a double portion, the Indians rode off. Anderson generally displayed little admiration for the Indians, but one of the four caught his attention: "The finest specimen of the animal man I ever looked upon. He was tall, straight, broad shouldered and tapering; had a well formed head and a remarkably thoughtful countenance." As with the slaves, he did not accept even the "finest specimen" of Native Americans as equals but rather saw them as "animal men."[16]

On May 17, Anderson's party reached Nebraska and settled by the Platte River. At first glance Anderson thought it resembled the Mississippi River, but then he came to see it as a "lie." More like a braided stream than a rushing river, it was unfit even for canoes, leading Anderson to exclaim, "This fussy, foaming, seething thing is like some big bragging men I have seen, all blubber and belly."[17]

The following day Anderson's party encountered a human skull on the trail. Others in his party simply rode past it, but he held onto it, imagining the living being that once embodied the skull: "This reflection came into my mind . . . that perhaps he had like myself been rejoicing in the beauties of nature, that impelled by the spirit of adventure, he had sought to behold the wonders of the mountains and the savage forest, but cruel fate had cut the thread of his existence & his head once the domicile of mind, was a loom-house for the spider to weave his curious silk." The whole scene reminded him of the gravesite in Shakespeare's *Hamlet* where, in a brief aside as he watched the gravedigger disinterring a skull that turned out to be Yorick, Hamlet reflected on the absurdity of presuming to own property in perpetuity when death waits for all: "This fellow might be in's time a great buyer of land, with his statutes, his recognizances, his fines, his double vouchers, his recoveries: is this the fine of his fines, and the recovery of his recoveries, to have his fine pate full of fine dirt?" Eventually Anderson laid the skull down because "in truth, the lonely sermon made the chill fear of death run through me, and I fancied the grinning skull moaned in my ear, *Momento homo tu es pulvis, et in pulverem reverteris.* Adieu, kind friend; I have no more time to moralize. . . . From Fancy, we have come to reality—a sad story."[18]

The next day the Sublette party passed a site of sixty or seventy Indian lodges with many red-painted twigs stuck into the ground. An Indian interpreter explained their significance: "We stand in the middle of a circle of blood-stained sticks, each bearing a lock of human hair. . . . At this spot there has lately been the scalp-dance." Anderson did not know it, but he was witnessing the aftermath of a long-held Indian tradition of the "Circle," within which victims were seated at the center and tortured to death. The red twigs confirmed their number. One gruesome account of the Circle dated back to King Philip's War in colonial New England:

> They first cut one of his Fingers round in the Joynt, at the Trunck of his Hand, with a sharp Knife, and then brake it off, as Men used to do with a slaughtered beast, before they uncase him; then they cut off another and another, till they had dismembered one Hand of all its Digits, the Blood sometimes spirting out in Streams a Yard from his Hand . . . yet did not the sufferer ever relent, or shew any Signs of Anguish. . . . At last they brake the Bones of his Legs, after which he was forced to sit down, which 'tis said he silently did, till they had knocked out his Brains.

A contrast indeed to William's "kind, natural, and hospitable" lodge visit.[19]

May 20, 1834, marked the one-month anniversary of Anderson's departure from St. Louis, and he capped it with his first buffalo chase. The scene of the chase was tumultuous and awe inspiring, buffalo as far as the eye could see coming "with sullen sound and endless roar." As the party neared the buffalo herd "everything was lost to sight. Below, around and above, clouds of dust . . . guided only by the snorts of the bulls as they scented their enemies." Anderson's inaugural hunt did not proceed easily. He lost his rifle after the first shot, but then he managed to empty his two pistols into a bull, so that "after a few desperate plunges, he staggered, bench-legged, and fell." In a story that repeated itself into environmental tragedy, he left the buffalo behind, did not even "go back and procure the evidence of my triumph, a buffalo's tongue." Euro-Americans condemned Indians because they left the land in a state of nature while themselves wiping out entire species for sport and profit.[20]

Anderson might have thought such an outcome impossible. The next day the numbers of buffalo multiplied dramatically so that he "could scarcely believe it possible for them to obtain subsistence."[21]

Anderson responded quite differently to the wild horses they encountered. Given that he would spend much of his adult life purchasing and breeding racehorses, it is not surprising that he took particular note of the horses. While he was delighted to view elk, antelope, deer, buffalo, and wolves, "all hitherto strangers to me," nothing compared with the "free horse—the masterless horse, fenced in by the horizon only, and with no rider but the wind."[22]

Meanwhile he observed, "The Platte is still the platte, from two to three miles wide, and fully knee-deep." When not crossing rivers, the Sublette party could make up to thirty miles a day, which, with the rival Wyeth company only a few hours behind, they needed to do. By May 28, Anderson's party was within three days of the Black Hills. In a somber note Anderson marked the spot as the location where a Mr. Scott, a superintendent of the Ashley Fur Company (not part of the Sublette party), had been left behind and abandoned after falling ill. He was later discovered attempting to crawl back to his father's cabin. An outraged Anderson reflected on the cowardly leader who had left him to die at the hands of wolves and raven: "Had such a being a father? I know not; for the sake of humanity, let us hope that he never had a mother, but 'dropped from the tail of a dung-cart.'" Anderson was not in Kentucky anymore.[23]

In one dramatic scene, Anderson happened upon a Sioux sepulcher among some cottonwoods: "I found to-day, a hawk's nest, on a scaffold which had been the resting place of a Sioux brave." The dead man remained "securely fastened in the boughs of a tree . . . wrapped in an honor-robe, his implements of battle . . . left to the companionship of the birds of the air and his brothers of the Spirit land."[24]

On May 31, the mountain men arrived at the Laramie River's fork at the Platte, where Sublette determined to build a fort. In a show of respect Sublette proposed to name the fort Anderson, in William's honor. William demurred, noting it should be named Fort Sublette, and as a mock bribe offered a bottle of New York champagne he had brought along. Sublette "stood by, cup reversed," until, as a compromise, they agreed that the fort be named in honor of their common first name. With that, "the foam flew, in honor of Fort William." Eventually the fort received its permanent name, Fort Laramie, and references to the original Fort William disappeared.[25]

On June 2, Anderson climbed to the top of the Black Hills and first glimpsed the Rocky Mountains. The spectacle slammed his heightened senses. He wrote:

> See towering up to Heaven, the Kremlin of the winter God! Pillars and arches of gold and silver, with the rose dyed glories of the setting sun, flashing from tower to tower. . . . Other portions of the range, not entirely wrapped in snow, were ever changing in form and color. . . . The center was darkened by moving clouds, which like mighty billows surged onward and upward, or rolled back with resistless power, as if to tear the giant Oregon from its base. To me these mimic battles of clouds and mountains are supremely grand, and whether serious thoughts or wild imaginings, I write them down.[26]

By June 5, Sublette's party had safely crossed the Platte at a point where shallow waters became a surging river. The threat of Indian attacks had heightened, and Anderson confessed that, while serving guard duty, "I did not breathe freely. . . . It would have been difficult to keep a better watch than I did last night. No wolf trotted in the moonlight; no elk whistled on the bliss that I did not see and hear." To his diary, Anderson admitted that he bore a brave "front," but if it came to a fight, he did not desire it. "I am not bloodthirsty," he confided, but "if it comes to the worst, I shall do as the rest—fight or run. I know one thing, however, I don't wan't to be 'tried and found' missing."[27]

The next day, with "my scalp still on," he marveled at yet another beautiful sight, "the snow-capped mountains of the Yellowstone." The West beckoned as it would for the many millions who would follow. In camp the mountain men treated themselves to a feast "at a beautiful spring, my skewer in the ground, at a hot fire of buffalo dung, a set of good, sweet hump-ribs roasting before me, legs crossed, knife drawn, and mouth watering." The repose also brought to mind "my sweetheart," a reference to Eliza McArthur, who was waiting back where he'd left her in Chillicothe.[28]

Communications assumed all shapes and sizes, and in the mountains Anderson discovered a "trappers post office" in the form of a huge boulder on which letters to absent friends, advertisements, and celebrations of "our national jubilee," the Fourth of July, were written in buffalo grease and powder. At the sight of this, Anderson "breathed the prayer, that my country's Union & Independence might be co-existent with that Rock." Another communications gap was breached when Sublette's party encountered six trappers who had been in the mountains for twelve years with no word from home. The mountain men gave "them news in broken doses; beginning with matters three years old. This was delightful, fresher by several years then any they had heard."[29]

Anderson was a strange addition to the company of mountain men, a lawyer with an esteemed frontier ancestry that dated back to Lewis and Clark. Even the Indians recognized him. One, "Little Chief, Insillah," pulled Anderson aside "and rapidly related his boyhood recollections of the Clark and Lewis expedition" in 1805. On another occasion Anderson witnessed a mock war dance "in compliment, I believe, to me. Baptiste Charboneau, a half-breed, & born of the squaw actor in this scene. Of him there is something whispered which makes him an object of much interest." The "whisper" Anderson refers to was the rumor that Jean Baptiste Charbonneau (Sacagawea's son) was the son of William Clark, though the timing of Clark's travel and Charbonneau's birth do not conform.[30] Regardless of whether Clark was Jean Baptiste's biological father, Clark did grow close to the son and adopted him when Sacagawea died.

On June 10, Sublette's party crossed the continental divide, or, as Anderson phrased it, the "Trans montane America," where "today I drink of the waters of the Atlantic, to morrow I quench my thirst from those of the Peaceful [Pacific] ocean." The crossing had been delayed a day because of threats from the Blackfeet tribes, but Anderson was now sufficiently inured to marvel at the Rocky Mountains, which he variously named the "American Andes" or the "American Alps." Still in its race with Wyeth, the party made straight for the Green River, site of the rendezvous. The sights continued to bedazzle Anderson, but one familiar beauty was missing—tree country, leading a homesick Anderson to confide, "How I long for a timbered country. In a thousand miles, I have not seen a hundred acres of wood. . . . These everlasting hills have an everlasting curse of barrenness." And with this nostalgia came renewed images of "a pair of pretty blue eyes, in Ohio."[31]

On the trail, Anderson rarely recorded personal philosophical and religious reflections in his journal. One entry, however, seems to foreshadow his conversion to Roman Catholicism, and with it his search for a meaningful life. The entry appeared on his twenty-seventh birthday, June 24. Instead of celebration he encountered "lonely & restless reflections." He was "regretting the little good which I have done for myself, my God, or my country. How vain have been my wishes & my hopes!" His present experiences and location left him "in a social waste, as soil-less and as desolate as the Desert which I dwell in." "Health, fortune and knowledge" seemed to be escaping him. As the child of a heroic Revolutionary War hero, the brother of a West Point officer and a Harvard graduate, and the nephew of William Clark, well known by Indians and whites alike, he could have judged himself lacking. Interestingly, Anderson traced his present rootlessness, in part, to being "soil-less." In time, land in abundance, good health, and Catholicism would fill that void, but not in 1834. Anderson would later convert to Roman Catholicism, but that intense piety was not evident in the mountain journal. On one occasion he did comment on religion, with regard to an encounter with Nez Perce Indians. He observed in his pocket diary: "This tribe like the Flat-heads is remarkable for their more than Christian [in margin: "I mean as practiced in what are called Christian countries"] practice of honesty, veracity and every moral virtue which every philosopher & professor so much laud, and practice so little." Also present were four missionaries who sought to Christianize the Indians according to Western standards, prompting Anderson to complain: "If they can only succeed in making them such as the white-men are, & not such as they should be, it would be charity for the messengers of civilization to desist." Contemplating "the only people on the globe [who] despise and discountenance lying, stealing and begging" challenged for Anderson the notion of the "white man's burden" to "Christianize" these people of apparent moral superiority. This religion entry in his diary did not appear in his subsequently edited narrative for magazines back home. But it does confirm the very different attitude Anderson displayed toward Indians than he would later display toward African Americans in the Civil War era.[32]

At the same time, Anderson was acutely sensitive to the racial intermingling in the West spanning diverse European and Indian ancestries. On June 18, the parties of Wyatt and Edmund T. Christy of the Rocky Mountain Fur Company and the Sublette party met together with some tribes, leading Anderson to observe, "We are a motley set, Whites, French, Yankees, Nes Perces, Flatheads, and Snakes." The gathering was jumbled and overlapping as conventions of dress and habit broke down in a sea of encounter, not that prejudice evaporated. In a later entry, Anderson reflected on Indian women, noting, "I have seen only one squaw that I can consider at all handsome. She [is] a Pierced-nose woman, belonging to [Dr.] Newell a trapper."[33]

The Sublette party had joined the rendezvous site at Ham's Fork, Wyoming, on June 20. On June 26, a still-depressed Anderson simply recorded, "There is nothing now in the camps but drunken brawls and songs, night and day." His greatest pleasure came from sharing buffalo with his horse, Blackhawk. He found the various Indian parties interesting and watched thirty of them "whooping, singing, and beating their rude drum."[34]

By July 8, Anderson was agonizing over whether to return from the rendezvous with Sublette or remain in the mountains with Thomas Fitzpatrick, a member of the Rocky Mountain Fur Company party. In the end, homesickness won and he opted to make his return with Sublette's party, even while exclaiming to his diary, "Great God, how wearisome & monotonous will be the way." The following day, Sublette split off from his party for St. Louis with seventy packs of beaver pelts to trade. An admiring Anderson summed up the qualities he had come to appreciate in his soon-to-be-separated mountain mate. His "prudence and courage" were unrivaled: "Every way, I think he is an estimable man, and I think I know him—I have slept with him, I have eat with him and if I have not fought with him, at least I have been with him, where we thought it would be done—There is no man in whose company I would rather do it."[35]

As he prepared to leave for home, Anderson changed his mind about some Indian tribes and conceded that American claims of looking after the Indians were mere arrogance. Clearly the Flathead and Nez Perce tribes won his loyalty as "incomparably the best people in the world," leading Anderson to lament, "I wish I could eloquently plead their cause before those who term themselves, 'fathers' of the Red-men."[36]

On August 8, as Anderson made preparations for the journey home, his mood suddenly shifted. He had much to be grateful for in his experience, not least of all the fact that he had gained fifty pounds, so that "I am stout and well." The next day the Sublette company (without Sublette) departed for home, led by the legendary mountain man James Bridger, who had earlier discovered the Great Salt Lake and was presently a principal in the Rocky Mountain Fur Company. The company made steady progress, between twelve and twenty-five miles a day. One of their best marksmen was appointed buffalo hunter to supply much-needed meat without discharging so many weapons as to alert hostile Indians.

By the end of August, they were on Whitetail Creek in Nebraska. By September, Anderson had had enough. Still hundreds of miles from home along the Platte, he wrote, "Curiosity can no more prompt me, and health I hope I never more shall require to take the trip again." In what had become a roller coaster of emotions, Anderson complained on September 14 that he continued to feel "restless" and "anxious," even as Louisville loomed ever closer. He feared "I shall never be settled & happy." But then, in the next sentence: "To see men with boots and shoes on, to dine at a table, and to eat with forks again is a right pleasant thing—Who would have thought, 8 months ago, that such would be my thoughts at this time?"[37]

On September 23, Anderson arrived at his original departure point at Lexington, Missouri. Now a seasoned mountain man, he proudly noted that his mountain looks offended more-polite eyes: "I supped this minute at a tavern table, amidst village politicians, pedantic doctors, and wise looking lawyers—My dirty hunting shirt and greesy leather

breeches seemed to offend their hypercritical eyes and too curious ol-
factories—God help them!" On September 29 he concluded his diary:
"This night I end where I began six months ago—in St. Louis—I shall
not stay to display my greasy carcass here—As soon as possible, un-
washed, uncombed I start for home. . . . Here ends my traveling notes."[38]

His trip complete, all that remained were the memories he would
lovingly preserve for the rest of his life. Later in life, in 1871, Anderson
wrote from his home in Circleville, Ohio, to an old mountain man acquaintance, Robert Campbell, in St. Louis. Campbell had fought with
Sublette in the Indian Wars and partnered with him in the fur trade; by
his death in 1879 he would be one of the wealthiest men in Missouri. In
his letter, William forwarded selections from his diary, confident that
"my journal, though covered with the dust of nearly forty years, may,
through the magic power of memory, bring before you, with all the life-
like vividness of yesterday, places and persons, almost forgotten. You and
I have looked upon the same noble and manly faces with expressions too
dear to die." How many of the mountain men, Anderson wondered, were
still alive, "how many are gone to the Spirit-land. . . . Who are left, Who
are gone?" He had no way of knowing, but of one thing he was certain:
"The survivors must follow their file-leaders. 'Time is passing and we are
passing with it.' The question is, not when, but where we shall go. Let us
be armed and prepared to march when the trumpet sounds."[39]

ANDERSON RETURNED TO OHIO a new man. In 1835, the twenty-eight-
year-old Anderson married his longtime sweetheart, Eliza McArthur.
Eliza was the daughter of General Duncan McArthur, a close friend
and working associate of Richard Sr. and Nathaniel Massie and a leading figure in the early political and military history of Ohio. Fabled to
have strength and speed, McArthur became renowned as a frontiersman and Indian fighter. From 1793 to 1794 he had been employed by
Kentucky as an Indian ranger, patrolling the Ohio River and tracing
the movements of the Indians. A year later he began his wildly successful career in land speculation, serving first as chain carrier for Nathaniel Massie in the Scioto Valley. There he surveyed—and eventually
owned—much of the land around what would become Chillicothe,
Ohio's original state capital, where he served several terms in the House

of Representatives. Already by 1804 he was one of the wealthiest land-holders in the Valley and had built a mansion north of Chillicothe he named Fruit Hill.

When he was not fighting to dispossess the Indians of their land, McArthur served in the critical post of commissioner for US negotiations with the Indians. The object of this commission was, of course, land. McArthur did not disappoint and negotiated two major treaties with the Indians in which they ceded virtually all of their remaining lands in Ohio and Indiana to the white inhabitants. Their removal, completed in 1830 with the federal Indian Removal Act (with McArthur sitting as Ohio governor), effectively marked the end of any major Indian cultural presence in the region.[40]

Soon after William's marriage to Eliza, younger brother Charles became engaged to another Eliza. In 1834 he'd met Elizabeth (Eliza) J. Brown, the daughter of a Dayton merchant. They were married in September 1835. In the same year, Charles attempted to partner with Robert on land their father had deeded them on the Ohio River, opposite the Wabash. In short order Robert discovered that farming was not in his blood, and he returned to West Point as an instructor of artillery. Charles agreed and headed to Louisville to complete his law training and briefly joined Larz's firm, Pirtle and Anderson.[41]

After gaining admittance to the bar in 1835, the ever-restless Charles had intended to settle in St. Louis, but instead he decided to move to Dayton, Ohio, to set up his own practice. For the next ten years he would practice a combination of half-time law and half-time farming. While in Dayton, Charles shifted his political loyalties from the Democratic Party to the recently founded Whig Party of family friends Henry Clay and John Crittenden.

The party leader, Clay, summarized the party platform as directly opposed to Jackson and Jacksonian politics, in particular his war on the Second Bank of the United States. Once engaged, the contest between the parties would be to the death. Clay, now returned to the House, proposed two resolutions. The first rejected and ridiculed Secretary of the Treasury Roger B. Taney's efforts to remove federal deposits from the bank. The second denounced Jackson personally for his executive overreach and disregard for the Constitution. The Whigs would also endorse Clay's American System.[42]

Charles was, in fact, the most devoted Whig supporter in the Anderson family. The Whig Party would be the only party the future governor of Ohio would ever profess his loyalty to. In a funeral oration for Clay delivered in 1852, Charles would sum up his sense of Clay's standing among the great triumvirate of leaders—Clay, John Calhoun, and Daniel Webster: "Calhoun excelled him decidedly, in his own sphere. Webster very far transcended him in many and in great respects. *But as a whole man, Henry Clay was the greatest of the Triumvirate—nay the greatest of his Age!*"[43]

In February 1835, however, Charles again had land on his mind and consulted with brother-in-law Latham. He was optimistic about property he owned in Franklin, Ohio, and wanted to preserve as much of his land as possible on the (mistaken) assumption that prices would continue to go up. Instead of selling his own land for a loss, he wanted to sell a town lot of Eliza's. He needed to use the proceeds to raise a mortgage to retain the Franklin land and needed Latham's advice: "Let me know immediately if you think it can be mortgaged to the Trust Company, as the person who made the offer for the lot has gone to Cincinnati, and wishes to know on his return next week. . . . Send me too if you please, the number of acres in my name. I have forgotten it." In the same year Charles and his mother, Sarah, assigned their power of attorney to Latham "to lease, let, or sell the said land to such person or persons and for such a lease or number of years and other rents as he shall think fit." In assuming power of attorney, Latham was consolidating the family's financial affairs. Despite the disparate activities and investments, the family remained integrated. A year later Charles was pleased to thank Latham for securing the mortgage and avoiding the necessity of "selling a piece of property which I think is as well to be in my possession as the sum offered for it." When Charles and Eliza had their first child, they named him Latham in honor of their brother-in-law.[44]

Another topic of great interest to Charles—and everyone else in Ohio—was the construction of a national road linking farmers to markets. In December 1835, Charles wrote Latham in the latter's capacity as a member of the National Road Committee, asking that Latham query "some of your Washington City or other friends on this subject." Any insider information regarding the construction of the Maysville Road would be valuable in locating lands that would connect to the road and from there to national markets. Later that year Charles noted some "cheering news on the subject of the National Road." Unlike private turnpikes built by corporations to secure tolls, the "national road" marked an internal project at federal expense—a favorite pursuit of Whig politicians.[45]

While Charles was exploring roads and markets, recently married brother William was considering his economic future. Now that he was married to a wealthy woman with an inheritance of her own, he contemplated alternatives to the law and his work as surveyor general, succeeding his father. In a letter to Latham written in May 1835, he asked for advice on "the subject of my transformation into a merchant." To accomplish such a goal, he further requested that Latham provide him a loan. There simply was not enough money to be made in law, and "to make money is now I confess the end and aim of my hopes." As evidence he pointed to his merchant friend Pope McNight and others who "within a five years have made themselves men of fortune." For William to do likewise, he had to abandon his "honorable beggary," and for that to happen he needed capital. At the same time he maintained his interest in land and farming, noting, "There is now for sale 3 miles from Louisville a farm of 8 hundred acres at $16 per acre. Tis beautifully situated and its rich grounds situate on part of said tract in North. At twice the distance on this side, there was sold yesterday 50 acres at $150 per acre." Then came the ask: "Can you loan me $5 or 6,000? To this I can add by November $2500 more with which I shall be content to begin."[46]

William was casting around for a meaningful investment that would bring him wealth. In time, religion would replace wealth as his *summum bonum*, but for the moment money ranked highest. In the same letter to Latham he commented on property, banks, and the exciting prospect of a railroad link to Lexington: "There is nothing new in these parts. Banks in great abundance—Larz and I subscribed for twenty shares . . . in the Bank of Ky. . . . Such [is] the mania for this kind of property. Our city will improve more this season than it had ever done—so say the men who do the building. The turnpike to Maysville and the railroad to Lexington will be commenced I don't know when." From this letter it is clear that "property" was an expansive term in the early republic that included banks. And like other property, banks had their booms and busts. William's investment with Larz in the Bank of

Kentucky would soon be challenged by a financial panic that would leave the banks reeling.[47]

There is some evidence that Latham used the family for his personal affairs along with helping its members with theirs. William did not enjoy the work of surveyor general at all but continued doing it because it benefitted Latham's land investments.[48]

Other family members continued buying and selling land. Apparently seldom-heard-from brother John Roy Anderson was not pursuing family land sales that he had earlier agreed to process for other family members. His nephew, Richard Anderson Logan, complained that he was not selling land for badly needed family income. Despite repeated requests to "dispose" of Logan's Ohio lands, John Roy had not acted, prompting another letter "requesting an immediate sale (if it can be done without a sacrifice). But provided a delay of a few months will make a material difference in sale you are requested so to act. . . . They wish to know immediately from you whether you have sold." Apparently Logan's letter worked, for John Roy turned the money over to Allen Latham in January 1836, leading Ann Logan to write to Latham noting she had received "your letter with the balance of the money enclosed in it. I am very much obliged to you for the trouble you have been at."[49]

In 1836, Robert wrote his mother from his teaching post at West Point to express his happiness at Charles's "fortunate choice" in a wife. Robert still hoped to marry at the right time, but military affairs would dictate when that time would be. The success of Texas's campaign for independence from Mexico in 1836 and prospect of its joining the Union provoked foreign policy issues of recognition with England and France. Until these were resolved, Robert continued, he would be committed to service: "I may remain single a year or two longer, at least until after we give France a good drubbing, and then I can, with a quiet conscience ask the hand of some fair maid." Robert hoped for peace: "If the mediation of GBritain has been accepted, I presume that we all have no war on the disputed question." If hostilities ensued, Anderson feared that US defenses were inadequate, adding, "Even in our Indian warfare, how shameful that no adequate preparations had been made to put down at once the threatened hostilities." He concluded that a foreign policy of cynical realism was problematic: "'Whatever is is right' is

I think a comfortable but a very dangerous doctrine as far as nations are concerned." Perhaps, but it did shape much of America's foreign policy. Like European nations, America often determined what was in its best interests and then pronounced it "right."[50]

National politics dominated the political scene historically with the rise of the Democratic Party and the triumph of Andrew Jackson. The Anderson family was divided, with Charles championing the Whigs and William a committed Democrat. The period from 1820 to 1860 marked the height of partisan politics, with voting participation rates at all-time highs for white males. A major reason for this heightened sensitivity was the increasing power of the market to focus attention on such major issues as tariffs, internal improvements at federal expense, a transportation revolution, and banks. The emergence of national and international markets for Ohio goods meant that the local face-to-face culture of Richards Sr. and Jr. increasingly gave way to more national networks and associations as more and more midwestern communities were integrated into the large markets, creating a strong middle class committed to the region's economic and social development."[51]

The financial panic of 1837 politicized huge numbers of previously disengaged citizens as banks crashed, businesses failed, and properties were foreclosed. As in 1819, many citizens saw the value of their property plummet even as they owed mortgages that placed them, in modern terms, underwater. Much of Andrew Jackson's popularity derived from popular discontent with a status quo that was betraying the promise of America. Land was the lifeblood of the young nation, but land was jeopardized by the markets and was the source of unending anxiety.

While the Andersons avoided financial ruin in the Panic of 1837 and resulting depression, all the residents of the burgeoning population of Ohio were put under severe strains. With reckless extensions of credit and speculation, Ohio banks were not exempted from the crisis. Banks flooded the country with paper currency, severely conscripting capital in hard specie. The trigger for the crash came with President Jackson's Specie Circular of July 11, 1836, directing land agents to accept nothing but specie in payment for public lands. At the same time, British creditors began calling in their American bank loans, causing a heavy drain of coin that could not be stopped. Soon banks suspended specie payment. As if all of this were not enough, extensive crop failures in 1837 and

1838 in Ohio threw the country into depression. At an Ohio bank convention in June 1837, twenty-three of Ohio's thirty-two chartered banks met and pledged not to part with any of their gold or silver and to receive the paper of the other banks. To contain the panic, Ohio passed the Bank Commissioner Law of 1839, requiring that banks limit the circulation of paper bills to less than three times the amount of specie, exclusive of deposits, in their vaults and actually belonging to the bank.[52]

The Panic of 1837 would continue for seven years beyond 1837, wreaking havoc for many of the same reasons as the previous panic: speculative lending by western banks, a sharp decline in cotton prices, a collapsing land economy, and restrictive lending policies in Great Britain. In the western states, financial crises proliferated, fueled by Jackson's war on the Second Bank of the United States and his Specie Circular of 1836 requiring payment in gold or silver, which most westerners did not possess in abundance. The value of land sales dropped precipitously, from $25 million in 1836 to $4 million in 1838 and $2.7 million in 1840.[53]

The predominant political issues in Ohio between 1820 and 1850 concerned the banks. If the land boom was to continue and thrive, banks would be indispensable partners for the purchase of land and the improvement of property. The firestorm between Jacksonians and Whigs over the Second Bank of the United States was only the most visible of related issues for banks issuing paper that would be creditworthy. Directors of local banks, like Larz, faced resentment on the part of citizens who perceived them as aristocrats and unfriendly to the people. Jacksonians, in particular, were hostile to banks and paper money. Whigs, who came to power in the aftermath of Jackson's veto of the Second Bank of the United States, tended to favor banks and paper money as essential to the commercial prosperity of the state. In fact, rhetoric aside, Democrats and Whigs were both elitists at heart and believed government was best placed in the hands of the better sort.[54]

Larz's move to Cincinnati to become the director of Citizens National Bank came in 1837, as financial panic loomed. It could not have been a more inopportune time, but it did not ruin him. In part, this was no doubt owing to the fact that his wealthy father-in-law, Nicholas Longworth, was still alive and able to help shore up the family reserves. Still, these were not easy times for anyone. In September 1837, Larz learned that sister Cecelia was pressed for money. In a letter to her, he wrote to say that he would do all he could even though "I am now very much pressed for money myself, having about five thousand dollars to pay for my house. I wish you would write to let me know how the matter stands."[55]

While Larz was managing the move to Cincinnati, brother Robert was pursuing Indian removal as assistant adjunct general on the staff of his commander, General Winfield Scott. Scott was tasked with removing the Cherokee from their native tribal lands in Georgia and Tennessee to the distant frontier territory of Oklahoma. By August 1838, three thousand Cherokees had left their homes by water toward Oklahoma. Another thirteen thousand remained in camps, where four thousand died before the others departed.

In a letter to his mother, Robert described his experiences with the brutal Cherokee removal ordered by President Jackson. Writing from the Cherokee Agency, he noted that the Cherokees "are about commencing their change of home." With this euphemism he went on to reflect at some length and with evident moral uneasiness about what he was participating in. He wrote that the first Cherokee party was nearly ready for removal, "abandoning at once its ancient home, and journeying to the wilderness to seek for another." Unlike voluntary moves by Americans who sought to "better their condition," this was involuntary, forced at gunpoint. While separations were painful and "griefs that all have felt, and some felt keenly," they were "slight" compared to what the Indians were suffering: "They go, not by their own free will and choice. The Treaty under the provisions of which they are emigrated, was not approved by this people. They go, compelled by stern unyielding necessity. Their homes are required by the whites—and they must seek others in a distant and strange land. With a heart susceptible of friendship and perhaps love, I can not but feel warmly for this poor people. Would to heaven that it was in my power to aid in exciting in their bosoms the kind feelings which I entertain of them." Then, echoing the rationale of many legislators, he closed with the hope that they would be better off leaving:

> The country to which they go, has many things to render it preferable to this; and after a few years I hope that they will be convinced that they have been benefitted by the changes. They have made

considerable progress in civilizations. Woman is with them rising above her mere menial pursuits, with which she is solely occupied in savage life. The men pay those little attention, which mark civilization. I have seen a Cherokee, stop in the road and tie his wife's shoo. Here I have seen the husband assist his wife in carrying the child. These are trifles, but 'trifles light as air' show the approach of change in civilization, as well as in weather.[56]

Though a professional soldier, Robert suffered the ache of a compassionate heart. The Cherokees were as civilized and accomplished as the Americans. As of 1838 they had adopted much of the technology and farming science of the Americans and, contrary to Americans' false definitions, "improved" the land they farmed.[57]

President Jackson did not share Robert's moral qualms and would not be deterred in his determination to secure complete removal of Indians to the west of the Mississippi River. In return, the nation would realize vast stretches of southern and midwestern land for sale to eager white purchasers. Despite the protests of powerful critics, especially among the Protestant clergy, Jackson prevailed, leaving the devastated Indians to follow their "trail of tears" west.

10

A Time of Testing

1839–1844

As Richard Anderson Sr.'s surviving children grew solidly into adulthood, with active careers, adventures, and marriages of their own, the management of family affairs grew necessarily more complicated. The "Andersons" now subsumed not only blood relations but also business partners, political associates, and—most decisively—in-laws. To a person, Larz's generation married well, financially speaking, and the new family connections brought with them both great advantages and challenging tangles. It was a wise Anderson, indeed, who managed to embrace the former while finessing the latter.

In addition to his surveying and speculation, William found himself in 1839 deeply involved in settling the estate of his father-in-law, Duncan McArthur. Larz had warned William to stay away and repeated his warning to Charles, pointing out that "William is in considerable trouble respecting the estate. I trust he will have nothing to do with the management of it. He would have a life plague of it if he did."[1] To Larz, the reason was plain: McArthur had put together a complicated will, assigning much of his considerable estate to his grandchildren and thereby bypassing his children—a provision certain to be contested in court.

William ignored Larz's advice. Larz wrote a follow-up letter to William warning that McArthur's son Allen would contest the will and suggesting that William remove himself and perhaps win a significant reward: "If as I presume you suspect and as indeed may be the case—he would like to have a hand himself in settling the estate, why not help him in it? By so doing you might at all events, entitle yourself to more consideration with him, than were you to make opposition. This I suggest for your reflection." Whether through his own stubbornness or the influence of his wife, Eliza, William chose to ignore his brother's wise advice and paid miserably for it. Thereafter, his correspondence groaned with requests for payments and court appearances. But William also reaped significant reward in the estate, vaulting William from the poorest of his brothers to second only to Larz.[2]

Larz's predictions proved prescient. Almost immediately Allen McArthur contested the will, arguing that it was written at a time when his father was not in possession of his faculties. The presiding judge, John H. Keith, ruled with Allen and decreed that the will should be broken and the property divided equally among the children. Much of the land was sold well below market prices because potential buyers feared the titles would not hold up to a challenge.

In fact, Judge Keith's verdict would not go unchallenged. There was too much land at stake and too much ambiguity surrounding the will. Eventually, the case reached the Supreme Court in 1885, where the justices determined that all lands must be given back to the McArthur grandchildren, including lost rents and profits. At this point, the property alone was worth more than $1 million, leaving numerous buyers adversely affected. In attempting to enforce the ruling, Allen McArthur was almost murdered, and soon thereafter he ended his life by shooting himself.[3]

The extent of William's involvement with these cases is unclear. What is clear, however, is that the suits left William emotionally broken and many of the McArthur heirs ruined by their father's landed wealth. William did not live to see the final adjudication in the Supreme Court.

While William was consumed with litigation, Robert Anderson had committed fully to his military career. Any thoughts of returning to a farm in Kentucky or Ohio were long departed. As a consequence of his West Point teaching experience and service in the Cherokee removal, Robert was appointed to General Winfield Scott's headquarters in Elizabethtown, New Jersey. From there he continued to monitor family affairs and keep himself in the loop. In an August 1840 letter to his mother, who was staying with her daughter Mary Louisa in Cincinnati, he noted: "Charles I see has entered the field of politics. I hope that he will remain as decided, as he has from the farm, in resisting the claims made on this point. If he enters as a politician now, he will keep his family poor as long as he remains in public life. He is young enough to make a competency at his profession and to serve his country as a public man afterwards." Robert questioned not only Charles's financial stability to undertake public office but also the very idea of politics as a useful career. Both he and his commander and friend General Scott (both Whigs) had had enough of the Jacksonian spoils system of political cronyism, leading Robert to complain bitterly, "The politicians of the present day are not the class of men he [Charles] would like to associate with. They are not <u>statesmen</u>, but men who act on the vile creed that <u>all is fair in politics</u>. They speak of their country—the rights and liberties of the people—but act for place and serve for themselves and their party. Their acts tend to demoralization and anarchy." In conclusion, he warned: "A few short years, and these men will be forgotten or remembered only to warn demagogues of the retribution which awaits them." Of course Robert was right about the motives of politicians, but wrong about the potential for anarchy. As long as America delivered on its promise of land and abundance, the ship would stay afloat.[4]

IN THE 1840 PRESIDENTIAL election, the Whig Ohioan William Henry Harrison defeated Martin Van Buren, but he died in April 1841, his second month of service, leaving Vice President John Tyler to succeed him. Charles Anderson would not be elected to the Ohio state senate until 1844, settling in the meantime for local Dayton politics, serving as township clerk and later as prosecuting attorney of the county.[5]

Larz—the patriarch of the family—dispensed advice to all his siblings from his home base in Cincinnati. The indecisive Charles, who was struggling to launch a coherent career, received a series of sympathetic, Dutch-uncle letters from Larz. In a letter written on May 9, 1839, Larz wrote: "Dear Charley, We hear from you so seldom these times, that I begin to augur that you have too much to do." By August Larz had not heard back and, somewhat indignantly, wrote again to wonder at "your apparent slight of me for the last 2 or 3 months. I am at a loss to conjecture. Perhaps I may have unthinkingly given you offence, if so I should like very much to know it." He closed with a brief note on wife Catherine (Kate): "Kate is still thin and delicate. I hope a little trip will do her good."[6]

Charles was married and a father, but still lacked direction. He favored pastimes over work, leaving Eliza to limit his fishing or hunting to no longer than two days away from home. This was no doubt a response to an ongoing complaint that Eliza had shared the year before in a letter to her mother-in-law, Sarah: "To begin with my troubles. Charles left home this morning to be gone nearly if not quite two weeks, and there is not a living creature in the house, but myself—and plenty of spiders and rats; not very pleasant company by the bye." Between his lawyering and hunting, "Charley" was "away from home so often that one is always either anxiously looking forward to their return or spending the time they are to leave home, so that there is not much pleasure in their society when at home. But I must cease complaining."[7]

Larz was not alone in trying to steer Charles into a settled, responsible life. Adding to the familial voices of advice was a letter from Robert cautioning Charles about leaving "familiar and friendly faces" for the unknown. The consequences would be costly and require local knowledge of land: "You must be prepared for living a little uncomfortably, being without clients, at first. Do you intend farming? Examine the land, select for yourself, see that it possesses most of these advantages, health, fertility, facility of communication, an outlet to a certain market, a comfortable cabin for your family. Having found such a spot (and not before) you may think of disposing of your property and moving to the 'far west.'"[8]

Larz and Robert knew their younger brother well. With Larz's marriage to Kate in 1834, material assistance would always be available—perhaps too available—but not always appreciated. A letter from Eliza to a traveling Charles made clear at least her feelings about her brother-in-law's largesse: "I send you $25.00 20 of which were given me by Larz—and done in such a way that I felt very unpleasantly at the time; nor can I get over it." Apparently he just stuffed the money in her hand, "and I could not help taking it." She thanked him but was not happy: "Now Charles what I am after, is, that you either return this to Larz for me with many thanks for his great kindness to <u>us</u>, or that you use it in paying Mrs. [Effie] Coones or any debt you see proper to pay with it."[9]

For his part, Larz did not miss a beat in offering Charles advice. In a familiar pattern, Charles was restless and disaffected with his work, leaving Larz to worry whether Charles could resist the allure of politics and what would happen if he succumbed. Larz began his letter of December 30, 1840, by invoking "a little maxim" of their father: "that whatever is worth doing at all, is worth doing well." From this invocation, Larz turned to Charles's indecision and openly wondered if farming would soon grow dull, so that "a little want of excitement would not have soon overtaken you in your retreat, and driven you, as it has many others of like turn with yourself into the great game of Politicks." Here, Larz could scarce contain his contempt for its politicians. To Charles, he offered a frank critique of the "nobility" of politics compared to the "greedy confines" of farming and lawyering and pointed out, "It is next to impossible for the politician to preserve himself pure, amid the despicable shifts and maneuvers which he sees his rivals systematically practice."

With that Larz returned to his larger point, namely, Charles's inability to commit to anything besides hunting and fishing: "You say that you are set down, after abandoning the practice almost entirely to make a living, you don't know how—this is exactly what I object to. You should know how. . . . I wish to bring you to something definite. I want a purpose, an end, a plan—wherever you may be. The plan is not as important a consideration as a plan. . . . You are better qualified for success at the bar, than in any other calling or craft whatever."

To assist Charles in fashioning a plan, Larz went on to offer his brother a partnership in his firm, noting, "I fancy and flatter myself, that our business would grow rapidly. Besides I should be willing to share with you the fees (if I ever get them) in cases yet undisposed of, in which I am now engaged." Larz made plain he did not want to pressure Charles into a commitment: "I only throw out these suggestions to help you, as far as I may do, to form the right conclusion." Despite the generous offer, Charles demurred, preferring to remain in Dayton, where his wife, Eliza, owned family property and where he engaged a legal partnership with John Howard.[10]

Meanwhile, amid the trauma of losing their child "little Sally," who died July 4, 1840, William and Eliza came to a momentous decision:

they would convert to the Roman Catholic faith. In the front of his notebook containing correspondence with the Episcopal minister Edward W. Peet, William noted, "I made my first communion Dec. 22nd 1839," and then added, "Received confirmation . . . July 4 1840." By one account a priest had visited the couple as they were mourning the death of their child and offered solace. That, together with their study of scripture and theology, persuaded them to convert. To this point, religion had not figured significantly in William's extant writings. The Episcopal Church was there more as an embellishment than any deeply felt faith. But all of this would change radically with his conversion, making him rival Robert in spirituality and exceed all in proselytizing energy—often at the cost of lost affections in his immediate and extended family.[11]

The religious changes appeared immediately in William's letters and the commonplace book that he began compiling in 1836, running through 1841. He turned on his Episcopal and Protestant beliefs with venom. The Protestant revivalists, he proclaimed, were rank emotional exploiters, out of all touch with the "important dogmas of Christianity—the mystery of the Divinity, the incarnation." Instead of truth, these Protestant hucksters made use of everything that "can stimulate and excite the feelings and passions of the convert to the highest pitch, and when reason is banished by frenzy to receive the irrational and frightened creature into half or whole communion with the faithful. Is not this the invariable practice of the most popular, if not the most prevalent sect of this country, the Methodist?"[12]

In addition to his fervent Catholic faith, William was also perennially the most racist of the Anderson brothers. He hated the Whig Party in part because he thought it was always more sympathetic to blacks than the Democrats. He was correct. Whig politicians were hardly abolitionists, but they did harbor preferences for colonizing freed slaves to Africa and condemned racial violence. In his notebook, Anderson also wrote on physiology, reflecting the notions of superior and inferior races. In matters of race he embraced the eugenics of his day, even as he rejected most other "modern" science in favor of revealed religion. Anderson confidently asserted that there are "four races of men, differing in the color of their skin and the proportions of their parts, the Caucasian, the Mongolian, the Ethiopian and the American [Indian]." From their jaws, William concluded that it was clear that "the Caucasian race is superior."[13]

William also remained a staunch Democrat, in contrast to other family members, and issued a states rights' critique of Henry Clay's American System, the same system his brothers Richard and Charles promoted. Not one to worry himself about alienating family members, William wrote: "The American system, or the right of Internal Improvements by the Genl. Government, was the first unscrupulous, unconstitutional chain, forged by that great and daring legislator Henry Clay, which bound the separate and separated states to the centralized power at Washington." In this, William believed, Clay had betrayed his region and diverged substantially from the revered Jefferson: "The brilliant but erratic genius of Clay, in striking out a new path which he hoped would conduct him to the triumph of fame [assigned himself] the impracticable if not impossible task of passing through the storms and hurricanes of the past revolution, without rudder or compass."[14]

While William scored deepening lines of division between himself and his clan, other family members continued to tug the network close. In September 1840 Larz wrote a chatty letter to his brother Robert, announcing the birth of a third son, whom Kate named William Pope Anderson. In politics, the 1840 presidential election was looming, with William Henry Harrison, Whig of Ohio, the overwhelming favorite. With a united party and a national economy still in tatters, the "Hero from Tippecanoe" was poised for a landslide victory, along with Whig candidates to state elections, and the Buckeye State was proud. Larz commented: "What a cause of exaltation it is to see the whole country thus rising as it were one man. . . . Heaven be thanked for the hope we have of a thorough Reformation." Larz went on to communicate that Richard Anderson, Charles's son, had visited until his maternal grandfather picked him up. Larz noted: "Master Richard is now a great talker, calls himself a 'log-cabin-man' and huzzahs for 'Tippecanoe' on all occasions." Larz closed with news from Chillicothe, where Sarah was expected to stay with sister Mary Louisa, who had been married again, to the famous judge James Hall.[15]

In Dayton, Charles continued his farming and law practice, including, as brother-in-law and family attorney Allen Latham explained, defending "a colored man by the name of Anthony Evans," who purchased a lot from a seller who had sold the same land to another party. Though "lazy" by his own admission, Charles was strikingly attractive and a born orator admirably suited for court trials and politics. Latham, in a letter to Charles, declared that rumor had it "Dayton is getting too small to hold the bags and that you talk of moving to Cincinnati." Charles would relocate to Cincinnati in 1847, not in partnership with Larz.[16]

On Christmas Eve 1842, William was in some financial distress over his land. In a letter to Latham, he asked: "Will you do me the favour to enquire what the amount of my taxes and penalties for non payment are? I would also like to be informed whether it is possible for me to pay them in Chillicothe money. . . . I have lost on the purchase $1400." The news on the McArthur estate was also not good, and again William turned to Latham: "At the earnest desire of Wm McDonald I write to request (if there is yet time) that you procure the passage in the legislature of a bill authorizing me to make deeds for lands sold in the life time of Gen. McArthur."[17]

On a brighter note, the long-single bachelor, Robert, had at last found a wife. In a Christmas 1841 letter to his sister Maria, he wrote: "I am engaged, yes little sister, I have thought well of the term engaged to be married to Miss Eliza Bayard Clinch—she is the daughter of an old and valued friend Genl. D. L. Clinch and is one of the noblest of our race—in fact, to say that we are engaged is to show that I find her all and desire in my partner for life." Although presently "confined in her sofa by an affliction of the spine," it was nothing serious. In a note of pique he closed, "You may tell the news to Sarah and Brother Allen— no one else near you, has any interest in the matter or any right to know any thing of it."[18]

On the home front, William was confronting problems with his firstborn son, Thomas. Already in 1843, when Thomas was only seven, William began to discern troubling signs that his son was resisting the religious indoctrination of priests and parents. In a letter to Robert he noted that all Thomas cared about was following his uncle Robert into an army career: "Tom's military enthusiasm is now at the highest. . . . It would have given him great happiness if he could have seen his war like uncle but I have no doubt the rest of us are gainers by his disappointment." Tom was learning how to read the Bible, "and what for do you suppose? He says he 'wishes to see the account of those glorious old battles which were fought in those days.'" William closed his letter to Robert with an ironic note that could only be appreciated in time: "I believe you have never been at old fort Moultrie. How delighted I should be to go over the ground where our brave fathers have endured so much danger and privation. Especially at Charleston and Savannah." Robert would indeed be stationed in command at Fort Moultrie, and from there, more ominously, at Fort Sumter. But other wars would be prosecuted first.[19]

As HENRY CLAY WAS angling once again for the presidency, Charles was persuaded to forgo his law practice and run for the Ohio state senate on the Whig ticket in 1844. As a gifted public speaker, Charles ran a dynamic campaign, crisscrossing the state and earning yet another complaint from Eliza that he was always away. But this time the travel paid off and Charles was easily elected in 1844, contributing to a Whig majority in the state senate. The Whig gubernatorial candidate, Mordecai Bradley, defeated the dynamic Democrat David Tod by a slim margin. Henry Clay, on the other hand, lost the presidential election to James K. Polk, who ran on a relentlessly expansionist ticket intended to gain yet more land as America's Manifest Destiny.[20]

Charles's victory once again had him moving, this time to the state capital in Columbus, in December 1844. Again land would come to preoccupy him, this time over the pressing national issue of annexing Texas. Charles, like his mentor Henry Clay, opposed annexation, but not to the extent of advocating disunion, as some Whigs advocated. In the end, the Democratic campaign for annexation prevailed, grounded, not surprisingly, in the prospect of limitless acres of cheap land.[21]

While Charles was serving in the Ohio senate, he wrote his sons Allen Latham Anderson and Clough Anderson an instructive letter from Columbus, with not a little guilt thrown in along with good-natured affection: "I write this letter to you now, to say that I am very glad indeed to learn that you have quit crying and also that you don't quarrel and fight any more. . . . I cannot stay away from home and work to feed and clothe you two great big boys while you are doing nothing.

You ought to work for us, as we work for you. You must clean up the yard and take messages for your mother and cousin Janet." He then closed with a little gender stereotyping characteristic of the age: "You must play out of doors too. Little girls must play in the house. But boys should play on the terrace, and the yard and in the orchard."[22]

Charles's parental advice echoed the prevailing wisdom of the day. Boys were encouraged to engage in rigorous outdoor play to build up their aggressiveness. The activities of girlhood were more limited to maternal domestic activities, including childcare and housework, which kept them inside the home more than their brothers. Few Americans— and certainly no Andersons—questioned the patriarchal structure of family life; they assumed that women would submit to their husbands and confine their activities to home and farm. Where many early American families experienced father-son tensions, sometimes boiling over into overt conflict, this did not happen to Charles. For brother William and William's son Thomas, as we shall see, it did.[23]

Besides immersing himself in issues of trade and markets involving railroads and turnpikes, Charles again took a stand on conscience that put him at odds with the party faithful and effectively ensured that he would be a one-term state senator. The issue was race. Ohio legislators, fearful of an influx of escaped slaves and free blacks, had passed a series of "Black Laws" in 1803 that were intended to block African Americans from access to the state. The laws remained in force and rendered even free blacks second-class citizens. Now far removed from his slaveholding past, Charles proposed eliminating one provision of the law—the prohibition on blacks testifying in civil and criminal court cases. The Senate passed the bill on February 20, 1845, but it failed in the House. Both the press and House immediately jumped on Charles and his "niggerology," and accused him of betraying his Kentucky heritage.[24]

The fusillade of race-based hatred and vituperation, together with Charles's ill health—in this instance, aggravated asthma—encouraged him to take a leave of absence in March 1845 and recover his health in a new setting. With leave from the Senate (and presumably Eliza), he embarked on a dream vacation through Europe's cultural centers that belied any notion of frontiersman or backcountry bumpkin. In a letter to his brother William he notified him that he would be a one-term senator, adding, "I care but little for it. If I had any political aspiration, it might be different, but it is not so. Let it pass."[25]

Anderson traveled to northern Spain and southern parts of France via the Rhône River, and then on to Mediterranean ports in Italy, Sicily, Greece, and the Ottoman Empire. He met the sultan of Constantinople twice, and from there sailed up the Danube River through Germany and northern France, concluding his travels in London. In November 1845, Charles wrote Eliza from the *St. Brittanie* "at sea" southwest of the Nova Scotia peninsula, noting his return from Europe: "We hope to reach Boston in time for the 4 o'clock train of boxes tomorrow evening. . . . I hope you have received my Dresden letter and will be ready, through some arrangement . . . to go with me straightway to Columbus." This would not be Charles's last trip to Europe alone. Of all the Anderson wives, Eliza appears to have been the most long-suffering, enduring her husband's frequent long absences, though not without complaint.[26]

In October 1845, Larz had reported to William that Charles had written from Constantinople and expected to be back in Boston in November. Larz wrote, in words that would not have been well received by Eliza: "This is delightful intelligence but I fear Master Charley is returning too soon. Let us however be happy for what we hear and hope for the best." By this point Larz was quite successful, and William was laboring under the costs and aggravations of the McArthur suit. To ease his way, Larz assured William that if he needed funds, "I presume we could get it for you here if requisite." Charles was also out of funds and returned to Ohio to rejoin the legislature in January 1846.[27]

Charles frequently commented on his wife Eliza's ill health, which tended to keep her homebound even as he traveled widely. But in 1846, she turned the tables on him when, despite her ailments, she decided to travel with her mother. Charles did not approve: "My wife, hardly able to walk ten feet, left in the stage yesterday with her mother, for Dayton. This movement is not according either to my judgment or wishes. But as both she and her mother were resolved, it couldn't be helped." By July, Charles wrote to his mother expressing regrets that summer travel to visit family would not be possible. His daughter Sally, he explained, "is too feeble," and "I can neither spare the money which I must expend in the visit, nor that which I should lose, by my absence from my office and profession." Sally's health continued to deteriorate and in September 1846 Charles wrote again: "My dearest mother . . . It is very painful duty to announce to you, the death of our dear little child, your namesake, Sally. She died on Friday morning at ½ past 7 oclock."[28]

The family buried Sally on Sunday, precluding many family members, including Charles's mother, Sarah, from attending because of the distance. No amount of experience with the death of loved ones, nor lengthy declines, could adequately prepare parents for the loss of a child. In a letter to his mother, Charles wrote, "Eliza, who was very much distressed at this separation from her poor, afflicted babe, seems reviving, in resignation to her loss, if not in cheerfulness. But protracted as it was, the illness of Sally, was a heavy blow to her even when it comes."[29]

Meanwhile, the family had to cope with their long-surviving widowed mother. This was not without contesting voices and sibling rivalry. In July 1846, son-in-law Allen Latham wrote to Sarah Anderson giving her a general warrantee deed for a lot and house in Cincinnati, which he had purchased from William Anderson "in consideration of 440 acres of land in Union County. Sarah has received possession by delivery of keys." Instead of moving from Cincinnati to Chillicothe to be with Allen and Maria, Sarah remained in Cincinnati. The reason was simple. Sarah never moved to Chillicothe because Charles and Mary Louisa thought she was better off in Cincinnati. In September, Sarah's youngest daughter, Sarah Anderson Kendrick, wrote a plaintive note to her mother explaining that Allen Latham had provided money to bring her to Chillicothe, but "Brother Charley and Sister Lou interfered to prevent it." The contest did not end there as Sarah Kendrick brought Maria directly into the picture with her offer to move to Chillicothe: "Sister Maria says that she never felt like interfering before but that she does now that they interfered in our arrangements and now she is determined if she can to get you home." Sarah then closed what she knew would be a provocative letter with the enjoinder, "Don't show this to any person burn it up as soon as you red [sic] it, only come home and ask nothing more. Brother Allen says that you must come right away."[30]

Upon returning to the States to complete his senatorial term, Charles took Larz's advice and relocated with his family to Cincinnati in 1847 to form a partnership with Rufus King, grandson of a signer of the Declaration of Independence and personal attorney to Larz's father-in-law, Nicholas Longworth. He would remain in Cincinnati for ten years. Thanks in part to Larz's connections, Charles participated in a thriving law practice and became well connected to Cincinnati's elite social circles. Anderson correspondence in these years affords a clear illustration of the ways early American families in the West dealt with the challenges of distance and mortality to forge a closely knit extended family. It reveals as well the sophistication the Andersons assumed both at home and in travels abroad. Sibling tensions and criticisms sound remarkably modern. In many ways, the commonalities between then and now are more striking than the differences. Of these commonalities, none loomed larger than Americans at war, as Robert was again to experience.[31]

11

Robert's Mexican War

1844–1848

Not surprisingly, the cause of the Mexican War was land—first Texas, then the ultimate prize, Mexico itself.

No land appeared more immediately desirable than Mexican land to abate the unceasing American appetite for land. The campaign to acquire Mexican territory actually began with the annexation of Texas in 1845. With that, the United States took over its public lands and property, assumed its debt, and declared the Rio Grande the boundary separating the United States and Mexico. In the 1844 presidential campaign, Democratic nominee James K. Polk emerged victorious, urging annexation and statehood, while his defeated Whig opponent, Henry Clay, argued to postpone annexation to avoid war with Mexico. War did not trouble Polk, however, and with his narrow victory he moved immediately to admit Texas as a state. On January 25, 1845, the US House of Representatives approved annexation and the stage was set for certain conflict. On March 4, Polk was inaugurated president. In one stroke, 268,596 square miles of land was added to American territory, making Texas the largest state in the Union.[1]

With Polk's mandate for expansion, the way forward with both Oregon and Mexico was fixed. As a flimsy rationale for claiming Texas, Polk, like Jefferson and Jackson earlier, argued disingenuously that the Louisiana Purchase included Texas. By 1845 demography alone had determined that Americans would dominate Texas, but Polk went on to assert ownership of the vast lands of California in addition to Texas. By this time Mexico, though badly divided and weakened, could not let such a claim stand uncontested. In his war message to Congress in May 1846, Polk proclaimed falsely that "Mexico has invaded our territory," and with that, the war began, despite fierce Whig opposition.[2]

Robert Anderson found himself once again facing the call to duty. For Robert, the deepening antagonism with Mexico meant an end to garrison duty in Fort Preble, Maine, and a return to war. Family members must have complained about Robert's frequent absences from home. He closed a letter to Charles with a note to his sister explaining why he was under such pressure: "In our profession we can not, without constant application, keep pace with the European powers. You would not love me if you thought me willing to exist as a drone, and will not, must not regard my absence as caused by indifference or neglect."[3]

That the United States would "keep pace" with Europe became dramatically clear in the Mexican War. Again Robert would play a central role. Because of illnesses he incurred in the Second Seminole War and the Cherokee removal, he could have excused himself from active duty on the front lines. Instead, he declined an offer from commanding general Winfield Scott to serve on his staff behind the lines and entered the fray.

The Mexican War sprung ultimately from President Polk's ambition to build on the dubious annexation of Texas in 1845 from Mexico—following the 1836 Texas Revolution—which created the independent Republic of Texas and expanded the country's borders to the Pacific coast. The fighting extended for a year and a half, from the spring of 1846 to the fall of 1847. From the start it was an uneven contest. American forces quickly occupied New Mexico and California, and followed that with armed invasions of northern Mexico. In May 1846, General Zachary Taylor defeated the forces of General Pedro de Ampudia at Palo Alto in Texas. In this engagement, American artillery proved decisive in supporting the infantry and cavalry. At the same time, America's Pacific Squadron blockaded Mexico's coast and took several garrisons, reaching south to Baja California.[4]

WHILE DEMOCRATS APPLAUDED THE imperialistic reach of President Polk, Whig anti-imperialists bitterly opposed it, both as an unjust war and as a war that would promote the Democratic Party's embrace of slavery. Henry David Thoreau, lifelong abolitionist and rabid opponent of the Mexican War, went to jail (briefly) rather than pay taxes to fund a war he did not believe in. Given the Andersons' predominantly Whig loyalties, it must have required a supreme sense of patriotism and duty for Robert to remain in the army and participate in the war. Not for the last time would he favor duty and patriotism over contrary sentiments.

Robert's Mexican war took place within the larger war at key moments. As commander of the Third Field Artillery Regiment, Battery G, he was ordered to Mexico with instructions to participate with General Scott in the campaign for the Mexican port city of Veracruz. The company moved from Fort Moultrie in the Charleston, South Carolina, harbor to Fort Marion in St. Augustine, Florida, and then to Fort Brooke, Florida. From there it embarked for Mexico. It was at this point that Anderson began a long-running correspondence with his wife Eliza, subsequently transcribed and published by his daughter, Eba Anderson Lawton.

The couple's correspondence begins with a letter from Robert, stationed at Fort Brooke, in which he tells her the company is awaiting transport to the American-controlled coastal city of Tampico in southeastern Mexico, due north of Veracruz. Eliza was staying at her father's plantation, The Refuge, on St. Marys River in Georgia.

Robert's "3rd Arty" would contribute to an overall force of seven thousand strong under the command of General Scott. This force easily outnumbered the four thousand or so Mexican soldiers at Veracruz. All of the men eagerly awaited Scott's arrival in Tampico so that the campaign could begin. Robert was prepared for engagement but not as eager as his untested forces: "My heart leaped with pride when I saw the United States flag flying over the City of Tampico, but that pride was soon checked when I thought of the power of the United States, and the weakness of Mexico." He pursued a similar line when describing a dinner he had with one Colonel Kinney, noting, "I was rejoiced to find no animosity in his conversation towards the Mexican common people, which I expected from him as the Texas Ranger; on the contrary he concurs with me in sympathizing with them."[5]

While in Tampico, Robert promoted his vision for a literal soldier's retreat or "army asylum" of his own by taking advantage of the concentration of officers to prepare a petition to Congress. He was assisted in his efforts by General Scott, who was a tireless advocate for a veterans' retreat. When Scott returned from the Mexican War with $100,000 paid by Mexico City for sparing the city from destruction, he dedicated some of the money to his and Robert's project. Eventually the dream would come true with the founding of the Soldiers' Home in Washington, DC, in 1851. The most famous building was Anderson Cottage, named for its advocate. President Abraham Lincoln would spend one-fourth of his presidency at Anderson Cottage and would write the last draft of the Emancipation Proclamation while in residence. Anderson Cottage has remained the core building in what is today the Armed Forces Retirement Home.

Meanwhile, Robert continued to await Scott's arrival in Tampico, fearing that if he did not arrive soon to assume command, any attack on Veracruz would have to wait until October. As for Tampico, "Col. Bankhead arrived to-day. . . . We think that he will be the Milty. Governor of this place. . . . He is an old friend and favorite of Genl. Scott's." Left out of this equation was Robert himself, also a "friend and favorite" of General Scott. Robert recognized that Scott would need judicious advisers, "and prudence is always a virtue in the Staff of a man like Genl. Scott, whose indignation, though justly excited, may sometimes lead him to express himself too harshly."[6]

By February 20, Robert could finally write to Eliza, "Thank God I have at last received letters from you. . . . With what gratitude do I thank our Heavenly Father for having restored you to health. And you have suffered so severely, my poor wife. . . . I do thank God for having given us relations with hearts so warm and so true." In the same letter, he conveyed the happy news that General Scott had arrived the day before, issuing orders "naming his Staff Officers." Left out of this account was the fact that these included Robert. In his letters to Eliza, Robert repeatedly noted he was telling her things he wouldn't tell others for fear of "egotism." As well, he would invariably note the uncertainty of the mail and regret that it caused her "many bitter hours of anxiety and uneasiness."[7]

Such was the warmth of their relations that Robert wanted Eliza to literally picture him in his surroundings. On February 27, he wrote from Tampico: "Before I stop I will take you [on] a walk through the market. . . . In the first place you see the 'Flag of our Country;' it is placed on a platform intended to receive a statue of [Mexican] Genl. Santa Anna." He could not have known how soon the American flag would come to assume an unprecedented centrality in American political culture, nor how centrally involved he himself would be.

By March 5, writing onboard the steamship *Alabama*, Robert noted that his troops were "about thirteen or eighteen miles south of Vera Cruz" and eager for action. When Taylor's army bogged down in battles with General Santa Anna on February 22 and 23, Scott prevailed on Polk to land his army at Veracruz and then march overland to capture Mexico City, following a path once blazed by the conquistador Hernán Cortés.[8]

While awaiting the order to go forward, Robert engaged in a frank reflection on war and his place in it. Recognizing that Eliza would be imagining constant dangers on all sides, he ruminated, "This will, I hope, be the last war I shall take an active part in. I think after the declaration of peace I may safely promise that I will go a-soldiering no more. I think that no more absurd scheme could be invented for settling national difficulties than the one we are now engaged in—killing each other to find out who is in the right!" This would not be Robert's final war, but the sentiments help explain his subsequent behavior at Fort Sumter to do everything in his power to prevent the "absurd scheme" of war.[9]

At last, on March 12, 1847, Robert reported that American forces had landed and were camped near Veracruz. The city itself was completely invested, with mortars due to be set in position the following day. Robert being a veteran artillery officer, the behavior of the Mexican army bemused him. Instead of meeting the Americans on the beach, it had held back, throwing harmless shells at too great a distance to have any significant effect. An optimistic Robert confided that Scott had fourteen thousand "anxious" soldiers ready to attack: "'Tis true that all our heavy Ordinance has not yet arrived, but still we have enough to bring them to terms before the sickly season commences." Once the heavy ordnance was in place, Scott decided not to invade the city but to open his batteries on the castle, forcing the Mexican army to surrender while minimizing the civilian casualties that would otherwise ensue were the city invaded. Robert concluded, with pride: "This is just like him, ever instigated by the most humane and generous feelings." Still,

Robert feared "that all Genl. Scott's foresight will not be able to guard against, and prevent the perpetration of most shocking acts of brutality in the taking of the City. I shall exert my powers to the utmost to aid him in stopping such unchristian and brutal acts."[10]

Robert shared Scott's intense dislike for Polk and realized that it would likely cost him a promotion to major: "From the decided hostility evinced by President Polk to the Army, and his eager desire to secure political influence in his appointments, I have no doubt that all the exertions which might have been made by my friends would have been disregarded." For the moment, a disillusioned Robert complained, "For myself, I am becoming pretty thoroughly disgusted with the way in which the Army is treated, and care very little about remaining in it after the close of the war." Those sentiments would not last.[11]

Throughout the Mexican campaign, Robert neglected writing to his larger family, save his mother, concentrating all of his attention on Eliza. When referencing family he addressed his father-in-law in place of his own deceased father, closing many letters with "love to father and the family." Throughout his correspondence, Robert sometimes had to "cross" his letters by writing horizontally over the initial draft to conserve paper and maximize efficiency, though he used separate sheets of paper whenever possible.

As an artillery officer, Robert was increasingly preoccupied with mortar fire in an effort to compel a surrender. Despite Scott's wishes to the contrary, any heavy bombardment of the city by mortars and heavy batteries inevitably put innocents at risk. A reluctant Robert confessed: "It really goes to my heart to be compelled to do my duty when I know that every shot either injures or seriously distresses the poor inoffensive women and children, who have neither part nor lot in the War. On our side the loss in numbers is trifling."[12]

Finally, on March 27, Robert could report that the Mexican forces at Veracruz had surrendered and would be moved inland as prisoners of war. As the soldiers of the conquered army laid down their arms and marched by his company, Robert reported in customarily humble words, "I did not look at them critically or closely, as I was afraid they might detect something of triumph in my countenance, when I thought them so humiliated by their surrender that none should have been exhibited, though we could not help feeling it."[13]

While awaiting word on his artillery company's next march, Robert strolled around Veracruz looking for something "fashionable" to send to Eliza. All he encountered were sullen merchants who had raised prices to exorbitant levels out of resentment for all the shelling and destruction. In an ironic aside, Robert commented: "Never, never do I wish to be one of a besieging army again. And faith, I have no great desire to be one of the army besieged!" This latter hope would be dashed in Charleston harbor in 1860.[14]

Robert intended to go to church on Sunday, April 11, 1847, but when the day dawned he demurred due to the excessive heat. Instead, "I have therefore gone through with an hour Sunday routine of readings (reading my part distinctly and your part silently), and after a loll of an hour am now ready for the duties of the day." He later referenced "my two Sunday books," suggesting the Bible and the Episcopal *Book of Common Prayer*.[15]

On April 13, Robert's company left Veracruz for a "healthy region" in the mountains, requiring some very hard marching through deep sand. But the route soon changed, and General Scott continued on toward Mexico City by crossing the Rio Antigua. To block him, General Antonio López de Santa Anna established fortifications with twelve thousand soldiers at Cerro Gordo. Scott's leading division, of which Robert's company was a part, was commanded by General David Twiggs. A frontal assault on Santa Anna's army would have been suicidal, but earlier, Lieutenant Pierre G. T. Beauregard of the Army Corps of Engineers had determined that Santa Anna's army could be turned—a plan confirmed by Captain Robert E. Lee, who discovered a path around the Mexican left. As part of the turning force, Robert marched at 1:00 a.m. on April 17 and took a hill. Captain John B. Magruder captured Mexican guns and turned them on the retreating Mexicans. Realizing they were surrounded, the Mexicans surrendered.[16]

In describing the battle to Eliza, Anderson noted the "heavy losses" sustained at Cerro Gordo, adding, "I was not in the engagement, as by some mismanagement we were delayed, and work intended for us was done by the 2nd and 7th Infys." In a later letter he praised how "civilized" the American army had been in treating the vanquished foe humanely: "It was delightful to see our officers and men giving food and drink to the wounded, and doing all in their power to smooth the hard pillow of the dying."[17]

From Cerro Gordo, Scott moved on to Jalapa, which Robert reached on April 23, encamping for a night before marching off the next morning for Puebla. By this point, Robert could confidently proclaim: "Mexico has no Army. May it please God to end this war, and to restore me to my own beloved family." By forbidding his troops to pillage, Robert believed that he produced "a favorable result on the common people. . . . As far as I can see the laboring Mexicans care very little about the War." Though sympathetic to the Mexicans, Anderson also considered them limited, writing to Eliza in words echoing the White Man's Burden: "Poor deluded Nation—the people are not fit for self-government, and we are, perhaps, instruments intended to open this country to the world and finally to establish enlightened and free government in it. Education must first be spread among the masses, who are now ignorant and idle. . . . God grant that I may soon complete my task in this great work, and be restored to my native land and my own beloved fireside."[18]

Robert had no doubt who would carry the White Man's Burden: "Our Army will be followed by active and enterprising men, who will remain in the Country. . . . They will give a stimulus which will finally produce good results and effect great changes in the people and Country." "Active and enterprising"—that encapsulated the Anderson ethos and the spirit of the emerging colossus to the north. It can be seen in every one of the Andersons, each in his or her own way, whether the men were blazing trails in the workforce or the women were managing the home economies—in Eliza's case, literally, due to Robert's frequent absences. The pragmatic sense of destiny is palpable—and typical of a generation of American entrepreneurs who would seek to shape two continents.[19]

Robert believed in a just war with protection of innocents, but he also recognized that irregular (guerrilla) warfare on the part of the enemy could transform strategy. Hearing the rumor that the Mexican Congress was issuing commissions to guerrilla officers led him to conclude: "If they commence that species of warfare, and wage it in the cruel manner their relations did in Spain, we shall be compelled to adopt a mode of warfare totally abhorrent to our feelings and wishes. God grant that I may never be engaged in so conducting a war as to be compelled to give no quarter, to take no prisoners." If so ordered, of course, he must be prepared to respond in kind, and indeed would do so in the American Civil War, whose "guerrilla" tactics he would encounter soon enough.[20]

On May 8, Robert wrote: "Anniversary of the battle of Palo Alto, the beginning of the War. Poor Mexico, what has she not lost during the past year." Along with that came thanksgiving and piety: "Genl. Scott has ordered a spirit of conciliation to be practiced, and among other things, we should seem to evince respect for the Sabbath. I hope, without very urgent necessity, we shall have no more drills on Sunday." Sabbatarian reverence was not unusual in the military and would recur in the Civil War, when losing battles would often be attributed to the fact that they were fought on the Sabbath.[21]

Given the Protestant biases of all but the Irish Americans, and the strong strain of anti-Catholicism, Scott repeatedly issued orders to respect the Mexican churches and monasteries. He recognized that the Church could be a powerful agent for peace if it did not feel its existence threatened. Robert understood that as well, writing Eliza: "The priests must know that if the war continues much longer, there will be great danger of their churches being reduced to the level of other denominations, which will be called into existence to satisfy the wants of tens of thousands of foreigners who will be attracted from every part of Europe by the reports of the richness of their lands, the delightful temperature of their climate, presenting the palate every delicacy of the most favored climes."[22]

Robert continued to give Eliza "tours" of all the sights he had seen and the manners of the people. One woman intrigued him for the "novel way of carrying a child." It brought to mind a comparison from his earlier days in the Second Seminole War and, of course, a moral: "You see them frequently carried here as the Indians do theirs in Florida, in blankets on the back. In fact the common people here resemble our Indians so strongly in their habits, it would be easy for them to assimilate at once." And then the moral: "Education would make them good citizens. Ignorance keeps them serfs." Cathedrals also intrigued Robert, as they later would his brother William when he explored Mexico after the Civil War. In Puebla de los Ángeles Robert marveled at the art and furnishings in the cathedral, writing that "the effect is grand beyond description." Later he described attending, by invitation, a High Mass at the cathedral, which reminded him of a service he had attended in New York: "The music was very fine, not so sweetly pleasant to the ear as the vespers as we heard them sung in St. Peter's Church in New York. You remember the time."[23]

On May 29, Robert called on General Scott and could not help noticing that "the Genl. does not look very well; he is, I presume, merely suffering from the fatigue of a rapid march." At the same time, American newspaper reports of the Battle of Cerro Gordo arrived. The excessively heroic reports put Robert off and prompted him to hope for less cheering and more reporting: "I hope that Capt. R[obert E.] Lee, U.S. Engineers, will write a Military Memoir on that battle. . . . The accurate description of that battle would place the science of our Army distinctly and most creditably before European Military readers." The next day Robert dined with General Scott, "my best friend." The general was taking quinine, suggesting a fever and causing Anderson to recall his own protracted recovery from fever. He added that "the Genl. has been as kind and affectionate as ever to me, and begs me to call whenever I can. But knowing how little time he has to spare to friendly intercourse, I cannot intrude often on him." Later, he and the general attended services at the cathedral.

In response to Eliza's last letter, Robert wrote: "I am rejoiced that your dear grandmother is well again after her dangerous attack. Of our friend Lt. [William Tecumseh] Sherman we have not heard, except through the newspaper which announces his arrival in California." Sherman was indeed in California with another rising star, Henry Halleck, and so missed the war. He would be one of the very few army generals in the Civil War who had not cut his teeth in the Mexican War. Later, Robert commented favorably on the glowing reputation General Scott was gaining, adding that Eliza's father, General Clinch, "knows the Genl. as well, indeed much better than I do, and he will not be astonished that at every battle, and by every important movement, he gains warm friends."[24]

On July 4, American forces celebrated with a national salute fired at noon. A jovial Robert responded with a query: "Will they give us rockets for each of the Mexican states we have annexed?" He looked forward to the end of hostilities and seeking peace and reconciliation with Mexico. The notion of annexing Mexican land did not concern him in the least. It was, rather, a matter for humor.

By July 26, Robert was still in Puebla de los Ángeles, hoping for peace but expecting to march in a few days if it was not forthcoming: "If we have a fight near [Mexico] City, it will probably be the great battle of the Mexican War. Pride to save their Capital from our grasp, a desire to revenge their repeated disastrous defeats, will urge them to exert their powers to the utmost." The next day Robert noted, "I purchased a Catholic Bible, 1742 A.D. for brother William."[25]

Robert's hope for a rapid peace proved short-lived. Whereas talk of peace was prevalent in early July, that happy prospect "which began to lighten up a few days since, has disappeared, and that over the lovely landscape we thought we could get a glimpse of, now hangs the dark and threatening cloud of War." The Mexican Congress, he continued, "characterize our invasion as the most unjust of all aggressions." As for Robert, he had no doubt of the justness of the cause and the perfidy of the "Spanish dons." In surveying the widely dispersed American armies, he again turned to the Bible: "I begin to liken our position to that of some of the Armies whose exploits are recorded in the bible, and hope that our operations are blessed by God, whose instruments we may be, to effect some wise scheme of His providence." This same faithful hope extended to his family. After receiving a letter from Eliza filled with "apprehensions," he replied with "gratitude to our Heavenly Father. He stayed, and, I hope, has dissipated, your burning fever, and over me He has always His protecting shield. What can we do without Him? Oh! Let us never cease to praise His holy name."[26]

On August 4, Robert wrote that his regiment was poised to advance on Mexico City, with his division and two others continuing on and stragglers left behind. By Monday, August 9, Robert's company had moved eleven miles from Puebla on the road to Mexico. At that point he was personally held back from the offensive by fevers, but "I determined at all risks to join my Compy." His commanding officer, General Worth, had reconnoitered the area and determined his plan of attack. Robert's division was assigned the lead. Again there were rumors of an armistice, leading Robert to write that "the sight of a sacked City either maddens the brain, or breaks the heart of a sensitive person." Once again the rumors proved unfounded. Robert was ready to fight and receive "some bauble of honor," which he craved. Though the prospect of battle both horrified and fascinated, "still, like the gambler, he ventures o'er and o'er, even health and life itself, to win that prize."[27]

By September 6 it became apparent that the temporary truce agreed upon earlier that day by Santa Anna was not being honored, leading General Scott to warn that unless an apology arrived tomorrow for violating the truce, "our batteries will open to-morrow at 12 AM." Despite suffering from "chill and fever," Robert was determined not to be left behind: "I <u>must</u> be in the next fight." A different sort of motivation drove patriots like Robert, one that counted survival less than honor and duty, and backed up patriotic bromides with resolve.[28]

Instead of accommodating General Scott's demand for an apology, Santa Anna marshaled his army for an attack on the Americans. The next day, with battle looming, Robert drew comfort from his certainty that God was on the Americans' side, so that "we may very well hope and believe that God is sighting our battles with us, or rather for us." He then closed his letter to Eliza: "Should God spare my life, I will resume this letter the earliest moment after victory. That he may continue to guard and guide you in your path to Heaven I humbly pray."[29]

The Battle of Molino del Rey, near Mexico City, began on September 7 when a large number of Mexican horsemen were observed around several large buildings there. Scott ordered General Worth's division to attack Santa Anna's army and destroy any ordnance it came across. At 5:45 a.m. on September 8, General Worth, with Robert in command of a lead company, moved out. The assault column soon came under intense artillery fire, killing many of Worth's officers. Robert was badly wounded in the attack. With the battle's conclusion, he became faint from loss of blood and was carried behind the lines to convalesce. The surgeon's report read that Robert suffered "a gun-shot wound in the right shoulder, received at the battle of Molino del Rey, and that, in my opinion, he will not recover the use of his right arm (it being now completely disabled) for at least two or three months to come." In fact, he would never fully recover from the wound. For his bravery under fire, Anderson received a brevet promotion to major.[30]

In a letter to Eliza written on September 22, "two weeks ago since I was wounded," he described the battle and how he received his wound. He characteristically began with thanks to God: "This day two weeks ago since I was wounded. Oh how devotedly I should offer thanks to our Heavenly Father for His preservation of my life on that dreadful day." He went on to describe his place in the battle, accompanied with a diagram of the battlefield. His regiment lay prone before a building known as the "Foundry" or "El Molino del Rey." His men's exposed position would not go unnoticed: "Within two hundred yards of the Foundry, we were received with an awful shower of grape and musketry." He continued, "Thanks be to Almighty God for my preservation; the fire was more severe than I ever thought it could be in battle. For a few moments I was apprehensive that we must either be cut down or driven back, but God gave us the victory." Robert immediately sheltered his troops against a wall of the Foundry. At this point, "for example's sake [more] than anything else," he manned one of the artillery guns until other men were in position. In the same spirit that would accompany Robert later in the Civil War, he lamented a fallen colleague: "Poor Lt. Col. Graham fell, gallantly cheering his men on."

No sooner had Robert rejoined the regiment then suddenly "I felt a severe blow against my right shoulder; it was like the blow from the ball in a leaded cane." At first Robert thought it was a spent ball that fell on his shoulder, but he soon realized that, in fact, he was severely wounded from fire originating on a rooftop. But the order rang out for the Third Artillery to advance on the Foundry and "I immediately called out 'Forward 3rd Arty.' And rushed forward." Despite being rendered "a little less vigorous," Robert continued to advance on the building: "As I passed through the passageway, a ball grazed my right leg, grazing the bone outside about three inches below the knee." Soon reinforcements arrived. With the adrenaline of battle worn off, Robert "realized that I felt discomfort from my wound," and, "in a few minutes I fell." His company was "cruelly cut up." In doing the math, he noted, "Leaving Vera Cruz with nearly a hundred in its ranks, I shall now find its privates reduced by death and absentees in the hospitals, to less than thirty."[31]

In his next letter, a convalescing Robert reflected on the meaning of the victory. In the first place, it marked the conquest of Mexico City and effectively ended the war. But there was something bigger afoot, something that Americans were programmed to believe of themselves since their first settlement in the New World: "I cannot but think that we are here to carry out some great scheme of Providence." On October 4 he reported that General Scott had appointed him assistant adjutant general with the rank of major, "to enable him to select me as Chief of his Staff."[32]

While maintaining great faith in the army and his commander, General Scott, Robert frequently criticized the Polk government. He repeatedly complained that it made political decisions rather than military decisions—and decisions designed to thwart the Whig general Scott at every turn. Upon reflecting on his career after Mexico, he confided: "I cannot return to the Army whilst this administration holds the reins of power. The news of every appointment shows us their prosecution of a plan to insult and break down the spirits of our Regular Army Officers." Although Robert did not follow through and resign, his disgust with the politics of patronage remained palpable.[33]

While convalescing, Robert enjoyed daily walks with General Scott, but he despaired of hearing news of his return to the States and to Eliza. The problem, as he saw it, fell to the Mexican people, who were incapable of self-rule, so that their incompetence "will keep us here for an indefinite time." But then, out of the blue, he wrote on October 24, "Can it be that I shall be the bearer of this letter? Lt. Lay told me this morning that Genl. Scott had directed his Acting Adjt. Genl. to order me to the United States." Anderson left Mexico on October 27, 1847, with orders from Scott to recover from his wounds while serving on recruiting duty.[34]

The war ended with the Treaty of Guadalupe Hidalgo, signed on February 2, 1848. The treaty forced the Mexican cession of the territories of Arizona, California, Colorado, Nevada, Utah, Wyoming, and New Mexico in exchange for $15 million. The total compensation was paltry even by American standards, as millions of acres were available for pennies each.

But millions of acres of conquered land did not bring the peace and prosperity that Polk had hoped for. America's greed and rapacity for land would ensure that the slavery question would not die, tied as it was to the nature of the expansion, but be transformed into a national debate that would lead to civil war. As in every other land grab, the acquisition of additional territories merely heightened anxieties and tempers. With every newly acquired territory and eventual state, the vexed question of slave or free emerged to torture American politics and drive the nation ever nearer to disunion. Robert would soon find himself at the center of the storm, which would temporarily render him the most famous man in America.

12

Andersons at Home

1848–1856

The war with Mexico had not preoccupied the Anderson family, though Robert's intimate involvement in it must certainly have engendered fears for his welfare until he was sent east. The day-to-day concerns of the extended family, on the other hand, seem to have claimed a significant amount of members' time and energy. The focus of attention in Anderson lives and correspondence concentrated on cementing careers, protecting wealth acquired from land, and bringing the next generation into responsible adulthood—and inheritances of their own.

With the exception of Robert, family members were settled into raising families, furthering their careers, and establishing stable households. The surviving children born to Richard Sr. and Betsy were now in their fifties. Of the children born to Richard Sr. and Sarah, Larz, Robert, and William were in their early forties, while Charles, John Roy, and Mary were in their thirties. Only Sarah, at age twenty-six, had not reached thirty. Despite his role as the new patriarch, letters to and from Larz are far less numerous than surviving letters from his siblings. In part this relative paucity of letters to and from Larz reflects the uneven preservation of family letters, and in part it reflects Larz's lack of official public correspondence from politicians Richard Jr. and Charles, or the military correspondence of Robert. The greatest volume of correspondence and diary entries are William's.

Richard Sr. and his two wives modeled the child-rearing practices that their children would emulate in their own homes. Physical punishment with a switch was a generally accepted mode of discipline. Love was dispensed in bountiful qualities, along with great expectations for success and distinction. The correspondence and diaries leave no evidence of withheld love or denigration. The goal of child-rearing was to instill middle-class habits of industry, responsibility, and love.

Soldier's Retreat remained the symbolic representation of the Anderson household. Though no family members purchased the property when it became available for sale in 1847, it loomed central in their shared memories. Soldier's Retreat was simultaneously a home, farm, and retreat for numerous veterans who visited and enjoyed the colonel's famous hospitality. It stood for wealth, independence, and the rising West. That "West" was never intended to be a "wild West" but a domesticated West that retained and emulated eastern elite life. Above all else, Soldier's Retreat stood for family. In his never-completed memoir of life at his childhood home, Charles described the grandeur of the mansion with its sixteen rooms, including a ballroom for weekly dances, often accompanied by Richard Sr. and his Stradivarius violin.[1]

By the time Charles penned his memoir, the grandeur of Soldier's Retreat was only a memory. In a letter to his mother, Charles captured a poignant moment of nostalgia when he visited Soldier's Retreat and found disarray and neglect: "We found the graves of our family utterly buried in briars and other brush. . . . The place of their rest, seems to me now, a minor question. The state in which affectionate attention is apathetic and neglect may preserve or desert them, is a far more tender and touching subject."

The physical state of affairs brought to the surface memories of another time that was lost but not forgotten:

All else is changed—oh! How sadly changed. And yet, there were glimpses, pregnant and precious, as Eve's remembering of paradise, of my childhood's house, smiles of my sunlit—morning—life, glaring through the sadness of change and the deeper gloom of neglect and decay! A strange circumstance overwhelmed me with grief. I passed the place of the old monumental poplar—the styles—the May cherry tree. Saw the substituted evergreen of the lane and yard;

the altered aspect of the walls of the house and door steps. I observed all these changes with but a general and undefined sense of melancholy.

In profound ways, Soldier's Retreat had defined all of the Andersons' sense of position and place. When he visited his old homestead, Charles was dismayed by the owners' complete disregard of the property. While Charles may have felt "melancholy" at the dilapidated state of the homestead, it was a melancholy infused with overwhelming nostalgia for the place and the parents who did so much to shape the family's collective identity.[2]

By the 1830s the process of child-rearing in America had largely been delegated to mothers or other female family members. This included discipline. In a letter to his mother and his sister Maria, Charles instructed them in properly disciplining his son, "Master William," during his absence. "Chastisements," he wrote, were "indispensable." Accordingly, "I remit their discipline to you, trusting that you will so far revive your earlier habits, as to try your hand. . . . I think too dear mother, that, as he is said to resemble his father very much, it must be very natural for you to whip him often and hard. . . . I fear, the same looks in both must be token similar deservings in each." Though discipline was necessary, it did not necessarily come easily to women whose instincts centered on affection rather than discipline. Maternal love came more naturally, even as the female had replaced the male in the social dynamics of child-rearing. On this key, Charles concluded his letter of instruction: "If he is a very good boy, pray let him sometimes visit his Uncle William and John."[3]

There are few surviving letters from children describing their world. But one letter from Ann Logan's daughter Catherine to her aunt Maria Latham, revealing a young girl's preoccupation with her social life, suggests that earlier "frontier" concerns that focused on creating a haven in a hostile environment had largely been supplanted:

Parties are generally uppermost in young girls minds—they are in mine and I am sure I involuntarily turn in that direction when I write a letter. I was at a small one on last Tuesday evening. . . . There was but eight ladies and ten gentlemen there, but it was very agreeable notwithstanding. . . . I was not very well and had to wear long sleeves, and had but one dress of my own . . . and it had worn a good many times. . . . I accepted the offer of Aunt Eliza to lend me her black silk and you may depend upon it was tight. Uncle had to squeeze me in to make it meet, while Mary Ann hooked it.

Religion also occupied her attention, in particular, a Methodist revival: "I suppose you have heard of the great revival in the Methodist church here, upwards of three hundred persons have joined."[4]

Childless families were rare in the West, but they did happen—not necessarily a welcome outcome in a culture whose "social security" depended largely on the family network over generations. The evidence points away from conscious birth control to infertility. In a letter to Maria Latham that her childhood friend Mary Sibley wrote from Linden Wood, where her husband, Major Langdon Sibley, was an Indian agent stationed at Fort Osage, she shared the fact that "Langdon tells me you have no children, in that we are alike. I have never had any. I am bringing up some orphan children but not as adopted children. I am happy to hear that the Lord has prospered your house and that you have much of this world's wealth." Unspoken here may be the thought that wealth was in some sense compensation for childlessness. Mary seems at pains to emphasize further compensations in her next remark. "As you are not encumbered with young children why can you not come over and make me a visit?"[5]

Another indication of the evolving ethos of the new nation was increased attention to its own history. Soon after Charles arrived in Cincinnati in 1847, he received a letter from the historian Lyman Draper, secretary of the Wisconsin Historical Society, describing a biography of George Rogers Clark that he was writing and wanting information on Clark's friend and brother-in-law Colonel Anderson. Apparently brother William had been approached and never replied to Draper's request:

If you, too, are not indifferent to your father's memory—and I am sure you are not—I shall hope for better things of you. . . . Let me know as well as you can, when and where your father was born—his ancestors—whether he was engaged in public life before the

Revolution—in what battles he fought and the date of his death—
when he settled at Chillicothe—whether he heard the news of your
brother's death . . . before his own departure, and whether that event
hastened his own?—and whether, too, the wound he suffered at Savannah troubled him in after life?

Draper's questions revealed specific knowledge of Anderson's life in the
Revolution, but little else. He was mistaken in locating Anderson Sr.
in Chillicothe, but not in inquiring about Anderson's wound, which
indeed did "trouble" him and led to his death soon after the unrelated
news of his son's demise.[6]

Property became increasingly important not only for settlement
and the accumulation of wealth but also for the multiplying of the institutions intrinsic to building a coherent and civilized nation. The family
continued to find common cause in acquiring domestic land. Men who
married into the family, such as Allen Latham and Andrew Kendrick,
worked closely with the brothers to survey and speculate. Included in
Latham's investments was a military land warrant originally invested
with naval hero John Paul Jones, acquired from Robert Bagby in 1849.
In April 1850, Charles wrote to Kendrick from Cincinnati on the subject of land: "I am going to sell my lots again at Auction on the 1st of
May. I will be obliged to you therefore if you will send me my plat or
plats of them, which you say I sent you."[7]

Charles owned land in Louisville, Kentucky, and in 1849 he received a letter from J. McMichael asking whether he would sell some of
it for a new church. Charles later reported in a letter to William that he
sold the lot to a Lutheran church. In the same letter, Charles referenced
a recent trip to Washington and highlighted his visit with boyhood
friend Zachary Taylor, recently inaugurated president: "At Washington,
and became quite encouraged by Old Zack and his family." Though politically inexperienced, Taylor had run as a Whig and won the election
largely on his popularity as a war hero.[8]

Charles told his sister Maria of the visit as well: "I have this moment returned from the President's House, where I have gotten upon
a very easy footing. He treated me with great kindness." Charles then
went on to describe his own ambitions for political office or a major
administrative appointment, perhaps with brother Richard Jr. in mind:

"I <u>cannot</u>, of course, under any circumstances, mention <u>my</u> ambition. He would think me very selfish, if I did, <u>at least</u>. . . . I am vain enough to believe I shall obtain high offices. At all events, I know I should have <u>your</u> vote and that of several other sisters. Good night, dear Sister, Minister or no Minister, I can pray for blessings of love upon you, with a sincere heart."[9]

President Taylor, meanwhile, had little time to consider the possible ambitions of his old friend. No sooner was Taylor in office than he alienated himself from southern Whigs by not pushing for the expansion of slavery, even as antislavery northern Whigs clung to him. Before he could act on the issue, he died of acute gastroenteritis on July 9, 1850, four months after his inauguration. Millard Fillmore succeeded him, and between the two of them, they did more to wreck the Whig Party than any Democrats could do. Their combined ineptitude and stubbornness was a direct precursor to the Compromise of 1850, engineered by Henry Clay, whereby California would be admitted to the Union as a free state, Washington, DC, would retain slavery, and the slave trade would be banned. Most controversially, the Compromise included the Fugitive Slave Act, forcing the North to return runaway slaves. Despite strident northern criticism, the laws passed, thus defusing, for the moment, sectional tensions that threatened to derail the Union.[10]

While raising his own family and engaging in his new Cincinnati law practice, Charles continued to maintain his mother in Dayton, where she had moved to be with him before he moved to Cincinnati. Other family members disapproved. In spring 1849, Sarah wrote her mother in life-and-death terms, urging her to join the family in Chillicothe. She was not pleased with where the elder Sarah was living in Dayton and raised a frightening specter: "I am very much afraid that you will take the cholera and die. Sister Eliza has been very much worse since you left but she was better yesterday. She says that she suffers from want of nourishment, that there is no one there to think of any thing nice for her to eat and that she cannot think herself." She closed with yet more pressure to escape the cholera, noting that brother John Roy would be traveling and "you had better come home with him."[11]

As always, family transmittals catalogued the wild swings of emotion that could not be evaded in the uncertain circumstances of mid-nineteenth-century America. In a letter written to his mother on March

9, 1848, Charles could scarcely contain his ebullient prose: "My beloved Mother, How constantly and rapidly are you becoming a grand mother to others. . . . My wife has another daughter—born at ½ past eleven this day, fat, pretty no—<u>beautiful</u> (I know you think that impossible) still, I say beautiful with black hair."[12]

But not even a year later the joy turned to mourning: "Dearest Mother, My Mary is dead. Oh! Think how afflicted how crushed I am? Thus to lose my little <u>favorite</u> my sweetest, best and prettiest child—so suddenly and unexpectedly—utterly overwhelms me. . . . Mother, My Mary is dead! Your affectionate son." Charles speculated that the cause of death was scarlet fever and took some consolation from the fact that she did not suffer long.[13]

In July 1849 Charles had more sad news to convey, this time regarding Larz and Kate's recent loss: "It is my painful duty, again, to announce to you, sad intelligence. We have lost another sweet little grand daughter! Larz and Kate must now endure the grieving suffering . . . which Eliza and I suffered." The toll on the family was heavy, especially the parents: "Poor Kate is, of course, sadly, bitterly grieved at the loss. It was her only girl. . . . Our dear Larz too had become deeply interested in her and devotedly fond of her, and, therefore, suffers very much."[14]

Charles also continued to be concerned over his war-hero brother Robert, who still suffered from the two wounds he'd received in a war whose purpose he did not believe in. Robert and wife Eliza had moved into a house inside Fort Preble, Maine, where he was stationed. In a letter to his sister Sarah, Robert confided that Eliza could not write, and she was "thus nearly deprived of one of her greatest pleasures and unfortunately I have not always leisure at my disposal, to allow me to act as her amaneucies, so that by a seemingly unpardonable neglect, she gives umbrage to, and loses, many valued correspondents." It is not clear why Eliza could not write, nor is it clear who served as her amanuensis, if anyone. But a determined Robert closed with the note, "I shall teach little Eba to write, as soon as practicable, so that she can assist her darling mother."[15]

Robert's disapproval of the war with Mexico compelled Charles to think twice about the highly vaunted doctrine of Manifest Destiny, which Richard Jr. had championed. Always in demand as a public speaker, Charles directly addressed the subject of America's self-proclaimed providential destiny in several lectures. One especially important speech, entitled "An Address on the Anglo-Saxon Destiny," was delivered before the Philomathesian Society of Kenyon College in August 1849. In that lecture Anderson addressed the "conceit" of Manifest Destiny that infected so many nations, including America. All of the European pretenders to supremacy were "sunk . . . rapidly and deeply, into the very abyss of oblivion." He then asked: "What shall henceforward be the actual destiny of our race?" His rhetorical question did not lead to cheerleading: "We cannot pretend to claim for it, either now or heretofore, higher power, or brighter glory, than those nations and races had all attained; shall we meet a different fate? If we continue in their courses of ambitious conquest—shall we not, also, reach that invariable goal, to which ambition has ever led?" Then, invoking a phrase from John Quincy Adams, he asked: "Has our star of empire yet culminated to its zenith? And is its course still higher, still onward? Or, is it already following in the descending track of preceding races and nations, and 'riding down the western sky,' to be, in its turn, quenched in an everlasting night of darkness and gloom?" Charles's speech reveals deep ambiguity about America's destiny in the world. He remained intensely nationalistic, but he was also concerned about the nation's relentless expansion.[16]

Charles's Kenyon address was the greatest of many outstanding orations he delivered in his storied career as politician and public speaker. Piece by piece, Charles relentlessly demolished the logic on which his brother and President John Quincy Adams had made their case. First, he pointed out correctly, the very notion of an Anglo-Saxon "race" was a lie. There was no such race. American stock, he countered, was "mongrel and heterogeneous." With no such thing as an Anglo-Saxon race, the jingoistic conclusions drawn from the concept were equally preposterous. Chief of these conceits was the idea of special divine favor as a "New Israel" that, like Israel of old, could take what it wanted with no accountability. Drawing on the Bible (which, personally, he did not embrace), Charles claimed God had no divine favorites. If some races and nations assumed dominance, it was less a question of divine preference than natural advantage. "Even" blacks, he asserted to widespread derision (including that of his brother Larz), might someday achieve as much as whites, given comparable advantages.[17]

From his travels, Charles wrote home in ways both admonishing and loving. In a September letter to Eliza, who was in Dayton with family, he expressed frustration: "Dear Wife, What is the matter with you and [son] Latham? Your tardiness in correspondence has spoiled me entirely. I am quite uneasy now, if I do not receive a letter every other day. And I have now been a week without a word from Dayton." Apparently it did not dawn on him that Eliza was preoccupied with the work that both of them should have been doing, while she was alone at home. Then, in a note that surely would have generated marital anxiety, he confided: "I went on Sunday and stayed all night at Warfields who resides in Kentucky. Some how or other I maintain a great fancy for that woman. . . . Elizabeth Breckenridge too is a much better and more interesting girl than she has credit for."[18]

Larz was also in Cincinnati when in February 1850 he wrote his well-connected friend Orlando Peterson with some advice on what was arguably the most famous sculpture in mid-nineteenth-century America. The artist, Hiram Powers, first came to the Andersons' attention in 1829 as a young sculptor of wax figures, whom brother Charles commissioned when a student at Miami College to create a bust of college president Robert Hamilton Bishop. He came to the attention of Larz's affluent father-in-law, Nicholas Longworth, as well. Longworth was so impressed with Powers that he sent him to Washington to secure portraits of Daniel Webster, John Calhoun, John Marshall, and Andrew Jackson. The two became friends and Longworth became Powers's patron, as well as the patron of another great American artist, Benjamin West. With Longworth's patronage, Powers moved to Florence, established a studio, and soon came to the attention of European artists.[19]

Powers's most famous creation, a marble sculpture entitled *The Greek Slave*, received the highest award at the London exposition at the Crystal Palace in 1851—a first for an American artist. When viewed in America, many saw a nude statue for the first time. Over one hundred thousand flocked to view it, with men and women segregated. The statue later became a potent symbol of the abolitionist movement. In all, Powers carved six marble statues of *The Greek Slave*, one of which was acquired by Longworth, which brought it into the Anderson domain. Longworth opened his mansion, the Taft House (now the Taft Museum of Art) to allow public viewings. In a letter to Peterson, Larz crowed: "The Greek

Slave came among us. . . . She is with us and submissively awaiting your commands. If, however, you are still in love with her—if you still yearn to possess and feed on her beauty without rivalry—if you feel that you must have her, or be miserable Why then resign your official servitude at once, hasten hither and I pledge myself to do all that men can do to have you appointed her—keeper! What say you? Shall I commence making interest for you?" It is not clear whether Larz ever lent the sculpture to his friend, but the evident joy that he gained in its acquisition testified to his and Kate's status in Cincinnati society.[20]

Increasingly, issues of status had play even within the family. In a letter to sister Elizabeth, a preening Charles declared: "Did you know that Wm. and Eliza had named their baby after me? I never heard of it, until last night, when Mrs. Mansfield told me he's my namesake." Charles himself would name yet another Anderson that year. As he wrote to "my beloved mother, You have once more a grand daughter— born in 10 minutes. It is large and fat—Mother and child seem well." But sad experience taught him not to be too ebullient: "I add no word since I know not whether it be a subject for joy or grief. Nevertheless, affectionately your son Charles."[21]

Charles maintained a multifaceted relationship with his mother that may in part explain his insistence on controlling where and how she lived. On September 8, 1851, Charles wrote from Cincinnati: "My beloved mother, below and enclosed you find, a certificate of deposit for $300 the amount (as I suppose of your pension due). I also send, to save some trouble, a blank form for the necessary affidavit, hereafter."[22]

Sarah would survive until 1854, but her health was precarious and, already in 1852, Charles and other family members were thinking of an appropriate memorial for her. A "set of proposals" from sister Elizabeth included a separate memorial for her in the family burial ground at Soldier's Retreat. Even though Soldier's Retreat had been sold outside the family, they were able to continue burying family members there. Charles checked with other family members and replied to Elizabeth: "But you may not be aware that where the present monument was designed, it was intended for mother as well as for father. And a side and spaces with blanks were left for her memorial also. I consulted with her on the subject and she told me that she desired to be buried at Soldier's Retreat. . . . We all agree, therefore, that a separate monument would be out of place and do not doubt that you will agree with us, when advised of these facts."[23]

The land that had given such joy in life would be her final resting place. Given its state of disarray, however, Charles proposed to take up a collection among family members and then go to the still-surviving family gravesite at Soldier's Retreat to commission a "firming up of the base of the monument . . . putting a top to it, planting roses and flowers etc as soon as the ground thaws in the spring. This I will do myself as a task of love and duty." Charles was gratified at the generous support from all the family members toward their matriarch: "I had never presumed to pressure upon the generous and affectionate disposition of you all . . . upon that pious regard which we ought all to have for the simplest wish of our departed mother. You do not know my dearest sister, how proud I felt when I received your letter proposing the remittance of these claims and where the brothers-in-law as well so heartfully gave their cheerful consent." He closed on a note of familial pride: "I did not feel that we were equals of our mother in disinterested, self-sacrificing generosity. But I did feel elated at the thought that we were all like her." The close family bonds persisted in the new generation. Charles closed the letter by noting his son Latham had followed in the steps of his uncle Robert and was a cadet at West Point, adding, "He is anxious to hear from you."[24]

A year later the monument restoration was complete, and Charles wrote his brother-in-law Allen Latham to acknowledge receipt of $330 to cover expenses: "We still get confirmations of the favorable respect of beauty and solidity. And I hope we shall feel proud of it when we see it ourselves. Besides, I thank you for your generous contribution towards it." Family members could indeed take pride in the way they followed in the steps of the founders. Clearly they aspired to be a rising dynasty.

NOT ONLY FAMILY TIES endured. In a letter to Allen Latham from Jackson, Kentucky, where there were significant coal deposits, Charles sought advice on speculating, this time not in land but in coal: "The school section it is said is for sale having been appraised at $5 per acre." It could be good for speculation. "My informant thought the coal good, but adjudged the marble to be soft. Write if you want the school section bought and what you think of the . . . coal mining." A key consideration in Charles's mind was the incoming railroad. "Speculation not a sure but a probable thing. Does this view of things alter your purposes?"[25]

By 1850, William was still involved in the McArthur estate, though no longer as executor, and deeply committed to his newfound Catholicism. In September, Richard Sr.'s fellow surveyor Henry Massie wrote to William on the absurd claims coming in for the McArthur estate. One in particular galled him: "The claim set up by Mr. Stokes is so preposterous, that I hardly think it worthy of notice. . . . It is really annoying to have absurd claims set up like this, but we see strange things take place every day."[26]

William had probably lived to regret his decision to engage the McArthur estate. Not so his religious conversion. The church was of far greater interest and reward for William. His correspondence contains numerous letters from priests. In September 1850, Bishop Henry Juncker wrote an affectionate letter with advice on William's son Thomas, recommending a Catholic college with a view toward turning William's eldest son into a priest: "The college in Missouri should be in my opinion the best for him, true valid knowledge and piety will go together. . . . I know Mrs. Anderson neither of you has any objection should he wish to become a priest after having finished his studies—everything is very cheap." When it came to Thomas, William and Bishop Juncker could not have been more misguided. Not only would Thomas show no interest in becoming a priest, but more dramatically, he would bitterly disavow the entire church.[27]

But William's faith burned bright. In March of 1851 he received a letter from Robert, who was still stationed at Fort Preble, Maine, and must have felt certain of William's interest in a meeting with the famous Catholic convert Orestes Brownson: "By the bye, I had the pleasure of seeing last week a man who has become somewhat famous in the theological literary world—Dr. Orestes Brownson called on me last week with the Catholic Priest of Portland. I had not much conversation with him but he is rather a remarkable looking man. You know his history or enough of it to know that he wields a powerful pen on any side of a question he may chance to advocate." Robert himself had probably read of Brownson. His reference to wielding a "powerful pen" echoes how Brownson described himself in the preface to his conversion narrative.[28]

William most certainly knew of Orestes Brownson, as the two had followed similar odysseys. Both had converted to the Catholic Church from Protestantism. Unlike William, Brownson was an internationally known public intellectual whose writings on philosophical theology reached wide audiences. But in temperament the two were similar— feisty and given to fierce debates that got them in trouble. Both, having found their home in the Catholic Church, never left for other pastures. While William published no theological musings, he ruminated constantly in notebooks and letters on the divine harmony he came to see between the natural and the supernatural. Even as science was moving steadily away from religious avowals of the supernatural world and toward scientific infidelity, Brownson and William were compelled to reunite the two and ascribe primacy to revelation and the miraculous. Both strenuously denied that the end of existence was natural and asserted instead that God created man for a supernatural end. To their dying days they repudiated the philosophical trinity of pantheism, naturalism, and absolute rationalism. Both agreed with the Syllabus of Errors articulated in Pius IX's encyclical, which condemned eighty heresies, including modernism and moral relativism. And both enjoyed the close friendships of bishops and clergy.

In January 1852, William received word from John Lampkin Taylor, Whig congressman from Chillicothe, on his possible appointment as minister to Rome. Taylor had lobbied with Secretary of State Daniel Webster to exert his influence with President Millard Fillmore, and learned that Webster would talk with the president if it became apparent that the current minister, Lewis Cass, would be recalled. In the same month, Robert weighed in, in typical Anderson fashion, on the question of the appointment. In the first place, he questioned whether William had the diplomatic skills for such a position, noting that younger brother Charles had far better skills for such a post (irrelevant, of course, since only William was a Roman Catholic). Then Robert added an economic consideration. Most diplomats were wealthy: "As you desire to go to the Eternal City, I should be most happy to see you settled for that position, but my advice would be for you to Americanize and to devote your undivided attention to your [current] office and your own affairs until you lay by a stock of [funds] sufficient to enable you when you desire it, to go abroad either on Govt. business or for your own pleasure." As it happened, William did not receive the coveted invitation, and the conversation withered.[29]

In the years preceding, William and Eliza had celebrated the birth of a daughter, Mary, in 1846, and in 1850, the birth of son, Charles, named for William's younger brother. In 1853, William and family moved from Chillicothe to Circleville, Ohio, eventually settling down at Seven Oaks Farm in Pickaway County. The farm was part of a two-thousand-acre gift that Eliza received from her father, Duncan McArthur. The farm got its name from seven trees that grew from a single oak acorn. Eliza lived only two years on the farm before dying in 1855. William would remain until his death.

Law and farming did not satisfy William, but he managed nevertheless to prosper with his two farms and lands. To a greater extent than anyone else in the family, he was a self-taught intellectual, reveling in the study of theology, science, and the arts. His 154-volume personal library contained works in history, philosophy, the classics, literature, and languages. He purchased few scientific works but became well informed on ornithology, botany, horticulture, and floriculture. His intellectual curiosity also carried him to the study of art and the exploration of archeological digs, where he pursued original research into the Mound Builders of Ohio. All of these interests appeared in his correspondence, but none more than religion. He was, in a word, fanatical on the subject of his Catholic faith, a sentiment shared by his second wife, Ellen Columba Ryan Anderson, whom he would marry in 1857.

William found time, in the midst of all this intellectual activity, to manage the legal and financial matters of the Archdiocese of Cincinnati with his brother Larz, and to represent his brother Robert's interests in various property investments. In turn, Robert sought his advice on land: "Mr. Mapie advised me by all means to keep this land, as he says that if I do not want the money, the land must improve in value for some time. I am not in want of the money, but think that an excellent offer might not be lightly rejected." Robert went on to complain that family communications were breaking down. William himself was not exempt, leading Robert to exclaim: "Aren't you a businessman? About six weeks have passed since I enclosed you a check for some of the money to enable you to help my house out of the mire, and you have not noticed it in any way. . . . I am a little interested in the matter too, for if the draft has been miscarried or lost, it behooves me to know it that I may at once give notice of that fact and have the payment thereof stopped." He then went on to complain that "the name even of my new nephew is not communicated. . . . Larz and Charles have become as uncertain in their correspondence as you are." The cause of Robert's displeasure is not clear, but it went back at least to his letter to Maria Latham announcing his engagement and forbidding her to mention it to her brothers.[30]

In June 1852, Charles attended the national Whig convention to support the nomination of Robert's close friend, General Winfield Scott. He was called upon to address the convention, which he did with a ringing endorsement of the general. Scott did indeed win the nomination, but the Whig Party was done, crashing on the shoals of sectional discord and slavery. To compound the sense of loss, family friend and Whig standard-bearer, Henry Clay, died of tuberculosis the same month. Charles addressed the memorial service, issuing a moving eulogy to his hero. With Clay's demise and the Whig crash, Charles would become an independent, refusing to join either party and endorsing no one.[31]

But if Charles was done with political parties, he was by no means done with politics, nor his flourishing social and professional life in Cincinnati, made possible through his connections to Larz and the Longworth family. By then, Larz no longer practiced law, concentrating all his efforts on managing Longworth's estate, valued at some $15 million. In 1854, Charles moved into a palatial new house close to Longworth's Taft House in the center of the city. He participated in its design, drawing inspiration from his European tour. Under Charles's direction, the architect designed the house on the model of an Italian villa. When completed, the house impressed guests with its tasteful design and creative architecture. In effect, Charles created a place reminiscent (in graciousness if not design) of his boyhood home at Soldier's Retreat.[32]

Yet not all of life among the Andersons centered on work, politics, or religion. Vacations, not a common occurrence in early-nineteenth-century American society among the working class, signaled the achievement of middle-class status. They remained elite preoccupations and afforded extended time away from home for pleasure and healing in elaborate spas and European getaways. Europe had its titled aristocrats, but America offered its own middle-class pretensions to wealth and status.[33] The Andersons, though from the "West," joined that middle-class elite and enjoyed vacations for pleasure and health, traveling, and touring both throughout the United States and abroad. In short, they absorbed the cultural habits and pursuits of the American elite. The basis for status was land. Only later in the nineteenth century would vacationing become democratized to include the working class.

In the summer of 1854, Charles embarked on a trip east that concluded with a stay in "that great London of America—New York." He noted the beauty of Sandusky Bay in northern Ohio as they traveled in "the finest boat propelled by the finest [steam] engines I ever saw." All of this was prelude to the grandest sight of all: "Then—then *the* Falls. How in the world any body could be disappointed at the first sight of them . . . I can't imagine." Charles concluded his trip with a visit to his son Latham at West Point and was equally impressed with the campus and setting along the Hudson River.[34]

Though no longer in public affairs, Charles felt deeply concerned over the national political scene and his own state's gubernatorial election in the autumn of 1855. The passage of Illinois senator Stephen A. Douglas's Kansas-Nebraska Act in 1854 effectively nullified Clay's Missouri Compromise in favor of a doctrine of "popular sovereignty." By leaving the question of slavery in territories open to popular opinion, slavery could be approved in all territories. Opposition to popular sovereignty appeared in the newly founded anti-Douglas and abolitionist Free-Soil Party, which put forward Salmon P. Chase for governor. An unhappy Charles condemned the Free-Soil Party and endorsed the Know-Nothing Party candidate, former governor Allen Trimble, a rabid racist and rabble-rouser. Continuing his maddeningly unpredictable political zigzag, Charles broke ranks with other former Whigs in the presidential election of 1856 and endorsed the ultimately victorious Democrat James Buchanan, all the while insisting he was no Democrat. But clearly neither was he a Republican, as many former Whigs and Free-Soilers now were. Should California senator John C. Fremont win on the antislavery Republican ticket, Charles feared, the Union would be dissolved, with war or secession as the result.[35]

In an omen of what was to come, the South virtually ignored the Republican Party, even as it recognized it could not prevent a Republican victory in future elections. A disgusted Larz railed against the failed Whig policies that led to the party's destruction, complaining that "the Whigs of Kentucky do not see how utterly illogical their recent course has been." His son Nick, then a student at Harvard, shared his views in a letter to his mother: "If [Salmon] Chase (the black, base, villainous abolitionist) is elected, the third state in the Union is disgraced; if [Allen] Trimble, the noble, old veteran, has succeeded and will occupy the gubernatorial chair again, Ohio is honored forever."[36]

As the presidential election loomed, William faced other, more pressing considerations. He had lost his wife to fever the year before and feared the loss of his son to unbelief. In April 1856, William received a letter from Archbishop John Purcell offering condolences for the death of Eliza, assuring William that "your love for your wife will be acknowledged and rewarded by her love for God." Six months later, William received another letter on very different subjects, namely the McArthur estate, politics, and the state of son Thomas's soul. Purcell referenced the "charitable purposes" of the estate and recommended that it be divided "part to the church of St. Mary, Chillicothe and part to the St. Peter's asylum." As for national politics, he made no partisan comment except to say, "We are as you may imagine, in the midst of the 'latest' kind of political excitement just now."

Purcell then turned to Thomas's religious state with a grim assessment from Thomas's parish priests. After noting that Thomas had gone to Portsmouth, Ohio, he added: "He makes himself very unamiable and ever disagreeable by his arrogance in introducing and seeking to obtrude upon topics in which he sets their judgment and even that of the church at defiance." Purcell then closed with fear for Thomas's soul, "lest he fall away from the true faith whose safeguards alone can preserve him from ruin. But age I hope will change him." For someone who dearly wished his son would enter the priesthood, this must have been extraordinarily difficult to hear. William would later abandon hopes for Thomas's soul and hope for better with his third son, Robert Marshall, who would be born to Ellen and William in 1862. Robert was deeply pious and would go on to attend Notre Dame University in 1883, after his father's death, but his chosen vocation would be engineering, not the priesthood.[37]

Though William was grieving the loss of Eliza, Bishop John Carrell soon introduced him to the deeply pious prodigy Ellen Columba

Ryan. Considered a beautiful woman, Ellen came to America with her parents and sister Frances (Fanny) from Londonderry, Ireland, in 1833 at the age of nine. The family settled on a farm near Urbana, Illinois, and Ellen distinguished herself as a young woman of alert mind. She and her sister were educated at the Nazareth Convent in Kentucky and at Sacred Heart in New Orleans and traveled extensively in the United States and Europe. Smitten with the young Ryan, William pursued her affections, and they were married on April 21, 1857. William was fifty years old and Ellen was thirty-three. Not unlike many Anderson in-laws, by the time of their marriage she had already inherited a sizable fortune from her father and uncle.

Charles's hopes resided in political connections, as volatile as they were. He trusted that his support for Buchanan would land him a cushy diplomatic appointment, preferably to Berlin or Naples, and went so far as to travel to DC to lobby for a successful outcome. But by then his principled and unpredictable stands had won him no strong following in any party, and the desired diplomatic assignments went to the party faithful.

While Charles was pursuing foreign postings, Larz was again taken up with land sales. In a letter to attorney Daniel Gregg, Larz discussed a portion of his land that had apparently been settled and improved upon by a squatter:

> My notion of the short time required to dispose of the land, arose from the offers which had been made for it and the opinion, expressed by Mr. Salthame, of its probable value from Mr. Stipp's representation of it. I leave the sale, however, entirely to your discretion. As to the improvements, I would rather pay for them . . . at a fair price than get possession without pay—whether they are, in strict law, entitled to pay or not. If you can settle with them on reasonable terms you may do so at once and draw on me for the required amount.

There was an ambiguous place for squatters in American property, and Larz's letter confirms that goodwill could exist between squatters and landowners.[38]

In Cincinnati, Larz continued to explore his own options for land. In a letter to Daniel Gregg, he gave him power of attorney with instructions to settle lands of his that had been acquired in Iowa. He authorized Gregg, if necessary, to evict the squatters, but in a humane fashion: "I have no objection to suit being brought against the occupant of my land. . . . I do not wish to eject them, without giving them something for the improvements they may have made upon the land." Larz's interest in Iowa land paralleled that of many other Ohio speculators, most notably his father-in-law, Longworth, who jumped from one frontier to the next on the heels of surveyors and land officers. Some of these gambles yielded spectacular returns, while others were in time losing propositions.[39]

Throughout 1855 and 1856, Robert employed Gregg to help him handle land warrants that went back to the Virginia Military District and land he inherited from his father: "Whereas Entry no. 2405 for 100 acres (in the Virginia Military District of Ohio) founded upon Virginia Military continental Land Warrant No 4493 for 100 acres was set off to me in generalty as one of the heirs of my father late Colonel Richard C. Anderson decd . . . I do hereby assign and convey Daniel Gregg . . . and request that surveys be recorded in his name and patents be issued to him or his assigns." These instructions confirm the mechanism by which land warrants surveyed and owned by Richard Clough Anderson Sr. were passed on to the children. In addition to assigning Gregg to be his representative, Robert's letter contained an official sealed document from May 1856 by Allen Latham and John R. Anderson, confirming that Robert Anderson "is son and heir at law of the late Col. Richard Clough Anderson and as such entitled to all the right and property in said Warrant."[40]

By 1856, Larz was well aware of William's son Thomas's hostility to the Church, and he wrote William a letter intended to reassure the father. It would appear that Larz was responding to William's concern regarding Thomas's questioning of religious belief, which began early and, William feared, could become a permanent condition. To this Larz commented: "I believe him safe in his principles . . . and habits. The tendency you speak of I am not, myself, afraid of. I believe it will correct itself. At any rate what I can do by precept or otherwise to right it shall be done. . . . He is very observant and sees weakness as well in manners as argument which will save him from giving faith to sentiments not founded in truth, or from following examples that are not <u>exemplary</u>." Larz went on to note optimistically that Thomas was a frequent, "well mannered" visitor to their home: "I think you need not fear for him—though, of course, your anxiety is an inevitable one." Larz's optimism was unfounded, and William remained both anxious and angry. Thomas would never become a priest or even return to church. He and his younger brother Harry would spend their lives as career army men.[41]

With lives and careers well established, the Anderson sons and daughters found themselves securely ensconced in America's upper middle class. Many of the greatest financial anxieties had passed by for most of them. There would be yet more panics and steep market fluctuations, but age and accumulated wealth would enable them to weather the financial storms. The political storms were another matter, as rising tensions between North and South drew the children and the adult grandchildren into their nation's greatest crisis.

13

Times of Trial

1857–1861

I n 1857 New York witnessed the arrival of yet another financial panic, this time triggered by a dramatic shortage of gold for banks to pay off their debts. The banks had invested in businesses that were failing, and the panic spread to ordinary people who worried that their accounts would collapse. As investors lost heavily in the stock market and railroads defaulted on substantial debts, land speculators who had counted on the construction of new railroad routes to open new markets suffered spectacular losses. The railroads went broke or unbuilt. Word of foreclosures spread, and depositors rushed to the banks to withdraw their money, only to find the banks lacked the gold. Support was supposed to arrive from a massive gold delivery by the sailing ship *Central America*, coming from California, but the ship sank in a violent hurricane, leaving banks unable to redeem deposits.[1]

At first, westerners thought that the crisis was an East Coast phenomenon brought on by irresponsible markets and speculators, but they soon found themselves caught up in the maelstrom. On August 24, 1857, the New York branch of the largest bank in Ohio, Ohio Life Insurance and Trust Company, failed. This precipitated a panic in New York that set in motion a chain reaction of banking collapses across the nation. Within two weeks the stock market fell 50 percent, with railroads especially hard hit. Thousands were thrown out of work. In Ohio, many small private banks were compelled to close shop, but paradoxically, the Ohio Life was the only major bank in Ohio to fail. While the majority of authorized Ohio banks survived the panic, that did not prevent a major depression that continued for three more years.[2]

The financial panic of 1857 was so severe that several scholars have linked it to the subsequent onset of civil war, because it occurred in a political context where the major issue was the institution of slavery, beloved in the Deep South, hated in the Northeast, and tolerated in the West. Southern Democrats, obsessed with protecting the "peculiar institution" of slavery, recognized that it was crucial to restrain the powers of the federal government that threatened slavery. They resisted federal power across the board, whether expressed through protective tariffs, national banks, bounties (subsidies) for manufacturers, aid to education, internal improvements at federal expense, or, most threatening to the West, free land for western settlers. In response, with the passage of the Kansas-Nebraska Act in 1854, a mélange of antislavery Whigs, nativists, Free-Soilers, and abolitionists had coalesced to form the Republican Party, which opposed any expansion of slavery into the territories.[3]

The Panic of 1857 undoubtedly affected the Anderson fortunes in serious ways, injecting financial anxiety alongside the rising political din. But in a curious lapse, there is hardly any surviving correspondence or diary entries for the years 1857–1860. The reason is clear in the case of Charles Anderson, whose immediate correspondence was seized by Confederate authorities after his removal to Texas in 1859. Larz's correspondence, always limited (especially letters to him), is virtually silent in the late antebellum years, as is that of Robert, preoccupied with marriage and mounting tensions between North and South. As bad as the depression was, Anderson family members seem to have escaped relatively unscathed, although William remained mired in the unending litigation over the McArthur estate. Although William was now happily married to the wealthy Ellen Columba Ryan, the steep toll of McArthur's land lingered.

There is slightly more correspondence surviving from William, virtually all of which is underscored by perturbation and profound anxiety over the McArthur litigation. A case in point concerned James R. Challen of Cincinnati, who was involved in a "vexatious suite" involving 6,662 acres of land in Portsmouth, Kentucky, claimed by both Challen and Anderson. His lawyer sought to "compromise this suit and thus amicably end it." Evidently William was not in an amicable frame of mind, for a subsequent letter from Challen, dated December 21, 1859, scolded William for a tart response: "I had almost concluded to pass by your last as utterly unworthy of notice. This is sent however to enlighten you." Challen went on to make William an offer: "The land is valuable and worth fighting for. But we will buy or sell. . . . I will take $80 an acre and clear off all encumbrances from our side, or give $80 an acre and you clear all encumbrances and present the title. I am willing to do what I ask to do and if you are of the same character we can soon come to terms." To this William replied: "As to the fifty eight acres, which I hold from the McArthur estate, I accept your offer of $80 per acre. I will make you general warrantee. . . . You may write me word when you can pay for it."[4]

Fortunately William held title to some McArthur lands given to his late wife before McArthur's death. In addition to her family wealth, Ellen had received word from her wealthy uncle Michael Boyce that he had established a trust for Ellen and her children, "hoping that the property will secure to each of you a payment of $1000 per annum." When William and Ellen lost their infant on July 4, 1840, Boyce again wrote: "Do not I beg of you I beg of you brood over your unhappiness for the death of your little one! Take exercise and exertion as much as your health will permit as the disease of mind always injures the health of the body. You should watch over yourself and keep cheerful!" Ellen, who would live until 1898, would mourn the deaths of all but one of her four children. With all these untimely deaths still to come, Boyce closed his letter on the happy note that his wife was traveling in Europe and was presently in Florence and Rome, attending "magnificent balls and suppers given by the Grand Duke."[5]

In February 1858, with sectional tensions reaching a fever pitch, Robert wrote William about land. In particular, he was concerned about a five-hundred-acre tract of land in Kentucky he had inherited from their father, whose tenant was "destroying more of the timber than I was aware of." A friend, Captain Edwards, who was supposed to monitor the estate, had moved to Texas, leaving the power of attorney with his son. Robert asked William whether Captain Edwards "has ever made any report to you, informing you on what terms he had given leases." The problems of absentee owners and squatters oblivious to property rights were, of course, endemic to the early republic, and Andersons were by no means exempt. Robert's experience illustrates how issues with squatters were not always peaceful and often generated unrest.[6]

Normally, William would have jumped all over the question. After all, at issue was a lot of land. But he was in too deep a depression to negotiate business as usual. With McArthur's grandchildren leapfrogging his offspring to claim his land for themselves, McArthur's children—including William's late wife, Eliza—were liable to pay the grandchildren if the case went against them (which it eventually did, after William died). He confessed to Robert: "My spirits sunk to such a depth of cowardly despondency that I gave up the attention to everything but the endless endeavor to extricate myself from the McArthur injustice and iniquity. I set to work, to sell or exchange anything and everything I had to pay off the $9000 which they claimed and secured against me. Partly with that view I exchanged with Anderson Hendrick my green river lands, for some poor, broken hills and lands in Scioto river. I surrendered up to him all my farmes." The loss would not be permanent, but at the moment Larz's advice to stay away from the estate must have haunted him.

Only after describing his sad situation did William address the question of Captain Edwards, saying: "I have no direct recollection of the details of any instructions to Capt. Edwards, but of this I am sure, that I must have been more just and judicious in any efforts to protect your rights than I would have been about my own." He then went on to denigrate squatters on the property: "I should like to see a copy of the paper I left with Capt. Edwards. Get your agent to demand the paper or a copy of it—The only recollection I have of the statement about our interests down there, that devastation and destruction was the order of the day with a set of lawless . . . squatters."[7]

On October 5, 1857, Robert had been promoted to major in the First Artillery in the Regular Army. Hearing that brother William had the "bious [bilious] fever" (a common family ailment), in August 1858 he wrote a note of sympathy and then went on to complain once again about how infrequent communications were. He noted that his wife Eliza's health was also poor and would probably preclude a trip to Ohio and Kentucky. This reflection led to an observation that belied his mere fifty-three years of age:

> As I go down the hill of life, my heart sometimes and not infrequently, yearns for companionship with my brothers and sisters. I would like to visit the scenes of my youth once more. And perhaps, for the last time the house where we were born and look upon the graves of our dearly beloved parents whom we shall soon follow. Oh how ardently do I pray that we may all be alive, that when we depart this life, it shall be with the full assurance that we are to be partakers of life in the better world.[8]

In 1858 Robert was stationed in Trenton, New Jersey, inspecting iron beams. In a letter to William he described political events heating up with regret and consternation that they were taking over his life. With Eliza ill, their daughter Maria was staying with Robert's sister Maria and her husband, Allen Latham. He hoped to have her back soon and all together: "We are anxious to have the children go to the same school. I can not bear the idea of our other children growing up without being together. This separation tends to wean them from each other and from us. I am very glad, though that our little Maria has enjoyed the privilege of becoming acquainted with so many of her cousins and relatives to the west."[9]

Despite difficulties in travel and communications, families made an effort to stay in touch. In November 1858 Larz's wife Kate wrote to William's wife Ellen to tell her she had met the aforementioned Uncle Boyce in St. Louis. The trip was occasioned by business that engaged Larz as a director of the Ohio and Mississippi Railway. The railroad's East St. Louis terminal, near the Mississippi River, had been completed in 1857, thus occasioning Larz's trip with Kate and some New York investors. Kate hoped that Ellen would soon visit. "I am almost ashamed to expose them [my letters], to one who writes so beautifully as you do, dear Ellen—but as I hope to know you very well and shall in the course of our acquaintance exhibit much more glaring faults I shall make no apologies but beg you to believe me. Affectionately yours, Kate." In an added note she shared news that the ever-restless Charles had "Texas fever" and was embarking for that state that year. She also thanked Ellen and William for entertaining their nephews and nieces and wished Ellen would meet Larz: "You have heard, no doubt, from William, of the absence of my husband, but you do not know him well enough fully to appreciate my loneliness."[10]

Kate was right about Charles's "Texas fever." The peripatetic brother was again on the move, placing him unknowingly in a state that would soon feel the full force of secession. Although his law practice was successful, Charles experienced ongoing concerns over his asthma that persuaded him a change in climate and vocation was necessary. Cincinnati held especial dangers for poor health. A travelogue on Texas prepared by the famed landscape architect Frederick Law Olmsted promised cheap land and adventure—just the combination that appealed to the entrepreneurial aspirations of all the Andersons. With very little real experience in more primitive settings and no history of raising horses, Charles determined to move to Texas to pursue farming and raise racehorses. Against the advice of friends and family alike, he set off for San Antonio in 1858. He soon found a beautiful piece of land in Worth Springs, north of San Antonio, and returned to Cincinnati to finalize arrangements. He turned his financial affairs over to his former law partner, Rufus King, and on January 8, 1859, set out for Texas, to be followed that fall by Eliza and their daughters.

The contrasts for Charles's family could not have been greater. Having deserted the sophisticated, industrial landscape of Cincinnati, they landed in a true frontier environment. A local military post provided some measure of security and commerce, but like most military towns it was also bedeviled with heavy drinking and violent single males.[11]

While Charles was moving to Texas, Larz received a letter from Joseph Holt, President Buchanan's secretary of war, in February 1860, inquiring into the whereabouts of Charles. Writing from Washington, DC, Holt asked Larz to forward a letter to Charles offering to make him "Minister plenipo. to Mexico." Larz did forward the letter to Charles and added: "I am obliged to transfer great attention to Mr. Longworth's taxes." It is not clear that Charles ever received the letter that offered him possibly the greatest entry to foreign service he would ever receive.[12]

Charles threw himself into the business of acquiring horses, cattle, and building a handsome ranchero's mansion. He named the farm River

Springs. But none of this could make Texas home. In a letter written on the Fourth of July 1860, he wrote his sister Elizabeth expressing his forebodings at political events from his very vulnerable location in Confederate-leaning Texas: "My very dear Sister, I write now on this national Holy day. Great God! Is it to be our last?"

Charles refused to run for public office in Texas due to its proslavery orientation, but he lacked the disdain for politics that brothers Robert, William, and Larz had acquired. In the same letter to Elizabeth, he wrote: "I am glad to hear that John [Roy] is once more away from towns and I hope from politics. So much has been said to me and at me by my family, indeed and friends against my having any thing to do with 'politics,' that I have been myself rather chary about scolding any body else in the same way." That said, Charles defended public service: "I think though, as I always thought, that Politics is a very respectable career to expend a fortune in—but a most dangerous life to seek a living by. Our dear brother [Richard Anderson Jr.] was, (with his warm social feelings) early beset with this passion . . . having, in an eminent degree, that talent (for electioneering) of which I seem wholly deprived by Nature." In fact, Charles was not deprived of political skills, but he lacked a party. Charles then closed his letter with a reflection on the times and his place in them. He remained a staunch patriot, but sectional discord threatened the grand experiment. In an extended lament he cried:

> But alas! I feel absolute dismay, when I contemplated our public and political affairs and tendencies. Disunion—horrid word—the most horrible thing of this or any other state, that I believe or fear—may be—appears close to hand. Webster said he sought not to penetrate that veil. To my apprehensions at least, that veil is rent—and what a hell of woes, do I see and hear, bleeding, blazing, groaning directly and boundlessly beyond it? Oh! My Country, my Country, through what perils, art thou passing—to what an end will thou come?

Charles was right to feel anxiety.[13]

THE PANIC OF 1857 set in motion the forces that would elevate Republicans in the North and weaken Democrats, whose financial policies, while making some economic sense, were politically disastrous. By opposing any upward tariff revisions, the Democrats lost the Northeast. Compounding the Democrats' problems was an intraparty division between northern and southern Democrats over slavery extension. With the Republican Party an exclusive northern preserve, the question emerged whether northern and southern Democrats could come together to defeat the Republican upstarts. The answer was no. Bitter divisions between the northwestern faction of the Democratic Party, led by Stephen Douglas, and the radical southern faction, led by Jefferson Davis, ensured a ruptured party. When it became obvious at the Democratic convention meeting in Charleston, West Virginia, on April 23, 1860, that Douglas was the unanimous choice of northwestern Democrats, southern Democrats, led by the "fire-eater" William L. Yancey of Alabama, marched out of the hall. A follow-up convention in Baltimore on June 18 could not heal the break, paving the way for a Republican victory in November.[14]

Having won a national reputation in his senatorial debates with Douglas, Lincoln had set his sights on the Republican nomination for president. His chief rivals were the easterners William Seward of New York and Charles Sumner of Massachusetts. At the nominating convention in Chicago on May 16, Republican delegates bypassed the favored Seward (weakened by his outspoken sympathy with the abolitionists) and nominated Lincoln on the third ballot, to the ecstatic joy of western delegates. In addition to opposing the spread of slavery in the territories, the Republican platform pleased westerners with a plank favoring protective tariffs.[15]

Despite receiving only 40 percent of the popular vote, Lincoln carried the Electoral College by an overwhelming majority over the divided Democrats. Lincoln's victory set the stage for southern secession. At a convention meeting at Columbia, South Carolina, on December 20, 1860, southern delegates adopted an ordinance of secession. Within six weeks, Mississippi, Florida, Louisiana, Georgia, and Texas followed South Carolina out of the Union. On February 4, 1861, the disaffected southern states created the Confederate States of America. Jefferson Davis of Mississippi was elected president and Alexander H. Stephens of Georgia, vice president.

No record remains as to whether any Andersons voted for Lincoln. William certainly voted Democratic, as did John Roy. Charles and Larz supported John Bell of Tennessee and Edward Everett of Massachusetts in the newly created Constitutional Union Party. Robert probably did not vote. But all of the family remained sympathetic to the Union their father had fought to create. In the summer and fall of 1860, Robert was back at his beloved West Point as a member of a commission examining the school's curriculum and its system of discipline. Included on the commission was his friend and classmate Senator Jefferson Davis of Mississippi. Davis had served as a colonel in the Mexican War and subsequently as secretary of war under Democratic president Franklin Pierce, and then as a Democratic US senator from Mississippi. He was an ardent defender of slavery but as senator had argued against secession. At the same time, he believed strenuously in states' rights, including the right (if not the prudence) of secession. Sovereignty, he argued, lay ultimately with the individual states and not the federal government. By the summer of 1860, Davis was reconsidering secession. After South Carolina adopted its ordinance of secession on December 20, Mississippi followed on January 9, 1861. On January 21, the day Davis called "the saddest day of my life," he delivered a farewell address to the US Senate and returned to Mississippi.[16]

In the same period, events were evolving rapidly in Robert's life. Despite his Kentucky origins, ownership of slaves, and marriage to the daughter of a Georgia plantation owner whom he admired greatly, Robert's sense of duty precluded supporting secession, and he remained with the army. Under different circumstances, the fifty-five-year-old Robert would have quietly finished out his career in the army and returned to his native Kentucky. But these were not ordinary times, and on November 15, 1860, he received an order: "Major Robert Anderson, First Artillery, will forthwith proceed to Fort Moultrie [in Charleston Harbor], and immediately relieve Bvt. [Brevet] Col. John Garner, lieutenant-colonel of First Artillery, in command thereof." The order was signed by Robert's friend and commander, General Winfield Scott, but it originated from the secretary of war, General John B. Floyd. Floyd would go on to become a Confederate general and probably chose Anderson thinking his Southern sympathies would prompt him to jump ship as well. Instead, Robert would sell the slaves inherited from his father-in-law and remain loyal to the Union.[17]

The story of Fort Sumter is usually framed as the consequence of a contest between newly elected Republican president Abraham Lincoln and Confederate president Jefferson Davis. But more immediately, it was also an unwanted contest between two friends, Jefferson Davis and Robert Anderson. Many in the newly formed Confederacy thought Anderson would accede to their demands to relinquish control of Forts Moultrie and Sumter in Charleston Harbor, but they miscalculated Anderson's West Point–bred sense of duty. Next to his Christian faith, duty to country remained his highest loyalty, and it guided his decision to honor the Union and its new president.

Neither Lincoln nor Davis expected to engage in a major war, but South Carolina was itching for a fight and would not back down. The focal points of Confederate aggression were Forts Moultrie and Sumter. As a new nation, the Confederacy believed that erstwhile federal property was henceforth South Carolina property, and soon after Christmas 1860, it demanded that federal forces, commanded by Robert, leave the forts. This Robert refused, but he was frustrated to have little advice or assistance from the Buchanan administration in its last days. On his own, Robert decided that the sturdy Fort Sumter offered better protection for his soldiers. On December 26, 1860, while Carolinians were preoccupied with Christmas, he spiked the cannons at Fort Moultrie and transferred his two-company garrison to the unfinished Fort Sumter, in the middle of the harbor. The fort was years in the making and formidable. Consisting of concrete slabs erected on an artificial island, it was capable of withstanding substantial assaults. But it could not provision itself. That would require federal deliveries, which South Carolina had vowed to resist.

To South Carolinian Confederates, provisioning federal forts in their new nation would constitute an act of war. In fact, they were convinced that the first blow had already been struck, when Anderson spiked the guns at Fort Moultrie. Neither did it help South Carolinians' pride to know that, despite their leadership for secession, theirs was the only secession state besides Florida that had failed to seize all federal properties on its soil.[18]

After the unannounced federal relief ship *Star of the West* was fired upon by Carolinian gunners on January 9, 1861, Anderson, not wishing to start a war, withheld his fire. But he refused to surrender the fort. Suddenly Fort Sumter emerged center stage as the dominant symbol of Union and Confederate pride.

In a letter to his Kentucky friend Charles Balance, Robert frankly explained his situation and the grave portent it represented: "Since my arrival in this harbor, all my energies have been devoted to an endeavor to prevent the shedding of blood. I saw that S. Carolina was determined to leave the Union, and know that if blood was shed in her severence from her sister states, or subsequent threats, it would involve the whole country in civil war, and render it impossible perhaps ever to reconstruct a Union of the States. I hope that my endeavors have not been in vain." He then concluded: "This is a subject on which I cannot think without emotions of the most painful character. God grant that our blessed land may not be bathed in blood. The fanaticism, the madness and folly of man are being exerted to ruin and disgrace our people."[19]

Soon after Robert's removal to Fort Sumter, William determined to meet Robert in Charleston Harbor. On February 18, Robert wrote his sister Maria from Fort Sumter. He was still hopeful that war could be avoided: "I was delighted to see our dear brother [William] when he came to see me. But to tell the truth, when word was brought, in the morning, that he was coming down and that the Governor said he could only see me in the presence of some gentlemen who were coming with him, it looked like a last visit to a doomed man." Clearly, already in February, Robert was a marked man, unable to escape Confederate monitoring.

He then returned to the theme of faith: "The older I am, the more I see, and the more trying the scenes, the stronger my belief, in the power and goodness of God becomes—Never mind how dark the appearance of the sky around me, I know that there is light beyond it, and that, as of the night time, the clouds will be dispersed, and all will go on well again." Robert closed with a note of thanks to brother Larz, who had sent an encouraging letter: "He says you think a great deal about me. God bless your warm and true heart. I only wish that you could, all of you who feel so deep an interest in me, only read my heart, and see how quietly I place my trust in God, and how sure I feel in that trust, and I think it would calm your own feelings and quiet your fear."[20]

While loathe to be the architect of civil war, Lincoln was not ready to vacate the fort peacefully, despite the advice of General Winfield

Scott. In his inaugural address on March 4, 1861, Lincoln asserted his intention to "hold, occupy, and possess" federal properties wherever they be found.[21]

Meanwhile, Major Anderson's plight grew worse by the day. On March 29, after suffering a sleepless night with a migraine headache, Lincoln authorized an unarmed flotilla of supply ships to relieve the fort. Most of his advisers counseled that such an action would be interpreted as an act of war, but Lincoln was determined to move forward. The expedition set sail by April 6. Nobody knew what Lincoln would do should South Carolina's response be hostile. Probably Lincoln himself did not know.[22]

When President Davis received word that Lincoln intended to provision Fort Sumter with nonmilitary supplies, he predictably declared the attempt an "act of aggression." Davis knew that the only way to lend plausibility to a real national independence for the Confederacy in the eyes of England and the uncommitted border states, including Robert's native Kentucky, was to make a strong response. Already the *Daily Richmond Enquirer* had responded to Lincoln's inaugural with a vitriolic declaration of war: "Sectional war, declared by Mr. Lincoln, awaits only the signal gun from the insulted Southern Confederacy, to light its horrid fires all along the border of Virginia." To fail to act would be to concede defeat. Davis felt the extreme tension of an ultimatum and went to bed with a migraine of his own.[23]

On April 11, crowds gathered along the shore, certain they would see a display of martial gallantry, only to be disappointed by quiet. But the storm was building. At Davis's order, Secretary of War Leroy P. Walker sent Confederate general—and Robert's fellow West Point graduate—Pierre G. T. Beauregard instructions to demand the immediate evacuation of Fort Sumter. Beauregard duly issued the demand. Despite his Southern friends, Major Anderson refused the order, maintaining his loyalties to duty—and the Union.

On April 12, just as a relief expedition of several federal ships was approaching, the Confederates opened fire on Anderson's fortress. The surprisingly feisty federal defenders returned fire and held out for two days. But with fires on all sides and depleted munitions, Robert had no choice but to surrender. From the shoreline hundreds of persons, principally ladies, rejoiced to see the palmetto flag of South Carolina replace the Stars and Stripes over the fortress. Despite the heavy bombardment, Robert lost none of his soldiers. Only one horse died.

With the firing on Fort Sumter, twenty years of accumulated frustration, sporadic violence, and bombastic rhetoric at last ignited a war whose outcome was unknown to everyone. Upon receiving word of the surrender, an uncertain President Davis confided that the bombardment would mark "either the beginning of a fearful war, or the end of a political contest." In fact, it brought about both.[24]

On April 18, Robert sent a dispatch after boarding the steamship *Baltic*, en route to Washington, DC: "Having defended Fort Sumter for thirty-four hours, until the quarters were entirely burned, the main gates destroyed by fire, the gorge walls seriously injured, the magazine surrounded by flames, and its door closed from the effects of heat, four barrels and three cartridges of powder only being available, and no provisions remaining but pork, I accepted terms of evacuation offered by General Beauregard." Anderson continued, noting that he marched out of the fort on April 14 with "colors flying and drums beating, bringing away company and private property, and saluting my flag with fifty guns."[25]

When Robert Anderson surrendered at Fort Sumter, the Civil War officially began, although as Charles Anderson pointed out, it actually began before that. Beneath the Civil War lay private property. First, and most obviously, was the vast property owned by the Public Land Survey, whose federal ownership was explicitly challenged by the Confederacy. Confederate leaders claimed ownership of the lands within the Confederacy and lands farther south that it intended to acquire through conquest. Second, and less obvious, was the private property represented in slaves. Just as the Confederacy threatened the Public Land Survey, so the war threatened the South's largest property valuation, next to the land itself, in the form of its slaves. Before secession, the primary responsibility of government was to protect the sanctity of private ownership, including "property in persons," even though such ownership ran contrary to free-enterprise capitalism because it precluded significant capital investment on the part of millions of slaves who could not own property. Emancipation would mark the first major breach of government's most important duty, and Confederates would resist it with their lives. When England abolished slavery in 1833, the former owners were compensated for their lost property. Civil War would ensure there would be no such compensation in the States. In social terms, the consequences were equally profound as four million former slaves suddenly became potential landowners, increasing the demands on property—and the profits.[26]

Robert returned to a hero's welcome. He brought the fort's thirty-three-star flag with him to New York, where a parade in his honor in Union Square was said to be the largest public assembly ever in North America up to then. Newspapers crowned him "the most popular man in America."

The returned American flag would mark the start of a new mythology that elevated the Stars and Stripes to levels of symbolic significance never before approached. Before Sumter, there were few symbols of national unity at all. Rather, state and local associations governed American life. In the early republic, the American flag, the clearest and most literal emblem of patriotism, was barely visible. Flags were limited largely to merchant and naval ships. None flew from homes or churches. But all this changed when Robert brought back the flag from Sumter. Now, the clearest and most literal emblem of patriotism and resolve was the national flag. Churches, storefronts, homes, and government buildings all waved flags as a sign of loyalty and support. On both sides of the conflict, flags assumed a transcendent significance as symbols of their respective nations' sacred importance.[27]

Robert himself was less sanguine than his fans. Going to war with his Southern friends was nothing he desired, and in fact, he felt a sense of failure for not having prevented the war. Of course, there was nothing he could have done, but the regret persisted even as duty called. Robert was promoted to brigadier general on May 15, 1861, and took command of the Department of Kentucky (later renamed the Department of the Cumberland) on May 28. He then moved his headquarters from Cincinnati to Louisville after Confederate general Leonidas Polk occupied Columbus on the Mississippi. In a letter to Hiram Barney from Cincinnati regarding "my native state of Kentucky," Robert wrote: "My impression is that that state will, if permitted to have her own way until after the August election, come out decidedly for the Union. It is important that no call should be made on her for troops until after that time, as the Union party . . . will show that Ky is all right." He closed with a note on his health. Between earlier war wounds and the ordeal at Sumter, he was struggling: "My health is, I regret to say, such that the Doctors say I must avoid soldiering, as any duty, and they have recommended my going to some high mountainous region. I am sir your respect, Robert Anderson."[28]

Anderson did not regain his health. In a letter to his brother William on June 23, he enclosed a fragment from the Fort Sumter flagstaff and confided, "I am now compelled to hurry at once to the mountains where my doctors say I must rest. God willing starting tomorrow morning for Cupen Pa. where I will remain, until I am well enough to report for duty or until in the opinion of the Union leader of Ky., my presence is needed in that state." Contained in the same letter to William is a letter from William to his wife Ellen, with which he enclosed the letter from Robert and added a note on Robert's health and their son Thomas, who was also in the army. Of Robert he wrote, "I send this letter to you, by which you will see that Robert's health is still not good. I hope any patron saint, on whose birthday he begins his journey may watch over and protect him. I feared that terrible ordeal would prove too much for his over vigorous body. God's will be done!" He then turned his attention to Thomas, noting, "Anything more from Tom— I will bring over his letter from fort Staufer near Green Castle, Pa if I do not forget it. I almost think he will fall in this horrible war."[29]

As Robert faced his moment of destiny, William at last confronted the question of secession. Born in Kentucky, the owner of slaves, and bitterly racist, William had deep and enduring ties to the South that would remain after the war. But he was also his father's son and had deep loyalties to the republic and its Constitution. Soon after the war erupted he was visited by an old Virginia friend and former neighbor, Robert McNemera, and their conversation was later summarized by brother Charles. McNemera began by playing off a probably apocryphal statement attributed to Lincoln's secretary of state, William H. Seward, in a meeting with British diplomat Lord Lyons: "I can touch a bell on my right hand and order the arrest of a citizen in Ohio. I can touch the bell again, and order the arrest of a citizen of New York. Can the Queen of England, in her dominions, do as much?" This quote was in reference to Lincoln's suspension of writs of habeus corpus soon after the war began, leaving McNemera to assert: "I hate all this tyranny of

[Secretary of War Edwin M.] Stanton and Seward and his little bell. I would rather see this Union smashed than that any man should lay violent hands on our beloved Constitution." To this William replied, "If the Union is destroyed the country is destroyed so far as government is concerned. And without a country of what use is a Constitution?" McNemera countered, "Perhaps you are right in your way of looking at it, but it is hard to know that your blood relations are being shot down in their homes and that the fields over which I have hunted as a boy and man are devastated and drenched with the blood of my family and neighbors." Again William replied, "I am thoroughly opposed to the ways of Seward and Stanton and many of their military underlings and always shall be, but it is futile to speak of upholding the Constitution and destroying the Union."[30]

Larz shared William's love for the Union and anxiousness for its preservation, but as late as 1860, with sectional tensions peaking, he had been deeply involved in land speculation. On October 2 he purchased six hundred acres in Iowa for $2,250, followed by another purchase in Iowa for $7,250. The purchases were shrewd. One quantitative analysis of land transactions in Iowa in the 1850s confirms that land speculation there paid handsomely and far exceeded average bond and stock returns.[31]

In Texas, the news for Charles was not good. He stood to lose virtually all the $30,000 he had invested in his ranch. In a letter to Rufus King he complained, "I am dead broke." He suspended construction of his ranch and hoped to borrow money from King. As well, he wrote his attorney, Daniel Gregg, that "I want to sell my Madison and Franklin lands. I hope to get $20 per acre for them—but will take the best that can be had. Will you undertake this office for me, for such compensation for your trouble as just? It is too expensive for me to cover so far. There is a plat of the land on the back totaling around 600 acres."[32]

With Texas's secession, Charles's days in San Antonio were numbered. He became deeply unpopular with slaveholding Texans for his vocal support for the Union and opposition to slavery. In an impassioned speech to "the people of Bexar county" gathered in Alamo Square, delivered soon after Lincoln's election, Charles came out blazing against Confederate Texans: "Has the madness of faction, the virulence of fanaticism, at last reached this point? Have sectional partisans finally

dared to make, or devise, an assault upon this beloved and most glorious Union, which our fathers of the South and the North shed their united blood to cement and establish?" And for what reason, he asked? So that they could confederate with territories south in the never-ending pursuit of land: "Alas! That independent States of our North American Union, should ever dream of crawling together with Honduras, the Belize, and the dissevered States of Central America, like a litter of timid whelps, with their backs all humped, and their tails all tightly tucked between their trembling legs, around, behind, and under the British Lion—for protection!" Then, in conclusion, he affirmed the position that President Jackson had assumed over South Carolina's threatened secession: "Secession was what General Jackson proclaimed: it's 'only revolution.'" Charles's rant made national news, but it did nothing to protect his interests in Texas. Indeed, it would mark the beginning of the end.[33]

In a letter written to "my very dear friend" William Corry on January 21, 1861, Charles offered a primer on the looming sectional crisis. He (wrongly) agreed with Corry's belief that "the main spring is in the tariff and trade policy and that the slavery is greatly with South Carolina, a pretense and maddening." But that did not absolve the South of culpability. Indeed, it increased its guilt: "Because, denounce the 'Protective Policy' with what truth or exaggeration we may, the culpability of the North is much less in its history, than in their courses, concerning slavery." The problem, as Charles saw it, was that "the whole country has grown rich beyond precedent because of slavery. If economic hardship accompanied slavery it would be a strange cause for subverting government and societies. As it is, it does seem to me—simple insanity or worse *a total incapacity for republican government!* And there my friend, there is the fundamental fact!"[34]

Unable to see the cancer of slavery and racism for what it was, Charles instead focused his rage on republican government generally. In words that could be perceived as denying the legacy for which his father had fought, he wrote to Corry, "Our form of government is a failure. We are now proved to be incapable of self-government." Conceding that he once "loved that dream" and "trusted that grand idea," he now concluded, "The idea is a fallacy. The dream is a mere mirage. As I *gaze* upon it—in admiration and in love—as I gaze upon it, does it not vanish? Alas! the day and hour that I should so write and you should so read. But it is ever so." The problem with the ideal was the depravity of human nature—a depravity that no form of government could undo. Charles confronted his ideals and judged them wanting: "Our system ostensibly *so national and benevolent*—like all other perfect theories—*fails in the experience,* through the amazing irrationality and malevolence of mankind. Woe is us!" He then closed with a reference to the March Convention, when Texas passed an ordinance of secession: "I must prefer it to the terrible realities which constitute the government, in its whole development from the whiskey insurrection to the ides of March. 'Remember the ides of March'!"[35]

As Charles was weighing his future in Texas, his friend General Robert E. Lee was also wrestling with his future. Lee was a close friend of Charles and brother Robert. The two served under General Winfield Scott in the Mexican War. Charles's relocation to San Antonio afforded multiple opportunities for Lee to attend frequent balls and parties at the Andersons'.[36] Lee himself had recently returned to Texas from his capture of John Brown at Harpers Ferry, Virginia, to assume temporary command of the US Army's Department of Texas, but he was surprisingly replaced by Major General David E. Twiggs, a Georgia native with stronger Confederate loyalties. With Texas out of the Union, a group of Texas commissioners approached Lee and informed him that if he would resign his commission and join the Confederacy, he would have command of the Confederate army, but if he refused he would not be allowed transportation to move his possessions. An incensed Lee responded that his allegiance was to Virginia and not to Texas. Uncertain what to do next, Lee sought out Charles and told him of the Texas offer. Apparently the commissioners had said nothing about detaining Lee personally. Lee asked Charles if he could entrust his belongings to him until they could be forwarded, to which Charles readily acceded.

On their way to the storage merchant, Lee asked Charles if he recalled their conversation in the presence of Charles's friend Doctor Willis G. Edwards, which Charles remembered distinctly. According to Lee's biographer Douglas Southall Freeman, Lee then replied:

> I think it but due to myself to say that I cannot be moved by the conduct of these people [Texans] from my sense of duty. I still think, as I then told you and Doctor Edwards, that my loyalty to Virginia

ought to take precedence over that which is due the Federal Government. And I shall so report myself at Washington. If Virginia stands by the old Union, so will I. But if she secedes (though I do not believe in secessions as a constitutional right, nor that there is sufficient cause for revolution), then I will still follow my native state with my sword, and if need be with my life. I know you think and feel very differently, but I can't help it. These are my principles and I must follow them.

Lee then returned to the commissioners to declare that he was neutral in the controversy between Texas and the Union and prepared to return to Virginia.

In recounting this seminal conversation, Freeman speculated about would have happened if Lee had been in command of the department of the army instead of General Twiggs when the Texans demanded surrender of Union property. Freeman suggested that Lee would almost certainly have refused to surrender government property, perhaps setting the stage for Lee's arrest. But Lee was not in charge, he did return to Virginia, and when Virginia seceded from the Union he cast his lot with the Confederacy.[37]

Charles would take the opposite course. He was sure that the Texas convention would mark the time when "we shall be preempted out of the Union." That posed an existential question for him. "Whither," he asked William Corry, would he go? "Texas—insanely disunited from *my* United States . . . what are her probabilities—and mine in her—and those of my posterity after me? Think—think—think of it all especially the last series. . . . And I doubt not, a few weeks' history will shew that I ought not to fix my generations to such a fate. What then? Where <u>ought</u> I to <u>go</u>? What ought I to <u>do</u>?" In closing his letter, Charles underscored his dilemma—a dilemma brought on by an impulsive decision to relocate across the continent: "What do I do to maintain my family—under a monarchy in England? Alas! for such a question with my inefficencies, could I make bread in the law? . . . Would lecturing 'pay' them? . . . But a few more days and the probability is that I must [go]."[38]

Fearing for his and his family's safety, he sought to escape to Mexico. The family was arrested in the attempt and taken back to San

Antonio, where they were confined in the Menger Hotel. Charles was imprisoned as an enemy of the new Confederate state. When arrested in October 1861, Charles demanded to know who ordered his arrest and was told that it was US marshal Henry Eustace McCulloch. He protested both his arrest and the seizure of all his money, save $100. In response to Charles's written protest, McCulloch noted he had no choice, but he would allow him parole within a ten-mile radius of San Antonio, to which Charles replied, "I wouldn't give my parole for one minute to save your soul from hell!" In addition, Charles addressed McCullough with a blistering attack on McCullough's character and the cause of the Confederacy, to which Marshal McCulloch replied in a condescending tone that must have infuriated Anderson: "Sir, Your long letter of yesterday, which I suppose you intend to be the last, is before me. . . . You certainly will not expect me to be so unmanly as to permit your harsh, bitter and undeserved allusions to myself, to excite the baser passion of the heart; if you do, you will find yourself as much mistaken in the last as circumstances rendered it necessary for you to be in the first." McCulloch closed with instructions for how Charles would be treated: "You will be limited to the boundaries of Capt. Michling's line of camp sentinels, permitted to associate with him and his officers (if agreeable to yourself and them) but to receive no visits from others, or to correspond with any one, except through these headquarters. Sincerely sir, very respectfully, your obedient servant."[39]

Charles was confined in two tents and closely monitored. With visitors and correspondence severely constrained, Charles was abandoned to his own devices. On the day following his arrest he managed to befriend one of his guards, a fellow Kentuckian with like sentiments, over a game of backgammon and enlisted him in his plan to escape. On the night of his escape, Charles feigned acute asthma, and when other guards were preoccupied, he slipped out the back of his tent, mounted a horse, and rode to the home of Ann Ludlam, a Unionist who gave him money and a disguise. The escape was dangerous, and Charles was accompanied by fellow prisoner William Bayard. The two traveled without fires and rode alongside river bottoms until reaching the Rio Grande, where they crossed into Mexico and were met by a friendly Mexican general, Jerónimo Treviño, who gave Charles a military escort to Monterrey. He arrived safely at the home of Governor Santiago Vidaurri on November 1, 1861.[40]

Meanwhile, Eliza and the children had been transported to Browns-
ville, Texas, and from there they traveled to Monterrey to be reunited
with Charles. From Monterrey, the family took a schooner bound for
Veracruz, arriving on November 28. From there they took a ship to
New York, arriving on December 11. Like his brother Robert earlier,
Charles quickly became the latest hero of the town. From New York,
he sent his family home to Dayton as he went on to Washington, DC,
again receiving a hero's welcome and invitations to speak. His earlier
sentiments against the republic having been firmly put to rest as quickly
as they had arisen, he reappeared a staunch patriot. Reversing his earlier attribution of sectional tensions to the tariff, he charged after his
arrest that the real cause of secession was "the slave interest striving to
obtain political power. It was the work of insane demagogues grasping
for power." Charles went on to praise the Revolution and its legitimate
heirs among the Unionists and denounce "in the most severe terms the
very thought of secession. He could weep tears of blood to see treason
in such men."[41]

On December 28, a relieved R. C. Anderson (Larz's son) wrote
from Moxley, Georgia: "Dear Uncle Charles, It is impossible to express
the anxiety and suspense which your troubles have kept Agnes and myself [in] or the gratification we experienced at the intelligence that you
had escaped from your enemies and safely arrived in N. York. Can you
not bring your family over and stay with us until you conclude upon
some plan for the future? If it suits your convenience, make our house
your home as long as you like." Charles's nephew closed by noting that
the only consolation he took from his uncle's trial "is the fact that fate
has thrown us together once more when I had begun to fear that we
might never meet again."[42]

With a newly born speaking schedule in hand, Charles traveled
throughout the East to praise and applause. His friend William Corry
hoped to meet him in New York and offered some warning along the
way. The war, he noted, would not be easy. Their native Kentucky would
probably not be spared: "Right here at home in Kentucky, the horriblest
of civil war battles may burst on our vision to sear our very eyeballs.
100,000 men at least wait but for the word of the leaders for self destruction. Andy and friends of mine are on both sides what a dreadful
crisis in human affairs."

He followed this with some advice to avoid political commentary except to "endorse the Lincoln menagerie," and not to "give a course of lectures on the war." Corry agreed with Larz that "we both want you to confine yourself to Texas and yourself." This, presumably, would be to set the course for any political office Charles might wish to run for in future elections.[43]

With Charles's reputation as a stirring speaker growing, President Lincoln commissioned him to go to England and promote the cause of the Union. In a letter to Eliza, written from Washington, DC, prior to departure, he described his meeting with President Lincoln and General George B. McClellan, general-in-chief of the Union army: "The Prest. strikes me as one of the most unreserved, honest men I ever saw. Gentl. McClellan impresses me exceedingly—which is reciprocated I believe." He then closed with an awkward praise of McClellan's wife: "Mrs. Mc-Clellan I find charming. She is natural, frank, [a] beauty—and that winning manner of the Army ladies so attractive to me. I am sure she and I should be friends, if we knew each other a life time."[44]

By March 1862, Charles was in New York, awaiting departure for Europe. With hatreds brimming, he wrote Eliza: "Alas! what a crime these Southern villains have created. Will the gallows ever have its full just due to society?" Two days later, about to embark on the *Glasgow*, he wrote, "Robert looks well. . . . She [Robert's wife Eliza] looks really badly—thin in the face—tho smart and agreeable as ever." He added, "Rufus [King] has invented a tobacco pouche. Perhaps I will take the British patent and make my fortune at last!" He then went on to question his purpose in serving: "What is the use of my going over there now? Can you tell?"[45]

A few days later, describing his "gloomy straits" in contemplating his journey, Charles expressed "my own relief at the information of our beloved son—first born and only—from actual and past dangers." The referenced son, Latham Anderson, served as a captain in the Fifth Infantry and later as a colonel in the Eighth California, where he spent much of the war largely out of harm's way.[46]

While en route to Liverpool, Charles wrote to Charles Francis Adams, son of President John Quincy Adams and Lincoln's minister to England, where he worked to ensure England's neutrality during the war. Charles's purpose was not political but rather to introduce himself and a colleague, William Hopes, in regard to business matters they wanted to pursue in London with the tobacco pouch. Hopes, formerly a British attaché at Washington, was also in London. Charles assured Adams, "We shall not unduly waste your time."[47]

In an update to Eliza, written from London on May 2, 1862, Charles shared his disappointment in not getting any of his essays published in England. Every paper he approached "declines publishing Union articles." He then went on to describe his work for Lincoln and his fear of failure with William Gladstone, then chancellor of the exchequer and British abolitionist: "Depend on it—we are by no means out of the woods with these people here. They are all opposed to our carrying on the war. . . . Any little accident might get the two-three—four into a war! I grieve to see such dangers, however improbable—with no power to help my country." He closed with his own uncertainty over what to do at home: "When I come home—what to do—where to go? Do you know? Not I."[48]

Whatever his future, Charles took advantage of his present to do some touring in England in May as a proper "western" gentleman. At one time or another, virtually all of the Anderson children spent time in Europe absorbing the civilization, admiring the beauty, and comparing themselves favorably to the Old World. In a letter to his daughter Kitty, Charles described visiting the National Gallery, the Royal Academy, the French Gallery, and Buckingham Palace. In addition, he wrote, "evenings were spent going to court to observe English law in action and attending evening sessions of Parliament." Further travel beckoned: "I had almost fixed to start on Thursday for Edinburgh—Glasgow—Belfast—Dublin and interesting places according to expenses—on my way home. Last night, however, I met a new friend of America, an editor, who insists on my going to Manchester to speak. I will if they want me and undertake to bring it about. What will come of this—who knows?"[49]

Three days later, Charles wrote Eliza to inform her that the Manchester trip proved fruitful for public speaking, encouraging him to stay on another month. For someone who had no clue what to do on return, he had no difficulty filling his dance card away from home. He was not, however, without disappointment: "My patent speculation has all come to naught. It is, really, a very cute and useful thing. But the English use a different tobacco and will not work in this pouch. Otherwise we might have made plenty of money out of it." In a note on health he complained, "I have now a suspicion that my asthma is more persistent, than I expected." He added that a trip to Paris was a possibility: "I can go to Paris for 30 shillings, I have a half mind, if event should accommodate me, to go over there to glance at its wonderful changes in the last 10 years. This is rather improbable. England is a fine enough country for me." Five days later, however, Charles was indeed enjoying Paris even though "I have no business exactly." We have no record of Eliza's response to his dilettante ways, but she had to have found them trying. In fact, Charles seems to have perfected a long-standing practice of the Anderson men. Even as the patriarch was often away from his family in ways replicated by Richard Jr., so also were Larz and William. Charles closed his letter by noting that he was glad to learn that Latham was unhurt, adding: "Oh! How I do wish he could be in my place among these arts. I think if he can get a furlough, we must afford to send him over, for a few months, this or next year after the War? It would improve him so much." The notion that "next year" would witness the end of Civil War demonstrated the extent to which Americans, North and South, underestimated the conflict on which they had embarked.[50]

From Paris, Charles moved on to Oxford, England, in late May, where he visited "cousin Die," who was in a nunnery there. In a letter to daughter Kitty he observed, "I think she is more for the church than formerly. But I am not sure of that, for she was always rather sectarian. She is evidently quite concerned for my soul . . . if I have soul." He then recounted the highlight of his European gambol: "Since I came here, nothing delights me so much as Oxford and Cambridge. This university passion of mine, is a strange thing for one who never was, nor could have been, a scholar. Nothing so much delights me, as to be about colleges." With characteristic hubris he closed, "I ought to be the president of a university." He would never attain that goal, though he would become an influential board member at his alma mater, Miami University of Ohio.[51]

En route to the States, Charles accounted his time in Europe a failure. This he blamed chiefly on the liberals in England who wished the war prosecuted on an abolitionist platform: "The government party . . . The liberals—a vast multitude . . . in their blind zeal and deep ignorance of means and consequences, wish the War prosecuted chiefly and directly for the forcible extirpation of <u>slavery</u>." Charles would later discover that his own president was entertaining similar notions. For himself, Charles finally answered, on his trip home, his earlier questions about what to do and where to go. He would, he determined, join the fight.[52]

While Charles was traveling and contemplating his future, the Confederacy had already become a nation. Lincoln's call for volunteers tipped the balance of Virginia fence-sitting, leading the state to secede on April 17. This would prove to be the most significant event in 1861, as it moved the nation's largest state into the Confederacy, and with it the Andersons' friend, Robert E. Lee, who assumed command of the state troops of Virginia and later became general-in-chief of all Confederate armies. As well, Virginia's secession convinced other states in the upper South to secede. Arkansas seceded on May 6, North Carolina on May 20, and Tennessee on June 8. The Anderson children's native state of Kentucky did not secede but remained a slave-owning border state with strong pockets of Confederate loyalty.[53]

The Confederacy immediately relocated its capital from Montgomery to Richmond and met on July 20, 1861. In the meantime, forty-eight counties in the western mountains of Virginia voted against secession and were admitted into the Union as the state of West Virginia. Hoping for an early, decisive victory and Confederate surrender, Lincoln rashly moved unproven troops to Bull Run, Virginia, just north of the city of Manassas, where they suffered a humiliating defeat before civilian crowds who gathered to watch from surrounding hills. With that defeat, three long years of unending battles were launched, with Andersons never far from the center of the fray.[54]

While Robert is the only Anderson remembered for his role in the Civil War, he had virtually no participation in the conflict after Fort Sumter. Injuries sustained during prior service to his country's wars left him unfit for active duty, and he was honorably discharged from the military for permanent convalescence in October 1863. But Richard Sr. directly and through example had taught his children and their adult children well regarding their duties to the nation. All of his children and grandchildren supported the Union. Many participated in major battles and fought with distinction. One daughter, Sarah A. Kendrick, youngest child of Anderson Sr. and Sarah, served as a zealous volunteer in the Christian Commission hospitals in the North, which were sponsored by evangelical churches. William would become a Copperhead—a Democrat with Southern sympathies—but he defended the Union and served for a short time in the state militia. William's son Thomas later compiled a family history that included a list of family members who served in the war. They included Thomas himself, who was wounded twice at Chancellorsville and at the "Bloody Angle" at Spotsylvania but survived to become commanding general in the first international expedition in the Philippine War in 1898; Charles and his son Latham Anderson, a West Point graduate, who commanded the Eighth California Volunteer Infantry; and Larz's sons Colonel Nicholas Longworth Anderson, who commanded the Sixth Ohio Volunteers, and Captain Edward Lowell Anderson. Also serving were Captain Fred Anderson and William's other son, Captain Harry Anderson. When not supporting his sons in uniform by buying winter clothing and supplies for all the troops, Larz continued to work for his ailing father-in-law's estate, managing lands and investments. As well, he traveled frequently to Washington and conferred with members of the Lincoln administration.[55]

14

Charles Anderson's Civil War

1862–1865

The Civil War had progressed for seventeen months when, on September 17, 1862, General George McClellan's Army of the Potomac faced off with General Robert E. Lee's and General Thomas "Stonewall" Jackson's Army of Northern Virginia in what would stand as the single bloodiest day in American history. The Battle of Antietam, near Sharpsburg, Maryland, implicitly rewrote the rules for acceptable losses in war. Twelve thousand four hundred Federals were killed or wounded alongside 11,724 Confederates, for a total of 24,000 casualties in little more than twelve hours.

Antietam also inspired the single most momentous act in Lincoln's presidency. On September 22, 1862, Lincoln issued his Emancipation Proclamation, effective January 1, 1863, declaring that "all persons held as slaves within said designated [rebellious] States, and parts of States, are, and henceforward shall be free."[1]

While Lincoln's Gettysburg Address and Second Inaugural remain ingrained in American memory, they did not occupy such exalted states in Lincoln's mind. Only his Emancipation Proclamation was accorded that special status, the most solemn and spiritual political decision of Lincoln's life. Of hundreds of presidential proclamations, including President Washington's famous proclamation of American neutrality, none exerted a greater impact on American history than Lincoln's Emancipation Proclamation. Events had conspired and the time had arrived for him to follow his personal instincts in an entirely fitting and legitimately constitutional manner.[2]

For Lincoln, emancipation and union were not contradictory goals. They were not separate goals. They were the same goal. Although hardly single-handedly responsible for emancipation and the end of slavery, Lincoln was indispensable—and he knew it. He realized the enormity of what he was doing. He caught the thunderbolt. This was the single most momentous outcome that he—and he alone—could ever accomplish in his lifetime.[3]

Lincoln's proclamation, together with the mounting carnage of ever-greater numbers of casualties, transformed the Civil War into something resembling a total war, where none would escape suffering. Indeed, the Civil War was the costliest war in American history. The revised death toll now stands at 750,000, 20 percent higher than the 618,000 figure that stood for over a century. The Southern economy, dependent on slave labor and exports, suffered devastation.[4]

Many of the Andersons and their fellow Kentucky citizens and friends still owned slaves. Yet, with the prominent exception of William, all brothers continued fervently to support the war effort, especially Charles, who enjoyed an expense-free celebration in New York through November and December. He was no abolitionist, and he harbored no doubts that slavery, which he came to oppose, had so degraded blacks as to render them inferior and unfit to vote. But as the casualties mounted at a mind-numbing rate, Charles felt his service abroad had not contributed enough to the war, and upon his return to the States he found his mission: he would enlist in the army and fight for his country, emancipation and all. Ohio governor David Tod, desperate for volunteers in the aftermath of severe Ohio losses at the Battle of Shiloh, permitted Charles, then in his forties, to raise, and command, a regiment, which he accomplished in just two weeks. In July 1862, Governor Tod commissioned Charles as a colonel in the Ninety-Third Ohio Volunteer Infantry in command of his own regiment. Like many other "political officers" in the Civil War, Charles had minimal training for such a mission and would pay a steep price. Many of his volunteers were also ill trained and ill equipped to step into the middle of a war.

Larz's oldest son, Nicholas, also fought in the war. He had graduated from Harvard in 1858. Although born to wealth, he maintained the frontier scorn for the pretensions of the aristocracy of New England. One classmate, Henry Adams, made it clear that he was not immediately impressed with his western classmate. Nicholas returned the insult, declaring that the Bostonians of his day "have three gods—Boston, money, and the Pilgrim Fathers." Especially irksome to Anderson was their Puritan snobbery: "Loyalty and attachment to ancestry is undoubtedly a valuable trait in any people. It implies faithfulness, honor and patriotism when moderately developed, but when too strongly cast, it implies idolatry, fanaticism and all sorts of ultraism." Despite his contempt for "Puritan" hypocrisy and egotism, Nicholas embraced the Union cause and fought with fellow Harvard graduates on the side of the Union.[5]

When the Civil War broke out, Nicholas had just commenced the study of law. He could have had a colonel's commission for the asking, as his father was one of the principal supporters of Ohio governor William Dennison. Instead he volunteered as a private in the ranks of the Cincinnati militia company the Guthrie Grays. On the organization of this militia company as the Sixth Ohio Regiment, he was elected a lieutenant. Before leaving Camp Dennison, the Sixth Ohio was reorganized as a three-years regiment, and Nicholas became its lieutenant colonel on June 21, 1861. Serving in western Virginia, he took part in the engagements at Laurel Hill, Corrick's Ford, Shiloh, Corinth, and Stones River.

The Sixth Ohio was transferred to the Army of the Ohio, and Lt. Col. Nicholas Anderson was with his men, serving under Cincinnati's General Jacob Ammen, on April 6, 1862, at Shiloh. After the first day of the Battle of Shiloh, Larz, with two or three friends, fitted out a steamboat as a free hospital for the wounded. Nicholas then fought through the second day and took part in the siege and occupation of Corinth. While Confederate general Braxton Bragg was unsuccessfully invading and leaving Kentucky, Nicholas and his regiment helped hold Nashville until after the Battle of Perryville, Kentucky, in October 1862. On the resignation of the Sixth Ohio's colonel, Nicholas became regimental commander with the rank of colonel on November 9, 1862.

Often family superseded sectional loyalties. In a letter from Charles's second daughter, Kitty, to Latham's wife Sallie—a Southerner by birth—she wrote plaintively about the deeply personal nature of the war: "You and I in all the sisterhood of true-hearted woman nature must pray for peace and love to reign over our unhappy country, and that we may meet where all dangers of earth are forgotten. Mother [Eliza] and kids now say as a farewell that you must never imagine that she has any animosity whatever to the South or Southerns—all her ancestors were southerners, and her mother, one of the most devoted Kentuckians ever born there."[6]

Scholars often write about the Civil War as the "last romantic war," noting the extreme patriotism and romance that accompanied the soldiers into battle. This was clearly reflected in a letter Charles received from "Kate Phillips and 32 other women," who presented him an American flag and a regimental banner to bring with him into battle: "With these flags accept our best wishes, and our prayers for your safety and glorious success, in the march, the camp, and the battle field."[7]

In the summer of 1862, Charles established a base near Dayton, where four companies had enlisted. He promptly began training his men (and himself). The troops next set up camp in Lexington, Kentucky, near William's alma mater, Transylvania College. On August 30, Charles received orders to move on Richmond, Kentucky. But when Confederate troops routed his soldiers, Charles was forced to order his regiment back to Lexington.

In a letter to daughter Kitty in September, Charles informed her that "the Regt it is supposed is under orders to march—after [General Braxton] Bragg I presume meanwhile we are all the time 'alarmed' with threats of an expected attack. . . . Last night we were assured that the enemy was 3 miles off our pickets." He and his men were in trenches "with no time or opportunity whatever for drills or instruction." Three days later he wrote his wife Eliza with the concerns that most commanders experienced: "When we go I know not. I hope to Lexington— or else somewhere for all of us to learn our new trade. We are sadly deficient. Adieu. Affectionately your husband, with love to Kitty, Belle and others of the family."[8]

Fortunately for Charles, his regiment did not make it to Perryville, Kentucky, in time for a horrific battle on October 8 with seven thousand casualties. When Charles's regiment arrived three days later, it was treated to a gruesome scene. Unlike veterans of World War II, who seldom mentioned their experiences in war, Civil War soldiers offered graphic descriptions of the carnage to loved ones, which surely alarmed them greatly. Of the Perryville battlefield, Charles wrote:

I have seen a field of battle after the excitements and dangers. What a sight for the imagination! Also poor human nature! How soon the most disgusting and appalling scenes, become common place and dull sights. A cornfield with not infrequent carcasses of horses, their straightened legs in the air, men dead, swollen, bursting; some blackened literally as the blackest Negroes and very like except, perhaps, somewhat bluer—these [look] more like some beast or monster than men. Others (those not shot in the heart, lungs, or brain) white, pale, thin, beautiful, in their narrow flexible hands and fingers, sometimes holding delicately, a straw or blade of grass. Some with their legs torn in shreds of fiber. . . . Others, with the entire skull blown away—the ball dragging out all the brains. These and such things made up the scene.

But then, to Anderson's surprise and shock, "in ten or fifteen minutes, all were reconciled—and, in a few minutes more, all without sadness and many in gaiety were actually eating our dinners in sight of some of the most contorted of these human forms! What think you of the living human nature of War?"[9]

On December 11, 1862, Charles again wrote to his daughter Kitty to note, "We have moved camp again from the lunatic asylum. . . . We [are] now only a half mile from your cousin Nick's camp." As Christmas 1862 approached, so did battle, but that was not Charles's focus. Army life and the war were driving him crazy. Twelve days later, on December 23, in another letter to Kitty, he wrote: "Another year gone. Twelve more months—365 more days—8760 more hours—525600 more of the precious minutes—moments—gone forever—and alas alas wasted all. Ah! Me." This led him to a more general meditation on war: "War upon us. War by us. War over, above, before, behind, around—Within us! Spreading through space—filling up time. Why should we care for or count its actual intervals? No—let the miserable legacy-impart and whole steal off, unheeded and forgotten, into that blank nothingness of the past which is so much better than the shameful present or the dismal future." Three days later Charles and Nick would both be launched in the fight of their life in the "western theater" near the town of Murfreesboro, Tennessee.[10]

THAT PROCLAIMING SLAVERY'S END would inevitably lead to total war received eerie confirmation when, on New Year's Day 1863, newspapers presented coverage of both the Emancipation Proclamation and a frightful new battle at Murfreesboro: the Battle of Stones River. Confederate forces in retreat from Perryville, Kentucky, under the command of General Braxton Bragg, met advancing Federal forces under General William Rosecrans. Both commanders were hot-tempered and eventually lost their commands, but not before clashing in a full-fledged bloodbath. Along with Charles, two of his nephews—Nicholas and his brother Edward (Ned)—were also involved in the battle. Having tasted combat at Perryville, Nicholas's regiment was the most seasoned and would be the most tested. Charles's regiment would be held in reserve.

On December 31, 1862, forty-nine thousand Yankees faced off against thirty-eight thousand Rebels just west of Stones River. That night, with battle looming, the contending bands played their rival national tunes. Then, in a poignant moment of shared brotherhood, both bands and armies joined together in singing "Home Sweet Home." Two armies, one home. The next day they met in battle.[11]

Ironically, both generals planned a morning attack on the other's right flank, hoping to get into his rear, cutting his army from its base. General Rosecrans ordered his attack to start at daybreak after breakfast. But as at the earlier Battle of Shiloh, the Confederates caught the coffee-sipping Yankees by surprise. With a burst of bloodcurdling Rebel yells, the Confederates advanced and drove the Federal right flank back three miles before they were finally stopped. A fierce holding action and counterattack by the young and extremely gifted General Philip Sheridan bought sufficient time for the Federals to regroup. In the course of a furious four-hour firefight, Sheridan lost one-third of his men and all of his brigade commanders to death or serious wounds, the latter including the wounded Nick Anderson. But the imperiled flank held, and with it Sheridan's and Nick Anderson's reputations.

By noon, the Union line had regrouped in a precarious position likened by military historians to a "jackknife with its blade nearly closed." If the Confederates could break the Federal line anywhere along the Nashville turnpike, the blade would snap shut and the Union army would be destroyed. The crucial angle where the blade joined the handle lay in a four-acre oak grove named Round Forest, which the soldiers would rename "Hell's Half Acre." Confederate corps commander and former Episcopal bishop Leonidas Polk ordered his Mississippi Rebels to charge across an open field to attack the Round Forest.[12]

On the other side, General George Thomas had placed lines of heavy artillery in the paths of the charging Confederates. In a single salvo of shattering noise, the artillery opened up and tore the advancing Confederates to shreds. A second Confederate charge penetrated the Union line west of Round Forest and succeeded in capturing one thousand prisoners and eleven guns. But still the midwesterners held Round Forest as a cigar-chomping General Rosecrans, in rumpled hat and bloodstained overcoat, rallied his forces up and down the line.

In a letter to Eliza, Charles described his regiment's role in the battle. The night before, he noted, "I put my Regt to bed and asleep at the very spot where the next morning's attack." Luckily, however, "I took the responsibility of moving it, without and rather against orders to a place where we last attacked. I really believe in the former camp, we would have been exterminated, almost to a man." The regiment was on observation point for Sheridan's cavalry and fires were prohibited. Again this worked to the regiment's advantage, as its men could not fall asleep and so were alert when the Rebels attacked. Soon the regiment found themselves "in the very thickest hail of balls of every shape and size—my horse was hit 3 times—2 by spent balls glancing from trees—I think once by a spent ball. One ball aimed at only 75 yards distance, as I turned to see . . . how the enemy were advancing—struck near the 2nd button—exactly of my coat over the pit of the stomach . . . the ball tore away the skin and flesh from the outside of the rib . . . and passed off harmless into the air, or else into some poor fugitive around me." Recognizing his dire straits, Charles continued: "I then took to my native heels and ran as if I were still a Whitehead [young boy]." He then closed: "You will call this providential deliverances, but as I see better men killed by similar glances—the other way—I still think them <u>accidents</u>. But I can't say much now of Anderson luck." Charles's reluctance to invoke "providential deliverance" was unusual in the Civil War as religion was central to both sides of the struggle. Charles stands in stark contrast to his brother Robert, whose invocation of Providence was a constant refrain.[13]

Bragg was so certain Rosecrans would retreat, weighed down as he was with many Union casualties and Confederate prisoners in tow, that he sent a victory message to President Jefferson Davis: "God has granted us a happy New Year." But Bragg's God proved to be a New Year's angel of darkness. Instead of retiring, Rosecrans decided to remain in the field overnight, moving his army from the Round Forest to higher ground perfectly suited for a strategic defensive position. From there the Federals launched a fierce counterattack that claimed 1,700 casualties in little over an hour.

With a third of his troops dead, wounded, or missing, Bragg could neither follow up his tactical victory with an attack on Rosecrans's larger army nor drive it back. Instead, badly humiliated, he called off the attack and retreated to a new position south of Murfreesboro, leaving carnage behind.

Nicholas's command was also distinguished on that day. The Sixth Ohio saw the regiment in front of it collapse in "in utter confusion." A stunned Nicholas faced a rebel onslaught only a hundred yards away. At first his ranks buckled, but then recovered and returned fire. For twenty minutes the two lines traded intense fire, until Nicholas, wounded minutes earlier, gave the command to fix bayonets and charge the Rebel stronghold. But just as they were about to charge, a volley of fire into their left flank compelled Nicholas to order his men to about-face, fire by the rear flank, and then retreat. Thanks to his leadership, the maneuver was accomplished in good order and, having held the Rebels for forty minutes, Nicholas reformed the ranks and engaged the youthful General Lucius Polk's brigade.[14]

Both Charles's and Nicholas's wounds were serious and removed them from the field of battle (in Nicholas's case, only temporarily). In addition, Charles reported eleven "of my poor braves killed—dead—and 47 wounded. Doubtless, more yet of each class to be subtracted from the unknown quantity of missing." We now know the totals. In all, Federal losses totaled 12,906 of 41,400 engaged. In proportional terms, this would prove to be the deadliest battle the North would fight. The Confederates lost 11,739 out of 34,739 engaged.

On January 2, the wounded Charles wrote to daughter Kitty that he was "so unwell, feverish and in pain from my wound, that I was on the verge of asking sick leave. . . . The Dr. thought I was tending to typhoid fever." On January 22 he wrote to Kitty again from Camp Sill near Washington, DC, saying he was "in considerable distress. The fact is, my wound, was always a more serious affair than I gave it credit for." He should have gone for a "softer bed . . . but, without any [available] field officer I could not think of leaving the Regiment. When I suffer now, I think, I will ask Leave and go home at once. But when I feel easier, I feel it impossible to go." The psychological damage from all of the suffering reached new depths: "Every hour my spirit of vengeance vanishes and my pity for this portion of them, softens and swells until at times, it quite unnerves me for such a warfare. It must come to that . . . Ah! What a Revolution is this?" He then referenced Kitty's brother: "As to Latham I have made up my mind, that I wish him to resign. He is too good for this work. Nor is this government, as now administered, worthy of controlling in heedless neglect—such an officer. I enclose to your mother his letter. Adieu Your Father." Charles's sympathy for the South and admiration for Confederate bravery was not unusual and was reciprocated. As he continued to recover, he doubted his ability to return to combat, and he resigned his commission on February 21, 1863. The decision probably saved his life. The new commander, Hiram Strong, would be mortally wounded at Chickamauga in September.[15]

IN JUNE 1863, CHARLES heard from John D. Caldwell, organizer of the Republican (or "Union") Party in Ohio, who was organizing opposition to the "Peace Democrats," led by the Copperhead Clement Vallandigham, who condemned Lincoln's emancipation policy and urged immediate peace no matter what the cost. When Vallandigham cleverly arranged his own arrest for "disloyalty" in 1863, rendering him a "martyr," Lincoln commuted his sentence from imprisonment to banishment. While in exile, Vallandigham ran in absentia for governor on the Ohio Democratic ticket. Ohio Republicans vowed to thwart this plan, and Charles was chosen to play a vital role. In his letter to Charles, Caldwell wrote that the party had nominated John Brough for governor and invited Charles to run for lieutenant governor as one ideally poised to "expose the fallacies which artful men have used to misguide a generous, noble people." Then, playing to Charles's family fame, Caldwell asserted that "this great opportunity—like that embraced by your patriotic kinsmen of the Revolution, will be as proud a one for exhibition of your love of Country, as that of your renowned brother in blood, the hero of Ft. Sumter. Charge 'Charlie' charge, again against the enemies of your country!"[16]

Charles accepted the nomination, prompting brother Larz to write a cautionary and typically critical note. But then Larz relented: "But upon consideration I give up [trying to persuade you]—believing that your mind is already made up. Joe says that there is no use in attempting to make any thing of you any how, and I believe he is more than half right. . . . However you are old enough and ought to be experienced enough to manage your own affairs wisely . . . so there is the end of it."[17]

A few weeks later, Larz softened his criticism with some constructive advice. In running for office, he recommended that Charles laud Vallandigham's arrest "and hold it up constantly and persistently on the question which it truly is, the existence or destruction of the Union, the acceptance and support of lawful government or of rank despotism. . . . If you permit them to set you upon the discussion of the other issue [emancipation], you will . . . lose much strength and unnecessarily weaken your cause."

In February 1863, Larz's father-in-law, Nicholas Longworth, had died, rendering Larz and Catherine two of the wealthiest people in Ohio. Knowing that Charles's resources were severely constrained and not likely to improve with a colonel's pay, Larz closed: "Knowing that you cannot afford to make this campaign without help I send you the enclosed contribution [in pencil "$500"]. Spend whatever may be necessary, without stint, and call on me without hesitation for any aid you may require. There is no cause—as I understand this juncture—to which true and honest citizens should more cheerfully contribute than this."[18]

Larz's advice was well taken, and in the ensuing election Brough and Anderson trounced Vallandigham. It did not hurt the Union cause that on the day Larz wrote to Charles, July 4, 1863, Union armies won crushing victories at Gettysburg and Vicksburg.

Soon after deciding to run for lieutenant governor, Charles had begun receiving letters of congratulations and well wishes, most on a very elevated plane. One exception was a letter from Joseph Geiger, whose relationship with Charles is unknown. Geiger assured Anderson he would win "because with your ability and personal bearing it will be almost if not surely the way to the United States Senate. . . . Every body knows you are patriotic, and you can have an irresistible host of friends." He then cautioned Charles to switch from smoking cigarettes to smoking cigars, adding that in this way he could "look like a man and not a female baby." In conclusion, Geiger attempted a note of humor: "I am going to make a speech in Dayton before long and want you to be there, but you must not speak after and diminish me or I will kick your damned ass." More typical was a letter from Edmund Davis, who, reflecting Republican opinion, wrote, "It is not necessary to say that I would consider, even the possibility of the election of such a man as Vallandigham a greater disaster at the present time than would be the gaining of a great victory by the Rebels." The publisher William Cooper Howells (father of the famed writer William Dean Howells) wrote urging that Charles display his antislavery (if not abolitionist) views and assuring him that they would serve him well: "You know that this has been a former anti slavery region, and it is so still, as to almost five sixths of our vote. You are just the man to do that [generate enthusiasm for antislavery]—as your Texas experience has given you a reputation with us as one who knows what the peculiar institution is, and is able to show it up in its true character." Howells may not have known that Charles did not have to travel to Texas to know the "peculiar institution," as he grew up with it in his family.[19]

When not complaining about the wastefulness of war, Charles was preoccupied with the prospects of becoming lieutenant governor, serving with Governor-Elect John Brough. On December 26, the then lieutenant governor Benjamin Stanton advised Charles on his inaugural speech. Stanton recommended that Charles not "launch into national politics" and instead choose to "keep it brief." Stanton added that he would be happy to consult on upcoming appointments.[20]

In August 1863, Charles received a letter from General William Tecumseh Sherman, an Ohio native whose brother John was an Ohio senator and friend of Charles. Sherman was serving under General Ulysses S. Grant, and the two had recently vanquished the Confederate fortress at Vicksburg. A speech by Charles had caught Sherman's attention and prompted the letter. He began: "Dear Sir I have not read a speech in two years, but accidentally finding one of yours published in Cincinnati paper of July 30, I read it all, the other night. You make some good points—war existed before Sumter—was just one." He then derided "peace talk" as "nonsense." "They are cowards and try to cover up this cowardice by a plea Peace. I have seen such men in battle, when bursting shells and hissing bullets made them uncomfortable they would discern suddenly that they were sick or had left something back in camp." He followed this up with extreme language: "Today I declare I have more sympathy with the misled but brave [Confederate] man who fights when I come within the range of his guns, than of the miscreant who tries to discern a Reason by calling his cowardice patriotism—Take the fore ground disfranchise all who will not help their country, you fight for it . . . and all true and brave and worthy Americans will cry aloud. Amen." He then concluded: "I am no voter. But I have some 20 lb rifles that have more sense than 4/10 of the voters of Ohio and if you want them say so. . . . I am for the regeneration of poor Ohio."[21]

SOMETIME AROUND LATE OCTOBER or early November 1863, Charles received a letter from William Wellen informing him that the New York Union Party State Committee wanted to take advantage of his great speaking ability in New York to boost the state's chances in the upcoming 1863 state election. Charles's response is not preserved, but at the bottom of Weller's letter he later penciled in: "A fool—I declined—to go and so lost the V. Presidency to A[ndrew] Johnson!"[22]

Again, Charles's abrupt reply betrayed him. Whether he would have actually been nominated is an open question, but given his pending position as the lieutenant governor of Ohio, it is entirely plausible. His star was in the ascendant and was reinforced by an invitation from Governor David Tod of Ohio to speak at "ceremonies of consecrating the ground" at Gettysburg, Pennsylvania, in November. Massachusetts educator, minister, and statesman Edward Everett would deliver the main address but the organizers also wanted someone from Ohio to speak: "Upon consultation with several of our mutual friends we can think of no one better fitted for that duty than yourself." This invitation Charles did accept, and in so doing assured that Everett and Lincoln would not be the only ones delivering a "Gettysburg address."[23]

Shortly after accepting the invitation, Charles received a letter from Rutherford B. Hayes, who would later become governor of Ohio and eventually assume the presidency. At the time of writing, Hayes was another political officer, but a most accomplished one who would be wounded five times in battles and promoted to major general for bravery. In his letter to Charles, while still in the army, he wrote on the necessity of a military draft: "The Gov. [Tod] is sound in feeling, but the last year of his term has been spent not in strengthening our armies but in avoiding the draft. . . . I hope Governor Brough will adopt sounder views. <u>We must get the great majority of men hereafter by drafting</u>. . . . In no other way can we raise the men who will be required to end the war." Again, we see what a small world these interconnected elites shared, with personal acquaintances at all levels, as high as the presidency.[24]

With the gubernatorial election nearing in late 1863, Charles wrote and published "A Letter Addressed to the Opera House Meeting in Cincinnati." His purpose was to discredit the Ohio Democrats and Vallandigham in particular. After recounting his escape from San Antonio, he proceeded to lambast those who denigrated the cause for which he had escaped and fought. To those seeking armistice he asked, "Why entrust these, the most cunning of all conspirators, the most faithless of all traitors in the course of all history, with time, place, and opportunity to refresh and reinforce themselves for a renewal of their energies in the same and other bad purposes and plans?" He then went on to argue, presciently, that an armistice would create unending struggles between the two sides, effectively turning the United States government into a "Military Republic." To the Peace Democrats in Ohio he defiantly proclaimed, in cadences reminiscent of Patrick Henry: "As for me, I should prefer to see this dreadful war go on, without a pause, until the last *white* man who is able to bear arms in the cause of the Union shall have impaled himself upon their last bayonet, before we shall consent to a division of this Union, or even an armistice for discussion." Soon enough, Charles would not be able to reference the "last white man," as African American soldiers would volunteer, fight, and die in the thousands. But the letter does confirm his reluctant antislavery sensibilities in 1862 and 1863.[25]

One major disappointment, which amazingly did not sour family affections, was William, who turned on his family and Republican friends to vote for Vallandigham. A chagrined Thomas wrote to his uncle Charles, torn between being a dutiful, if challenging, son and being a loyal American patriot under arms who loved his uncle. After acknowledging numerous differences over the years, he wrote, he'd learned to respect his father's "honesty." He continued, "You know my Dear Uncle that it has often been my misfortune to differ with my father on many important questions and never more widely than now." Then, he pointed to one instance where his father had actually admitted he was wrong, in regard to a "family matter" apparently involving his stepmother, Ellen. From the letter it appears that both William and Thomas thought William had made a mistake in taking Ellen's counsel in favor of Vallandigham. Thomas continued: "Would to God, for his happiness it had been otherwise. But that misfortune without his knowing it, has very decidedly influenced his political opinions. No man can have certain opinions songs or chimes in his ears from morning to night without their producing some impression on him. I fear I have not so excellent an opinion of the sex as the rest of my family, but I know the influence they can exert when they have a man at a matrimonial disadvantage." How could that be? Ellen was very close to her uncle Bryce, a Confederate slaveholder, and he may have induced her to support the Vallandigham platform of peace at any cost. That said, Thomas concluded, "Come what, come may; no one can question the honor of our tribe, while our women are all chaste and the men are all loyal and brave."[26]

This would not mark the end of William's sympathies for the Confederacy. Though he never betrayed the Union, he ventured extremely close. Thomas's letter suggests that he held William's second wife, Ellen, at least partly to blame. But not solely. William probably detested the Republican Party as the descendant of primarily Protestant Whigs, and for Lincoln's sympathy for people of color, whom he routinely labeled "niggers." But in a testimony to the power of family loyalty, Thomas, who had no sympathy with the cause of the Confederacy, refused to break ranks against "our tribe." Nor, for that matter, did Charles, who later in life confirmed his love for William.

ON NOVEMBER 19, 1863, political and military luminaries met at the Soldiers' National Cemetery in Gettysburg, Pennsylvania, four and a half months after the climactic three-day Battle of Gettysburg. The extremely long oration of Edward Everett is well known, and even more so the considerably shorter Lincoln speech destined to become American secular scripture. But few know that Charles delivered his address that day as well.

At the conclusion of his four-minute address, Lincoln—suffering at the time from variola, a mild form of smallpox—walked arm in arm with John Burns, a Gettysburg civilian who fought with the Union, to the Presbyterian church, accompanied by Secretary of State William Seward and the Marine Band. Four and a half months earlier the church had become a makeshift hospital for Union and Confederate wounded. But in November, the battle past, it was time for one more remembrance. Awaiting the president was the Ohio delegation and its chosen speaker, Colonel Charles Anderson, the lieutenant governor–elect of the state.

In many ways, each of the orations addressed different sentiments, and each contributed something unique. Everett offered an extended, neo-classical oration modeled on the ancients.[27] Lincoln offered a sacred meditation for the ages. Anderson spoke later at the Presbyterian church. In his speech, he made clear that with the war not yet over, he was angry. The Confederates were leading a rebellion after all, which had led to unimaginable destruction and suffering, with hatred aplenty on both sides.

Charles opened his oration by proclaiming what everyone already knew: that Gettysburg represented the turning point of the war. Here, "the Army of Patriotism and Liberty was victorious. The army of Treason and Despotism was decisively beaten." In contrast to Lincoln's soaring invocation of a "new birth of freedom," Anderson roared: "*The Dead must have justice at their own graves as in all history.*" The Confederate leaders were not republicans, as they claimed, but "despots." Nor were they Christians, "but followers of Judas Iscariot." Anderson then made clear he was not including his friend Robert E. Lee in his condemnation, recognizing instead "the excellent moral character of the commanding General of that army." Nor did he condemn "the great body of the Southern people," including his own countrymen. Rather, he blamed the "junta of insane slavery oligarchs," as distinct from ordinary slaveholders, who committed no offense. No doubt with his own family uppermost in mind, Charles simply could not identify slavery per se as a "sin." With no idea of the looming Thirteenth Amendment, he proclaimed: "I am willing to tolerate this monster-disease [of slavery] and crime within the Union, until Providence may, in his own good time and way, mitigate or remove it." The moral contradictions embedded in slavery were deep.[28]

In contrast to his earlier expressions of disillusionment with America, Charles now proclaimed, "Here then was the first and only fair trial of self-government, of a government of the people, for the people, ever made on earth." This noble experiment, he continued, would be "our example to all other peoples in all future times." Then, repeating a term that would be used with numbing regularity on both sides of the conflict, those who died "were martyred. . . . They died in the cause of our civil and religious liberties." He concluded by extemporizing on Lincoln's address, proclaiming America as "God's best hope on earth."

On December 3, Charles received a letter from S. Hine, editor of the *Ohio Commercial Gazette*, apologizing for not printing his Gettysburg address. The space required to print Everett's long oration precluded Charles's speech, so Hine had sent it to the *Commercial* for publication. But the original was apparently lost, leading Charles to write in pencil over Hine's letter in May 1893: "apology for not printing my Gettysburg Address. Where is it now?"[29]

In November 1864—one year after his address—Charles would receive a complimentary letter from Abraham Stagg. In rereading Everett's address, Stagg recalled Anderson's and wanted to publish it: "You are aware of what I am about to say; that you are deemed by the best literary men, one among the best speakers in the West. Would it not be best to put it into the hands of those publishers who solicited the publication of your speeches years ago?" In fact, Charles's speech would not be discovered and printed until the twenty-first century.[30]

In January 1864 Charles Anderson took office as lieutenant governor of Ohio. Two months earlier he had been thrilled to speak at Gettysburg. Now in Columbus, with his family in Dayton, Charles was bored. He saw no important work to do as a lieutenant governor, and he began planning to finish his term and leave politics for an uncertain future. As Governor Brough set out to raise thirty thousand additional volunteers, Charles sat idle, punctuating his time with occasional visits to Larz in Cincinnati.

In May 1864, Charles received a letter from his nephew-soldier Thomas. Defying the wishes of his father, William, and his priest, Thomas wanted nothing other than an army career and served with distinction. After being wounded in the Battles of the Wilderness, he wrote to Charles in some discomfort: "It is very difficult for me to write while lying in bed. . . . The Doctor tortures me considerably to prevent my joints from getting stiff." He then sounded a note of frustration with the family: "I do feel somewhat disappointed that I have not received a single line from home. I know that Father knows I am here wounded, for he telegraphed his member of congress to know whether he should come on or not. Except a short note from Aunt Maria I have not received a line from any relation although I have been in this hospital two weeks."[31]

Charles did write back to Thomas in regard to the wording of a memorial for Colonel Anderson, with several options, including a non-specified "number 2" that Thomas favored. But then, Thomas added, "I doubt whether it would agree with my father's theology. He wrote me the other day; that God judged by his justice not by our sympathies, ergo we could not take for granted the future happiness of any human being."[32]

In August, Charles was invited by Godwin Volney Dorsey, Ohio state treasurer and member of the Republican convention of 1864, to deliver a speech at the Republican national convention. Again Charles turned down the offer, claiming, "I have not the heart." And then, in words that would inevitably sour him with the Republican leadership and end any hope for a diplomatic assignment, he took off after Lincoln: "As for Mr. Lincoln, he might as well attempt to row up the Niagra Chute in a particularly frail birch canoe, with a particularly weak feather for a paddle, as to talk . . . of abolishing slavery as a sine qua non and condition precedent to re-union." Then, in a monumental act of disrespect, Charles closed by saying he had better things to do with his time: "I leave tomorrow for a two-weeks hunt in Indiana—filled with some foreboding—almost despair—for my country." In a stroke, Charles effectively ended any hopes he may have harbored for political advancement.[33]

As he viewed events in Washington, Charles was horrified to see the Radical Republicans lead the charge for Lincoln's reelection on an emancipationist platform. As he had said a year earlier at Gettysburg, emancipation would prompt an invasion of freedmen into Ohio, turning it into "a vast cloaca Maxima [gutter] for their overflowing filth." Adding to Charles's frustration was the realization that his boss, Governor Brough, had backtracked on emancipation and was supporting Lincoln's bid for reelection. For Brough, the choice was easy, given that the alternative was Ohio native son and radical abolitionist Salmon P. Chase. To Charles's extreme discomfort, Lincoln was indeed reelected, and the Thirteenth Amendment, abolishing slavery everywhere, was passed by Congress on January 31, 1865, and ratified on December 6, 1865. In January 1865, Charles heard from his nephew Richard Clough Anderson in relation to land recommended for purchase, owned by a man named "Mr. Mahun." R. C. Anderson wrote: "All I know against this man's judgment is that he not only sympathizes with your Brother William's political notions but also went so far in his follies as to agree with him on the cashmere goat question—with a view to the propagation of this animal in connection with sheep." (Apparently William was exploring raising goats for cashmere, though it does not show up in his correspondence.) He then closed in words that led Charles to pencil in "alas" years later: "My heart understands once for all is set upon spending the remainder of my days near all or most of you. . . . I am still quite unwell but think a few bright days will bring me out." In fact, he would die young.[34]

Though serving as lieutenant governor and soon to be acting governor, Charles continued to set his sights on a European diplomatic appointment, which paid far better and offered greater ease. In February 1865 he received a letter from his friend John Markley that said, "I enclose a letter addressed to the President in favor of your appointment as Minister in Spain." Two days later, James Speed, Radical Republican from Kentucky and longtime friend of Lincoln, sent a similar note, saying he would be happy to help after Congress adjourned, when Charles's chances would be better. How Charles could think he would have even a remote chance for an appointment with an administration he reviled is hard to understand. To paraphrase Charles's own insult to the Republican Party, he might as well row up the Niagara chute in a frail birch canoe as win favor in the Republican administration.[35]

On March 7, 1865, John Sherman wrote, "Yesterday I had a talk with the President about your appointment. He says he would like to satisfy you, but you must first find the plan. . . . Changes will only be made for some specific concern." Two weeks later, Rutherford B. Hayes wrote to his friend Charles from camp near Cumberland, Maryland: "Dear Friend I shall as suggested write to the President a general letter requesting that an appointment of the kind be made. I am glad to know that the Spanish Mission was not a particular object of desire on your part." Hayes noted that he would be going soon to Washington, DC, to meet with President Lincoln: "I will then hand a formal letter to the Pres. Please [do] not speak of my purpose to visit W." It is not clear whether Hayes ever wrote the letter. Sadly for Charles, all of the interventions would prove too late to promote his cause.[36]

In July 1865, Charles abruptly learned that in all likelihood he would imminently be appointed governor. In late June Brough had taken a fall in the garden, badly bruising his hand and ankle. In a short time, gangrene had set in. In a letter from the "Executive Department" on July 19, Sidney D. Maxwell notified Anderson that the governor's illness had taken a turn for the worse. Apparently he had suffered two severe hemorrhages in his foot that were followed by "a congestive chill that came near terminating fatally. We hope for the best, but I am very much afraid that he will not recover. I know you must be anxious concerning him, and I have consequently, now decided to write you this hurriedly. I will keep you advised of his situation." By August it was clear that the end was near. In a letter from Benjamin Cowen, Charles learned that the amputation scheduled to take place on August 26 had to be postponed due to a "local inflammation" and the end was near.[37]

On August 29, Brough died and Charles was sworn in as governor of Ohio. His term in office was brief, lasting less than five months, until January 8, 1866. Much of Charles's correspondence while in office consisted of letters from favor-seekers looking for appointments for themselves or their friends.

As Charles wound down the governorship, he made it clear he had no intention of joining the Republican Party and running for reelection. In his annual State of the State message, delivered on January 1, 1866, he opposed full black citizenship indirectly by refusing to endorse the Republican resolutions to strike the word *white* from the state convention. The stand was petulant and, in the end, rendered moot by the Fifteenth Amendment, which prohibited states from denying the franchise on the basis of race. And once again, as he had done in his Kenyon address, Charles attacked the Monroe Doctrine, even as France moved to impose a Catholic-sponsored government in Mexico led by Ferdinand Maximilian. Charles adamantly opposed any meddling in Mexican affairs.

How do we understand the self-righteous anger and contempt Charles manifested? What could explain his repeated indiscretions? An impulsive personality lacking cautionary filters? A false sense of honor that suggested only he had the integrity to act on his conscience? A racism so virulent that it matched that of his brother William? Perhaps all of the above. Charles would later reiterate that he had no religious faith, and his love affair with America would continue on-again, off-again. His only sure loyalty besides family was the Whig Party. When it died, he was left rudderless. He had no trouble identifying who and what he loathed—and they were legion. But he could not submit and bow to anyone but his beloved Henry Clay, now long dead. Even his dead half brother Richard was implicitly smeared by his disavowal of Manifest Destiny. His obsessive certainty that he and he alone was right, and his willingness to martyr himself, made him lose virtually all political allies in the aftermath of America's trial by fire.

In November 1865, Larz, ever the patriarch, wrote a concerned letter to the ailing Charles. Columbus did not do Charles's asthma well and Larz offered assistance: "Why do you not come down here, where you are free to visit every week and stay a day or two, or as much longer as you can? . . . I think you would be much the better for it, and we would be delighted to have you with us for any time you could spare." Four days later, Larz arranged for a medical specialist to consult with Charles.[38]

The wartime preoccupations of the Andersons allowed little time or occasion for their beloved speculation even as the larger purpose of the war involved the acquisition and preservation of private property. Their mania would resume in the postwar republic, with eyes set on the West and, in William's case, back on Mexico.

15

An Ex-Confederate Colony

1865–1866

Family may have dictated that William would be a strong Unionist, but it also dictated that he would be a harsh critic of Lincoln, abolitionists, and the Union's conduct of the war. He did not hesitate to enter the raging debates surrounding the war in conversation and newspaper opinion pieces. Emancipation he labeled a campaign to "Africanize the South and make the whites the serfs and vassals of the negro population." Apparently William's nephew R. C. Anderson harbored similar sentiments. On January 14, 1866, he wrote to William from Ohio that his experiences in Ohio and Kentucky persuaded him that "farming in Ohio will never suit me. I cannot get over old prejudices and old habits. In bringing negroes here I fear I have tried an impracticable experiment—a free state is not the air or the soil in which this kind of labor thrives. The branch is unsuited to the bud. . . . I have been back to my 'old Ky home' about Lexington and Frankfort and most of my friends." Once back in Kentucky, Richard discovered that emancipation had left the state without a labor base, so that whites "now have all the evils without any of the benefits of servitude. The minds of men are greatly exercised and this approach seems seriously awakened. What the end will be no body pretends to know. . . . Clearly there is uncertainty and disorientation with the disappearance of slavery and the continued presence of 'negroes.'"[1]

Given William's antipathy to abolition, Lincoln, and the Thirteenth Amendment, it is not surprising that he detested Radical Republican

rule, which sought to impose harsh terms on white former Confederates while granting full citizenship to the freedmen. Backed by military
force, Radical Republicans imposed forcible "reconstruction," fired by
an emancipationist vision. His resentment far exceeded any evidenced
by other family members, including Charles, and set the stage for an
enigmatic trip to Mexico. With relatively short notice, he wrote a will
conveying all his property to his wife Ellen and departed alone for
Mexico on March 29, 1865. Nothing in the surviving letters provides a
complete answer as to why he would leave Ellen behind and travel to a
dangerous country. Surely William did not intend to leave Ellen, whom
he supported and whose shared fervent Catholicism was a strong bond.
But then why effectively desert her? It seems unlikely that at age fifty-
eight the desire for adventure had suddenly overcome him. Nor does his
professed interest in undertaking an archeological expedition ring true.
Perhaps curiosity about Mexico as a Catholic nation drove him. More
likely his fundamental alienation from the Republican Party in power
bred in him a desire to possibly move to Mexico permanently as part of
a Confederate community in exile.

Throughout the nineteenth century, Mexico witnessed a bloody
struggle between French-backed Conservatives and anti-French Liberals, who wanted to destroy the Catholic Church and nationalize its
considerable lands. The Liberals located their government in Veracruz
while the Conservatives controlled Mexico City. Their struggle for
dominance erupted into a full-scale civil war. Eventually the Liberals
prevailed, forcing Conservative forces to surrender in December 1860,
but that did not stop the Conservatives from conspiring with French
forces to install Maximilian I of Austria as emperor.

Unlike Charles, who supported US neutrality in Mexico, William
actively placed his bet on the Catholic monarchy of Maximilian and
against the Liberals seeking to topple the monarchy and establish a republic. In December 1865, William received a commission from Maximilian to survey lands in northeastern Mexico for a possible colony for
ex-Confederates, hundreds of whom had exiled themselves in Mexico
following the surrender of the Confederacy in April 1865. Included
among them were the scientist (and leader) Matthew Fontaine Maury;
Confederate generals Joseph Selby, John B. Magruder, and Sterling
Price; and displaced politicians Governor Henry Allen of Louisiana

and Judge David Terry. Settlement in Mexico, as in the United States, would require lots of land. Land titles depended on the emperor, who, in turn, required settlers to pledge loyalty to Napoleon and his French forces, incurring the wrath of American leaders. Of course, William's commission and the promised lands were only as good as Maximilian's power over the country, and that was increasingly tenuous. Maximilian had come to power as the only monarch of the Second Mexican Empire with French backing (and the absence of American opposition from a nation preoccupied with the Civil War). The Monroe Doctrine prevented any US recognition of his French-based "empire," and with the end of the Civil War, the United States was providing unconcealed support for Liberal forces of mestizos (people of mixed race) and Indians under President Benito Juárez, who led them to war against foreign occupation under the emperor Maximilian.[2]

William's experience with surveying, land, and farming made him the ideal candidate to do in Mexico what he and his father had done with the Virginia Military District. Carlos Sanchez Navarro, a wealthy landowner from Coahuila and ally of Maximilian, had offered two million acres for sale to potential colonists, which Maximilian readily accepted. When Maury, acting for Maximilian, offered William the commission, he eagerly agreed and established a land office. Once again an Anderson was at the center of a vast land grab involving millions of acres, but this one would ultimately go unrewarded.

As WITH ALL OTHER Andersons, land was William's métier. If he did not engage in as much speculation as his father or brothers, it was probably because he inherited substantial lands through his two wives. He was commissioned on November 20, 1865, to work with Jacob Kuchler, another surveyor and engineer who knew Manuel Maynez, the administrator of the Hacienda de Patos, the property of Carlos Sanchez Navarro.

The surveyors explored and surveyed lands in Coahuila, close to the US border. They concentrated on the Hacienda de Nacimiento, a landed estate of substantial size. William reported that the land appeared especially adapted to grain and grass, but "the quantity of farming land [is] diminishing, and the yield of grain by no means satisfactory." What was badly needed was "industry and irrigation." Immigrants could supply both with a strong work ethic and the construction of a dam to supply water to thousands of acres. A dam could also power mills and manufacturing establishments "to supply the wants of a large population."[3]

The richest and most fertile lands came from Palado, part of the vast landholdings of Don Jacob's grandfather, Don Melchior Sanchez. Volcanic rock and lime in the adjacent lomas (hills) increased the land's fertility, which reminded William of cotton lands in Texas, Louisiana, and Mississippi. But here too civil war, thieves, and neglect had taken their toll: "The once opulent home of Don Melchior is now in ruins." William blamed the Liberals who, under the guise of "military necessity," stripped the hacienda bare of horses, cattle, and pigs. But he remained optimistic, asserting that "whenever this curse of nations shall have ceased, whatever this war for a theory [i.e., republicanism] shall be ended, I see no reason to doubt that this will become one of the most prosperous portions of Mexico."[4]

As with his earlier trip through the Rocky Mountains, William kept a journal of his time in Mexico, filling six notebooks. The journal was subsequently published in the twentieth century. With minimal Spanish-language skills and no means of communicating with home, his diary represented his primary conversation partner. His fictional "archeological dig" took place around the lands of Coahuila. The territory vacillated between French and Republican rule, making it extremely volatile and dangerous for partisans of both sides. When read in the light of internal Mexican tensions and larger international relations, the diaries present a fabulous adventure of travel, capture, escape, and homecoming.

William dedicated his diaries to Ellen's sister, Frances (Fanny) Ketchum, perhaps because Ellen never approved of the mission. In a preface to his diary, written in the form of a romantically ambiguous letter to Fanny on March 29, 1865, he projected a great exploit and asked Fanny to share it with him: "Let us now begin, & sail on, ride on, walk on, as steam, horse, or foot power shall require." To Fanny, who with Ellen shared Southern roots, William did not hesitate to display his rampant bigotry. His first night out en route to Veracruz, he was seasick and wrote, "I suppose I ought to thank old green-head for not giving me a free pass across his pond, as I, like 'the nigger with his kicked shin, feel so good gittin well.'" Of one of the female passengers he wrote, "She looks as if she might make a dead nigger turn pale with fear."[5]

On April 13, William arrived in Veracruz and, as was his custom, went immediately to Mass. The Catholic Church was itself an institution under siege by the Republicans, who were eager to expropriate its vast holdings for their followers. On the following day, Good Friday, he worshipped at the Church of San Antonia, regretting the paucity of male parishioners. That night, Lincoln was assassinated at Ford's Theater. The next day he worshipped at the old cathedral church of Veracruz and "was delighted to find the whole concourse respectful & wrapped in pious devotion." He observed mixed races in the congregation and in ignorance wrote: "Old Abe [Lincoln] ought to sympathize and fraternize with Maximilian, as this population is miscegenated to his heart's content!" Throughout, William recorded endearments for Fanny—phrases such as "Ah, Fanny, dear 'hermana mia,'" or "dear Sister," or, in Spanish, "Cunada" (sister-in-law). He told her he would happily be "willing to waste words, if it can give you pleasure." When he reached the top of a mountain ridge he wrote, "How I wished for Minnie [his sister Mary Louisa], & Fanny or Charley [his son]!" Conspicuously absent from his list of wished-for companions was Ellen. In a curious choice of metaphor, he employed a reference to a narcotic to describe his enchantment with the scene: "All the haschisch [hashish] and whiskey in the world, used to a point just below mental madness, could not conjure up such a lovely chaos." The flirtatious tone of his letters makes it clear there was more on William's mind than giving Fanny a travelogue.[6]

At points William barely restrained his joy at being out of a United States he could no longer love, and a Protestant nation at that: "Sister Fanny, dream! Dream your best, dream, dream your prettiest dream, and you will be behind any reality." His rare comments regarding Ellen stood in stark contrast. On April 30, 1865, William wrote: "I received a most lugubrious letter from my wife. Two thousand miles away from home—Alone!—I could not help thinking & feeling that as husband, father, or friend, a more unsuitable letter never was sent by mail. Well, I will do my best and trust in God." In contrast, on May 4, he wrote: "Ah, dear Fanny, how I wish for your smiling, good natured face & amiable palet. . . . What a paradise this would be!"[7]

Politically, Mexico seemed less of a paradise. Mexican emancipation dated to 1829, and as far as William was concerned, it was misbegotten. Writing from Córdoba he observed: "The negroes were said to have been numerous hereabouts; where are they now? A few crawl about here, as ancient landmarks. They have disappeared & so has that great wealth which came & went with them. Has the civilized or Christian world gained by it? . . . And what has the world gained by it? A principle? Yes, the principle of freedom—the principle of independence, starvation, & death." Anderson was correct on the decline of the region, but its cause was hardly emancipation. Poor colonial administration, incompetent officials, and a decadent mother country had robbed and diminished it. The races were more mingled in Mexico, in large part because Spain, unlike England, did not discourage miscegenation of all races. But by assigning blame to emancipation, William could proceed to his main argument: "I pray God that negro slavery may be re-established all through tropical America for the health, the happiness, & the preservation of the African race, & for the cultivation of lands now waste and desert."[8]

William was more accommodating to the paler-skinned Mexican people. Where American Protestants saw only ignorant and superstitious Mexican Catholics, William witnessed inspiring churches filled with "reverential beings." Where Protestants saw filth, Anderson saw piety and happiness: "Poor, naked, dirty creatures! But who can tell how bright, how beautiful are their souls." Even within his own family, most notably his deceased brother Richard and sister Louisa, strong strains of anti-Catholicism signaled stark disagreements, but never to the extent of rending the family fabric.[9]

William made little reference to the Civil War in his notations. Lincoln's assassination was not registered, but on May 15, 1865, he reported the sad news of defeat: "A report reached here last night that [Generals] Johnson and Beauregard have surrendered to [General] Sherman, on the same terms & conditions that Lee did to Grant. If such proves the fact, what will come of it? Will vulgar power crush the weak, or will magnanimity and generosity be extended to the conquered foe?" With Confederate surrender, Maximilian had to rethink his earlier overtures to Confederates. The Confederate exiles had defied Washington's policy on Mexico, and now they had no country to claim.

Maximilian had enough problems without enraging American officials, and he began reversing his welcome in the few remaining months he had to live.[10]

By August, William was complaining that he had received no letters from his wife and children, save one from Thomas "as was right and proper." At that time, Thomas was in the army, recovering from his Civil War wound. In the same month William sought to purchase sixty acres of farm land: "I have closed a contract for a small piece of land near the latter city [Córdoba], which I shall ask God's blessing on before I go." It would seem that William had hopes of remaining in Mexico, perhaps permanently, as long as Maximilian offered protection. Such was his self-absorption that he never considered just how jolting his departure must have been to the family. His adventure was their trial. And now it was his trial as well, not only relationally, but also because he had counted on money to support his purchase of Mexican land. It never arrived, forcing him to abandon the purchase and rely solely on his position with Maximilian to survey the lands of Sanchez Navarro for purchase.[11]

On August 18, William attended two Masses offered by the bishop of Veracruz. Three nights later, "just after lamp lighting," while listening to an entertaining book reading, William's merriment was cut short when French soldiers appeared in his room. He soon found himself under arrest without any charges put forward. In response, he decided to "show my spunk" and "try my hand at bragg." He demanded an explanation in writing from the commander, together with his immediate release. With only one trump card to play—"the American flag"—he got lucky. That night an orderly waited on him with a letter from the *comandante*, apologizing for the arrest and explaining that he thought some Mexicans who were assaulting his troops were in the room. As soon as he learned the identity of the American—"the brother of General Anderson"—"I gave the order to set you in liberty" and promised "a similar thing shall not happen again." To this, William responded: "Respected Sir, Within the hour, I have been a prisoner and liberated, without being informed how, or whom I have offended. . . . As an American citizen I demand to know why I have been deprived of my liberty, and why released without examination or hearing." There is no record of a response.[12]

On December 1, William left Córdoba and arrived in Mexico City, where he met prominent ex-Confederates, including General John B. Magruder and former Louisiana governor Henry W. Allen. Magruder had been appointed chief of the land office of colonization and was technically William's superior. In practice, William, the more experienced surveyor, organized the survey. By December 13, William had arrived in Querétaro, a strongly Catholic and Conservative bastion of Maximilian and the site of his last stand. Sounding like a salesman, William praised the plains and prairie lands, the "beautifully paved roads," and a marvelous aqueduct built in the colonial period and designed to carry water into the city. In design and beauty the structure was reminiscent of the Roman aqueducts, leading William to exclaim, "There is no question, no denial, that noble Hidalgos have executed a work worthy of all praise and honor." Everywhere he looked, he saw "brilliant and beautiful" sites, be they cathedrals or farms or, most notably, the "Mexicans pure," who, contrary to the views of most Southerners in Mexico, were not a "weak and effete race" but nature's noblemen: "For men of their size, I have never seen their equals in strength or activity." Most American Protestants in Mexico failed to see William's perspective on the country and people. For example, David S. Terry, formerly a judge of the California Supreme Court, had a very different view of the Mexican people: "I am not in love with the people, who, like most of those in countries where the earth produces abundantly and with little labor are indolent and ignorant."[13]

By January 1866, William was still on the move. All references to Fanny were gone from his journals and regrets at receiving no mail from home no longer appeared. By February 17 he could report completing "our first days survey & exploration in the Hermanas," part of the two million acres assigned for sale by Don Carlos Sanchez Navarro. He was assisted by "our faithful service boy" Mozo Juan, who, like manual laborers, received little pay and no assurance of security from his government. William complained, "There are sighs and sobs & hypocritical howls for the poor negro, but who doles out one hundred psalms for the poor Mozo?" The next day he visited the silver and gold mines in the Cerro with Juan as a packman, but, a rueful William noted, Juan "was entrusted with a bottle of Mescal & got drunk before eleven o'clock this morning."[14]

On February 26 William's explorations were coming to an end, and he wrote, "We are now at La Mota making preparations to start in the morning for Monclova on my return home." William knew he was in dangerous territory, as support for Maximilian had steadily waned and America was now pressing France to remove its troops under the terms of the Monroe Doctrine. In William's only surviving letter to Ellen from Mexico, written on April 6, 1866, he wrote of encountering a "company of Liberals. . . . As soon as they saw us coming they confiscated our horses and immediately divided them out among themselves. Two days before, they had stopped a private citizen near that spot and robbed him of 2 horses seven pistals as many guns and stripped him down as close as his knife." In response to this theft, he wrote, "I have been strongly tempted to make a break for Texas, but in that case, I would not only lose my wages, but little momentos . . . which I might some day treasure."[15]

William soon came to regret his decision not to break away. On April 20, he encountered two officers from the Republican army and heard them "utter . . . ominous words" that threatened his well-being. This time bravado did not work. He was held under guard and forced to make a difficult decision: "My mind was instantly made up. To save my papers & my arms I must sacrifice everything else & make my escape that night & cross the mountain ridge that separated me from Patos." Taking advantage of a drunken guard who fell asleep, William ran. As later described by his son Robert Marshall Anderson, who inherited William's papers and diaries, William stepped over the sleeping guards and began walking toward the mountains. About an hour into his escape he heard men on horseback and two bloodhounds hot on his trail. He hid in a small rock opening but was discovered by one of the hounds. William had two pistols, but knew if he fired he would be discovered. Then, as summarized by Robert, "during what . . . seemed long hours the dog stood still giving forth low growls. Suddenly the brute stopped growling, [and] wagging his tail turned around and trotted off." Over the next twenty-four hours William traveled forty miles across a mountain range and completed his escape.[16]

By May 18, 1866, while he was making his way to Mexico City and from there back home, William would sadly report that "things are going to pieces here." Napoleon had announced the recall of his troops from Mexico, leaving both Maximilian and the ex-Confederates in an untenable position and forcing them to desert the Confederate settlement in Carlota. On May 19, William reported in one curt sentence: "Got a letter from my wife which has been here a half year & I could never get it before." Where Frances was always "Fanny," Ellen's name is not referenced, only "my wife." He made no further elaboration as to the contents of the letter, and we can suppose it probably was not pleasant. In the next sentence William announced, "I am done with my journal," though he would continue adding "memoranda and scraps which I wish to preserve." He began his return trip via Mexico City on April 15. All hope for land and colony gone, William could only complete his report, collect his fees, and return home.[17]

On May 21, William submitted his report evaluating the lands offered by Carlos Sanchez Navarro to the minister of commerce. Maximilian had been convinced that for Mexico to improve, the population had to be leavened with immigrants from abroad, including former Southern Confederates. But this would not happen. In summarizing his report, William noted that the lands were suitable for tobacco, sugar, cotton, "and every cereal of the temperate zone." But in evaluating its worth, he considered the price of civil war such that "the man of capital will invest at no price, & the poor man will require a strong inducement." William recommended such inducements. If the government, or the present owner, would "lay off 5000 acres of land in a square form every ten or fifteen leagues, with a village in the centre . . . these lands might be safely & speedily settled." In particular, he recommended that French, Belgian, and German soldiers be offered such inducements and come prepared to defend themselves by maintaining a sort of militia. The same would apply to former Confederate soldiers.[18]

William closed his "memoranda and scraps" on a political note. He remained leery of American intervention. The people of Mexico, he wrote, "are very anxious for the army of America to drive out the army of France, but they are very apprehensive that if ever the American man shall straddle the Mexican horse, & thereby conquer the Gallican lion, they will never be able to persuade him to dismount again."[19]

William evidenced no sense that the Maximilian regime was in its death throes. Instead he hoped that once the Liberals were neutralized, the good people of Mexico would be freed to build a strong society. He had no faith in the Liberals, asserting that "if the republic is revived, with it will also be revived disorder, confusion, & anarchy." In fact, the republic was revived, sooner than William imagined. The Liberals captured and executed Maximilian in 1867, after William had left Mexico. This left the hundreds of exiled Confederates who had settled their colony of Carlota without legal or political protection.[20]

Meanwhile, William arrived in Veracruz on June 6, 1866, only to discover that his ship had sailed. He secured passage on another vessel soon after, but the day after his departure he suffered another attack of yellow fever and had to disembark in Cuba to recover his health. He did not reach Ohio until late summer of 1866, and then discovered that Ellen and the children had left Seven Oaks Farm and moved into Circleville, Ohio. William reluctantly moved into the Circleville homestead, but he made daily visits to the Seven Oaks farm. He may have put one of his farms up for sale. A letter from the banker Thomas Dugan to William in November closed by advising him, "In regard to the sale of your Farm . . . I think you would do best to make a sale if you could get a fair price."[21]

In a letter intended for publication in a newspaper, the perennially disenchanted William reflected on the state of the Union, arguing, "I believe the center and soul of all our sorrows and sufferings are, and have been, the manufactories of New England." The former Copperhead could scarcely restrain his contempt for New England's Puritan heritage:

> On their banners they have inscribed "liberty, equality and the rights of man." With this appeal to the world of progress they deem themselves secure. The "liberty" is granted for every man to believe that Jesus Christ might have been as smart a man as [the Unitarian abolitionist] Theodore Parker, if he had received a Yankee education; that all New Englanders are "equal" if they can prove they are as good as a full blooded negro; and that every outsider has the "right" to pay ten dollars a yard for Yankee cloth which he could buy in England for three dollars.[22]

In a letter to Ellen from her uncle Henry Boyce, she received news from the South that could only have deepened her husband's disgust. He wrote, "I fear it will be some time before we have much prosperity in the South again. This has been a bad year for us."[23]

WHILE WILLIAM WAS IN Mexico, the Civil War was winding down, with a Union victory in reach. In a note to Charles dated April 3, Senator John Sherman wrote of his brother: "Gen. S[herman] is at last through and I spent two days with him at Goldsboro. . . . Since I saw his and Grant's army I am sure the rebellion is on its last legs." Goldsboro did indeed mark the wind-down of the war. With Columbia and Charleston in smoke and rubble behind him, Sherman turned his troops to the north in March. As he moved on to North Carolina, it was plain that Confederate forces were in no shape to block Sherman or to come to the relief of General Robert E. Lee's starving army. With food supplies captured at Appomattox Station, the only choice facing the Army of Northern Virginia was surrender or starvation. But there would be one last try. When Sherman moved his two-winged juggernaut toward Goldsboro, North Carolina, Confederate general Joseph E. Johnston concentrated his seventeen-thousand-man army on Sherman's left wing near Bentonville, North Carolina. After some initial gains, his assault was pushed back on March 19, allowing Sherman to rest his weary troops. Soon thereafter, Sherman marched to Virginia to link up with Grant's Army of the Potomac and destroy Lee's Army of Northern Virginia. But Grant blocked Sherman's desire to join forces, determined to "get Lee" on his own. On April 3, a triumphant Grant notified Lincoln from Richmond that the capital city was now in Federal hands and invited him down from City Point (Hopewell), Virginia, for a visit—an invitation Lincoln accepted.[24]

In the march through a burning Richmond, Grant and the president met a phalanx of ecstatic slaves welcoming Lincoln as the messiah. On April 14, 1865, Good Friday, Lincoln was assassinated by John Wilkes Booth while attending a play at Ford's Theater. Immediately, Washington was thrown into complete disarray. Among myriad other consequences, Lincoln's assassination put all federal appointments on hold. Inevitably, this put Charles Anderson's hopes for a diplomatic appointment on hold as well.[25]

But the business of government continued. On April 22, William Deshler, chair of the Columbus Chamber of Commerce, wrote Charles to inform him that his peerless oratory was once more desired: "Our committee being in charge [of the] program for Saturday April 29, when the remains of Prest. Lincoln will be here—have selected you to deliver the oration upon that occasion." It is not clear why Anderson was invited, given his hostility to Lincoln. In any event, Charles injudiciously declined the invitation, even as he pressed the Republican administration for a diplomatic post.[26]

On April 9 General Lee surrendered the Army of Northern Virginia, which, in turn, triggered a series of surrenders across the South, signaling the looming end of the war. April 14 found much of the Anderson family, including Charles, in Charleston, South Carolina, in what would prove to be a glorious day for the Union. With Lincoln's assassination not yet widely known, the celebrants met on April 14 and listened with rapt excitement as the famous minister Henry Ward Beecher deliver a conciliatory sermon preparing the way for peace. That was followed by a ceremony featuring brother Robert Anderson raising the Federal banner over Fort Sumter—almost exactly four years after lowering the same flag before the victorious Rebels.[27]

In July 1865 Charles enlisted the aid of Benjamin Franklin Wade in securing an appointment, with disappointing results. Wade, a Radical Republican senator from Ohio and president pro tempore of the Senate, was not a favorite with Secretary of State William Seward, as he wrote to Anderson: "I cannot say that I have received what I consider encouragement that the appointment would be made so that I fear this with all others of the same kind, of any importance, will be reserved for the favorites of the Secretary of State." Charles, who had often benefited from his connections, was discovering in this case that he was on the losing end. Any doubts were resolved in a follow-up letter from John Sherman. Sherman was incredulous to learn "that Seward says he did not know of our application. I presented it to him myself. . . . I wrote to Hunter the acting secretary with a view to learn the status of affairs and he informed me that nothing had been done in the way of appointments since the attack upon Mr. S[eward]. You ask what is the best course to pursue. I can only answer that it is best to keep the matter constantly before his mind. . . . I know no other way."[28]

Meanwhile, with the Civil War over, questions of reconstruction under President Andrew Johnson continued to press on the government. Following the celebratory trip to Fort Sumter, Charles received a letter from one "L. Hall" from Altoona, Pennsylvania, who had met Charles at the celebration and wrote with a request: "I want you to send me a copy of the resolutions you offered lately before your Convention in Dayton on Negro Suffrage and reconstruction of the southern states. Will you oblige me by so doing: what will your state convention be likely to do on this question, if anything? When is it held? I see Mr. Sherman has been defining himself on it lately at Cincinnati."[29]

What was Anderson's position? While Charles was happy with freedmen testifying in court and with Ohio ending the Black Codes, he was not convinced that immediate suffrage for blacks would be good for either of the races. In this he echoed the other Sherman, General William Tecumseh Sherman. In responding to a "long and most interesting letter" from Charles on the subject of the "eternal Negro" question, Sherman learned that remarks he made in a "purely social" context had been overheard by "some newspaper spy" and printed in the press. Nevertheless, General Sherman continued to express his view privately to Anderson: "I fear the attempt to appease the enfranchisement negro to a political equality . . . will make much strife and trouble. The negroes are in our country and opinions vary so widely that I profess to await the action of those whose duty it is to initiate measures for the final solution. When in Georgia I began a system of segregation and settlement that seemed to work well. . . . I want to see the two races gradually part." And they did. The concept of segregation led to a sort of second enslavement by other means. Americans' love affair with land could not breach race. Slaves were property and land was property. Freed slaves wanted land, and many whites perceived black-owned land as a contradiction in terms. Private property and the issue of redistribution of Confederate lands all concerned what was going to be given to ex-slaves and what would be available for whites. Already in March 1865, the Radical Republican representative Thaddeus Stevens of Pennsylvania had proposed that all planter lands in the Confederacy be confiscated and redistributed to ex-slaves and poor whites, but the question never came to a vote in the House.[30]

As for the white South, Sherman favored immediate clemency, the restoration of former Confederate states to full membership in the reunited nation, and, of course, the ongoing protection of private property—against Stevens' and other Radical Republicans' calls for redistribution of Confederate lands. Sherman wrote that the South had "acted fairly" in surrender and deserved leniency. He then went on to accuse President Johnson of acting foolishly in exempting a large class of Confederate leaders from amnesty because eventually he would have to "restore all to the condition of citizens and trust to the national strengths to overcome any little opposition still left at the South. In the end he must pardon all combatants and leave to the laws . . . to punish all new 'crises and disorders.'"[31]

In response to a Thanksgiving proclamation Charles issued in November 1865, Salmon P. Chase, former secretary of state under Lincoln and current chief justice of the United States, wrote a letter of thanks for his "excellent proclamation. We have indeed passed great trials. . . . But prosperity lies before." This may have been the only praise ardent abolitionist Salmon Chase ever offered to Charles.[32]

John Porter Brown, a friend of Larz and an "oriental" scholar born in Chillicothe, agreed with General Sherman. Writing to Charles from Constantinople, he noted that while he was antislavery, he was concerned that a declaration of "universal suffrage" could be premature: "As we have the colored population and must keep them, I suppose the best policy is to 'make the best of it' and this can only be done by improving the mental faculties of the blacks. . . . But this requires time and I cannot see how the freed slaves of the South, can become electors with any practical utility in themselves, as to the country at large."[33]

While Brown's perspective demonstrated some improvement on America's defining racial tension, it also showed how very much the defeat of the Confederacy had left the issue ambiguous and unresolved. Much had occurred in 1865 for the nation and for the Andersons. William's sojourn to Mexico would extend into 1866, but for the rest of the Andersons, local and national issues prevailed at home. What would transpire in the war's aftermath, as President Johnson engaged the issue of reconstructing a Union that had nearly been riven violently apart, remained uncertain.

16

Andersons in Transition

1866–1870

With the surrender of the Confederacy, the victorious North faced the daunting challenge of reconstructing the nation and restoring a fragmented union in disarray. To that end, the Radical Republican Congress pushed through the Fourteenth and Fifteenth Amendments. The Fourteenth Amendment, proposed in 1866 and ratified in 1868, guaranteed citizenship and equal protection of the law for all persons born or naturalized in the United States. The Fifteenth Amendment, ratified on February 3, 1870, prohibited federal and state governments from denying a citizen the right to vote based on that citizen's "race, color, or previous condition of servitude." Other Radicals, including Thaddeus Stevens, continued to push for the redistribution of the lands of former Confederate plantation owners and oligarchs. But the sanctity of land and private property in the nation by now could not be shaken. Northern and Southern landowners alike realized that if Congress could seize and redistribute former Confederates' lands, it could seize and redistribute anyone's land and the principle of private ownership would be mortally wounded. There would be no redistribution of land; millions of acres remained in the same white hands. As a result, in the overwhelmingly agricultural South, freedmen who did not already own land would have to work as tenants for those who did, leaving them, as always, vulnerable to economic exploitation, political intimidation, and violence.[1]

In support of the Fourteenth and Fifteenth Amendments, the Radical Republican Congress passed the Military Reconstruction Act of 1867, which divided the former Confederacy into five militia districts administered by the US Army. Freedmen and Radical Republicans rejoiced, believing that justice at last would be served. Former Confederates and antiabolitionist Northerners—like many of the Andersons—were devastated. Instead of a reunited republic "with malice towards none," they imagined the prospect of a centralized police state governed by military despots. When newly installed president Andrew Johnson, himself a Southern sympathizer, urged leniency toward former Confederates, he was tried and impeached for removing his critic, Secretary of War Edwin Stanton. Instead of leniency, Radicals sought to remove former Confederate leaders and install freedmen in their place. Under the direction of the Freedmen's Bureau, the legal rights of freedmen were protected and Northern missionaries and educators were sent south to train the former slaves. Eventually the Republican efforts foundered amid another financial depression and a violent white Southern response, leading to the "redemption" of former Confederate states in 1877 and a return to white supremacy enforced at the end of a gun or a lynching rope. This would mark the failure of Reconstruction and calamity for blacks. The Andersons were opposed to Reconstruction and Radical Republicans because they deemed themselves patriotic in their opposition to racial equality.[2]

When Charles's term as governor of Ohio ended on January 8, 1866, he delivered a stinging indictment of the Monroe Doctrine, which his deceased brother Richard had done so much to promote. The trigger for Anderson's wrath was congressional voices' advocating an invasion of Mexico to forcibly remove the French and their Catholic-sponsored government headed by Ferdinand Maximilian. But Charles was having none of it. In opposing Mexican intervention and, with it, the Monroe doctrine, he reached back to Washington's Farewell Address with its enjoinder to avoid "entangling alliances." Circumstances had changed dramatically from 1826, when Richard Anderson Jr. was serving in Colombia, and the United States was in no position to fight another war, especially, Charles sneered, a war to liberate the "imbeciles" in Mexico. In stark opposition to brother William, who was in Mexico at the time the governor addressed the issue, Charles had neither sympathy nor respect for the "inferior" race of Mexican "barbarians."[3]

Unlike William, who sought to work with Maximilian, Charles opposed any incursion into Mexico for or against Maximilian. He received a strong letter of support from L. D. McCabe, a teacher of politics: "I send thousand thanks and ten thousand blessings upon you for your noble utterances relating to Mexico. . . . Thank God for the splendid blast of your trumpet. It sounds to me like the solemn warnings of a prophet of God."[4]

Equally strong support came from General William Tecumseh Sherman, who in 1866, on the heels of a brutal civil war, shared Charles's strongly isolationist sentiments: "I take the liberty now to express to you my complete endorsement of your views on our Mexican question. . . . It is a simple folly for us to crusade and especially now would it be suicide for us as a nation to engage in a new war with an old one yet smoldering." Aware that General Grant differed with him, Sherman commented: "I don't care." He then concluded: "It will require the common opinion of all good men in this country to keep us from flying off on some foolish caper and I will willingly share with your popularity if we can keep this in mind. . . . We have but thirty millions of whites not even civilized and it would be ridiculous for us to undertake to impose our thoughts on twelve hundred million [Mexicans]. Better, far better mind our own business."[5]

Another veteran of the Civil War, M. Wheeler of Findlay, Ohio, offered similar praise for Charles's "timely rebuke to the filibustering spirit of some of our people." Ohio had suffered enough, and so had Wheeler: "I am suffering greatly from my old Chickamauga wound, which will ever keep my mind too vividly in memory of war for me to wish to see my country involved in another."[6]

Of course, not everyone agreed with Charles's criticism. War Hawks, formerly led by Henry Clay, again beat the drum for war. His old friend Ephraim George Squier wrote him from New York that at a large dinner, "I had the honor of reading your letter, or rather the passages which attacked the 'Monroe Doctrine,' which were received with mingled groans and hisses—and cries of 'turn him out!' On being informed that the author was not present, there were loud demands 'send a policeman for him!'"[7]

But another voice from New York was more positive. William M. Smith wrote to thank Charles "for the bold and emphatic tone of your message in condemnation of that absurd dogma—the so called Monroe Doctrine. That stirring portion of your message was copied into the N.Y. Times."[8]

Charles Anderson's departure from his brother's embrace of the Monroe Doctrine is not surprising. The Monroe Doctrine, articulated by Monroe and John Quincy Adams, was determined more by domestic political consideration than abstract foreign policy reflections or preoccupation with other nations. Forty years later, much had changed. Having come off an unprecedented civil war, which made the Revolution and War of 1812 look like child's play, national leaders like Sherman and Charles were reflecting a very different domestic scene, one dominated by caution and exhaustion as much as patriotism and reach. As well, and relatedly, Southern hatred of the North continued to burn bright and clearly trumped foreign policy preoccupations. Frederick Hassaurek, US minister to Ecuador, wrote "to congratulate you on your message, that is to say on that part of it which refers to the Monroe Doctrine. . . . Your view of the Mexican question entirely coincides with mine."[9]

The Civil War had ended when Charles stepped down as governor on January 8, 1866. That month, Charles's nephew Richard wrote Charles about a significant land purchase he had made in a large tract of iron-mining lands in Lyon County, Kentucky. Richard began, "I am suffering a great deal and indeed ought and would if I could spare the time, be in bed." But business called, especially a proposal that Charles move to Kentucky, near Eddyville, and breed sheep. The main draw, Richard suggested, was that "its cheap lands, mild climate, acceptability and other recommendations have the advantage of Minnesota or any other country we have yet discussed." Having already lived in Kentucky, Dayton, Cincinnati, San Antonio, and Columbus, the well-traveled Charles was easily encouraged to consider this next move. He now conceived an interest in returning to his native Kentucky for his retirement. With no love for Ohio and the Republican Party, he deemed Kentucky a perfect retreat, where perhaps he could finally realize his lifelong dream of wealth and ease. To that end, he too purchased a significant tract of land in Eddyville, in 1866, close to nephew Richard's iron lands.[10]

To fund the purchase, Charles considered selling some land he owned in Iowa, but on the advice of his lawyer, H. W. Maxwell, he delayed. In his letter of May 26, 1866, Maxwell advised: "There are very few land buyers in the country this spring, and very few sales made. We are now making a great effort to get a R.R. from St. Paul Min. to Kansas City Mo, which if made, will run through our county. . . . Now my idea is that in the fall will be a much better time than now to sell land." Apparently, Charles was looking for yet more land, in addition to the Eddyville land purchase, for in July 1866 he heard from John Stacker of Eddyville, Kentucky, about land that could total 8,500 acres. He could have it surveyed for $200.[11]

Despite his purchase of land in Kentucky, Charles returned to his law practice in Dayton, where he would work from 1866 to 1870. Much of his time would be spent with his practice, viewing politics from afar, although family affairs, as always, remained a preoccupation. Late in 1866, Charles wrote his wife Eliza to say that son Latham might be court-martialed for an (unspecified) "offence" that Anderson did not consider worthy of concern: "I do not consider a dismissal for this 'offence' at all dishonorable. . . . We can support him and his family just as well now as later. And what else is our estate for except our children?" He then added a cautionary note on Latham: "It is true I do not think he will be of as much service in this business as you do. He is too much like his daddy—a little lazy—procrastinish and incurably dreamy— ever to be 'a man of business.' Moreover he does not have money enough. But all that makes no difference. He is our son." Whatever Latham's offense, the court-martial never happened and he retained his promotion to brevet brigadier general, which had been issued on March 13, 1856.[12]

Many of Charles's former cronies wrote regarding the politics of Reconstruction, which he intended to keep at arm's length. One particularly exercised congressman was Abraham Rencher from North Carolina, father-in-law to Charles's son Latham. Rencher wrote with particular distress about the prospect of "breaking up an old home," a direct consequence of the Radical Republicans' pro-black policies: "Almost anything would be preferable to that of having your property and character and even life itself to depend upon stupid negroes but recently emerged from a state of slavery, and directed and controlled, as they would be, by those who would feel for us nothing but bitter hatred." The "reconstructed" South possessed neither hard currency nor willing land purchasers, thus devastating land's value. What Rencher failed to acknowledge was the fact that whites had no compunction whatsoever about breaking up black homes. Faced with the prospect of being forced to "look for a new home," he favored Kentucky, where the "white people" would be allowed "to give laws to their former slaves and not the negroe to their former masters." He then closed on a bitter note: "I may take too dark a view of the future—I hope I do, but I can not but feel that the South, for many years to come, must be a . . . lost country, even under the kindest and most parental care by the Federal Government. But under the rancorous spirit of hatred and revenge which seems to actuate the people of the north, God only knows what bitterness is reserved for them."[13]

Wisconsin historian Lyman Draper, though no Rebel and a friend of the Union, was also unsettled. After writing Charles about a memorial for Anderson kinsman George Rogers Clark, he concluded: "While I have no sympathies with the modern Radicals, I sympathized thoroughly with the national efforts to preserve the Union—and I cannot but think that Radicalism is doing its best not to heal the festering sores of disunion, but to initiate them more and more."[14]

Charles's successor as governor of Ohio, Jacob Dolson Cox, was a Republican Civil War veteran but an uninspiring governor. In the beginning he had supported President Andrew Johnson, a Democrat, and the Fourteenth Amendment. He also resisted the Republican opposition. When the Ohio Union Party convention met in Columbus on June 20, 1866, Cox urged Johnson to support the amendment, and when Johnson vetoed the bill, his fate was sealed along with Cox's. By September Cox had formally broken with Johnson, but it was too late. Senator John Sherman, a Republican, wrote of Cox: "I do not doubt Mr. Cox's entire uprightness, but his superserviceable zeal in behalf of Johnson has fatally compromised his influence with the party."[15]

In January 26, 1867, Cox announced he would not be a candidate for reelection as governor. The following December he wrote a long letter to Charles expressing his frustration and sense of failure. In fact, the two had similar views and both felt abandoned: "I have been working as a soldier who knows he is moving upon certain destruction and that his superiors have overruled him in issuing the order." In words that would be anathema to Radical Republicans, he insisted on adhering "to the belief in the necessity of the political separation of the races."

Cox continued his letter by pointing out that in May 1866, he had written to Congressman James Garfield and John Sherman opposing the disenfranchisement of former Confederate leaders as a part of Radical Reconstruction: "Our Republicanism has come to this, that in our impotency to provide a civil government for ten millions of our people we would inflict a military despotism upon them now completely freed from any check or restraint than European tyrants ever dared put upon Poland." At the same time, he remained convinced that racial integration would mark the death knell of the black race "and that the negro has only been lured to destruction by the delusive hope of his absorption into the 'nation of whites.'"

Apparently stung by an earlier letter of Charles's that criticized him for his timidity, he went on to justify his action, pointing out that the present "drift" toward social equality would be "as fatal to the negro as our civilization has been to the Indian." He continued in the same vein to argue that the great majority of white Northerners were not radicals and were not committed to racial equality: "The moment that drift is fully seen and comprehended by the northern people, their 'negrophobia' will be of the most ultra copperhead type, and their instincts of race will make them pitiless toward the poor blacks who will only be working out the legitimate consequences of <u>our</u> policy." Cox predicted that Radical Reconstruction would not endure and that blacks would suffer on the heels of a "revolution in the Southern States." Elected black officials would be driven from office, and black voters from the ballot box. The whites would seize all power and Congress would accept whatever they would do, ignoring Radical Reconstruction. He concluded: "If the negroes show themselves men enough to fight for the power they will be losing so much the worse for them: their fate will be that of the Spanish Moors. If they submit at once, they become a degraded class of low caste laborers, making toil disgraceful and perpetuating the chief social evils of slavery. Cox's fears proved right about the consequences of Reconstruction, even as he was deeply deceived about segregation as the best alternative. Charles would find himself in the same position.[16]

Charles continued to be frustrated in his efforts to find diplomatic assignments. Once again Larz offered criticism rather than condolence: "I regret to learn that your expectations have not been fulfilled. I even feared that you were too sanguine. But that is your temperament and that is all that need be said about it." Larz thought that if Charles had befriended Andrew Johnson more, "you might have stood some chance for a mission. . . . Poor Andy is in a bad way himself—shorn of his powers and now about to be shorn of his office. It is enough to make one weep to think of affairs at Washington—Johnson and Stanton— all this bother about two such men! Heaven shield us."[17]

Three months later, on June 4, 1868, Larz wrote Charles that he had secured a portrait painter named Webber to produce sketches of the governors of Ohio. Apparently Larz was a patron of Webber and informed Charles that "he is desirous of giving something character-istic, or at least something interesting in connection with each one. In relation to yourself, he would like you to choose some event in your Texas life—for example, your confinement in Camp, your arrival in Rio Grande, or some other incident, and give a description of it such as he could introduce in a picture." A follow-up letter from Larz conveyed the encouraging news that wife Kate's health had taken a favorable turn, which they hoped to build on by traveling through the mountains: "If that should not benefit her, she will then probably go to the sea shore." For Larz and Kate there were no limits on travel, and both believed in its healing qualities.[18]

If his government seemed to sideline Charles, his family did not. While Larz was delivering yet another moral lesson, his nephew Rich-ard was worrying about him in the background. In a letter to William, Richard discussed "Uncle Charles" and his plan to farm sheep, fearing that it would come to naught but confident that the farmland itself would soar in value (which it did). In October 1868, Charles himself re-ceived a letter from his nephew Larz Anderson, son of his brother Larz, that he and his wife came to visit so that "I might have her with you, to know better and love more—while I prospected for ore." Larz Jr. was not destined to have the life his uncle would eventually enjoy. In 1902 he would commit suicide at his brother's house in Connecticut.[19]

Despite physical separations, the Anderson family as a whole lived a remarkably entwined existence. In April 1868, Sarah wrote to daugh-ter Maria from Louisville in characteristically staccato prose with local news: "I am with Elizabeth she says she cannot bear the thought of my leaving her I told if she would go home with me I would stay a week or two longer, she has consented to go, I think it will be of service to her, she mentions so often. . . . I can't bear thought of you leaving me."[20]

For his part, William continued to have economic issues with Ellen, dating back to expenses incurred during his trip to Mexico. Apparently she had funded much of his travel expenses. In May 1868 he issued her a promissory note for $1,716.00, stating, "Therefore I acknowledge myself to be indebted to my wife in the above mentioned sum, and I obligate myself . . ." William's action suggests that all had not healed in his relationship with Ellen, and the two may have been living separately for a period of time.[21]

Charles never got over his unhappiness with the Republican Party and never joined it. In November 1868 he turned down an invitation to "address a meeting of the soldiers and sailors national committee" because "my peculiar opinions [prevent] me from keeping further company with the 'Union' Party." One invitation Charles did not turn down came from soldiers at the "Home." The request was from a fellow soldier who noted, correctly, "I don't think it will be possible for you to ride through the grounds without giving your old comrades an opportunity to hear the sound of your voice again. If you feel that you can't resist the wish of so many brave veterans, and you ought not, I will notify Col. Brown privately of your contemplated visit and you will be sure of a cordial welcome."[22]

Another concession Charles made was to follow up on Larz's suggestion and commission the family portraitist "Mr. Webber" to paint his portrait in response to a request from the new Ohio governor, Rutherford B. Hayes, who added that he would contribute $150.00 to the artist. William also had his portrait painted by the same artist.[23]

Sadness again came to the Anderson family when sister Betsy died after a brief illness in 1870. Sarah Kendrick informed her brother Charles that "Eliza is very very much distressed—but bears it much better than we thought that she would. She has this to comfort her. She was the best the very best daughter that I ever saw in my life."[24]

Of all the Andersons, William wrote and preserved the most. In addition to his significant correspondence he kept several diaries and memorandum books with commentary on everything from weather and topography to politics and religion. Throughout 1869 he kept a memorandum book with miscellaneous entries inside the pages of his account book with the First National Bank of Circleville. Besides observations on nature, he included political commentary. Ulysses S. Grant was about to be inaugurated, leading William to comment acidly: "Grant is to be inaugurated today. He will be either dictator or congress will dictate to him. We shall see. . . . Poor Grant! You will either wish yourself in hell, before six months, or those who made you President will wish it. . . . Here is Grant, who was considered one of the most vulgar subjects of the educated army, is now the top of the lot. Does that mean the scum? If so, perhaps he may again be thrown out."[25]

William had one more journey's diary in him. His scientific interests in archeology had led to some original research on the Mound Builders of Ohio. In 1870–1871, he was again engaged in archeological explorations south of Memphis. At the time, he was sixty-four and in good health. Many of the details of his trip down the Mississippi are recorded in a pocket diary he kept for 1870–1871. On New Year's Eve 1869 he left Circleville on the railroad, ruing the loss of a couple of trunks. Four days later he passed through Louisville and found "everything in that part of our country very much the same as it was forty years ago." He arrived in Memphis on January 5 and shifted from train to boat and was pleasantly surprised: "This is a very neat boat, well furnished and I believe provided with every convenience for safety in case of accidents. We have a good table, good beds and respectful, on time waiters."[26]

In a style reminiscent of his Rocky Mountain journal, William could grow positively lyrical in recording the sights he experienced down the Mississippi. On February I, he observed, "This evening's sunset was certainly one of the most beautiful I ever beheld. The lake was perfectly calm, as unruffled, as unchanged as a mirror. Had it been a shard of silver covered glass, it would not have reflected, the varied and varying clouds with all their bands layers . . . just before the disappearance of the day." A bank of dark brown clouds appeared on the horizon "with only a narrow line of yellow light above the horizon . . . which gradually deepened into a lovely rose color . . . until the whole heavens, which hung over or bordered up the lake was painted upon the water."

By March 18, William was the only elderly passenger on the boat. The quality of the passengers' conversation did not impress him. He marveled at the triteness of conversation and the obsession with money—a universal American trait: "I have often observed that more men and women, when abroad, do and say more silly things than you could suppose possible in an enlightened age. But most of the thinking is about money—the hard thinking is 'how can I make more?'" The answer to that, as often as not, was "by acquiring more land." Of the women, he noted: "The fashionable dames, with their trains, remind me of mares with long tails switching them to the right or the left, just as they are spurred."

In his diary, William said little of his scientific discoveries, preferring to present them in the form of scholarly papers. On March 21 he made his last entry from St. Louis. The arrival was nostalgic, reminding him of his first visit to St. Louis with the Rocky Mountain mountain men. He closed the diary abruptly: "As soon as I have rested a while, I will go forth, to see what difference there is between the St. Louis of 1834 and 1871—a space of thirty seven years. Left St. Louis Thursday evening about 6 o/clock and reached Urbana Friday morning at 9 o'clock."

William's early preoccupations with land and wealth never completely disappeared, but they were eclipsed by his embrace of Catholicism, which, on occasion, he could turn on himself. In a later "statement of penance," contained in a memorandum book, William asked, "Is it possible, that I am the creature and hate my Maker! Have I not been cherishing the hope, the vain, the delusion, of fame, wealth & honor—and caring nothing for my true happiness here and here after? . . . I feel that since I have sinned every moment of my life, I should suffer unspeakable torments for an immeasurable eternity."[27]

What he applied to himself, William leveled also at his son Thomas, who stridently rejected his parents' Catholicism. For some years William and his clerical friends were gravely concerned about the state of Thomas's faith. But in 1870 concern and charity were replaced by a rancorous debate between father and son. The first surviving salvo was fired by Thomas in a letter from Laredo, Texas, on April 7, 1870. Thomas was then thirty-four years old, a veteran of the Civil War and career army officer. The letter was clearly in response to a harsh letter William had sent that is not preserved. In tone and philosophical sophistication it is apparent that, however distant he was from his father intellectually and theologically, he had learned a lot more from him than soldiering. Indeed, the heated correspondence that ensued proved him the intellectual equal of his father, at the same time confirming to his father his "infidel" status.

At the head of Thomas's April 1870 letter William penciled on the envelope: "My foolish boy's silly letter." In responding to his father's earlier assertion that he had no faith, Thomas mounted his defense: "So I am an Infidel! Without Faith. No father I have faith [WMA in pencil: 'what faith?'] A deep strong one. One I often fall from in practice. Yet still it is a faith. [WMA in pencil: 'in yourself?']." The problem, Thomas asserted, was that William confused faith with dogma: "God knows I hope you will not take offense at the distinction you have not faith, but a creed. A creed which you keep and cherish. Perhaps it is better to have a creed which you keep than a faith which you fall from. Who knows but God?" Thomas here distinguished what modern voices might term "spirituality" in contradistinction to creedal formulations and church doctrines. Thomas tried to articulate a faith that included a God who was not mechanistic or materialistic. He resented William's labeling him an atheist or a transcendentalist, citing Paine, Voltaire, Hume, and Emerson, even though "I have never read one of their books in my life and am not a materialist."[28]

Among the Andersons, none seemed to struggle in so painful a fashion as William and his son. In fact, though, none of the Andersons altogether escaped the scourge of suffering, with Southern kinsmen, financial panics, political upheaval, sickness, and death. The nation struggled to reconstruct itself, and change continued to play out on local, familial levels. The war had settled once and for all the question of secession, but land continued to preoccupy family wealth and independence.

17

Legacies

1871–1888

The era of failed Reconstruction saw the passing of members of the first Anderson generation to live their entire lives as US citizens. In these years, the next generation picked up the mantle of family leadership and brought yet another generation into being, while occupying offices of state and chasing those perennial carrots of wealth and land.

William's archeological research involved him in a wide web of correspondents. He collected artifacts with a view toward studying them and then giving them to a worthy society. He first favored historical societies in New York, especially the Anthropological Institute of New York, which elected him to membership in 1872. But local pride soon took over and Ohio boosters pressured him to consider giving his collections to Ohio repositories. Manning Ferguson Force, director of the Historical and Philosophical Society of Ohio, wrote Anderson in 1872 to express concerns that "the relics of the mound builders and other stone implements collected in Ohio, were all finding their way to the east." Calling on William's local pride, Force hoped "that some might be preserved in a permanent place here." Force went on to demonstrate the limits of his own knowledge, asking if the Mound Builders were Indians, not realizing the Mound Builders were an advanced civilization whose mounds antedated by a thousand years the pyramids of Egypt. In commenting on artifacts from the Mound Builders, brother Larz evidenced his own ignorance toward other cultures when responding to William's description of ornate tiles with inscriptions that he'd discovered in his digging: "I cannot conceive how tiles, of the form you describe, could be put together," Larz asserted. "I have but little doubt that the French, or some other civilized people, had a settlement there or thereabouts some hundred or more years since. It would be a pity if the evidence of such a fact after having been discovered should be lost."[1]

William received a similar plea for local privilege from Charles's former law partner, Rufus King. Confusing William with Colonel Anderson, he began, "Dear Colonel," though he clearly had William in mind. King recognized, as historian Frederick Jackson Turner would in 1893, that the frontier was coming to an end. On this basis, he appealed to Anderson to favor the Ohio Historical Society with artifacts and writings on behalf of "all of us who witness the rapid oblivion, if I may be pardoned the expression which is gathering over the pioneer age of the West."[2]

While the sense of a passing era grew among the old frontier people, they sensed as well the passing of their own generation. William's older brother Robert had never regained his health after the rigors of war and Fort Sumter. There is no evidence that he ever second-guessed the sacrifice. On October 8, 1871, Robert wrote his last surviving letter to William from Vevey, Switzerland, where he sought healing that would at last prove unreachable: "My dear Brother, I have sent you by the hands of Lt. Manson of the Navy a mosaic which was shipped especially for you by the Pope. It is to be sent to you by my agent, Col. Stinson. I am I hope doing well though very weak. One of the family will write you more fully. God grant that I may ere long be enabled to return home where I may meet you all again. Your loving brother, Robert Anderson."[3]

Robert never made it home. In the same month, sister Sarah Kendrick had bad news to convey to Charles: "Our dear brother Robert has gone to his home in heaven. . . . His remains are to be sent home by a ship of war. Brother Larz and Sister Kate went to Dayton yesterday will be at home tonight—they both look badly. I do not think that either of them are well, the rest over there appear to be very well." She closed: "My comfort is that brother Robert was a true Christian he had confessed Jesus before man and had given himself to his Lord."[4]

In describing Robert's last days to Charles, Larz wrote that "our brother was then in the perfect possession of his faculties, but stranger to see does not dream that it is the weakness of death that is stealing over him." His wife, Eliza, he continued, "has not seen fit to tell him. I think she fears that with his last words he might reproach her as the cause of his dying among strangers."[5]

Four months later, Larz wrote Charles of Robert's daughter: "Eba was behaving as we might have anticipated, in a most extraordinary way . . . was talking in the most unreasonable style." The Andersons never really warmed to Eliza, but instinctive family loyalties kept them engaged. After asking Charles to meet him in New York, Larz closed, "Expect that we shall be compelled to defer to the caprice of our sister-in-law as to the place of burial. I should like to consult you about that. But I do not suppose she has considered me in the matter. Come and accompany me if you can." Clearly Larz wanted to be with his brother at the internment. On March 25, 1872, Larz wrote to Charles, "My special object in writing, is to get you, if possible, to accompany me to the final ceremonies for the internment of our beloved brother, which are to take place on the 3rd of April. I trust you will be able to go."[6]

WHILE CONGRESS PRESERVED FORMER Confederate landowners' property rights, it could not prevent foreclosures as Confederate currency lost all value and lands lay fallow without seed money and slaves. The anxiety of landownership hit home for former Confederates who found their lands foreclosed in order to satisfy old judgments. Fellow lawyer Henry Parrish wrote to Charles from Farmville, Virginia, commenting that "it is remarkably sad to see the old home lands going into the hands of strangers, and the old families, many of whose names are associated with all of which Virginians are proud, turned aside—homeless and hopeless to make a precarious living the best way they can."[7]

While he was often financially beset, Charles's experience was quite other than that of the Confederacy's leading families. By 1871, the fifty-seven-year-old Charles had once again relocated, to a family farm in Kuttawa, Kentucky. He had first purchased the farm and founded the town in 1866, immediately after the Civil War. The city was formally incorporated by the state assembly in 1872.[8]

This is not to say that Charles's freedom from the brutal reparations of the post–Civil War South had yet brought him prosperity. On

June 6, 1874, his seventy-one-year-old brother Larz had reason again to serve hard advice to Charles. Written at the top of a letter from his brother, in pencil and in Charles's hand, is the comment, "Larz Anderson sound and good advice." After acknowledging receipt of a letter from Charles, Larz wrote, "But as it was mainly an expression of regrets for doing what you ought not to have done and not doing what you ought to have done with your life, I could add nothing on the subject but a homily which would have been more wearying than welcome perhaps, and productive of no good." Then came the advice in regard to Charles's expressed idea of selling land in Dayton. Larz wrote: "If you sell the first now, cutting off your principal source of livelihood, you would soon have to sell off the rest by piece meal in order to pay current expenses. Is it not wiser to sell at once the little productive or the unproductive property at whatever sacrifice, than to dispose of your income bringing property because it will sell more easily than the other?"

Larz then recommended that Charles take care of matters by himself and not rely on the family: "You ought to attend to this yourself, and not put this duty upon any one else. You have acted all along upon a strong principle—never doing yourself what you could possibly make somebody else do for you—and the consequence has been either that your business has not become done at all, or not nearly so well done as if you had acted for yourself." If Charles would only "do your own business," Larz continued, he would realize success: "I see nothing discouraging in your affairs except your habitual indolence, and your over indulged disposition to do work vicariously. . . . It is high time for you to sacrifice your love of ease to the interests of your family."[9]

Words like these had consequences. Later in life, after Larz had died, Charles confessed to William that his admiration for Larz was misplaced. It was William he most resembled: "I must tell you, dear brother, that I do greatly honor and love you. As I am somewhat 'upon honor' in these confessions (which are for you alone). I feel bound to disclose to you, the further selfishness of my nature in admitting that I fear a part of my admiration and affection, may arise from a truth which I have long known and which I suppose nobody has ever suspected, via: that my nature and character are more like yours than any body's besides." As for Larz: "My relations to Larz (which ridiculously enough, I long and vainly strove to make my model) have certainly molded my whole destiny, personal, social, professional and perhaps public (certainly <u>political</u>). But in character or disposition I never resembled him or Robert at all. The brother I have greatly and always resembled [is] you. I sometimes think more than any two brothers I ever knew, are we alike. Is it not natural, that I should love you?"[10]

The Andersons' inclination to record their place in these early days of US nationhood is understandable. The Andersons clearly had a sense of history and a sense that their records needed to be preserved for the national record, an effort begun on behalf of their half brother Richard upon his death in Colombia in 1826. Brother Robert had brought Richard's journal back from Colombia and bound it with Richard's earlier entries in Kentucky. Apparently, Larz then received the journals and gave them to Richard's children. In 1874, Larz wrote Charles that "the 'journal' of our dear Brother Richard—which you supposed still in my possession—was given by me long since to his daughter. I presume that one or the other of her daughters must have it at this time." In response, Richard's daughter wrote Charles that she could not locate her father's journal but "will search for it myself, on my first visit to Kentucky."[11]

THE 1876 PRESIDENTIAL ELECTION was one of the most contested—and controversial—in American history, and an Anderson once again had a role to play. The contest pitted the Republican Buckeye Rutherford B. Hayes against the Democrat Samuel Tilden, the latter nominated at his party's convention in St. Louis—the first held west of the Mississippi River. Hayes was elected in what was later labeled the "Compromise of 1877." Tilden won the majority of the popular vote, but some Democrats cast their electoral votes for Hayes with the understanding that he would remove all the Reconstruction agencies in the South and "redeem" the region for white supremacy. Throughout the election, Charles refused to endorse either party, but he did endorse fellow Ohio governor Rutherford Hayes.

After Charles refused to support Tilden, a Democratic official, S. Leonard, wrote to thank him for "setting forth your reasons for denying a request which I so hopefully made." Not one to give up easily, however, Leonard pressed on, reiterating his request that Charles support the party and telling Charles he could be a "prophet crying to the people to turn away from their brazen idols and join themselves with the cause of the righteous. I feel that I do not overestimate the strength you could bring to the party in Indiana."[12]

Charles's disillusionment with "the party" only partly explained his reluctance to be the party's "prophet." He was also caught up with affairs in his own family. In January 1877, his son Latham wrote Charles on the death of Larz's son Richard: "I am apprehensive of the effect that dear cousin Dick's death may have had upon you for I know it must have been a sad shock. . . . I leave in the morning to attend the funeral, returning in the evening. This blow cannot fail to have a bad effect on Uncle Larz's health as he is quite sick, but he bears it nobly, being as quiet and gentle as a little child. He is wonderfully comforted by his religion." In fact, Larz would die the next year and was piously religious until the end in ways Charles never would be.

From Richard and other family matters, Latham turned to the great family preoccupation with land. With another financial panic— the Panic of 1873—in full force, he warned his father: "I know of no real estate man who is so sanguine as to believe that property has yet reached its lowest figure. I think also you make a great mistake in selling any of your . . . land [having] sacrificed all the best years of your life to hold it and are selling it or giving it away at a ruinous sacrifice." Instead of selling land at steep losses he advised, "Get out of debt and get a house. . . . The interest you are now paying on your debt is greater than any rise in the value of property you could possibly expect."[13]

Diplomatic openings also continued to draw Charles, who, no doubt like his brother Richard earlier, hoped such an appointment would end his financial mess. Included in his correspondence is an 1877 letter from William M. Carry, former governor of Iowa and current member of the US House of Representatives, to President Hayes suggesting that "one of the most fit . . . appointments that can be made would be that of Mr. Charles Anderson of Ky. to Mexico as minister." Again nothing came of the overture, leaving Charles on his farm without political appointment.[14]

Apparently, Charles was deeply in land debt from the Kuttawa venture. Again the roller coaster of anxiety roared to life. In June 1877, the sixty-three-year-old Charles received a letter from his friend George Drake thanking him for the letter in which Charles had informed him of his debt. Though he was grateful, "it saddened me to learn that fate had been so unkind to you. At your time of life—a load of debt. . . . I believe in prayer—which I fear you do not—and I fervently pray that you may be prospered and happy." He then went on to reflect on why Charles was not more successful in his search for diplomatic positions and earlier political efforts. The problem, in brief, was that Charles did not know how to be diplomatic: "You see and talk plainly as of old. You were given brilliant talents—and had you been able to bear with the political follies of others, there were no good reasons why you should not have continued in political life. You were not well treated I grant—I think not properly appreciated, nor do I think when in public office you quite realized the necessity of yielding and suppressing your notions of politics and men. But I do not presume a lecture." Apparently, Drake's lecture was well received, for Charles penciled in at the top of letter "quite sound too." Meanwhile, the Panic of 1873 would grind on for six years.[15]

Drake's references to politics no doubt referred to Charles's wish to create, in his words, a new "National Party out of the wreck of the Confederate Democracy." With no Whig Party to revive, Charles had hoped for a new party, but those hopes were dashed by the 1876 election, which returned white supremacy to the South. Charles viewed the whole sordid affair with unconcealed contempt that impulsively erupted in a letter to daughter Kitty repudiating the whole election. In words that would not have surprised Drake, Charles spewed out the sentiment in apocalyptic terms: "I will see both parties eternally damned first— as they will be, if God rules. And this thought thrusts another up on me. . . . Has he delivered us over to Satan's providence in his thousand years of perdition?"[16]

In June 1877, Larz's thirty-four-year-old son Ned wrote to Charles from New York City, asking for information about the family's patriarch, Colonel Richard Clough Anderson. Apparently he had written William twice and gotten no response, and he wrote that he would appreciate "any information you can give me, no matter how trifling it may seem to you." He made plain the reason for his request: "I am about to write a memoir of grandfather Anderson. I have already secured valuable facts that would soon have been in the limbo of forgotten events. Can you aid me from your own recollection and tell me where I can seek more information. I cannot use my eyes at present and beg you to excuse this little note. Your aff nephew."[17]

Sometime in late 1877, William suffered severe injuries in a train accident, from which he would never fully recover. On January 8, 1878, his nephew Richard Clough Anderson wrote to William to say when he read of the railroad accident in the newspaper he was sick, but with returning health he assured him of his love in no uncertain terms: "You were very kind to me when I was a little motherless boy, very kind and considerate as I grew older and are one of the few persons in the world for whom my love will never grow cold. Your painful accident aroused a strong desire in my heart to see you once more and had I been well and able to travel I would have hastened to you at once."[18]

In March 1878, Charles heard from Marcellus Anderson (no relation), an unemployed genealogist of questionable character whom Ned had hired to do genealogical research: "It would be very agreeable to me for a suitable compensation to devote myself entirely to the service of your nephew Mr. E. L. Anderson in seeking such information as he desires and making a formal report of the results all of my discoveries of historic interest, as well as every thing relating to his family and for his own exclusive use." While Ned was planning a family memoir, his father Larz was growing weak. In what might have been his final letter, Larz wrote his sister Maria from Wheeling, West Virginia: "I promised you to pass by Chillicothe on my way home—but that is now impossible! I am so much exhausted with travelling in these miserable stages that I can not without a great exertion of being, continue that mode of going. . . . I assure you I would make any sacrifice to see you but I am too unwell to get on immediately."[19]

Larz died on February 27, 1878, and was buried at Spring Grove Cemetery in Cincinnati. His passing marked the end of an era. Two brothers and two sisters outlived him, but he was the first and last patriarch of his generation. Henceforth, the adult children would take their place as family leaders and dispense advice—and arguments—to their parents.

WHILE LARZ'S DEATH MARKED the end of an era, it does not mark the end of this story. William and Charles had one final chapter to contribute.

In a June 1878 letter to Charles, Ned wrote on black-ribbon letterhead commemorating the loss of his father. He informed Charles he would accept Marcellus Anderson's offer and in turn go to England in search of more distant ancestral records. Apparently Ned suffered from nervous ailments, for he closed his letter to Charles noting, "I am too nervous to write more, excuse my brevity. With love to all I am your aff nephew." In January 1879, Ned was happy to write from London: "In a few days after you receive this you will get 'Soldier and Pioneer.' I hope that you will like the book. I did not dare go into genealogy yet. But I leave here on Saturday for Europe, and I promise you that I shall get something in Scotland."[20]

It is impossible to know for sure what prompted Ned's (and brother Nick's) nervousness or Larz Jr.'s suicide. Perhaps part of the answer for Ned and Nick was post-traumatic stress from their Civil War experiences. Larz Jr.'s "melancholy," reported in his obituary, no doubt had deeper sources, perhaps a continuation of that prevalent in the older generation. All family members suffered anxiety of one sort or another—feelings not unusual for the offspring of a wealthy family. One thing that is certain is the continuation of "founding" families as the nineteenth century wore on and accumulation of wealth and property became the only true end.

Despite his nervousness, Ned kept Marcellus Anderson digging into genealogies, sending him fifty dollars and promising "$200 to trace back the Andersons to a family and county in his country [England]." Ned was hoping to discover a family coat of arms to "prove that we are descended from that noble family." By April 1879, Marcellus was asking Ned for the stupendous sum of $5,000, which led Ned to confide in a letter to Charles, "I do not put any faith in Marcellus."[21]

As usual, Charles had his own concerns. He made one more attempt at a diplomatic assignment, but again met with no success. After asking Lincoln's attorney general, James Speed, to intercede on his behalf with President Hayes, he heard in August 1879 that there was no hope: "The President read to me a list of the names of the applicants and I am sure your name was not among them. After what I have done you will see my dear sir that anything I might do or say would not avail you." Speed went on to note that a "Mr. Barr" was on the list, so he felt duty bound to support him: "It often happens in this life that we are forced to choose between friends and I hold that where choice is once made it should be faithfully adhered to." Separately, Charles wrote to wife Eliza that "some think that the demand for more and more lands will soon blaze out. I don't quite think so." Charles still hoped to eventually collect on his land.[22]

Meanwhile news of Charles's agnosticism spread to the grandchildren, leaving a pious (and ultimately suicidal) Larz Jr. to write Charles that Latham had recently visited and informed him of his father's lack of faith. In his letter, Larz Jr. referenced a book, *Beyond the Grave*, by a Methodist bishop and implored Charles to convert: "Can you not say, it is not true! . . . Then let us . . . acknowledge our loyalty to God; before men and in our lives! I write this to you because I love you! And for years have been looking forward with prayerfulness, for your conversion. Since Father's death I thought you believed with him. . . . Forgive me if I presume—whatever you may think—believe I respect and love you."[23]

In a letter to William written in June 1879, Charles confessed his unbelief: "I see all of my brothers and sisters in the church safe and happy in a Christian faith whilst I stand out, alone, cheerless and alas! Heedless—a mere personified negation a vacuum in faith. I ask myself why is this? How came it to be so? At times I surmise that one accidental difference of . . . circumstances . . . may have produced this startling difference of results."[24]

Charles did not know it, but as he was baring his soul to William, William, age seventy-two, was nearing his own death. Whatever issues had divided William and Ellen were largely gone by 1879. Letters to William from Ellen were signed "Nellie," an affectionate nickname not seen in the earlier years. In a letter written from Urbana, Ohio, in August 1879, she reported time spent with her mother and the always present priests: "Father Walker rode up to the house with us, dined, played croquet, and in the afternoon went over to Father Kearneys. . . . Father K had him out riding."[25]

Writing from Washington, DC, in February 1880, Ellen curiously noted a trip to a market stall where "I had my first attack of panic since I came, while walking through the market house. As soon as I was back in the carriage, it left me." She reported as well that she went to the eleven o'clock Mass at St. Dominic's: "The interior is beautiful, but of course I only took things in by a general glance coming out. I saw the stations were in bas relief, but cannot say more until I see them nearer. . . . The mysteries in the blessed Mother's life painted on those walls and overhead are beautiful." She signed it, "Always devotedly your wife, Nellie."[26]

In December 1880 William received a letter from problem son Thomas, who was stationed at Fort McKinney in the Wyoming Territory. In pencil across the envelope, someone wrote, "the last letter to his father." It appears that William had asked that Thomas return a book that Father Bowen had given to his mother. Originally, William had asked Thomas to give it to one of his children. Perhaps he had given up any hope that any of them would convert to Catholicism. Thomas replied that if William had not requested its return, "I would otherwise have given it to Arlene on her birthday. She will be eleven on the 17th of this month. She is quite a bright child and learns her lessons very well. But she is much harder to manage than any of the others. Her disposition being I fear too much like my own." Thomas added a troubled thought on a wildly insensitive and hurtful statement of his father's that Thomas's mother, Eliza, loved his brother Harry more than him. To this, Thomas responded: "Harry is a very fine man and is giving you great credit as a son. You surprised me somewhat, nevertheless, by telling me that he was his mothers favorite. I never could see that Mother made any distinctions between her children in her affection." In fact, Thomas continued, "she told Aunt Maria that she feared more for Harry because she thought his success in life would depend more on chance than opportunity. She hoped more from me because I was more self reliant. I knew I was far more self reliant in comparison to Harry."[27]

In the same way that he resisted his father's proselytizing, Thomas refused to let William use his mother as a weapon against him: "I hear my Dear Father you think I have disappointed her hopes. I do not think so. . . . Believe in her sincerity. She would have no more have reproached one with differences from her views [words 'her views' underlined in pencil by William] than her parents . . . could have reproached either of you with a departure from theirs."[28]

Thomas's letter was the last straw for William in his tortured relationship with his eldest son. In what would prove to be the final letter preserved in his collection, and probably the final letter he wrote, William let loose with a salvo of vituperative rage, issuing a self-defense against the perceived slights and offenses he had received at the hand of Thomas. In what stands out as the harshest letter in any of the Andersons' correspondence, and the longest, William crystallized all the arguments he had been rehearsing for years. In all likelihood, William realized he was dying as he wrote: "You may take offense, at what may prove the dying words of your decrepit father. I will speak tho it kill me. I mean no offense, therefore take none."[29]

Contained in William's letter to Thomas was nothing less than sheer rejection, combined with a dying plea to see faith the way he saw it and repent from the error of his ways. This he would take to his grave, and probably Thomas as well. One can only imagine Thomas's burden in this, the final testimony of his alienated father. On January 7, 1881, wracked with double pneumonia and suffering great pain, William received the last rites and died. In contrast to other fallen Andersons with adult children, no family members were pallbearers at his funeral.

Ellen and Thomas were left to pick up their lives, each in their own way. Different as they were, the two came together in a loving letter that Ellen sent to Thomas describing his father's last days. In stark contrast to William's faith and fury, Ellen demonstrated a strong faith but with the love of a stepmother to a suffering child forced to live out his days with the knowledge of his father's rejection. Perhaps in this moment, Ellen felt herself in some sense a kindred spirit, having lost William's support when he left for Mexico fourteen years earlier.

In recounting William's last days and hours, Ellen noted that his health was never the same after the train accident three years prior, "and only those with him, knew of his sufferings of the last months, unable to lie in bed and sleep any more, but rest as well he could on a lounge or chair, catching a little sleep, and then the oppressed breathing keeping him awake for hours of the long night, but he never complained." Wracked with the pain of a kidney ailment and breathing with difficulty, William still held on until an "irritation of the lower bowel" left him "too weak to rally, and [he] passed away as calmly as a tired child goes to sleep." In his final moments, William was surrounded by his son Robert, Ellen, and her beloved sister Fanny.[30]

As Ellen's letter made clear, Thomas did not attend the funeral. In his later "monography" of the family, Thomas heaped praise and love on his natural mother, Eliza, but of William he listed only the bare bones facts of his life. He gave none of his children his father's name.

After William's death, there follows a ten-year gap in Charles's correspondence file. By 1890, the seventy-six-year-old had recovered his financial affairs and was settling down to a life of ease in Kuttawa. For once Charles had bucked the national trends. A new railroad meant access to markets. The model town he'd envisioned in Kuttawa was realizing tangible returns with the creation of the Kuttawa Mineral Springs business, which Charles had opened in 1880. Equally successful was his Kuttawa Iron Ore Company, which grew steadily. In 1890 Charles sold all but one thousand acres for the princely sum of $160,000. Larz did not live to see the triumph of his "indolent" younger brother, but clearly he would have been pleased to see his advice at last vindicated.[31]

The final letter in Charles's collection was, fittingly, a reflection on the patriarch, Richard Clough Anderson Sr. In that letter, dated November 15, 1893, Reuben Thomas Durrett, a Kentucky-born lawyer and writer, clarified an Anderson family legend that Lafayette had visited Soldier's Retreat in his fabled American tour. Durrett correctly explained that Lafayette never visited Soldier's Retreat. However, as a member of the "committee of citizens" and "committee of entertainment" for the Frenchman, Richard Sr. entertained Lafayette at Washington Hall in Louisville on June 24, 1819, by his fellow Masons. Colonel Anderson then proposed a toast: "The Floridas; we wish them not in a spirit of acquisition, but to widen the field for free principles and free government." Durrett concluded: "I hope that you will take the time and the trouble to get up a good sketch of Col. Richard C. Anderson. He was not only a distinguished citizen, but was one of that class of good men who ought to be remembered in the history and the biography of his country.[32]

Two years later Charles died. The funeral was presided over by a Presbyterian minister. No copy of the eulogy survives.

IN THE END, THE Anderson children fulfilled the promise of their father and the republic he fought and bled to create. We are left, however, with a series of "buts." As surveyor general, Richard Sr. acquired a fortune in land and the love of all who lived and visited at Soldier's Retreat. But his love of speculation lost him much of what he had travailed to gain. Richard Jr., "the sage," landslide-winning congressman and American diplomat to South America, almost certainly would have risen to even greater national prominence had he lived long enough. But his addiction to land speculation forced him to make decisions that, in the end, cost him his life. The brilliant Harvard graduate and talented penman Larz, whose considerable banking talents and marriage alignments took him to the very top of Ohio's economic elite, maintained his humility and loyalty to the family. But he could also be a harsh judge, and his younger brother Charles was not exempt from his criticisms. Robert, the West Point graduate, wounded warrior, and unstintingly dutiful soldier, and "the most famous man in America" at one point, also managed to acquire significant land through marriage and partnerships with his brothers. But in the end, he subjugated his compassion to his duty, and his wounds—suffered in wars in which he did not believe—rendered him an invalid. William, the family renegade "mountain man," whose Southern loyalties and staunch Catholicism would strain and, in Thomas's case, break his ties with his family, also inherited and married into substantial land and wealth. But his hateful racism and rejection of fellow family members over religion and politics left him largely alienated, embraced at the end only by his wife, son Robert, and brother Charles. And finally, Charles, the "lazy" brother, managed to become a war hero, governor of Ohio, and much-sought-after speaker. At the end of his life he also found wealth in land that he would pass on to his heirs. But his impulsive judgments often rendered his talents ineffective, denying him both political influence and a diplomatic assignment, and delaying by many decades the financial security he longed to achieve.

The Anderson women, by birth and marriage, are largely remembered—as described in family correspondence—in relation to their intrafamily roles. Of Richard's daughters born to Elizabeth, Ann (Nancy) married John Logan against her father's wishes, but in the end his fears for her financial welfare proved unwarranted. Cecelia never married and we know little of her life. Elizabeth (Betsy) married her first cousin Isaac Gwathmey and suffered frequent ailments that left family members thinking she was on death's door at least ten years before she actually died in 1870.

The daughters born to Sarah included Maria, the childless family networker who married the highly successful lawyer Allen Latham. Maria remained close to her mother and provided a reference point and rock of stability for the larger family network. In her second marriage, Mary Louisa wed the famous judge James Hall of Cincinnati. She remained a strong Episcopalian and on several occasions confronted William about his Catholicism—which she took to be heresy. She engaged in bitter debates with William that rivaled his debates with son Thomas.

The Anderson wives, like their contemporaries in the "West," evidenced little decision-making regarding where and how they would live. They tended to follow the career paths of their husbands. On the domestic front, they were fully equal partners in the running of the family businesses. Betsy accepted Richard's decisions to enter politics and diplomacy. She endured months of his absence with only her children for company. She assumed all the household responsibilities, from overseeing the slaves and their labor to managing the farm and tending to her indispensable pig business. Despite the dangers of dwelling in Colombia, she willingly undertook the difficult journey with her children. In the end she paid for her loyalty with her life, as did her husband, leaving the children orphans.

Larz's two wives had fewer domestic responsibilities but also endured the deaths of children and frequent separations. Larz's success as a lawyer, bank director, estate manager, and legate of his second wife Kate Longworth's immense fortune allowed for frequent travel to Europe and US vacation spots, often in attempts to recover from sickly constitutions. Of all the families, the Larz Andersons and the Longworths were the most famous.

Robert married Eliza Clinch late in life and she never enjoyed frequent interactions with the other Andersons—a fact of some irritation to Robert. Her Southern loyalties probably challenged her husband's standing among Northern officers but meant a lot to family members with Southern connections. Her illiteracy meant there would be no surviving correspondence. With Robert's death, his daughter Eba edited his letters from the Mexican War years through Fort Sumter.

William also had two wives who brought him wealth and spiritual consolation. His first wife, Eliza, daughter of Governor Duncan

McArthur, grew up wealthy, only to see the family fortune dissipated by unending litigation over her father's estate. His second wife, Ellen Columba Ryan, was a woman of deep Catholic piety that matched William's. But she too had to endure marriage to a difficult man that peaked with his desertion and travel to Mexico after the Civil War. Following William's death she reconciled with William's estranged son, Thomas, and lived out her long life in devotion to the Church.

Charles's wife, Eliza Brown, endured trials with her marriage. Her husband's self-described "laziness" and frequent moves left her often alone as Charles traveled widely for pleasure and sport. His move to Texas proved to be a disaster that ended in terrifying escapes from pursuing Confederates and steep financial losses that were never recovered until the end of his life.

So what do we say in closing? The Andersons' lives embodied the good, the bad, and the ugly that marked America's great experiment in republicanism, capitalism, and continental expansion. They fought for their country with uncommon valor even as those wars included immoral ones on Mexicans and Indians. Neither great saints nor irredeemable sinners, they were merely human, pursuing their self-interested dreams with dexterity.

One American family, one generation removed from the fight for independence, helped to wed the meaning of America to unending hunger for land and personal wealth. And, like the generations that have followed, the family paid the price of lives motivated by acquisition, speculation, and the possibility of greatness. The anxiety that has become emblematic of modern American life and its capitalist ethos had already sunk deep roots into American soil during that first generation. The Andersons were a reasonably good-hearted, loyal family whose members participated freely in the early republic's ugliest chapters for the sake of personal gain.

In the Anderson family's story, replicated many times over in the newly minted United States, the insatiable nature of American life today, and the epidemic of anxiety that plagues it, seem inevitable.

Afterword

In 2015, I visited the site of the original Soldier's Retreat at Beargrass Creek, ten miles outside of Louisville off present-day Hurstbourne Lane and Shelbyville Road. Earthquakes in 1811 and 1812 weakened the main structure, and in 1840 it was torn down after a lightning strike burned it beyond repair. Several outbuildings still stand, most notably one slave quarters. The current owners have built a house that replicates many aspects of the original home, and the prominent properties that surround it testify to the ongoing power of land to shape the environment. At the end of the original Soldier's Retreat property stands the exclusive Hurstbourne Country Club and its championship golf course, covering grounds that once contained Richard Anderson Sr.'s vegetable garden, vineyard, smokehouse, storehouse, detached office (for Richard's surveying business), washhouse, and various artisan buildings, including those of the cobbler, cooper, and blacksmith. Of the dozen houses built for slaves, one survives intact.

A small burial ground remains, containing fifteen graves of Anderson family members. A monument to Richard Sr. and Sarah stands on the location, with an inscription penned by second patriarch Larz Anderson. After summarizing Richard Sr.'s renowned service in the Revolution and removal to Kentucky as surveyor general of the Virginia Military District, it closes: "He lived a life of usefulness and honor, leaving to his children and country the memory of a good citizen, a true patriot, and a just man." On the west side of the monument lies the grave of his first wife, Elizabeth Clark Anderson, and on the south side that of his second wife, Sarah Marshall Anderson.

Manicured neighborhoods and sprawling shopping malls have long since overtaken the early farms and settlements of the Kentucky and Ohio frontier. The allure of consumption is now inextricably woven into even the open landscapes of modern farms, riverside estates, and natural preserves. To the east of the old Soldier's Retreat lies the inner city. There the ongoing inequalities of opportunity and advantages bear witness to the legacy of slavery and racism, testifying to the winners and losers of America's great land stakes.

Acknowledgments

This book owes an immeasurable debt of gratitude to the Huntington Library, its generous benefactors—in particular Steve Rogers and his late wife Janet—and its incomparable staff. When Director of Research Roy Ritchie offered me a Rogers Distinguished Fellowship for the 2011–2012 academic year, I had no idea what I would pursue except that it would focus on an archive in their unsurpassed manuscript collections of Americana. My heartfelt thanks to the Huntington historical archivist, Olga Tsapina, who introduced me to the largely neglected but wonderfully rich collection of letters, diaries, and writings by members of a frontier family named Anderson. I opened the Anderson files on day one in September and did not stop until my final day at the Huntington the following Memorial Day. Throughout the course of the year I profited as well from coffee and lunchtime conversations with resident fellows and the newly installed director of research, Steve Hindle.

Other research libraries also proved unfailingly helpful and patient as I sought to fill in the historical gaps to create a narrative from a trove of letters. Yale's unsurpassed libraries and diligent staff provided resources on the West in American history that proved indispensable in the writing of this book.

The most important Anderson archive after the Huntington—Louisville's Filson Historical Society, not far removed from the Anderson ancestral homestead at Soldier's Retreat—offered up missing links and valuable insights. My gratitude goes to Jana Meyer, who employed her archival skills to prepare bibliographic searches ahead of my arrival that made it possible to maximize my stay at that worthy archive. I am also grateful to Mark Wetherington and Jim Holberg, whose leadership of the Filson has vaulted it to the top ranks of research archives. Other Anderson materials are housed at the Ohio Historical Society (now the Ohio History Collection), the Ohio Manuscripts in the University of Illinois Library, the Library of Congress, the Library of Virginia, and the King Library of Miami University.

Many friends and family have shared in this project since its inception. I would especially thank Emily Bingham and Stephen Reily, who gave new meaning to southern hospitality by opening their home to my wife and me during our stay in Louisville. For their friendship and moral support, my thanks to James Early, Victor Ferrante, Mark Messier, Peter Huckins, and the late Vincent Ferrucci. My children, Deborah and James, and their children have been a constant joy. To my brother-in-law, Terry Jenkins, who wants a book by me that he can "read for fun," this is as close as it gets!

Throughout the process of writing this book, many colleagues supplied critical readings and encouragement. I must begin by acknowledging my undergraduate and graduate mentor, Robert P. Swierenga. My first undergraduate college seminar with Bob introduced me to his specialty, the frontier in American history. My encounter with the Anderson family rekindled my fascination and curiosity with the subject. Over the years Bob has continued to inspire me with his dogged research skills and string of seminal books spanning the frontier and American immigration.

More recently, I owe a great debt to friends and fellow scholars who commented helpfully on the manuscript from their various bases of expertise. Catherine A. Brekus, Richard D. Brown, and Peter S. Onuf read portions of the manuscript at an early stage and convinced me that I had a book. For reading the manuscript in its entirety and offering deep criticism I thank Grant Wacker, Laurie Maffly-Kipp, Ken Minkema, and Kathryn Lofton.

My colleagues at Yale, in particular Jon Butler, Elli Stern, Glenda Gilmore, John Demos, David Blight, Naomi Lamoreaux, and Johnny Faragher, offered me the benefit of their wisdom over frequent coffees and lunches in New Haven. The American Religious History workshop and the Yale Early American History reading group graciously allowed me a preliminary reading of my argument and offered helpful advice and suggestions. I am grateful to Jan Stieverman, who generously hosted me for a month in residence at the Center for American Studies, University of Heidelberg, where the final draft was completed. It goes (almost) without saying that I am responsible for whatever faults may remain.

I owe a great debt of gratitude to my publisher at Basic Books, Lara Heimert. When I described this project, her enthusiasm was contagious. Her thorough critical reading improved the style and organization of the book immensely. So too, did the superb editorial insights of Roger Labrie and Erin Granville, whose corrections, questions, and suggestions are unrivaled in my writing career. Melissa Veronesi has been a superb project manager.

Finally, and most important, I thank my wife, Deborah H. DeFord, whose astute editing, constant encouragement in times of self-doubt, and all-around love and support made the work of this book fun. In dedicating the book to her I offer one small token of thanks.

Notes

The following abbreviations are used throughout the notes:

HL—Anderson Family Papers, Huntington Library, San Marino, California. All citations with "AND" or "AN" are from this collection.

Filson—Anderson-Latham Papers, Filson Historical Society Library, Louisville, Kentucky.

AL—Allen Latham

CA—Charles Anderson

LA—Larz Anderson

RA—Robert Anderson

RCA Sr.—Richard Clough Anderson Sr.

RCA Jr.—Richard Clough Anderson Jr.

WA—William Anderson

INTRODUCTION

1. On microhistory in recent scholarship, see Jill Lepore, "Historians Who Love Too Much: Reflections on Microhistory and Biography," *Journal of American History* 88, no. 1 (2001): 129–144; and Richard D. Brown, "Microhistory and the Post-Modern Challenge," *Journal of the Early Republic* 23, no. 1 (2003): 1–20.

2. For works detailing middle-class family ideals for women, see, e.g., Mary P. Ryan, *Cradle of the Middle Class: The Family in Oneida County, New York, 1790–1865* (New York: Cambridge University Press, 1981); Steven Mintz, *A Prison of Expectations: The Family in Victorian Culture* (New York: NYU Press, 1983); Elisabeth Donaghy Garrett, *At Home: The American Family, 1750–1870* (New York: Harry N. Abrams, 1990); Jan Lewis, *The Pursuit of Happiness: Family and*

Values in Jefferson's Virginia (New York: Cambridge University Press, 1983); or Emily Bingham, *Mordecai: An Early American Family* (New York: Hill and Wang, 2003).

3. Frederick Jackson Turner, *The Frontier in American History* (New York: Henry Holt and Company, 1921). The literature on the frontier is immense. For a sampling, see Ray Allen Billington, *America's Frontier Heritage* (New York: Holt, Rinehart and Winston, 1966); John Mack Faragher, ed., *Rereading Frederick Jackson Turner* (New York: Henry Holt and Company, 1994; New Haven, CT: Yale University Press, 1998); Thomas Clark and John D. W. Guice, *The Old Southwest, 1795–1830: Frontiers in Conflict* (Norman: University of Oklahoma Press, 1996); Gregory Nobles, *American Frontiers: Cultural Encounters and Continental Conquest* (New York: Hill and Wang, 1997); and Richard White, *The Middle Ground: Indians, Empires, and Republics in the Great Lakes Region, 1650–1815* (New York: Cambridge University Press, 1991).

4. See Andro Linklater, *Measuring America: How the United States Was Shaped by the Greatest Land Sale in History* (New York: Plume, 2003), 5. Of course, "relatively egalitarian" land distribution did not mean that large swaths of Americans were not closed out of landownership. On those left out, see Nancy Isenberg's provocative book *White Trash: The 400-Year Untold History of Class in America* (New York: Viking, 2016).

5. See Hernando de Soto, *The Mystery of Capital: Why Capitalism Triumphs in the West and Fails Everywhere Else* (New York: Basic Books, 2000).

6. Marvin Meyers, *The Jacksonian Persuasion: Politics and Belief* (Stanford, CA: Stanford University Press, 1957), 126–127, 135.

7. See Charles Lloyd Cohen, *God's Caress: The Psychology of Puritan Religious Experience* (New York: Oxford University Press, 1986).

8. David M. Potter, *People of Plenty: Economic Abundance and the American Character* (Chicago: University of Chicago Press, 1954). One recent critique of Potter by Donald Worster labels him an American "exceptionalist" but misses Potter's central argument that abundance doesn't make Americans exceptionally triumphant but exceptionally anxious. See Worster, *Shrinking the Earth: The Rise and Decline of American Abundance* (New York: Oxford University Press, 2016), 152–157.

CHAPTER 1: RICHARD CLOUGH ANDERSON, THE PATRIARCH: 1750–1787

1. For two outstanding overviews of the Revolutionary era, see Gordon S. Wood, *The Radicalism of the American Revolution* (New York: Alfred A. Knopf,

1991); and Alan Taylor, *American Revolutions: A Continental History, 1750–1804* (New York: W. W. Norton, 2016).

2. In today's dollars the tea was worth at least $1.7 million. Benjamin L. Carp lists the participants of the Boston Tea Party in his book *Defiance of the Patriots: The Boston Tea Party and the Making of America* (New Haven, CT: Yale University Press, 2010), 234–239. For a brilliant re-creation of one participant, see Alfred F. Young, *The Shoemaker and the Tea Party: Memory and the American Revolution* (Boston: Beacon Press, 1999). Also useful is Benjamin Woods Labaree, *The Boston Tea Party* (New York: Oxford University Press, 1964), 126–145.

3. John Adams, *Diary and Autobiography of John Adams*, ed. Lyman Butterfield, vol. 1 (Cambridge, MA: Belknap Press, 1961), 85–86.

4. It is not clear exactly how knowledgeable Anderson was about the particular events of the Boston Tea Party. Family legend has him as a keen observer—and supporter—of the event, while a more recent biographer of Anderson's son, Charles, is more cautious. What is clear is that Anderson was wrestling with the question of resistance and revolution, and by the time he arrived back in Richmond he, along with his older friend, neighbor, and fellow parishioner Patrick Henry, had become an ardent patriot. David T. Dixon, *The Lost Gettysburg Address: Charles Anderson's Civil War Odyssey* (Santa Barbara, CA: B-List History, 2015), 6.

5. See Greg Grandin, *The Empire of Necessity: Slavery, Freedom, and Deception in the New World* (New York: Metropolitan Books, 2014).

6. The term "spiritual holocaust" is taken from Jon Butler, *Awash in a Sea of Faith: Christianizing the American People* (Cambridge, MA: Harvard University Press, 1992).

7. See Philip D. Morgan, *Slave Counterpoint: Black Culture in the Eighteenth-Century Chesapeake and Lowcountry* (Chapel Hill: University of North Carolina Press, 1998); and Peter Kolchin, *American Slavery: 1619–1877* (New York: Hill and Wang, 1993), 19–20.

8. See Ira Berlin, *Generations of Captivity: A History of African-American Slaves* (Cambridge, MA: Harvard University Press, 2003), 80–88; Kolchin, *American Slavery*, 30.

9. Quoted in Alfred F. Young, *The Liberty Tree: Ordinary People and the American Revolution* (New York: New York University Press, 2006), foreword.

10. See especially Bernard Bailyn, *The Ideological Origins of the American Revolution* (Cambridge, MA: Harvard University Press, 1967).

11. W. P. Anderson, *Anderson Family Records* (Cincinnati, OH: Press of W. F. Schaefer and Company, 1936), 43.

12. On the limited participation of American volunteers, see John Shy, *A People Numerous and Armed: Reflections on the Military Struggle for American Independence* (New York: Oxford University Press, 1976), 13.

13. See Robert Middlekauff, *Washington's Revolution: The Making of America's First Leader* (New York: Alfred A. Knopf, 2015). On deference in colonial Virginia, see Rhys Isaac, *The Transformation of Virginia, 1740–1790* (Chapel Hill: University of North Carolina Press, 1999).

14. Harry Ammon, *James Monroe: The Quest for National Identity* (New York: McGraw-Hill, 1971), 11.

15. Edward Lowell Anderson, *Soldier and Pioneer: A Biographical Sketch of Lt.-Col. Richard C. Anderson of the Continental Army* (New York: G. P. Putnam's Sons, 1879), 18; and Anderson, *Anderson Family Records*, 43.

16. See Russell Freedman, *Washington at Valley Forge* (New York: Holiday House, 2008); and Paul Lockhart, *The Drillmaster of Valley Forge: The Baron de Steuben and the Making of the American Army* (New York: HarperCollins, 2008).

17. Anderson's role in the battle is traced in Dixon, *The Lost Gettysburg Address*, 9–10.

18. Lafayette is quoted in Henry P. Johnston, *The Yorktown Campaign and the Surrender of Cornwallis, 1781* (1881; repr. Freeport, NY: Books for Libraries Press, 1971), 37. On France's entry into the war, see Samuel Flagg Bemis, *The Diplomacy of the American Revolution* (New Haven, CT: D. Appleton-Century Company, 1935); Jonathan Dull, *A Diplomatic History of the Revolution* (New Haven, CT: Yale University Press, 1985); and Ronald Hoffman and Peter Albert, eds., *Diplomacy and Revolution: The Franco-American Alliance of 1778* (Charlottesville, VA: University Press of Virginia, 1981).

19. Anderson, *Anderson Family Records*, 36–37.

20. Johnston, *The Yorktown Campaign and the Surrender of Cornwallis*, 45.

21. For example, see Richard L. Bushman, *From Puritan to Yankee: Character and the Social Order in Connecticut, 1690–1765* (Cambridge, MA: Harvard University Press, 1967).

22. See Dixon, *The Lost Gettysburg Address*, 13–14.

23. See Miles DuVal, *George Rogers Clark: Conqueror of the Old Northwest* (n.p., 1969); and Honor Sachs, *Home Rule: Households, Manhood, and National Expansion on the Eighteenth-Century Kentucky Frontier* (New Haven, CT: Yale University Press, 2015), 98–109.

24. Elizabeth (Clark) Anderson to Anna Gwathmey AND 144 4-25-1788.

CHAPTER 2: MEASURING THE LAND: 1787–1796

I. William H. Bergmann, *The American National State and the Early West* (New York: Cambridge University Press, 2012), 6.

2. See Andrew R. L. Cayton and Peter S. Onuf, "The Significance of the Northwest Ordinance," in *The Midwest and the Nation: Rethinking the History of an American Region* (Bloomington: Indiana University Press, 1990), 1–24.

3. See Andro Linklater, *The Fabric of America: How Our Borders and Boundaries Shaped the Country and Forged Our National Identity* (New York: Walker and Company, 2007), 6–14.

4. See John C. Weaver, *The Great Land Rush and the Making of the Modern World, 1690–1900* (Montreal: McGill-Queen's University, 2003), 27.

5. David Potter, *People of Plenty: Economic Abundance and the American Character* (Chicago: University of Chicago Press, 1954), xxvi, 67, 116, 154.

6. For the working out of this in Kentucky, see Honor Sachs, *Home Rule: Households, Manhood, and National Expansion on the Eighteenth-Century Kentucky Frontier* (New Haven, CT: Yale University Press, 2015). On American treaties with Indians, see Dorothy V. Jones, *License for Empire: Colonialism by Treaty in Early America* (Chicago: University of Chicago Press, 1982); and Leonard J. Sadosky, *Revolutionary Negotiations: Indians, Empires, and Diplomats in the Founding of America* (Charlottesville: University of Virginia Press, 2009). On British colonists' purchase of Indian lands, see Stuart Banner, *How the Indians Lost Their Land: Law and Power on the Frontier* (Cambridge, MA: Harvard University Press, 2005), 85.

7. See Reginald Horsman, *Expansion and American Indian Policy* (Lansing: Michigan State University Press, 1967), 6–7.

8. Locke is quoted in Weaver, *The Great Land Rush and the Making of the Modern World,* 62. On preemption, see Banner, *How the Indians Lost Their Land,* 46–47; and Alan Taylor, *The Divided Ground: Indians, Settlers, and the Northern Borderland of the American Revolution* (New York: Alfred A. Knopf, 2006), 10.

9. In Stephen Aron's words, "Unlike pioneer men, Indian women did not claim permanent, individual ownership of the fields they farmed. Theirs was a group right and a use right, not an individuated and perpetual tenure." Stephen Aron, *How the West Was Lost: The Transformation of Kentucky from Daniel Boone to Henry Clay* (Baltimore, MD: Johns Hopkins University Press, 1996), 65. See also Wilcomb E. Washburn, "The Moral and Legal Justification for Dispossessing the Indians," in *Seventeenth-Century America: Essays in Colonial History,* ed. James Morton Smith (Chapel Hill: University of North Carolina Press, 1959), 15–32.

10. Banner, *How the Indians Lost Their Land*, 16. I have traced the evolution of the concept of discovery and America as a "New Israel" in *The New England Soul: Preaching and Religious Culture in Colonial New England* (New York: Oxford University Press, 1986). The literature on America as a New Israel is enormous and underscores major events from the rise of Puritanism to colonial wars with Indians to Manifest Destiny and global expansion. For a sampling of relevant sources, see Conrad Cherry, ed., *God's New Israel: Religious Interpretations of American Destiny*, rev. ed. (Chapel Hill: University of North Carolina Press, 1998).

11. See Aron, *How the West Was Lost*, 1.

12. The event is recounted in William Marshall Anderson, *The Rocky Mountain Journals of William Marshall Anderson*, ed. Dale L. Morgan and Eleanor Towles Harris (San Marino, CA: The Huntington Library, 1967), 45; and Landon Y. Jones, *William Clark and the Shaping of the West* (New York: Hill and Wang, 2004), 56–57.

13. Patricia Watlington, *The Partisan Spirit: Kentucky Politics, 1779–1792* (New York: Atheneum, 1972), 21–22.

14. Ibid., 27–30.

15. The four land speculators were the Ohio Company of Associates, the Scioto Group, the Connecticut Land Company, and John Cleves Symmes.

16. See Timothy J. Shannon, "'This Unpleasant Business': The Transformation of Land Speculation in the Ohio Country, 1787–1820," in *The Pursuit of Public Power: Political Culture in Ohio, 1787–1861*, ed. Jeffrey P. Brown and Andrew R. L. Cayton (Kent, OH: Kent State University Press, 1994), 17.

17. See Alan D. Gaff, *Bayonets in the Wilderness: Anthony Wayne's Legion in the Old Northwest* (Norman: University of Oklahoma Press, 2004); and R. Douglas Hurt, *The Ohio Frontier: Crucible of the Old Northwest, 1720–1830* (Bloomington: Indiana University Press, 1996), 120–142. On the defeat of St. Clair's forces, see Aron, *How the West Was Lost*, 50.

18. See Cayton and Onuf, *The Midwest and the Nation*, 29.

19. Shannon, "'This Unpleasant Business,'" 25.

20. Many of Anderson's surveys and transactions are preserved at the Filson Historical Society Library, the University Library at the University of Illinois at Urbana-Champaign, and the Library of Virginia.

21. The process of securing warrants is described in Watlington, *The Partisan Spirit*, 13–14. See also Aron, *How the West Was Lost*, 82–101.

22. John King AND 1197 5-15-1780 from Kentucky; RCA to [Captain] Robert Zankias AND 367 7-30-1784 from Louisville.

23. For a comprehensive survey of land mania in many states, see Michael Blaakman, "Speculation Nation: Land and Mania in the Revolutionary American Republic, 1776–1803," PhD diss., Yale University, 2016.

24. For a summary of the early administrative procedures for surveying the land, see Paul Wallace Gates, *History of Public Land Law Development* (Washington, DC: Public Land Law Review Commission, 1968), 126–128, 251.

25. William Waller Hening, ed., *Statutes at Large*, 13 vols. (Richmond, VA: 1819–1823), x, 331.

26. A number of Anderson's warrants are contained at Filson in the Anderson-Latham Papers 1771–1811 Mss. A A548C 4, and at the Library of Virginia. Among Anderson's deputies were John Cleves Symmes, Nathaniel Massie, Duncan McArthur, Major John O'Bannion, Lucas Sullivant, James Taylor, and Arthur Fox.

27. Andrew R. L. Cayton, *The Frontier Republic: Ideology and Politics in the Ohio Country, 1780–1825* (Kent, OH: Kent State University Press, 1986), 54–55; William Hutchinson, "The Bounty Lands of the American Revolution in Ohio" (New York: Arno Press, 1979).

28. Thomas Perkins Abernethy, *Western Lands and the American Revolution* (New York: Russell and Russell, 1959), viii.

29. Malcolm J. Rohrbough, *The Land Office Business: The Settlement and Administration of American Public Lands, 1789–1837* (New York: Oxford University Press, 1968), 17. On the benefits of indiscriminate location, see Ellen Susan Wilson, "Speculators and Land Development in the Virginia Military Tract: The Territorial Period," PhD diss., Miami University, 1982, 29–30.

30. Weaver, *The Great Land Rush and the Making of the Modern World*, 226–228. On Gunter's system, see Andro Linklater, *Measuring America: How the United States Was Shaped by the Greatest Land Sale in History* (New York: Plume, 2003), 16–17; and Linklater, *The Fabric of America*, 67.

31. Gates, *History of Public Land Law Development*, 255; Rohrbough, *The Land Office Business*, 8–9.

32. See Shannon, "'This Unpleasant Business,'" 29.

33. Edward Lowell Anderson, *Soldier and Pioneer: A Biographical Sketch of Lt.-Col. Richard C. Anderson of the Continental Army* (New York: G. P. Putnam's Sons, 1879), 16. Wilkinson is quoted in Watlington, *The Partisan Spirit*, 140, 147.

34. W. P. Anderson, *Anderson Family Records* (Cincinnati, OH: Press of W. F. Schaefer and Company, 1936), 47.

35. RCA Sr. to Betsy Anderson AND 317 12-8-1810.

36. Elizabeth Clark Anderson to George Rogers Clark AND 184 5-14-1787. On the importance of family and friends to frontier women, see John Mack Faragher, *Women and Men on the Overland Trail* (New Haven, CT: Yale University Press, 1979); Joan E. Cashin, *A Family Venture: Men and Women on the Southern Frontier* (New York: Oxford University Press, 1991), 40–52; and Hazel Dicken Garcia, *To Western Worlds: The Breckinridge Family Moves to Kentucky in 1793* (Rutherford, NJ: Fairleigh Dickinson University Press, 1991), 129–132.

37. Elizabeth Clark Anderson to Anna Gwathmey AND 145 1789. Elizabeth's father lived in Louisville.

38. Elizabeth Clark Anderson to RCA Sr. AND 139 1794. At end: "This letter was written by Mrs. Elizabeth Anderson copied by her grand daughter, Mrs. Sarah Gamble, Oct. 10, 1891."

39. RCA Sr. to Owen Gwathmey AND 364 2-7-1795.

40. William Croghan to RCA 11-4-1795 in Anderson-Latham Collection at the Library of Virginia; Thomas Parker to RCA Sr. 5-16-1795 in Anderson-Latham Collection at the Library of Virginia.

41. See David T. Dixon, *The Lost Gettysburg Address: Charles Anderson's Civil War Odyssey* (Santa Barbara, CA: B-List History, 2015), 15–16.

CHAPTER 3: A NEW GENERATION: 1797–1812

1. Joyce Appleby, *Inheriting the Revolution: The First Generation of Americans* (Cambridge, MA: Harvard University Press, 2000), 63.

2. Thomas McArthur Anderson, *A Monograph of the Anderson, Clark, Marshall and McArthur Collection* [1900] (Charleston, SC: Bibliolife, 2014), 13. Little Turtle's Miami name was Michikinikwa, and his forces inflicted major defeats on federal armies in 1790 and 1791. See Andro Linklater, *The Fabric of America: How Our Borders and Boundaries Shaped the Country and Forged Our National Identity* (New York: Walker and Company, 2007), 86.

3. RCA Sr. to Elizabeth Clark (Anderson) Gwathmey AND 312 3-11-1810; RCA Sr. to Elizabeth Clark (Anderson) Gwathmey AND 313 5-28-1810.

4. RCA Sr. to Elizabeth Clark (Anderson) Gwathmey AND 315 7-25-1810.

5. RCA Sr. to Elizabeth Clark (Anderson) Gwathmey AND 316 7-25-1810; Sarah Anderson to Elizabeth Clark (Anderson) Gwathmey AND 489 7-25-1810.

6. Richard Clough Anderson Jr., *The Diary and Journal of Richard Clough Anderson Jr. 1814–1826*, ed. Alfred Rischendorf and E. Taylor Parks (Durham,

NC: Duke University Press, 1964), 4. Hereafter cited as *Diary*. On Maury and Jefferson, see Annette Gordon-Reed and Peter S. Onuf, *'Most Blessed of the Patriarchs': Thomas Jefferson and the Empire of the Imagination* (New York: Liveright, 2016), 31.

7. Charles Sellers, *The Market Revolution: Jacksonian America, 1815–1846* (New York: Oxford University Press, 1991), 36–37.

8. See Sellers, *The Market Revolution*, 36.

9. My account of the Louisiana Purchase relies heavily on Marshall Smelser, *The Democratic Republic, 1801–1815* (New York: Harper & Row, 1968), 83–103; Gregory H. Nobles, *American Frontiers: Cultural Encounters and Continental Conquest* (New York: Hill and Wang, 1997); and Drew McCoy, *The Elusive Republic: Political Economy in Jeffersonian America* (Chapel Hill: University of North Carolina Press, 1980).

10. See Beckles Willson, *America's Ambassadors to France, 1777–1927* (London: Frederick A. Stokes Company, 1928), 86–92.

11. In Marshall Smelser's apt metaphor, "The Louisiana Purchase echoes like a thunder clap in America's story." Smelser, *The Democratic Republic*, 92–93.

12. Landon Y. Jones, *William Clark and the Shaping of the West* (New York: Hill and Wang, 2004), 55.

13. Quoted in Jones, *William Clark and the Shaping of the West*, 113.

14. William Marshall Anderson, *The Rocky Mountain Journals of William Marshall Anderson*, ed. Dale L. Morgan and Eleanor Towles Harris (San Marino, CA: The Huntington Library, 1967), 283–287.

15. In fact, York assumed a special sexual status with the Indians. See Jones, *William Clark and the Shaping of the West*, 137.

16. Jones, *William Clark and the Shaping of the West*, 141.

17. See Smelser, *The Democratic Republic*, 128–129.

18. See Patricia Watlington, *The Partisan Spirit: Kentucky Politics, 1779–1792* (New York: Atheneum, 1972), 198–199. On Richard's accommodations at college, see Smelser, *The Democratic Republic*, 6. William and Mary's curriculum is described in Albert D. Kirwan, *John J. Crittenden: The Struggle for the Union* (Lexington: University of Kentucky Press, 1962), 11–12. See also Amanda Porterfield, *Conceived in Doubt: Religion and Politics in the New American Nation* (Chicago: University of Chicago Press, 2012), 5.

19. Richard is quoted in Kirwan, *John J. Crittenden*, 6.

20. RCA Sr. to RCA Jr. AND 323 11-20-1808; RCA Sr. to RCA Jr. AND 324 12-4-1808; Richard Gamble to RCA Jr. AND 937 1-26-1809.

21. Quoted in Linklater, *The Fabric of America*, 113.

22. See Lawrence S. Kaplan, "Jefferson, the Napoleonic Wars, and the Balance of Power," *William and Mary Quarterly* 14, no. 2 (1957): 196–217; and Bradford Perkins, "Embargo: Alternative to War," in *Prologue to War: England and the United States, 1805–1812* (Berkeley: University of California Press, 1970), 140–183.

23. On the visit to Soldier's Retreat, see Jones, *William Clark and the Shaping of the West*, 178.

24. RCA Sr. to Elizabeth Clark (Anderson) Gwathmey AND 313 5-28-1810. On William Marshall's journey, see Chapter 9.

25. Smelser, *The Democratic Republic*, 133–134.

26. Benjamin Horace Hibbard, *A History of the Public Land Policies* (New York: Macmillan, 1924; Madison: University of Wisconsin Press, 1965), 73–78.

27. William O. Allen to RCA Jr. AND 19 1808.

28. Benjamin Watkins to RCA Jr. AND 1758 7-19-1808. On adolescence in the era, see Laurence Steinberg, *Adolescence*, 9th ed. (New York: McGraw-Hill, 2011); and Erik Erikson, *Identity: Youth and Crisis* (New York: W. W. Norton and Company, 1968).

29. RCA Jr. to Nancy Anderson AND 378 1808. On women writers, see Mary P. Ryan, *Cradle of the Middle Class: The Family in Oneida County, New York, 1790–1865* (New York: Cambridge University Press, 1981), 209–210, 221–222; and Appleby, *Inheriting the Revolution*, 96–98, 167.

30. See John Mack Faragher, *Women and Men on the Overland Trail*, 2nd ed. (New Haven, CT: Yale University Press, 2001), 144–178; Richard Brown to RCA Jr. AND 616 n.d.

31. John Crittenden to RCA Jr. AND 743 11-30-1810.

32. Alexander Bullitt to Helen B. Massie 2-24-1810, in Orlando Brown Papers, Filson.

33. See Kirwan, *John J. Crittenden*, 64–65. On consanguinity in the early republic, see Brian Connolly, *Domestic Intimacies: Incest and the Liberal Subject in Nineteenth-Century America* (Philadelphia: University of Pennsylvania Press, 2014).

34. Benjamin Watkins to RCA Jr. AND 1759 7-24-1809; Benjamin Watkins to RCA Jr. AND 1760 10-19-1809.

35. On fathers and sons in the early republic, see Appleby, *Inheriting the Revolution*, 172–173.

36. RCA Jr. to RCA Sr. AND 379 3-4-1810. On the formal and deferential language that characterized nineteenth-century letters, see Hazel Dicken

Garcia, *To Western Woods: The Breckinridge Family Moves to Kentucky in 1793* (Rutherford, NJ: Fairleigh Dickinson University Press, 1991), 63.

37. Sarah Anderson to Elizabeth Clark (Anderson) Gwathmey and Maria (Anderson) Latham AND 491 12-7-1810; RCA Jr. to Elizabeth Clark (Anderson) Gwathmey AND 369 11-8-10.

38. *Diary*, 6.

39. Thomas Boswell to RCA Jr. AND 582 4-9-1811.

40. John Crittenden to RCA Jr. AND 744 7-26-1811.

41. Donald R. Hickey, *The War of 1812: A Forgotten Conflict* (Urbana-Champaign: University of Illinois Press, 2012), 29–30; Benjamin Watkins to RCA Jr. AND 1766 8-21-1812; Kirwan, *John J. Crittenden*, 21–25.

42. Stephen Ormsby to RCA Jr. AND 104 12-24-1811.

CHAPTER 4: RICHARD THE SAGE: 1812–1817

1. *Diary*, 6; Elizabeth Clark (Gwathmey) Anderson to RCA Jr. AND 147 4-23-1812.

2. Owen Gwathmey to RCA Jr. AND 1026 7-10-1812; RCA Jr. to "Dear Sir" AND 443 6-12-1812. Later, Anderson would support Pope's successful contest for a seat on the board of directors of the Kentucky Bank and turn that support into banking credit for his problematic land deals. See *Diary*, xviii. On Pope's decision to oppose the War of 1812, see Orval W. Baylor, *John Pope, Kentuckian, His Life and Times, 1770–1845 : A Saga of Kentucky Politics from 1792 to 1850* (Cynthiana, KY: The Hobson Press, 1943), 82–93.

3. *Diary*, xviii.

4. Thomas Crittenden Jr. to RCA Jr. AND 766 11-19-1812.

5. Stephen Ormsby to RCA Jr. AND 1406 12-10-1812. Actually, the engagement was fought on October 15. See Donald R. Hickey, *The War of 1812: A Forgotten Conflict* (Urbana-Champaign: University of Illinois Press, 2012), 95.

6. Elizabeth Clark (Gwathmey) Anderson to RCA Jr. AND 148 12-12-1812.

7. Elizabeth Clark (Gwathmey) Anderson to RCA Jr. AND 149 12-19-1812. On the greater discontent that women suffered in the West, see Mary P. Ryan, *Cradle of the Middle Class: The Family in Oneida County, New York, 1790–1865* (New York: Cambridge University Press, 1981), 58–59; and John Mack Faragher, *Women and Men on the Overland Trail*, 2nd ed. (New Haven, CT: Yale University Press, 2001), 180–181.

8. Elizabeth Clark (Gwathmey) Anderson to RCA Jr. AND 150 1-5-1813.

9. Elizabeth Clark (Gwathmey) Anderson to RCA Jr. AND 151 1-12-1813; Stephen Aron, *How the West Was Lost: The Transformation of Kentucky from Daniel Boone to Henry Clay* (Baltimore, MD: Johns Hopkins University Press, 1996), 22–23.

10. *Diary*, 37.

11. *Diary*, 11–12.

12. *Diary*, 12, 16.

13. See Adam Jortner, *The Gods of Prophetstown: The Battle of Tippecanoe and the Holy War for the American Frontier* (New York: Oxford University Press, 2012).

14. Mary Anderson to RCA Jr. AND 294 7-25-1814.

15. *Diary*, 13–14.

16. Ibid., 13, 18. For a general treatment of child mortality in the era, see Sheldon Watts, *Epidemics and History: Disease, Power, and Imperialism* (New Haven, CT: Yale University Press, 1997). For statistics on health and life expectancy, see Daniel Walker Howe, *What Hath God Wrought: The Transformation of America, 1815–1848* (New York: Oxford University Press, 2007), 473.

17. The evolution is traced in Aron, *How the West Was Lost*, 195.

18. RCA Sr. to RCA Jr. AND 329 12-13-1814.

19. George Clark Gwathmey to RCA Jr. in Frankfort AND 963 12-13-1814.

20. *Diary*, 16; RCA Jr. to Peter Funk AND 402 1813; Thomas Crittenden Jr. to RCA Jr. AND 770 11-23-1814.

21. *Diary*, 16–17. See Sherry Keith Jelsma, "An Unexpected Nightmare: Charles S. Todd and United States Diplomacy in South America, 1820–1824," *Filson Historical Quarterly* 76, no. 3 (2002): 381–425.

22. *Diary*, 17.

23. Elizabeth Clark (Gwathmey) Anderson to RCA Jr. AND 152 11-10-1814. On women's roles in the domestic economy, see Ryan, *Cradle of the Middle Class*, 198–203; and Faragher, *Women and Men on the Overland Trail*, 59: "By no means were men the 'breadwinners' of this economy. Both women and men actively participated in the production of family subsistence. Indeed, women were engaged in from one-third to one-half of all the food production of the farm."

24. John J. Crittenden to RCA Jr. AND 746 12-14-1814.

25. John J. Crittenden to RCA Jr. AND 747 12-24-1814.

26. See Walter A. McDougall, *Promised Land, Crusader State: The American Encounter with the World Since 1776* (New York: Houghton Mifflin, 1997), 57–75.

Clay is quoted in Robert V. Remini, *Henry Clay: Statesman for the Union* (New York: W. W. Norton and Company, 1991), 154. See also Arthur P. Whitaker, *The United States and the Independence of Latin America, 1800–1830* (Baltimore, MD: Johns Hopkins University Press, 1941).

27. *Diary*, 19–20; Howe, *What Hath God Wrought*, 140–141.

28. *Diary*, 21–22.

29. Elizabeth Clark (Gwathmey) Anderson to RCA Jr. AND 153 1-8-1815.

30. Ibid.

31. See John William Ward, *Andrew Jackson: Symbol for an Age* (New York: Oxford University Press, 1962), 213.

32. William Taylor Barry to RCA Jr. AND 537 2-16-1815.

33. Isaac Gwathmey to RCA Jr. AND 999 2-28-1815.

34. *Diary*, 22–23.

35. *Diary*, 24–25. On the rise of well-paid professional politicians, see Richard Hofstadter's classic *The Idea of a Party System: The Rise of Legitimate Opposition in the United States, 1780-1840* (Berkeley: University of California Press, 1969). In Kentucky, Patricia Watlington found seeds of a party system earlier. See her book *The Partisan Spirit: Kentucky Politics, 1779–1792* (New York: Atheneum, 1972), 263.

36. *Diary*, 27, 29.

37. On slavery debates surrounding Kentucky's entry into the Union, see Watlington, *The Partisan Spirit*.

38. Brooke Hill to RCA Jr. AND 1106 10-12-1809.

39. *Diary*, 31.

40. Ibid., 31–32.

41. Ibid., 44, 50.

42. Ibid., 36, 41.

43. Ibid., 44.

44. Ibid., 34–35.

45. Remini, *Henry Clay*, 52–53; *Diary*, 41–43. Antebellum bank directors were not neutral agents and often favored family and friends. See Naomi R. Lamoreaux, *Insider Lending: Banks, Personal Connections, and Economic Development in Industrial New England* (New York: Cambridge University Press, 1994).

46. *Diary*, 28.

47. John J. Crittenden to RCA Jr. AND 748 11-10-1815.

48. *Diary*, 45; Albert D. Kirwan, *John J. Crittenden: The Struggle for the Union* (Lexington: University of Kentucky Press, 1962), 30–31.

49. *Diary*, 46; John Gwathmey to RCA Jr. AND 1017 12-11-1815.

50. See Robert V. Remini, *Andrew Jackson and the Bank War* (New York: W. W. Norton and Company, 1967), 26.

51. Remini, *Henry Clay*, 140–141; Anderson recorded his reservations in *Diary*, 50.

52. *Diary*, 52–53.

53. Henry Clay to RCA Jr. AND 1865 7-1-1817.

54. Remini, *Henry Clay*, 140–141.

55. John Jordan Crittenden to RCA Jr. AND 749 10-1-1816.

56. Elizabeth Clark (Gwathmey) Anderson to RCA Jr. AND 156 1-4-1816; Elizabeth Clark (Gwathmey) Anderson to RCA Jr. AND 157 1-18-1816.

57. Elizabeth Clark (Gwathmey) Anderson to RCA Jr AND 155 1-26-1816; RCA Jr. to Elizabeth Clark (Gwathmey) Anderson AND 372 2-3-1816.

58. Owen Gwathmey to Elizabeth Clark (Gwathmey) Anderson AND 1023 3-17-1816.

59. On Cane Ridge, see Paul K. Conkin, *Cane Ridge: America's Pentecost* (Madison: University of Wisconsin Press, 1990). The classic article on American civil religion is Robert N. Bellah, "Civil Religion in America," *Daedalus* 96, no. 1 (Winter 1967), 1–21. See also Martin E. Marty, *Religion and Republic: The American Circumstance* (New York: Beacon Press, 1989).

60. Howe, *What Hath God Wrought*, 225; *Diary*, 55.

61. See Remini, *Henry Clay*, 210–233.

62. Isaac Gwathmey to Elizabeth Clark (Gwathmey) Anderson AND 997 7-10-1817; *Diary*, 56–57.

63. *Diary*, 90.

64. Ibid., 42.

65. Ibid., 63. See Benjamin Horace Hibbard, *A History of the Public Land Policies* (New York: Macmillan, 1924; Madison: University of Wisconsin Press, 1965), 16–17.

66. *Diary*, 64. On Harrison's role in Indian removal, see Jortner, *Gods of Prophetstown*.

67. *Diary*, 65.

68. Ibid., 68.

69. Ibid., 71. On the groupings of congressional messes by region, see James Sterling Young, *The Washington Community 1800–1828* (New York: Columbia University Press, 1966), 98–102.

CHAPTER 5: "MY DEBTS MUST BE PAID!": POLITICS AND LAND IN THE EVOLVING WEST: 1817–1822

1. See Robert V. Remini, *Henry Clay: Statesman for the Union* (New York: W. W. Norton and Company, 1991), 134–135.

2. *Diary*, 73.

3. Ibid.

4. *Diary*, 74, 77; Benjamin Horace Hibbard, *A History of the Public Land Policies* (New York: Macmillan, 1924; Madison: University of Wisconsin Press, 1965), 70. On the friendship between Anderson Sr. and Monroe, see James Sterling Young, *The Washington Community 1800–1828* (New York: Columbia University Press, 1966).

5. *Diary*, 74 and footnote 157.

6. Samuel Gwathmey to RCA Jr. AND 1050 1-3-1818.

7. LA to Elizabeth Clark (Anderson) Gwathmey AND 241 1-28-1818.

8. RCA Jr. to "Dear Sir" [RCA Sr.] AND 445 2-14-1818.

9. *Diary*, 78.

10. Harry Ammon, *James Monroe: The Quest for National Identity* (New York: McGraw-Hill, 1971), 388. See also Remini, *Henry Clay*, 154–168.

11. *Diary*, 78.

12. Ibid., 79, 80. On General Clark, see John Mack Faragher, *Daniel Boone: The Life and Legend of an American Pioneer* (New York: Henry Holt and Company, 1992), 299–300.

13. *Diary*, 79, 80. On the evolving role of steam power in river travel, see Daniel Walker Howe, *What Hath God Wrought: The Transformation of America, 1815–1848* (New York: Oxford University Press, 2007), 214–215; and Henry Clay to RCA Jr. AND 1866 4-29-1818.

14. LA to RCA Jr. AND 246 8-2-1818.

15. John J. Crittenden to RCA Jr. AND 752 6-21-1818; John J. Crittenden to RCA Jr. AND 754 8-8-1818.

16. Henry Clay to RCA Jr. AND 1867 9-15-1818.

17. *Diary*, 83, 85.

18. *Diary*, 84; Howe, *What Hath God Wrought*, 98–103; and Ammon, *James Monroe*, 421–423.

19. *Diary*, 91; Howe, *What Hath God Wrought*, 101–102.

20. Hibbard, *A History of the Public Lands Policies*, 16–17. On Monroe and Adams on the question of Florida, see Ammon, *James Monroe*, 422–423; and

Walter A. McDougall, *Promised Land, Crusader State: The American Encounter with the World Since 1776* (New York: Houghton Mifflin, 1997), 66–69.

21. Andro Linklater, *The Fabric of America: How Our Borders and Boundaries Shaped the Country and Forged Our National Identity* (New York: Walker and Company, 2007), 185–186.

22. Quoted in Linklater, *The Fabric of America*, 187. On Manifest Destiny in the American West, see McDougall, *Promised Land, Crusader State*, 57–75.

23. See especially Donald G. Mathews, "The Second Great Awakening as an Organizing Process, 1780–1830: An Hypothesis," *American Quarterly* 21, no. 1 (Spring 1969): 23–43. The literature on the Second Great Awakening is enormous, but works central to this topic include: T. Scott Miyakawa, *Protestants and Pioneers: Individualism and Conformity on the American Frontier* (Chicago: University of Chicago Press, 1964); Howe, *What Hath God Wrought*, 164–202; Andrew R. L. Cayton, *The Frontier Republic: Ideology and Politics in the Ohio Country, 1780–1825* (Kent, OH: Kent State University Press, 1986), 138; Stephen Aron, *How the West Was Lost: The Transformation of Kentucky from Daniel Boone to Henry Clay* (Baltimore, MD: Johns Hopkins University Press, 1996), 171–186; Paul K. Conkin, *Cane Ridge: America's Pentecost* (Madison: University of Wisconsin Press, 1990).

24. On the intersections of frontier revivalism, egalitarian politics, and landownership, see Sam Haselby, *The Origins of American Religious Nationalism* (New York: Oxford University Press, 2015).

25. See Linklater, *The Fabric of America*, 190.

26. *Diary*, 87. See Brian Connolly, *Domestic Intimacies: Incest and the Liberal Subject in Nineteenth-Century America* (Philadelphia: University of Pennsylvania Press, 2014).

27. John J. Crittenden to RCA Jr. AND 753 7-15-1818.

28. *Diary*, 86.

29. Ibid., 87.

30. Ibid., 87, 89.

31. Ibid., 87.

32. Ibid., 87–88.

33. Ibid., 89.

34. Illinois Treasury Dept. to RCA Jr. AND 1141 9-8-1818; George Clark Gwathmey to RCA Jr. AND 964 11-25-1818.

35. Elizabeth Clark (Gwathmey) Anderson to RCA Jr. AND 160 12-2-1818.

36. *Diary*, 91. See Jonathan Levy, *Freaks of Fortune: The Emerging World of Capitalism and Risk in America* (Cambridge, MA: Harvard University Press, 2012).

37. Albert D. Kirwan, *John Jordan Crittenden: The Struggle for the Union* (Lexington: University of Kentucky Press, 1962), 46–65.

38. Elizabeth Clark (Gwathmey) Anderson to RCA Jr. AND 158 11-20-1818. Two days later Betsy wrote in a follow-up: "Four weeks this day since you left home, and not one line from you, for me, We are all well yours truly Elizabeth Anderson."

39. Elizabeth Clark (Gwathmey) Anderson to RCA Jr. AND 161 12-16-1818.

40. Elizabeth Clark (Gwathmey) Anderson to RCA Jr. AND 162 12-20-1818.

41. *Diary*, 91.

42. Elizabeth Clark (Gwathmey) Anderson to RCA Jr. AND 163 12-26-1818; Isaac Gwathmey to RCA Jr. AND 1003 12-15-1818.

43. *Diary*, 92; Elizabeth Clark (Gwathmey) Anderson to RCA Jr. AND 164 1-2-1819.

44. William Crogham to RCA Jr. AND 777 1-2-1819. See Landon Y. Jones, *William Clark and the Shaping of the West* (New York: Hill and Wang, 2004), 290–291.

45. William Clark to RCA Jr. AND 694 1-5-1819.

46. Ibid.

47. Jones, *William Clark*, 290, 325–326.

48. Ibid., 248.

49. RCA Jr. to Isaac Gwathmey AND 411 1-25-1819.

50. RCA Sr. to RCA Jr. AND 341 1-31-1819.

51. For a thorough account of the functions and abuses of Anderson's tenure in office, see Asa Lee Rubenstein, "Richard Clough Anderson, Nathaniel Massie, and the Impact of Government on Western Land Speculation and Settlement, 1774–1830," PhD diss., University of Illinois, 1986, 22–79. While correctly pointing out Anderson's shortcomings as surveyor general, he understates the unrealistic burdens that all surveyors suffered under in what amounted to the greatest land sale transaction in history.

52. *Diary*, 94.

53. Owen Gwathmey to RCA Jr. AND 1039 2-3-1819.

54. John J. Crittenden to RCA Jr. AND 757 5-21-1819.

55. John J Crittenden to RCA Jr. AND 758 7-17-1819. Despite Anderson's "correct" advice, Crittenden did resign his Senate post due to hard times. See Kirwan, *John Jordan Crittenden*, 35–36.

56. George Gwathmey to RCA Jr. AND 968 6-4-1819.

57. RCA Jr. to Isaac Gwathmey AND 413 12-24-1819.

58. See Remini, *Henry Clay*, 169–192; and Robert Pierce Forbes, *The Missouri Compromise and Its Aftermath: Slavery and the Meaning of America* (Chapel Hill: University of North Carolina Press, 2007).

59. E. C. Berry to RCA Jr. AND 558 1-14-1821. On the Panic of 1819 in Kentucky, see Aron, *How the West Was Lost*, 192.

60. *Diary*, 97.

61. Ibid., 96. Edward Coles to RCA Jr. AND 703, 10-14-1821.

62. RCA Sr. to Isaac Gwathmey AND 362 11-18-1820; *Diary*, 100.

63. RCA Jr. to Isaac Gwathmey AND 421 7-2-1821.

64. *Diary*, 97–98.

65. James Monroe to RCA Jr. AND 1369 3-1821. See also *Diary*, 98; and Ammon, *James Monroe*, 471–472.

66. RCA Jr. to James Monroe AND 433 4-20-1821.

67. James Monroe to RCA Jr. 9-26-1820.

68. *Diary*, 99.

69. Elizabeth Clark (Gwathmey) Anderson to RCA Jr. AND 169 10-21-1821.

70. *Diary*, 103–104; Remini, *Henry Clay*, 200.

71. Elizabeth Clark (Gwathmey) Anderson to RCA AND 176 12-2-1821.

72. Jesse Burgess Thomas to RCA Jr. AND 1652 1-24-1822.

73. Henry Clay to RCA Jr. AND 1870 2-26-1822.

74. Remini, *Henry Clay*, 196–197, 219.

CHAPTER 6: AN ILL-FATED MISSION: 1822–1824

1. See Walter A. McDougall, *Promised Land, Crusader State: The American Encounter with the World Since 1776* (New York: Houghton Mifflin, 1997), 76–100.

2. James Monroe to RCA Jr. 12-18-1822 AND 1371.

3. *Diary*, 107.

4. For a description of women's experiences on western migrations, see Gregory H. Nobles, *American Frontiers: Cultural Encounters and Continental Conquest* (New York: Hill and Wang, 1997), 181–184, 270.

5. *Diary*, 107.

6. Henry Clay to RCA Jr. in Louisville AND 1873 1-5-1823; Robert V. Remini, *Henry Clay: Statesman for the Union* (New York: W. W. Norton and Company, 1991), 213.

7. Charles Stewart Todd to John Quincy Adams, Washington City AND 1669 1-2-1823. This official document is included in Anderson's personal papers, suggesting it was forwarded to him as a form of background summary. Anderson's notes on his slaves are from *Diary*, 120–121. I assume that Denis Hite was Spencer Hite's son.

8. John Quincy Adams to RCA Jr. AND 5 2-1-1823; and Richard Mentor Johnson to RCA Jr. AND 1167 2-3-1823.

9. Extracts from Adams's memorandum are reprinted in *Diary*, 109–119. All quotations in the following paragraphs are taken from this extract.

10. George Clark Gwathmey to RCA Jr. AND 972 4-12-1823.

11. See Alvin O. Thompson, *Flight to Freedom: African Runaways and Maroons in the Americas* (Kingston, Jamaica: University of the West Indies Press, 2006); and Sylviane A. Diouf, *Slavery's Exiles: The Story of the American Maroons* (New York: NYU Press, 2014).

12. George Gwathmey to RCA Jr. AND 973 5-4-1823.

13. AL to RCA Jr. AND 1209 5-12-1823.

14. RCA Sr. to RCA Jr. AND 464 5-17-1823.

15. RCA Jr. to Thomas Bullitt AND 388 5-20-1823.

16. James Monroe to RCA Jr. (also signed by John Quincy Adams) AND 1372 5-22-1823.

17. RCA Jr. to RCA Sr. AND 382 5-27-1823.

18. John Quincy Adams to Baring Brothers and Co. AND 10 5-29-1823.

19. *Diary*, 123.

20. Ibid., 125–126, 130.

21. See *Historical Statistics of the United States*, Table Bb212, Average Slave Price.

22. *Diary*, 128.

23. Ibid., 129.

24. Ibid., 133.

25. Sherry Keith Jelsma, "An Unexpected Nightmare: Charles S. Todd and U.S. Diplomacy in South America, 1820–1824," *Filson History Quarterly* 76 (2002): 417–418.

26. *Diary*, 132–134.

27. Ibid., 133–134.

28. Ibid., 134–135.

29. RCA Sr. to RCA Jr. AND 346 10-11-1823; Sam Anderson to RCA Sr. AND 480 9-1823; LA to RCA Jr. AND 250 10-28-1823.

30. Isaac Gwathmey to RCA Jr. AND 1008 10-31-1823.

31. Charles Todd to RCA Jr. AND 1673 12-7-1823; RCA Jr. to Elizabeth Clark (Gwathmey) Anderson AND 375 12-12-1823.

32. RCA Jr. "Extract from the General Instructions Given to Anderson" AND 446 1823.

33. Samuel Gwathmey to RCA Jr. AND 1052 9-15-1823.

34. See Remini, *Henry Clay*, 234–301.

35. George Gwathmey to RCA Jr. AND 977 1-4-1824.

36. RCA Jr. to George Gwathmey AND 404 1-22-1824; RCA Jr. to Thomas Bullitt enclosed in RCA Jr. to George Gwathmey AND 390 2-19-1824.

37. Isaac Gwathmey to RCA Jr. AND 1010 4-30-1824.

38. *Diary*, 138–139, 144.

39. Ibid., 140–141.

40. Ibid., 139, 142–143.

41. John Quincy Adams to RCA AND 8 3-31-1824; Jared Sparks to RCA Jr. AND 1588 7-2-1824. Sparks retired from the faculty of Harvard to work on the review. Anderson would publish his "Constitution of Colombia" in the *North American Review* 23 (1826): 314–349.

42. *Diary*, 172, 174.

43. George Gwathmey to RCA Jr. AND 979 4-10-1824.

44. Owen Gwathmey to Elizabeth and RCA Jr. AND 1024 4-16-1824; Owen Gwathmey to Elizabeth and RCA Jr. AND 1025 4-18-1824.

45. RCA Sr. to RCA Jr. AND 350 4-27-1824.

46. William Robinson to RCA Jr. AND 1508 4-26-1824.

47. *Diary*, 154.

48. Ibid., 178.

49. Ibid., 148.

50. Ibid., 148–149.

51. RCA Jr. to Isaac Gwathmey AND 425 5-21-1824.

CHAPTER 7: A TRAGIC END: 1824–1826

1. *Diary*, 157.

2. Ibid., 164.

3. Ibid., 160.

4. LA to RCA Jr. AND 252 6-10-1824.

5. LA to RCA Jr. AND 254 9-1-1824.

6. LA to RCA Jr. AND 255 9-20-1824; *Diary*, 166.

7. RA to RCA Jr. AND 465 9-11-1824.

8. Ibid.

9. For a description of the event, see James A. Ramage and Andrea S. Watkins, *Kentucky Rising: Democracy, Slavery, and Culture from the Early Republic to the Civil War* (Lexington: University Press of Kentucky, 2011), 9–11.

10. *Diary*, 167.

11. Ibid., 168–169.

12. RCA Jr. to Thomas Bullitt AND 391 n.d. 1824.

13. Anderson's letter to his father is reprinted in *Diary*, 168.

14. William Robinson to RCA Jr. AND 1511 9-26-1824.

15. LA to RCA Jr. AND 256 10-20-1824.

16. LA to RCA Jr. AND 257 11-2-1824.

17. *Diary*, 178. Anderson was correct. Nineteenth-century mothers played dominant roles in establishing what Mary Ryan terms the "rituals of community mourning," which served to provide emotional bonding in the loss of a child. This was certainly true in the experiences of Anderson women, led by Betsy. See Mary P. Ryan, *Cradle of the Middle Class: The Family in Oneida County, New York, 1790–1865* (New York: Cambridge University Press, 1981), 219–220.

18. LA to RCA Jr. AND 258 12-12-1824; *Diary*, 179.

19. *Diary*, 181.

20. RA to RCA AND 467 12-24-1824; John J. Crittenden to RCA Jr AND 761 12-30-1824.

21. *Diary*, 183.

22. LA to RCA Jr. AND 260 1-15-1825.

23. George Gwathmey to RCA Jr. AND 985 2-5-1825.

24. Ibid.

25. George Gwathmey to Elizabeth Clark (Gwathmey) Anderson AND 985 2-5-1825.

26. LA to RCA Jr. AND 262 2-22-1825.

27. LA to RCA Jr. AND 265 2-29-1825.

28. *Diary*, 188, 194.

29. LA to RCA Jr. AND 266 3-6-1825.

30. AL to Isaac Gwathmey AND 1211 3-7-1825; George Gwathmey to RCA Jr. AND 987 5-7-1825.

31. *Diary*, 200.

32. Ibid., 201.

33. *Diary*, 206.

34. *Diary*, 206; Remini, *Henry Clay*, 290–291.

35. Remini, *Henry Clay*, 293; John MacPherson to RCA Jr. AND 1316 5-10-1826.

36. Clay's challenge is quoted in Remini, *Henry Clay,* 293.

37. Remini, *Henry Clay,* 297–299.

38. *Diary,* 211.

39. Ibid., 209–210.

40. Elizabeth Clark Anderson to RCA Jr. AND 905 8-15-1825; Elizabeth Clark Anderson to RCA Jr. AND 906 8-22-1825.

41. LA to RCA Jr. AND 268 8-30-1825; George Gwathmey to RCA Jr. AND 989 8-30-1825; RCA Jr. to Elizabeth Clark Anderson AND 396 9-9-1825.

42. RCA Jr. to Diana Moore Bullitt AND 385 9-12-1825.

43. John Quincy Adams to RCA Jr. AND 9 9-16-1825; *Diary,* 213.

44. B. Tompkins to RCA Jr. 1689 9-18-1825; RCA Jr. to Elizabeth Clark Anderson AND 397 10-8-1825.

45. *Diary,* 217, 228–229.

46. Ibid., 222–223, 238.

47. Elizabeth Clark Anderson to RCA Jr. AND 907 12-7-1825.

48. *Diary,* 258.

49. Ibid., 240, 243.

50. Ibid., 240.

51. *Diary,* 244; Ann Clark (Anderson) Logan to RCA Jr. AND 1240 6-10-1826.

52. Remini, *Henry Clay,* 301; *Diary,* 245.

53. *Diary,* 268, 269.

54. RA to RCA Jr. AND 469 7-12-1826; *Diary,* 270; Brooke Young to RCA Jr. AND 1835 1826 from Cartagena.

55. *Diary,* 271.

56. *Diary,* 271–272.

57. Ibid.

58. AL to Maria (Anderson) Latham at Soldier's Retreat, 8 September 1826, Filson.

59. AL to Maria (Anderson) Latham, 13 September 1826, Filson.

60. Allen Trimble to RCA Sr. AND 1694 9-16-1826.

CHAPTER 8: THE NEW PATRIARCH: 1826–1834

1. On the positive contributions of speculators and nonresident investors on the frontier, see Robert P. Swierenga, *Pioneers and Profits: Land Speculation on the Iowa Frontier* (Ames: Iowa State University Press, 1968).

2. AL to Maria (Anderson) Latham, 26 September 1826, Filson.

3. See Mary P. Ryan, *Cradle of the Middle Class: The Family in Oneida County, New York, 1790–1865* (New York: Cambridge University Press, 1981), 21–59.

4. For a fine overview, see James L. Huston, *The British Gentry, The Southern Planter, and the Northern Family Farmer: Agriculture and Sectional Antagonism in North America* (Baton Rouge: Louisiana State University Press, 2015).

5. Charles's recollections are preserved in his "The Story of Soldier's Retreat: A Memoir," unpubl. mss., Filson Historical Society, Louisville, Kentucky.

6. Edward Lowell to LA AND 1275 8-22-1824.

7. See Chaim M. Rosenberg, *The Life and Times of Francis Cabot Lowell, 1775–1817* (Lanham, MD: Lexington Books, 2011), 286.

8. Sarah Anderson to Maria (Anderson) Latham, 13 September 1829; LA to AL, 7 November 1829, Filson.

9. LA to AL, 18 June 1826, Filson.

10. LA to AL, 26 July 1826, Filson.

11. Ibid.

12. AL to Maria (Anderson) Latham, 5 September 1826, Filson.

13. RCA Sr. to William Beasley, 24 October 1826, Filson.

14. See letters by Larz on Soldier's Retreat in William Marshall Anderson, *The Rocky Mountain Journals of William Marshall Anderson*, ed. Dale L. Morgan and Eleanor Towles Harris (Lincoln: University of Nebraska Press, 1987), 49–50. Hereafter cited as *Rocky Mountain Journals*.

15. Sarah Anderson to AL, 20 November 1826, Filson.

16. WA to AL, 20 December 1826, Filson.

17. RA to AL, 7 May 1828; RA to Maria (Anderson) Latham 2 January 1827, Filson.

18. LA to Isaac Gwathmey AND 361 2-26-1827.

19. LA to AL, 2 March 1827, from Louisville, Filson.

20. LA to AL, 2 July 1827, Filson.

21. LA to AL, 22 July 1826, Filson.

22. AL to Isaac Gwathmey AND 1212 9-1-1827. On the economic rights and limitations of widowhood, see Ryan, *Cradle of the Middle Class*, 27–28.

23. LA to AL, 7 December 1827, Filson.

24. Ibid.

25. LA to AL, 29 February 1828, Filson. The printed announcement of Latham's appointment is also preserved at the Filson Historical Society.

26. Sarah Anderson to Maria (Anderson) Latham, 9 August 1828, Filson.

27. LA to AL, 11 November 1828 and 9 March 1829, Filson.

28. Sarah Anderson to Maria (Anderson) Latham, 11 March 1829, Filson.

29. LA to Isaac Gwathmey AND 276 3-13-1829.

30. WA to AL, 4 April 1829, Filson.

31. Sarah Anderson to Maria (Anderson) Latham 13 September 1829; Sarah Anderson to AL 11 December 1829, Filson.

32. Mary Louisa (Anderson) Alexander to AL, n.d. 1831, Filson. The term "domestic currency" is taken from Anne F. Hyde, *Empires, Nations, and Families: A History of the North American West, 1800–1860* (Lincoln: University of Nebraska Press, 2011), 21.

33. Quoted in Steven T. Newcomb, *Pagans in the Promised Land: Decoding the Doctrine of Christian Discovery* (Golden, CO: Fulcrum Publishing, 2008), 74. Modern legal historians tend to situate *Johnson v. M'Intosh* in secular law and distinguish the secular categories "Indians" and "Europeans." The word *Christian*, so central to the case, does not typically appear in contemporary law because if it did, it would have clear implications for the separation of church and state and the whole law would be thrown out. See Newcomb, *Pagans in the Promised Land*, xvi.

34. Quoted in Newcomb, *Pagans in the Promised Land*, 76. For a thorough analysis of *Johnson v. M'Intosh*, see Stuart Banner, *How the Indians Lost Their Land: Law and Power on the Frontier* (Cambridge, MA: Harvard University Press, 2005), 178–188.

35. See Reginald Horsman, *Race and Manifest Destiny: The Origins of American Racial Anglo-Saxonism* (Cambridge, MA: Harvard University Press, 1981), 1.

36. See Banner, *How the Indians Lost Their Land*, 178–179.

37. Andro Linklater, *Measuring America: How an Untamed Wilderness Shaped the United States and Fulfilled the Promise of Democracy* (New York: Walker Publishing Company, 2002), 215.

38. Edward Pessen, *Jacksonian America: Society, Personality, and Politics* (Homewood, IL: Dorsey Press, 1969), 317–318; Daniel Walker Howe, *What Hath God Wrought: The Transformation of America, 1815–1848* (New York: Oxford University Press, 2007), 342–357.

39. See Robert V. Remini, *Andrew Jackson and His Indian Wars* (New York: Viking, 2001).

40. Banner, *How the Indians Lost Their Land*, 202–205.

41. Jay H. Buckley, *William Clark: Indian Diplomat* (Norman: University of Oklahoma Press, 2008), 184–211.

42. Landon Y. Jones, *William Clark and the Shaping of the West* (New York: Hill and Wang, 2004), 279–281.

43. LA to AL, 30 August 1831, Filson.

44. RA to Maria (Anderson) Latham, from Baton Route, 8 October 1831, Filson.

45. Jones, *William Clark and the Shaping of the West*, 311–315.

46. See Howe, *What Hath God Wrought*, 418–419; and William T. Hagan, *The Sac and Fox Indians* (Norman: University of Oklahoma Press, 1958), 153–191.

47. RA to LA AND 316 8-16-1832.

48. Jones, *William Clark and the Shaping of the West*, 315.

49. RA to CA AND 450 1-7-1832.

50. LA to WA AD 26 4-28-1832.

51. Ibid.; Kenneth J. Winkle, *The Politics of Community: Migration and Politics in Antebellum Ohio* (Cambridge, UK: Cambridge University Press, 1988), 176–177.

52. LA to Isaac Gwathmey AND 277 3-12-1832.

53. WA to AL, 9 April 1833, Filson.

54. WA to Isaac Gwathmey AND 506 12-12-1832.

55. John Roy Anderson to AL, 29 November 1832, Filson.

56. RA to Sarah Anderson, 7 September 1834, Filson.

57. Ibid.

CHAPTER 9: ROCKY MOUNTAIN HIGHS AND REAL ESTATE LOWS: 1835–1838

1. Andrew R. L. Cayton, *The Frontier Republic: Ideology and Politics in the Ohio Country, 1780–1825* (Kent, OH: Kent State University Press, 1986), 139–141; and Andrew R. L. Cayton and Peter S. Onuf, *The Midwest and the Nation: Rethinking the History of an American Region* (Bloomington: Indiana University Press, 1990), 28–29. The statistics are taken from Cayton and Onuf, *The Midwest and the Nation*, 28–29. On the impact of migration on politics, see Kenneth J. Winkle, *The Politics of Community: Migration and Politics in Antebellum Ohio* (Cambridge, UK: Cambridge University Press, 1988), 171.

2. *Rocky Mountain Journals*, 48.

3. LA to WA AD 25 4-18-1825.

4. RA to WA AD 42 5-24-1825.

5. Robert V. Remini, *Henry Clay: Statesman for the Union* (New York: W. W. Norton and Company, 1991), 32.

6. On Sublette's life, see John E. Sunder, *Bill Sublette, Mountain Man* (Norman: University of Oklahoma Press, 1959). On Jedediah Smith, see Dale L. Morgan, *Jedediah Smith and the Opening of the West* (Lincoln: University of Nebraska Press, 1953), 215–235.

7. *Rocky Mountain Journals*, 52. Richard White famously described the middle ground in the *pays d'en haut* in *The Middle Ground: Indians, Empires, and Republics in the Great Lakes Region, 1650–1815* (New York: Cambridge University Press, 1991).

On the Rocky Mountain cultures, see Anne F. Hyde, *Empires, Nations, and Families: A New History of the North American West, 1800–1860* (Lincoln: University of Nebraska Press, 2011), 13.

8. *Rocky Mountain Journals*, 71.

9. *Rocky Mountain Journals*, 12, 73. On the brawl between Mormons and non-Mormons, see Richard L. Bushman, *Joseph Smith: Rough Stone Rolling, A Cultural Biography of Mormonism's Founder* (New York: Alfred A. Knopf, 2005).

10. *Rocky Mountain Journals*, 72–73.

11. Ibid., 74, 78.

12. Ibid., 75.

13. Ibid., 77.

14. Ibid., 81.

15. Ibid., 80–81.

16. Ibid., 85.

17. Ibid., 87.

18. Ibid., 89. On Shakespeare and landownership, see Andro Linklater, *Owning the Earth: The Transforming History of Land Ownership* (New York: Bloomsbury USA, 2013), 34.

19. *Rocky Mountain Journals*, 91. The description of the Circle is from William Hubbard, *Narrative of the Troubles with the Indians in New-England* (Boston, 1676), quoted in Jill Lepore, *The Name of War: King Philip's War and the Origins of American Identity* (New York: Alfred A. Knopf, 1998), 3.

20. *Rocky Mountain Journals*, 93. On the immense wastage wrought by Americans' buffalo hunting, see Hyde, *Empires, Nations, and Families*, 344.

21. *Rocky Mountain Journals*, 93.

22. Ibid., 95, 101.

23. Ibid., 105.

24. Ibid., 107.

25. Ibid., 109. On Fort William, see Hyde, *Empires, Nations, and Families*, 66.

26. *Rocky Mountain Journals*, 111.

27. Ibid., 115, 117.

28. Ibid., 117.

29. Ibid., 121, 129.

30. Ibid., 133, 142. On the unlikelihood of Clark's parenthood, see *Rocky Mountain Journals*, 142.

31. Ibid., 129.

32. Ibid., 132, 144.

33. Ibid., 135, 151.

34. Ibid., 149–150.

35. Ibid., 147, 156–157.

36. Ibid., 173.

37. Ibid., 209.

38. Ibid., 221, 227.

39. WA to Robert Campbell AD 89 9-15-1871.

40. Daniel Walker Howe, *What Hath God Wrought: The Transformation of America, 1815–1848* (New York: Oxford University Press, 2007), 372.

41. David T. Dixon, *The Lost Gettysburg Address: Charles Anderson's Civil War Odyssey* (Santa Barbara, CA: B-List History, 2015), 30–31.

42. On Whig origins, see Michael F. Holt's magisterial *The Rise and Fall of the American Whig Party: Jacksonian Politics and the Onset of the Civil War* (New York: Oxford University Press, 1999), 26–27.

43. Quoted in Abraham Stagg, *Biographical Sketches of the Fifty-Sixth Ohio Senate* (Columbus, OH: Glenn & Heide, 1864), 63.

44. CA to AL, 20 February 1835; CA to AL, 4 March 1836, Filson.

45. CA to AL, 19 December 1835; CA to AL, 4 March 1836, Filson. On the National Road, see George Rogers Taylor, *The Transportation Revolution 1815–1860* (New York: M. E. Sharpe, 1951), 15–31.

46. WA to AL, 22 May 1835, Filson.

47. Ibid.

48. Later, in March 1840, he wrote to Latham: "I am very anxious to be rid of the office. I can not consent to be harried by the cares of it much longer. I will again prepare a letter of resignation. Will you please think of this and make such arrangements as you may think best. Nothing but the hope and belief that the office might be profitable to you would have made me continue it this long." In the same month that he wrote Latham he also wrote President Martin Van Buren formally resigning the office: "I have endeavored to discharge the duties of it, with honesty and impartiality. How far I have succeeded in satisfying others I know not, but I am very sure, that from ill-health and inexperience I have not given satisfaction to myself." WA to AL, 24 March 1840, and WA to Martin Van Buren, 25 March 1840, Filson.

49. R. A. Logan to John Anderson, 8 September 1835; Ann Logan to AL, 27 January 1836, Filson.

50. RA to Sarah Anderson, 5 February 1836, Filson. On the path to Texas annexation in 1836, see Walter Nugent, *Habits of Empire: A History of American Expansionism* (New York: Alfred A. Knopf, 2008), 153–156.

51. See Cayton and Onuf, *The Midwest and the Nation*, 73.

52. See Charles Clifford Huntington, *A History of Banking and Currency in Ohio Before the Civil War* (Columbus, OH: Heer, 1915), 160–164.

53. See Peter Temin, *The Jacksonian Economy* (New York: W. W. Norton and Company, 1969), 113–147.

54. See Edward Pessen, *Jacksonian America: Society, Personality, and Politics* (Homewood, IL: Dorsey Press, 1969), 211–247.

55. LA to Cecelia Anderson AND 214 9-7-1837.

56. RA to Sarah Anderson, 28 August 1838, Filson. On white arguments that removed Indians would be better off, see Stuart Banner, *How the Indians Lost Their Land: Law and Power on the Frontier* (Cambridge, MA: Harvard University Press, 2005), 212.

57. On the Cherokee's adoption of European customs, see William G. McLoughlin, *Cherokee Renascence in the New Republic* (Princeton, NJ: Princeton University Press, 1992); and Howe, *What Hath God Wrought*, 343–346.

CHAPTER 10: A TIME OF TESTING: 1839–1844

1. LA to CA AND 215 5-9-1839.

2. LA to WA AD 27 5-1-1839; LA to WA AD 27 5-3-1839.

3. The case is summarized in *Rocky Mountain Journals,* 57.

4. RA to Sarah Anderson, 17 August 1840, Filson.

5. See Abraham Stagg, *Biographical Sketches of the Fifty-Sixth Ohio Senate* (Columbus, OH: Glenn & Heide, 1864), 56–57.

6. LA to CA AND 216 8-21-1839.

7. Elizabeth (Brown) Anderson to CA AND 185 11-29-1840.

8. RA to CA AND 457 12-13-1839.

9. Elizabeth (Brown) Anderson to CA AND 185 11-29-1840.

10. LA to CA AND 217 12-30-1840; see David T. Dixon, *The Lost Gettysburg Address: Charles Anderson's Civil War Odyssey* (Santa Barbara, CA: B-List History, 2015), 35.

11. William Anderson Letters to Edward W. Peet, Miscellaneous Writings, HL.

12. William Marshall Anderson Commonplace Book Religion, Physiology, Medicine, 1836–1841, HL.

13. Anderson, Commonplace Book, 37. On the attitude of Whigs toward race, see Michael A. Morrison and James Brewer Stewart, *Race and the Early Republic: Racial Consciousness and Nation-Building in the Early Republic* (Latham, MD: Rowman and Littlefield, 2001), 122–127.

14. Anderson, Commonplace Book, 140–141.

15. LA to RA, 29 September 1840, Filson.

16. AL to CA AND 1206 2-15-1841.

17. WA to AL, 24 December 1842; WA to AL 1 March 1843, Filson.

18. RA to Maria (Anderson) Latham, 28 December 1841, Filson.

19. WA to RA AD 416 12-29-1843.

20. Dixon, *The Lost Gettysburg Address*, 37; Michael F. Holt, *The Rise and Fall of the American Whig Party: Jacksonian Politics and the Onset of the Civil War* (New York: Oxford University Press, 1999), 206–207.

21. CA to WA AD 3 12-30-1844. On the Texas problem, see Holt, *The Rise and Fall of the American Whig Party*, 178–179.

22. CA to AL Anderson and Clough Anderson AND 33 2-20-1845.

23. See Howard Chudacoff, *Children at Play: An American History* (New York: New York University Press, 2007), 43; On generational tensions and gender roles, see Joyce Appleby, *Inheriting the Revolution: The First Generation of Americans* (Cambridge, MA: Harvard University Press, 2000), 169–177.

24. Dixon, *The Lost Gettysburg Address*, 39.

25. CA to WA AD 154 2-4-45; on Charles's trip to Europe, see Stagg, *Biographical Sketches of the Fifty-Sixth Ohio Senate*, 57–58.

26. CA to Elizabeth Anderson AND 51 11-13-1845; see Dixon, *The Lost Gettysburg Address*, 39–40.

27. LA to WA AD 28 10-11-1845.

28. CA to Sarah Anderson AND 74 7-26-1846; CA to Sarah Anderson AND 75 9-15-1846.

29. CA to Sarah Anderson AND 75 9-15-1846.

30. AL to Sarah Anderson, 9 July 1846; Sarah (Anderson) Kendrick to Sarah Anderson, 7 November 1846, Filson.

31. Dixon, *The Lost Gettysburg Address*, 41.

CHAPTER 11: ROBERT'S MEXICAN WAR: 1844–1848

1. On the annexation of Texas, see Walter Nugent, *Habits of Empire: A History of American Expansionism* (New York: Alfred A. Knopf, 2008), 131–156.

2. See Nugent, *Habits of Empire*, 195–197; and Walter A. McDougall, *Promised Land, Crusader State: The American Encounter with the World Since 1776* (New York: Houghton Mifflin, 1997), 93–96.

3. RA to CA AND 457 12-13-1839.

4. On the Mexican War, see John C. Pinheiro, *Manifest Ambition: James K. Polk and Civil-Military Relations During the Mexican War* (Westport, CT: Praeger Security International, 2007).

5. Eba Anderson Lawton, ed., *An Artillery Officer in the Mexican War 1846–7: Letters of Robert Anderson* (New York: Knickerbocker Press, 1911), 15, 19, 21.

6. Ibid., 41, 43–44.

7. Ibid., 59–64.

8. For good biographies of Scott, see John S. D. Eisenhower, *Agent of Destiny: The Life and Times of General Winfield Scott* (New York: Free Press, 1997); and Timothy D. Johnson, *Winfield Scott: The Quest for Military Glory* (Lawrence: University Press of Kansas, 1998).

9. Lawton, *An Artillery Officer in the Mexican War*, 71.

10. Ibid., 73, 81.

11. Ibid., 81–84.

12. Ibid., 91.

13. Ibid., 91, 102–103.

14. Ibid., 127.

15. Ibid., 129, 131.

16. On the battle of Cerro Gordo, see Johnson, *Winfield Scott*, 181–186; and Eisenhower, *Agent of Destiny*, 249–258.

17. Lawton, *An Artillery Officer in Mexico*, 179.

18. Ibid., 146, 179, 160.

19. Ibid., 160.

20. Ibid., 161.

21. See Harry S. Stout, *Upon the Altar of the Nation: A Moral History of the Civil War* (New York: Viking Penguin, 2006), 70.

22. *An Artillery Officer in Mexico*, 169, 175.

23. Ibid., 185.

24. Ibid., 181–193.

25. Ibid., 193–266.

26. Ibid., 266–273.

27. Ibid., 298.

28. Ibid., 301, 308–309.

29. Ibid., 310.

30. Ibid., 312–313.

31. Ibid., 314, 317.

32. Ibid., 315, 319.

33. Ibid., 333.

34. Ibid., 335–336.

CHAPTER 12: ANDERSONS AT HOME: 1848–1856

1. Charles's memoir was transcribed by Mary Tougher and is housed at the Filson Historical Society Library, Louisville, Kentucky.

2. CA to Sarah Anderson AND 83 5-16-1852.

3. See Mary Ryan, *Cradle of the Middle Class: The Family in Oneida County, New York, 1790–1865* (New York: Cambridge University Press, 1981), 157–159; CA to Sarah Anderson AND 77 7-19-1847.

4. Catherine Logan to Maria (Anderson) Latham, 5 February 1849, Filson. On Methodism's frontier appeal, see Richard P. Heitzenrater, *Wesley and the People Called Methodists*, 2nd ed. (Nashville, TN: Abingdon Press, 2013).

5. Mary Sibley to Maria (Anderson) Latham, 25 May 1847, Filson.

6. Lyman Draper to CA AD 154 1-28-1848. Draper planned to write a biography of Clark and other early settlers in the Trans-Allegheny region but never finished due to his founding work with the Wisconsin Historical Society. See William B. Hesseltine, *Pioneer's Mission: The Story of Lyman Copeland Draper* (Madison, WI: State Historical Society of Wisconsin, 1954).

7. CA to Andrew Kendrick, 17 April 1850, Filson. The warrant is located in the Anderson-Latham Collection, Library of Virginia.

8. J. McMichael to CA AD 257 4-7-1849; CA to WA, AD 4 (1 and 2), 4-10 and 6-19, 1849.

9. CA to Maria (Anderson) Latham AND 106 5-4-1849.

10. Michael F. Holt, *The Rise and Fall of the American Whig Party: Jacksonian Politics and the Onset of the Civil War* (New York: Oxford University Press, 1999), 519–522. On the Compromise of 1850, see Holman Hamilton, *Prologue to Conflict: The Crisis and Compromise of 1850* (Lexington: University Press of Kentucky, 1964); David M. Potter, *The Impending Crisis: America Before the Civil War, 1848–1861* (New York: Harper Colophon, 1976), 90–120; and Michael F. Holt, *The Fate of Their Country: Politicians, Slavery Extension, and the Coming of the Civil War* (New York: Hill and Wang, 2005).

11. Sarah (Anderson) Kendrick to Sarah Anderson, 5 May 1849, Filson.

12. CA to Sarah Anderson AND 79 3-9-1848.

13. CA to Sarah Anderson AND 80 1-24-1849.

14. CA to Sarah Anderson, 19 July 1849, Filson.

15. RA to Sarah (Anderson) Kendrick, 19 July 1849, Filson. Eba Anderson would, in fact, edit her father's letters from his Mexican War experience.

16. Quoted in Abraham Stagg, *Biographical Sketches of the Fifty-Sixth Ohio Senate* (Columbus, OH: Glenn & Heide, 1864), 64.

17. David T. Dixon assesses the significance of the Kenyon address in *The Lost Gettysburg Address: Charles Anderson's Civil War Odyssey* (Santa Barbara, CA: B-List History, 2015), 42–44. Larz expressed his skepticism in LA to Orlando Brown, 5 February 1850, Orlando Brown Papers, Filson Historical Society Library, Louisville, Kentucky.

18. CA to Elizabeth (Brown) Anderson AND 52 9-4-1850.

19. On Longworth and Powers's friendship and patronage, see Clara Longworth de Chambrun, *The Making of Nicholas Longworth: Annals of an American Family* (New York: R. Long & R. R. Smith, Inc., 1933), 86–88.

20. LA to Orlando Brown, 5 February 1850, Filson.

21. CA to Sarah Anderson AND 81 9-4-1850.

22. CA to Sarah Anderson AND 82 9-8-1851.

23. CA to Elizabeth (Anderson) Gwathmey AND 90 12-14-1852.

24. Ibid.

25. CA to AL, 28 July 1851, Filson.

26. Henry Massie to WA AD 260 9-20-1850.

27. Henry Demian Bp Juncker to WA AD 220 9-17-1850. Junker was probably referring to St. Louis University, a Jesuit college founded in 1818.

28. RA to WA AD 44 3-5-1851; Orestes A. Brownson, *The Convert; or, Leaves from My Experience* (New York: E. Dunigan & Brother, 1877). On Brownson's life, see Arthur M. Schlesinger Jr., *Orestes Brownson: A Pilgrim's Progress* (New York: Little, Brown and Company, 1939; New York: Octagon Books, 1963).

29. John Lampkin Taylor to WA AD 343 1-17-1852; RA to WA AD 45 1-12 and 13-1852.

30. RA to WA AD 43 12-19-1850.

31. See Holt, *The Rise and Fall of the American Whig Party*, 958.

32. Dixon, *The Lost Gettysburg Address*, 48.

33. See Cindy S. Aron, *Working at Play: A History of Vacations in the United States* (New York: Oxford University Press, 1999).

34. CA to Elizabeth (Brown) Anderson AND 27 8-25-1854.

35. Dixon, *The Lost Gettysburg Address*, 50–51.

36. LA to Orlando Brown, 3 November 1856, Filson; Nicholas Longworth Anderson, *The Letters and Journals of Nicholas Longworth Anderson*, edited by Isabel Anderson (New York: F. H. Revell, 1942), 65.

37. John Purcell to WA, AD 319 4-21-1856; John Purcell to WA AD 320 10-12-1856.

38. LA to Daniel Gregg, 3 September 1855, Filson. On squatters and pre-emption, see Paul Wallace Gates, *History of Public Land Law Development* (Washington, DC: Public Land Law Review Commission, 1968), 219–247.

39. LA to Daniel Gregg, 6 May 1856, Filson.

40. RA, no recipient listed, 25 March 1856, Filson.

4I. LA to WA AD 3I I-27-1856.

Chapter 13: Times of Trial: 1857–1861

I. See James L. Huston, *The Panic of 1857 and the Coming of the Civil War* (Baton Rouge: Louisiana State University Press, 1987), 16.

2. Ibid., 23; Charles Clifford Huntington, *A History of Banking and Currency in Ohio Before the Civil War* (Columbus, OH: F. J. Heer Printing Co., 1915), 242–249.

3. See, e.g., Roy M. Robbins, *Our Landed Heritage: The Public Domain, 1776–1936* (Princeton, NJ: Princeton University Press, 1942); William J. Cooper Jr., *The South and the Politics of Slavery, 1828–1856* (Baton Rouge: Louisiana State University Press, 1978); or Allen Kaufman, *Capitalism, Slavery, and Republican Values: Antebellum Political Economists, 1819–1848* (Austin: University of Texas Press, 1982). On the formation of the Republican Party, see Eric Foner, *Free Soil, Free Labor, Free Men: The Ideology of the Republican Party Before the Civil War* (New York: Oxford University Press, 1995), 103–225.

4. WA to James R. Challen AD 79 12-24-1859.

5. Michael Boyce to Ellen Columba Ryan Anderson AD III 9-27-1854; Michael Boyce to Ellen Columba Ryan Anderson AD II2 3-28-1858.

6. RA to WA AD 46 2-2-1858.

7. WA to RA AD 400 2-7-1858.

8. RA to WA AD 47 8-22-1858.

9. Ibid.

10. Catherine (Longworth) Anderson to Ellen Columba Anderson AD I II-7-1858.

II. David T. Dixon, *The Lost Gettysburg Address: Charles Anderson's Civil War Odyssey* (Santa Barbara, CA: B-List History, 2015), 54–57.

12. LA to R. P. Brown AND 273 I-9-1862.

13. CA to Elizabeth (Anderson) Gwathmey AND 9I 7-4-1860.

14. On the Democrats' financial policies, see Huston, *The Panic of 1857 and the Coming of the Civil War*, 265–266. The literature on the 1860 presidential election is immense. For a sampling of key works, see William Freehling, *The Road to Disunion*, vol. 2, *Secessionists Triumphant, 1854–1861* (New York: Oxford University Press, 2007); Roy Franklin Nichols, *The Disruption of American Democracy* (New York: Macmillan, 1948); or David M. Potter, *The Impending Crisis: America Before the Civil War, 1848–1861* (New York: Harper Colophon, 1976).

15. Again, the literature on Lincoln's election is immense, but key works include: Allan Nevins, *Ordeal of the Union*, vol. 4: *The Emergence of Lincoln: Prologue to Civil War, 1859–1861* (New York: Charles Scribner's Sons, 1950); Richard Carwardine, *Lincoln: A Life of Purpose and Power* (New York, 2003); David Herbert Donald, *Lincoln* (New York: Touchstone, 1996); and Michael S. Green, *Lincoln and the Election of 1860* (Carbondale: Southern Illinois University, 2011).

16. On Davis and the Civil War, see Clement Eaton, *Jefferson Davis* (New York: The Free Press, 1977); and James M. McPherson, *Embattled Rebel: Jefferson Davis as Commander in Chief* (New York: Penguin, 2014).

17. On Anderson's Sumter experience, see Eba Anderson Lawton, *Major Robert Anderson and Fort Sumter* (New York: The Knickerbocker Press, 1911).

18. The best account of the fall of Fort Sumter is Richard N. Current, *Lincoln and the First Shot* (New York: Harper & Row, 1963). Also useful is David M. Potter, *Lincoln and His Party in the Secession Crisis* (New Haven, CT: Yale University Press, 1942).

19. RA to Charles Balance, Fac. 61 1-16-1861, HL.

20. RA to Maria (Anderson) Latham, CW 7 2-18-1861, Anderson Family Papers, HL.

21. The issue of Lincoln's motives in moving to supply Sumter has been hotly debated. From a Northern perspective, it was an innocent attempt to save a federal property. From a Southern perspective, it was a ruse to force the South to act and, in so doing, cement Northern support for the looming war. A middle path that I find especially persuasive is discussed in Kenneth M. Stampp, *And the War Came: The North and the Secession Crisis, 1860–1861* (Baton Rouge: Louisiana State University Press, 1950), 280–286.

22. For an analysis of the factors influencing Lincoln's decision, see Donald, *Lincoln*, 288–292.

23. *Richmond Enquirer*, March 9, 1861. For a thorough description of the Confederate government in the days immediately prior to the attack on Sumter, see Current, *Lincoln and the First Shot*, 126–153.

24. Quoted in William C. Davis, *Jefferson Davis: The Man and His Hour* (New York: HarperCollins, 1991), 325.

25. Quoted in Current, *Lincoln and the First Shot*, 112.

26. Andro Linklater, *Owning the Earth: The Transforming History of Land Ownership* (New York: Bloomsbury USA, 2013), 256, 267.

27. See Cecilia O'Leary, *To Die For: The Paradox of American Patriotism* (Princeton, NJ: Princeton University Press, 1999), 20–25.

28. RA to Hiram Barney HB Box 1 (10) 6-1-1861, HL.

29. RA to WA AD 48 6-23-1861.

30. Charles Anderson, *Ye Andersons of Virginia and Some of Their Descendants* (np, 1908), 63.

31. See Robert P. Swierenga, *Pioneers and Profits: Land Speculation on the Iowa Frontier* (Ames: Iowa State University Press, 1968), 203–204.

32. CA to Rufus King, 7 December 1860, Rufus King Papers, Cincinnati Historical Society; CA to Daniel Gregg, 20 November 1860, Filson.

33. Quoted in Abraham Stagg, *Biographical Sketches of the Fifty-Sixth Ohio Senate* (Columbus, OH: Glenn & Heide, 1864), 65–66.

34. CA to William Corry AND 713 1-21-1861.

35. Ibid.

36. On Lee and Anderson socializing in Texas, see Dixon, *The Lost Gettysburg Address*, 67–69.

37. Douglas Southall Freeman, *R. E. Lee: A Biography*, vol. 1 (New York: Charles Scribner's Sons, 1934), 428–429.

38. CA to William Corry AND 86 1-21-1861. See also Walter Havighurst, *Men of Old Miami, 1809–1873* (New York: Putnam, 1974), 49–63.

39. Charles is quoted in Dixon, *The Lost Gettysburg Address*, 79; Henry Eustace McCulloch to CA AND 1299 10-4-1861.

40. For an account of the escape, see Dixon, *The Lost Gettysburg Address*, 86–98.

41. On Charles's welcome in Washington, DC, see, e.g., his letter to Peter Cooper in New York in which he replied to their invitation to speak about his escape: "I believe that it may be instructive for your fellow citizens to learn some of these facts and references, from a new point of view, I readily accept your flattering invitation." CA to Peter Cooper and others AND 85 12-19-1861. The account of Anderson's imprisonment and escape below is taken from the speech he delivered at Cooper Union, which is summarized in the *New York Times*, December 22, 1861.

42. R. C. Anderson to CA AND 299 12-28-1861.

43. William Corry to "My dear friend" AND 717 12-18-1861.

44. CA to Elizabeth (Brown) Anderson AND 54 1-18-1862.

45. CA to Elizabeth (Brown) Anderson AND 55 3-22-1862; CA to Elizabeth (Brown) Anderson AND 56 3-24-1862.

46. Thomas McArthur Anderson, *A Monograph of the Anderson, Clark, Marshall, and McArthur Connection* (n.p., 1900), 19.

47. CA to Charles Francis Adams AND 31 4-24-1862.

48. CA to Elizabeth (Brown) Anderson AND 59 5-2-1862.

49. CA to Catherine Anderson AND 36 5-13-1862.

50. CA to Elizabeth (Brown) Anderson AND 60 5-16-1862; CA to Elizabeth (Brown) Anderson AND 61 5-21-1862.

51. CA to Catherine Anderson AND 37 5-30-1862.

52. CA to Elizabeth (Brown) Anderson AND 62 6-23-1862.

53. See Luke E. Harlow, *Religion, Race, and the Making of Confederate Kentucky, 1830–1880* (Cambridge, UK: Cambridge University Press, 2014).

54. The best account of Civil War battles is James McPherson, *Battle Cry of Freedom: The Civil War Era* (New York: Oxford University Press, 1988).

55. LA to R. P. Brown AND 273 1-9-1862.

CHAPTER 14: CHARLES ANDERSON'S CIVIL WAR: 1862–1865

1. Lincoln's proclamation did not extend to the border states and slavery was not completely abolished until the Thirteenth Amendment was passed on January 31, 1865.

2. I discuss the significance of the Emancipation Proclamation in "Lincoln's God and the Emancipation Proclamation," University of Heidelberg Pennington Lecture, forthcoming 2017.

3. See John Burt, *Lincoln's Tragic Pragmatism: Lincoln, Douglas, and Moral Conflict* (Cambridge, MA: Belknap Press, 2013), 365.

4. The revised figures were computed by historical demographer J. David Hacker in "A Census-Based Count of the Civil War Dead," *Civil War History* 57, no. 4 (December 2011): 306–347.

5. Nicholas Longworth Anderson, *The Letters and Journals of Nicholas Longworth Anderson*, edited by Isabel Anderson (New York: F. H. Revell, 1942), 125; Henry Adams, *The Education of Henry Adams*, (New York: Library of America, 1983), 771. Adams later reversed his criticism, and the two families remained friends for three generations.

6. Kitty's letter is folded into a letter Charles wrote to a friend [in pencil "Governor Reuler"?] AND 116 8-9-1862.

7. "Kate Phillips and 32 other women" to CA AND 1432 8-22-1862.

8. CA to Catherine Anderson AND 38 9-28-1862; CA to Elizabeth (Brown) Anderson AND 63 9-30-1862.

9. CA to Elizabeth (Brown) Anderson AND 64 10-16-1862.

10. CA to Catherine Anderson AND 43 12-11-1862; CA to Catherine Anderson AND 45 12-23-1862.

11. For accounts of this battle I have relied chiefly on Charles Anderson's account and James McPherson, *Battle Cry of Freedom: The Civil War Era* (New

York: Oxford University Press, 1988), 580–583; Peter Cozzens, *No Better Place to Die: The Battle of Stones River* (Urbana: University of Illinois Press, 1990); and Bruce Catton, *Never Call Retreat* (Garden City, NY: Doubleday, 1965), 35–47. I also describe the battle in *Upon the Altar of the Nation: A Moral History of the Civil War* (New York: Viking Penguin, 2006), 201–205.

12. Catton, *Never Call Retreat*, 42.

13. CA to Elizabeth (Brown) Anderson AND 45 1-7-1863. On religion and war, see George C. Rable, *God's Almost Chosen Peoples: A Religious History of the American Civil War* (Chapel Hill: University of North Carolina Press, 2010); Mark A. Noll, *The Civil War as a Theological Crisis* (Chapel Hill: University of North Carolina Press, 2006); and Stout, *Upon the Altar of the Nation*.

14. Cozzens, *No Better Place to Die*, 139–140.

15. CA to Catherine Anderson AND 35 1-2-1863; CA to Catherine Anderson AND 46 1-22-1863.

16. John D. Caldwell to CA AND 655 6-18-1863. See Frank L. Klement, *The Limits of Dissent: Clement L. Vallandigham and the Civil War* (Lexington: University Press of Kentucky, 1970), 243–245.

17. LA to CA AND 223 6-26-1863 . The "Joe" Larz references could be Nicholas Longworth's eldest son, Joseph.

18. LA to CA AND 224 7-4-1863.

19. Joseph Geiger to CA AND 941 7-10-1863; Edmund Davis [of Texas] to CA AND 786 7-15-1863; William Cooper Howells to CA AND 11-24 8-10-1863.

20. Benjamin Stanton to CA AND 1606 12-26-1863.

21. William Tecumseh Sherman to CA AND 1556 8-1863.

22. William Wellen to CA AND 1785 10-19-1863.

23. David Tod to CA AND 1668 10-27-1863.

24. Rutherford B. Hayes to CA AND 1088 11-6-1863.

25. Charles Anderson, *Letter Addressed to the Opera House Meeting* (New York: William C. Bryant and Company, 1863), 5–12.

26. Thomas McArthur Anderson to CA AND 498 11-7-1863.

27. See Garry Wills, *Lincoln at Gettysburg*.

28. The text of Anderson's address is reprinted in David T. Dixon, *The Lost Gettysburg Address: Charles Anderson's Civil War Odyssey* (Santa Barbara, CA: B-List History, 2015), appendix, 194–208. Anderson's speech is also summarized in Gabor Boritt, *The Gettysburg Gospel: The Lincoln Speech That Nobody Knows* (New York: Simon & Schuster, 2006), 126.

29. S. Hine to CA AND 1110 12-3-1863.

30. Abraham Stagg to CA AND 1603 11-17-1864.

31. Thomas McArthur Anderson to CA AND 499 5-28-1864.

32. Thomas McArthur Anderson to CA AND 500 8-6-1864.

33. CA to Godwin Volney Dorsey AND 88, 8-22-1864.

34. Dixon, *The Lost Gettysburg Address*, 162–173, 215; R. C. Anderson to CA AND 300 1-28-1865.

35. John Markley to CA AND 1327 2-25-1865; James Speed to CA AND 1595 2-27-1865.

36. John Sherman to CA AND 1550 3-7-1865; Rutherford B. Hayes to CA AND 1089 3-25-1865.

37. Sidney D. Maxwell to CA AND 1341 7-19-1865; Benjamin Cowen to CA AND 726 8-26-1865.

38. LA to CA AND 229 11-7-1865.

CHAPTER 15: AN EX-CONFEDERATE COLONY: 1865–1866

1. R. C. Anderson to WA AD 37 1-14-1866. William is quoted in *Rocky Mountain Journals*, 64.

2. William Marshall Anderson, *An American in Maximilian's Mexico 1865–1866: The Diaries of William Marshall Anderson*, ed. Ramón Eduardo Ruiz (San Marino, CA: Huntington Library, 1959), xxiii–xxiv. Hereafter cited as *An American in Maximilian's Mexico*.

3. Ibid., 119–120.

4. Ibid., 120–122.

5. Ibid., 5–6, 11.

6. Ibid., 13–14, 17–18.

7. Ibid., 21, 25, 29.

8. Ibid., 33.

9. Ibid., 37.

10. Ibid., 41.

11. Ibid., 63.

12. Ibid., 62–63; WA to L. Berge retained copy AD 82 8-21-1865.

13. *An American in Maximilian's Mexico*, 64–67, 73; Terry quoted in *Times-Picayune*, March 1, 1866.

14. *An American in Maximilian's Mexico*.

15. *An American in Maximilian's Mexico*, 99, 101; WA to Ellen Columba (Ryan) Anderson AD 85 4-6-1866.

16. *An American in Maximilian's Mexico*, 107.

17. *An American in Maximilian's Mexico*, 115. On Napoleon's recalling troops from Mexico, see Todd William Wahlstrom, "A Vision for Colonization: The Southern Migration Movement to Mexico After the U.S. Civil War," *Southern Historian* 30 (2009), 50–66.

18. *An American in Maximilian's Mexico*, 124.

19. Ibid., 117.

20. Ibid.

21. Thomas Dugan to WA AD 156 11-6-1866.

22. William's essay is contained in the Anderson Family Collection, 1930–1938 Miscellaneous and Ephemeral, HL.

23. Henry Boyce to Ellen Columba (Ryan) Anderson AD 110 10-15-1866.

24. John Sherman to CA AND 1552 4-3-1865; Harry S. Stout, *Upon the Altar of the Nation: A Moral History of the Civil War* (New York: Viking Penguin, 2006), 428–430.

25. See Martha Hodes, *Mourning Lincoln* (New Haven, CT: Yale University Press, 2015).

26. William Deshler to CA AND 814 4-22-1865.

27. Harry S. Stout, *Upon the Altar of the Nation*, 445.

28. Benjamin Franklin Wade to CA AND 1730 7-29-1865; John Sherman to CA AND 1553 8-2-1865. Seward was nearly killed by assassins on April 14 and was left permanently disabled.

29. L. Hall to CA AND 1062 6-17-1865.

30. See Eric Foner, *Reconstruction: America's Unfinished Revolution, 1863–1877* (New York: Harper and Row, 1988).

31. William Tecumseh Sherman to CA AND 1557 7-28-1865.

32. Salmon P. Chase to CA AND 677 11-20-1865.

33. John Porter Brown to CA AND 614 10-27-1865.

CHAPTER 16: ANDERSONS IN TRANSITION: 1866–1870

1. See Howard Zinn, *A People's History of the United States* (New York: Harper-Collins, 1980), 192–205.

2. See Eric Foner, *Reconstruction: America's Unfinished Revolution, 1863–1877* (New York: Harper and Row, 1988), 409. See also C. Vann Woodward, *Reunion and Reaction: The Compromise of 1877 and the End of Reconstruction* (New York: Oxford University Press, 1966).

3. Charles Anderson, "Annual Message of the Governor of Ohio, to the Fifty-Seventh General Assembly," January 1, 1866. Copy in HL.

4. L. D. McCabe to CA AND 1295 1-2-1866.

5. William Tecumseh Sherman to CA AND 1558 1-4-1866. It is not clear what Sherman meant when he referenced "twelve hundred million."

6. M. Wheeler to CA AND 1734 1-4-1866.

7. Ephraim George Squier to CA AND 1601 1-9-1866.

8. William M. Smith to CA AND 1586 1-16-1866.

9. Frederick Hassaurek to CA AND 1083 3-10-1866. See Ernest R. May, *The Making of the Monroe Doctrine* (Cambridge, MA: Harvard University Press, 1975).

10. R. C. Anderson to CA AND 302 1-7-1866.

11. John Stacker to CA AND 1602 7-26-1866.

12. CA to Elizabeth (Brown) Anderson AND 69 12-1-1866.

13. Abraham Rencher to CA AND 1485 2-4-1867.

14. Lyman Draper to CA AND 829 7-5-1867.

15. Eugene D. Schmiel, *Citizen-General: Jacob Dolson Cox and the Civil War Era* (Athens: Ohio University Press, 2014), 194–196.

16. Jacob D. Cox to CA AND 731 12-6-1867.

17. LA to CA AND 230 3-21-1868.

18. LA to CA AND 232 6-4-1868; LA to CA AND 234 7-25-1868.

19. A special to the *New York Times* on June 27, 1902, noted: "It was a case of suicide due to melancholia. From the meager details obtained Mr. Anderson, at some time early on Thursday morning, cut his throat while in a bedroom of the residence of his brother Dr. Joseph L. Anderson at Ridgefield, Conn."

20. Sarah Anderson to Maria (Anderson) Latham, 10 April 1868, Filson.

21. WA promissory note AD 401 5-1-1868.

22. C. McDermont to CA AND 1300 7-29-1870. The invitation to address the "soldiers and sailors national committee" appears in Andrew Gregg to CA AND 780 9-12-1868. and Anderson's reply in CA to Andrew G. Curtin AND 87 11-25-1868.

23. Rutherford B. Hayes to CA AND 1091 1-20-1870.

24. Sarah Kendrick to "My Dear Brother" [CA] AND 1189 3-30-1870.

25. All quotations are from the William Marshall Anderson memorandum book of 1869, held at the HL.

26. The pocket diary is included in the Anderson papers at the HL.

27. WA, "Statement of Penance," AD 99 n.d.

28. Thomas McArthur Anderson to WA AD 68 4-7-1870.

CHAPTER 17: LEGACIES: 1871–1888

1. Ephrim Squirer to WA AD 336 2-17-1872; Manning Ferguson Force to WA AD 176 10-6-1872; LA to WA AD 33 11-19-1873.

2. Rufus King to WA AD 237 10-7-1872. Ohio got its wish when son Robert Marshall donated William's papers to Ohio archives.

3. RA to WA AD 49 10-8-1871.

4. Sarah Kendrick to "My dear Brother" [CA] AND 1190 10-27-1871.

5. LA to CA AND 235 11-19-1871.

6. LA to CA AND 236 3-25-1872.

7. Henry T. Parrish to CA AND 1417 2-13-1871.

8. Commonwealth of Kentucky. Office of the Secretary of State. Land Office. "Kuttawa, Kentucky."

9. LA to CA AND 237 6-6-1874.

10. CA to WA AD 10 1-10-1879.

11. LA to CA AND 239 11-18-1875; R. C. A. Flournay to CA AND 913 1-12-1876.

12. S. Leonard to CA AND 1223 7-18-1876.

13. Allen Latham Anderson to CA AND 26 1-13-1877.

14. William M. Carry to [President] Rutherford B. Hayes AND 716 6-5-1877.

15. George Drake to CA AND 828 6-14-1877.

16. CA to Catherine Anderson AND 48 11-16-1876.

17. Edward Lowell Anderson to CA AND 128 10-24-1877; Edward Lowell Anderson to CA AND 129 1877.

18. R. C. Anderson to WA AD 40 1-8-1878.

19. Marcellus Anderson to CA AND 283 3-27-1878; LA to Maria (Anderson) Latham, 23 October 1878, Filson.

20. Edward Lowell Anderson to CA AND 130 6-12-1878; Edward Lowell Anderson to CA AND 131 1-8-1879. Anderson's book appeared under the title *Soldier and Pioneer: A Biographical Sketch of Lt.-Colonel Richard C. Anderson of the Continental Army* (New York: G. P. Putnam's Sons, 1879).

21. Edward Lowell Anderson to CA AND 132; Edward Lowell Anderson to CA AND 133 3-17-1879; Edward Lowell Anderson to CA AND 134 4-24-1879.

22. James Speed to CA AND 1596 8-15-1879; CA to Elizabeth (Brown) Anderson AND 70 10-3-1879.

23. Larz Anderson Jr. "to my dear Uncle" [CA] AND 281 1879.

24. CA to WA AND 282 6-13-1879.

25. Ellen Columba (Ryan) Anderson to WA AD 15 8-17-1879.

26. Ellen Columba (Ryan) Anderson to WA AD 16 2-9-1880.

27. The writer of the penciled note on the envelope was quite probably Robert Anderson, who inherited his father's papers.

28. Thomas McArthur Anderson to WA AD 69 12-12-1880.

29. WA to Thomas M. Anderson AD 95 12-27-1880.

30. Ellen Columba (Ryan) Anderson to Thomas McArthur Anderson, AD 20 2-25-1881.

31. David T. Dixon, *The Lost Gettysburg Address: Charles Anderson's Civil War Odyssey* (Santa Barbara, CA: B-List History, 2015), 181.

32. Reuben Thomas Durrett to CA AND 854 11-15-1893.

Index

HARRY S. STOUT is the Jonathan Edwards Professor of American Religious History at Yale University and lives in Branford, Connecticut.